21st Century Information Systems

21st Century Information Systems

Edited by
Roberts Goddings

WILLFORD PRESS

www.willfordpress.com

Published by Willford Press,
118-35 Queens Blvd., Suite 400,
Forest Hills, NY 11375, USA

ISBN: 978-1-68285-349-8

Cataloging-in-Publication Data

21st century information systems / edited by Roberts Goddings.
    p. cm.
Includes bibliographical references and index.
ISBN 978-1-68285-349-8
1. Management information systems. 2. Information technology. 3. Computer networks.
4. Information storage and retrieval systems. 5. Electronic information resources. I. Goddings, Roberts.
T58.6 .A125 2017
658.403 8--dc23

For information on all Willford Press publications
visit our website at www.willfordpress.com

Printed in the United States of America.

Contents

Permissions

List of Contributors

Index

Preface

It is often said that books are a boon to mankind. They document every progress and pass on the knowledge from one generation to the other. They play a crucial role in our lives. Thus I was both excited and nervous while editing this book. I was pleased by the thought of being able to make a mark but I was also nervous to do it right because the future of students depends upon it. Hence, I took a few months to research further into the discipline, revise my knowledge and also explore some more aspects. Post this process, I began with the editing of this book.

Information systems are a set of systems that can process and organize large amounts of data and information. This book on information systems discusses the distribution and collection of data in all stages and its process in the business sector. This book studies, analyses and upholds the pillars of information systems and its utmost significance in modern times. Contents in this book highlight the importance of accurate data distribution and data retrieval as a method to reduce the margin of error. It is a complete source of knowledge on the present status of this important field. Coherent flow of topics, student-friendly language and extensive use of examples make this book an invaluable source of knowledge.

I thank my publisher with all my heart for considering me worthy of this unparalleled opportunity and for showing unwavering faith in my skills. I would also like to thank the editorial team who worked closely with me at every step and contributed immensely towards the successful completion of this book. Last but not the least, I wish to thank my friends and colleagues for their support.

Editor

Application in composite machine using RBF neural network based on PID control

Jia Chunying[1], Chen Yuchen[1], Ding Zhigang[2]

[1]College of Electronic and Electric Engineering, Shanghai University of Engineering Science, Shanghai, China
[2]Shanghai Computer Software Technology Development Center, Shanghai, China

Email address
Chuningjia@163.com (Jia Chunying)

Abstract: In the absence of solvent composite machine, because the radius of drum winding and rewinding roller in the transmission process is changing. With the coiled material rolls diameter more and more large, and put the curly size getting smaller and smaller, this has the certain difficulty for the tension control. Therefore, good tension control is non solvent composite is very important. Analyzed the reason and the tension control mathematical model generation composite machine tension in the BOPP production line, for the constant tension control of composite machine, put forward a kind of improved PID control method based on RBF neural network. By the method of Jacobian information identification of RBF neural network, combined with the incremental PID algorithm to realize the self-tuning tension control parameters, control simulation and implementation of the model using Matlab software programming. The simulation results show that, the improved algorithm has better control effect than the general PID.

Keywords: Control PID Algorithm, Jacobian Information Identification, RBF Neural Network, Matlab

1. Introduction

Composite machine is a kind of important processing equipment in packaging industry, Non solvent composite has high production efficiency, energy saving, safety, environmental protection and other advantages and gradually attracted the concern of the industry. In which the film high speed, smooth coiling in multi-layer coextrusion drooling film production is especially important. According to these characteristics, this article in order to maintain constant tension as the core, dynamic relationship between the size and speed of tension and linear speed. Study on the variation regularity of receive roll when changing winding motor, by controlling the motor speed difference of indirect tension control. At the same time using RBF neural network PID controller regulates the collection of direct compensation of tension roll speed. So as to realize the high-speed collecting film in roll when changing the constant tension control. Simulation and experiments show that, the presented control method has good control effect.

1.1. Analysis of Tension and Tension Control

1.1.1. Analysis of Composite Machine for Tension

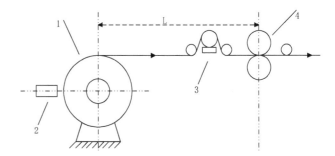

1. Unwinding roller 2. The distance sensor 3. Tension sensor 4.Drag roller

Fig 1. The reeling tension analysis chart

Tension control system of cast film processing equipment machine usually by the unwinding and rewinding and a series of interstand tension roller, etc.. In order to ensure the wrinkles and cutting the material phenomenon does not occur and to run at a certain speed. The constant tension control play a decisive role. Tension exists mainly in the parent roll unwinding and finished products in the process of winding roll.

Tension arises mainly from between the film Friction and the reel and the effect of driving force. This paper focuses on the analysis of composite machine control tension, as shown in Figure 1 for the winding tension process analysis.

1.2. Dynamic Relationship between Tension and Linear Velocity

Design the raw materials from the unwinding roll out time is t_1, Line speed is v_1. The arrival of materials drag roll moments is t_2, Line speed is v, Elastic modulus of the film is E, the cross-sectional area is A, the hin film from the traction roll to the winding roller length is L, the tension is F. In the period time of t_2-t_1, elongation of the films is $dL = \int_{t_1}^{t_2}(v - v_1)dt$. According to Hooke's law, film tension can be expressed is:

$$F = EA\frac{dL}{L} = \frac{EA}{L}\int_{t_1}^{t_2}(v - v_1)dt \qquad (1)$$

By formula (1) shows, we must control the line speed $v - v_1$ size to control the film tension of F, Visible tension control system is actually a linear velocity tracking system. Through the control of traction between the roller and the unwinding roller speed differential winding tension to indirect control of film.

1.3. The Tension Control of Composite Machine

Tension control system of composite machine is a time-varying, multi input, multi output, nonlinear system. According to the algorithm and improved PID neural network control algorithm of the traditional PID control algorithm, fuzzy control algorithm, the main tension control algorithm composite machine. However, tension control using conventional models are composite machine. If the operating condition changes, the control quality will decline, and even affect the normal operation of the control system.

Kee-hyun Shin proposed an eccentric eccentricity compensation assessment and an adaptive method to eliminate the interference produced by the drum shape [7]. Wei Xinming by using BP neural network PID control to reduce the system overshoot and improve the anti-interference performance of the system [8]. Chen Zuojie the design of fuzzy PI controller, study the actual value and the tension tension change range. According to the actual value and the change range of size and output of different KP and KI values, and further improve product technology level [9]. Deng Xiao uses a single output SPIDNN, enables the system to quickly achieve good dynamic and static performance [10].

Using nonlinear tension control model of the BP neural network has obtained satisfactory results, but because of the multilayer neural network are used in the large amount of computation, slow convergence, and are easy to fall into local minimum point, so the effect of its application. And by radial basis function neural network (RBF) with computational modeling process capability, the algorithm can approximate any nonlinear mapping is simple and practical, small volume, high precision of the model, but also solves the difficult

problem of PID parameter setting.

2. The PID Control of RBF Neural Network

RBF network is a kind of three layer feedforward neural network for solving pattern classification, including input layer, hidden layer and output layer. The input layer to the hidden layer weights between the input layer is fixed at 1, which is the information without any treatment [1], only the input variable assigned to the hidden layer, the hidden layer of each neuron represents a radial basis function. The hidden layer to the output layer weights can be adjusted. The hidden layer nodes by like Gauss function radial function as the composition, the number of nodes do not need to like the BP network that are set in advance, but increased in the learning process until it meets the error index so far, the output layer nodes usually is a simple linear function. RBF network PID control consists of two parts: RBF neural network identifier and controller based on PID. Identification RBF neural network through the controlled input and output data to identify the object in an approximate model of the controlled object, and the relationship between input and output instead of the controlled object. The parameters of the PID controller adaptive tuning through identification RBF neural network. RBF network PID control block diagram as shown in figure 2.

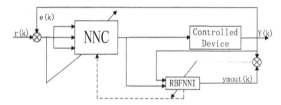

Fig 2. Block Diagram of RBF network tuning PID control

2.1. The Design of the System Structure

RBF network setting PID control structure as shown in Figure 2, there are two neural network system. Among them, NNC is a self-tuning PID controller, direct close loop control of the controlled object; RBFNNI for online identification system. The realization of controlled Jacobian information recognizing object, on the sensitivity of the control input output control object of observation in order to dynamically, to provide adaptive PID controller. The working principle of the system is based on the controlled object online identification by RBFNNI, power system through the adjustment of NNC in real time, so that the system is adaptive, achieve the purpose of effective control.

2.2. Design of Neural Network PID Controller

2.2.1. Neural Network PID Controller

PID control is a mature technology, widely used control method, which has the advantages of simple structure, and for most process has better control effect. The discrete PID control law is:

$$u(k) = K_P e(k) + K_I \sum_{j=1}^{k-1} e(i) + K_D[e(k) - e(k-1)] \quad (2)$$

In the formula, u(k) is the value output controller on k moment; K_P, K_I, K_D respectively the proportion coefficient, integral coefficient and Differential coefficient; e(k) as Position and the expectation of AC servo system in current time difference in the value of the moment; e(k-1) as Position and expected the last sampling of AC servo system, the difference in the value of the moment.

By formula (3) can be obtained between the increment of control volume u(k-1) controller output the first K cycle time control of the amount of u(k) and the k-1 cycle time is:

$$\Delta u(k) = u(k) - u(k-1) = K_P[e(k) - e(k-1)] + K_I e(k) + K_D[e(k) - 2e(k-1)] + e(k-2) \quad (3)$$

The traditional PID control, the main problem is the parameter tuning problem, once the setting calculation of good, are fixed in the whole control process. But in the practical system, because the system state and parameter changes, the emergence of state and parameters are the uncertainty in the process, the system is difficult to achieve the best control effect. In this paper, using two layers of linear neural network of three parameters of PID controller is adjusted online [2]. The input of the neural network is:

$$\begin{cases} X_1(k) = e(k) - e(k-1) \\ X_2(k) = e(k) \\ X_3(k) = e(k) - 2e(k-1) + e(k-2) \end{cases} \quad (4)$$

The performance index was defined as the NNC:

$$E(k) = \frac{1}{2}[\theta_d(k) - \theta(k)]^2 \quad (5)$$

So:

$$K_P(k) = K_P(k-1) - \eta_1 \frac{\partial E}{\partial K_P} = K_P(k-1) - \eta_1[\theta_d(k) - \theta(k)] \cdot \frac{\partial \theta}{\partial u} \cdot \frac{\partial u}{\partial K_P} = K_P(k-1) - \eta_1[\theta_d(k) - \theta(k)] \frac{\partial \theta}{\partial u} X_1(k) \quad (6)$$

$$K_I(k) = K_I(k-1) - \eta_2 \frac{\partial E}{\partial K_I} = K_I(k-1) - \eta_2[\theta_d(k) - \theta(k)] \frac{\partial \theta}{\partial u} X_2(k) \quad (7)$$

$$K_D(k) = K_D(k-1) - \eta_3 \frac{\partial E}{\partial K_D} = K_D(k-1) - \eta_3[\theta_d(k) - \theta(k)] \frac{\partial \theta}{\partial u} X_3(k) \quad (8)$$

Among them, η_1、η_2、η_3 is the learning rate, The $\frac{\partial \theta}{\partial u}$ for object Jacobian information, The information can be used by RBFNN network identification.

2.3. RBF Network Identifier

In the RBF network identifier structure, $X = [x_1, x_2, \cdots, x_n]^T$ as the input vectors of the network. Radial basis vector set $H = [h_1, h_2, \cdots, h_j, \cdots, h_m]^T$ RBF network for the Gauss function, available:

$$h_j = \exp\left(\frac{\|x - c_j\|^2}{2b_j^2}\right) \quad (j = 1,2,\cdots,n) \quad (9)$$

The center vector network of the first j node $C_j = [c_{j1}, c_{j2}, \cdots, c_{ji}, \cdots, c_{jm}]^T$ $i = 1,2,\cdots,n$. Design the base width set for vector network is:

$$B = [b_1, b_2, \cdots, b_j, \cdots, b_m]^T \quad (10)$$

In the formula: b_j as the width parameter for node J, and a number greater than 0. The weight vector network is:

$$W = [w_1, w_2, \cdots, w_j, \cdots, w_m]^T \quad (11)$$

The output for the identification network is:

$$y_{mout}(k) = w_1 h_1 + w_2 h_2 + \cdots + w_m h_m \quad (12)$$

In the neural network algorithm composite machine tension control, the control precision demand is not high, not precise part can be modified by adjusting the weight of the network parameters and. The tension of PID controller, the incremental

PID controller, the control error is expressed as:

$$error(k) = r_{in}(k) - y_{out}(k) \quad (13)$$

Neural network tuning index is:

$$E(k) = \frac{1}{2}error(k)^2 \quad (14)$$

The control algorithm uses the incremental PID algorithm [3], i.e.:

$$\Delta u(k) = k_p[error(k) - error(k-1)] + k_i[error(k)] + k_d[error(k) - 2error(k-1) + error(k-2)] \quad (15)$$

Adjustment of k_p、k_i、k_d by using the gradient descent method, i.e.:

$$\Delta k_p = -\eta \frac{\partial E}{\partial k_p} = -\eta \frac{\partial E}{\partial y_{out}} \times \frac{\partial y_{out}}{\partial \Delta u} \times \frac{\partial \Delta u}{\partial k_p} = \eta error(k) \frac{\partial y_{out}}{\partial \Delta u} xc(1) \quad (16)$$

$$\Delta k_i = -\eta \frac{\partial E}{\partial k_i} = -\eta \frac{\partial E}{\partial y_{out}} \times \frac{\partial y_{out}}{\partial \Delta u} \times \frac{\partial \Delta u}{\partial k_i} = \eta error(k) \frac{\partial y_{out}}{\partial \Delta u} xc(2) \quad (17)$$

$$\Delta k_d = -\eta \frac{\partial E}{\partial k_d} = -\eta \frac{\partial E}{\partial y_{out}} \times \frac{\partial y_{out}}{\partial \Delta u} \times \frac{\partial \Delta u}{\partial k_d} = \eta error(k) \frac{\partial y_{out}}{\partial \Delta u} xc(1) \quad (18)$$

Type: $\frac{\partial y_{out}}{\partial \Delta u}$ as the object of the Jacobian information, namely the object output sensitivity to input changes control. The sensitivity is obtained through identification of neural network, i.e.:

$$\frac{\partial y_{out}}{\partial \Delta u} \approx \frac{\partial y_{mout}}{\partial \Delta u} = \sum_{j=1}^{m} w_j h_j \frac{c_{ji} - \Delta u(k)}{b_j^2} \quad (19)$$

3. Tension Control Model and Simulation

3.1. The Establishment of tension Control Model

In the tension of composite machine control, RBF neural network define n=3, m=6; Input instruction signals, namely cutting machine winding tension set value r_{in}=1(Equivalent to the field winding tension of 150 N); Define $\Delta u(k)$、 $y_{out}(k)$ and $y_{out}(k) - y_{mout}(k)$ as the input of RBF network identification, among them: $\Delta u(k)$ is PID increment, $y_{out}(k)$ as the value of cutting machine at the moment the actual output tension. $y_{out}(k) - y_{mout}(k)$ Is the difference for cutting machine at the moment the actual output tension and RBF neural network to identify the output tension. To define the network center vector for $C_j = [0,0,\cdots,0,\cdots,0]_n^T$, Base width vector network for $B = [0,0,\cdots,0,\cdots,0]_m^T$, According to the definition of $\eta = 3.5$ experience learning rate, the momentum factor $\alpha = 0.05$. This paper selects salivation mathematic model of tension control system is:

$$y_{out}(k) = \frac{-0.2 y_{out}(k-1) + u(k-1)}{1 + y_{out}(k-1)^2} \quad (20)$$

To construct the simulation model of the system Using field data to train the RBF neural network controller. Firstly normalized sample data, in the tension control model design. In order to put the 100 groups of measured unreeling constant tension $T = \begin{bmatrix} 150.00 & 149.90 & 149.80 & 148.90 & 150.00 \cdots \\ 149.90 & 150.00 & 149.90 & 149.80 & 149.90 \end{bmatrix}$ are mapped to [0, 1], select one of the 80 sets of data as training data, and the remaining 20 groups stay on neural network controller test. In this paper, set the data of the minimum value is set to -1 (The number of selected is based on the tension set value is 1), Set the data of the middle value is set to 0. Thus, the measured normalized data can fall in the interval [0, 1], get the normalized data after T=[1.00 0.99 0.98 0.99 1.00···0.99 1.00 0.99 0.98 0.99]. And then to build a RBF network using radial basis function, which can match with the known sample points. Radial basis function neural network has two layers, that is the hidden layer radial basis neurons and the output layer of linear neurons.

Design radial basis transfer function for the hidden layer of:

$$\alpha = \text{radbas}(P) \quad (21)$$

Each neuron in the hidden layer weights and the thresholds of the center position vector of radial basis function $C_j = [c_{j1}, c_{j2}, \cdots, c_{ji}, \cdots, c_{jm}]^T$ and based wide vector $B = [b_1, b_2, \cdots, b_j, \cdots, b_m]^T$ corresponding to the specified. Every linear output neurons by weighting these radial basis function and composition. As long as each layer has the correct weights and thresholds, and have enough neurons in hidden layer, function as radial basis function networks to any arbitrary accuracy to approximate arbitrary. The completion of the training of the network in the learning process of neural network set up, in order to achieve the goal of error, the

sample point parameter approximation function reaches the target parameter requirements.

3.2. The Simulation Results of Tension Control

According to the above are derived by the RBF neural network controller and model identification learning algorithm, using Matlab simulation. The sampling period $t_s = 0.001$ s. The RBF tuning of PID after the output response as shown in Figure 3, figure y_{out} for cutting machine at the moment the actual output tension value, and the tension of the given r_{in} as desired value.

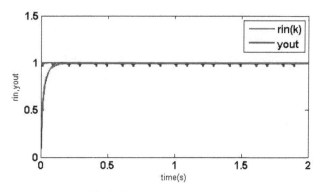

Fig 3. PID output response curves

As you can see from Figure 3, the RBF identification system identification RBF neural network controller has fast response speed, can play fast tracking effect model identification online.

This paper did simulation results were obtained in the absence of any field interference situations, therefore, the stability of the system and this is a scene with no comparable. After the PID tuning output tension curve, the output curve is better in overshoot, adjust time characteristics still than the actual site setup PID more.

As shown in Figure 4 for The traditional PID control curves, these curves reflect the convergence speed is slow. Robustness is not good, we can see that the superiority of RBF neural network PID control.

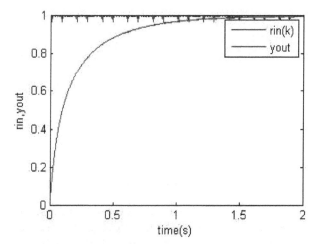

Fig 4. Traditional PID control curves

4. Conclusion

Because the traditional PID control algorithm in the proportion, integral, differential coefficient in the design stage set after week constant, do not have the ability to learn, self adaptive. Therefore, the robustness of using traditional PID tension controller of poor control performance needs to be improved. Simulation results show that PID tension control based on RBF neural network, through online identification process model is established and provide gradient information for the neuron controller, realizes the online identification and online control purposes; and high control accuracy, good dynamic characteristic, has self adaptability and robustness.

References

[1] Iman Poultangari, Reza Shahnazi ,Mansour Sheikhan RBF neural network based PI pitch controller for a class of 5-MW wind turbines using particle swarm optimization algorithm. ISA Transactions 51 (2012) 641–648.

[2] Ismail Yabanova, Ali Keçebas, Development of ANN model for geothermal district heating system and a novel PID-based control strategy. Applied Thermal Engineering 51 (2013) 908-916.

[3] LIU Hong-mei, WANG Shao-ping, OUYANG Ping-chao, Fault Diagnosis in a Hydraulic Position Servo System Using RBF Neural Network. 2006, 19(4), 346-353.

[4] Shi Zhongzhao. Neural network control theory [M]. Xi'an: Northwestern Polytechnical University press, 1999:85-90.

[5] Wang Jiangjiang, Zhang Chunfa, Jing Youyin. Self-adaptive RBF neural network PID control in exhaust temperature of micro-turbine[C] Proceedings of the Seventh International Conference on Machine Learning and Cybernetics,2008:2131-2136.

[6] Elanayar V T S, Shin Y C. Radial basis function neural network for approximation and estimation of nonlinear stochastic dynamic systems [J].IEEE Transactions on Neural Network, 1994, 5 (4):594-603.

[7] Kee-Hyun Shin, Jeung-In Jang, et al. Compensation Method for Tension Disturbance Due to an Unknown Roll Shape in a Web Transport System [C].IEEE Transactions on industry applications. 2003, 5(39): 1422-1428.

[8] Wei Xinming. Take the tension control system for machine based on BP neural network volume [D]. Northeastern University. 2014

[9] Deng Xiao, Hu Muyi, PID neural network application in the roll paper roll tension control system. China paper journal [J]. 2014.29(1).44-48

[10] Chen Zuojie, Wu Peide, Zhang Yihong. Application of fuzzy PI controller in the study of film tension control system [J]. 2014.3(1).42-44

Performance evaluation and operation of enterprise resource planning (ERP) software security system

Diponkar Paul[1], Md. Rafel Mridha[2], Md. Rashedul Hasan[2]

[1]Department of EEE, Prime University, Mirput-1, Dhaka, Bangladesh
[2]World University of Bangladesh, Dhanmondi, Dhaka, Bangladesh

Email address:
dipo0001@ntu.edu.sg (D. Paul)

Abstract: The criteria for selecting the specific systems are - containment of most common sources for attacks, knowledge of the exact location of each security hole, accessibility to the source code and selection of a typical web application such as a human resource management. We followed the human resource (recruiting and working procedure) to integrate all the facilities in a single programmable platform. The applied framework has been used to map a commercial security library to the target mobile application SoC (System-of-Chip). The applicability of our framework to software architecture has been explored in other multiprocessor scenarios. ERP software (or enterprise resource planning software) is an integrated system used by businesses to combine, organize and maintain the data necessary for operations. The fundamental advantage of ERP is that integrating the myriad processes by which businesses operate saves time and expenses. The whole process has been automated using a methodology that extracts the risk of ERP system by analyzing the class diagram of the system. ERP for the business to develop innovative services for new and existing organizations, has achieved operational excellence with streamlined logistics and manufacturing improve financial performance with tighter internal controls and insights connect headquarters, subsidiaries and partners in a single network. Any type of small and large organization who to maintain their work flow in an organized way and having an intensity of clear book keeping like as business & educational institutions as well as social organizations.

Keywords: ERP, SecureCL, Trigger, Cursor etc

1. Introduction

Short for enterprise resource planning, ERP is an organization's management system which uses a software application to incorporate all facets of the business, and automate and facilitate the flow of data between critical back-office functions, which may include financing, distribution, accounting, inventory management, sales, marketing, planning, human resources, manufacturing, and other operating units. ERP software, in turn, is designed to improve both external customer relationships and internal collaborations by automating tasks and activities that streamline work processes, shorten business process cycles, and increase user productivity. A method for standardized processing, an ERP software application can both store and recall information when it is required in a real-time environment. Companies often seek out ERP software systems to pinpoint and mend inefficiencies in a business process or when a number of complex issues exist in the business environment. ERP software systems are also implemented to enhance operational efficiencies, achieve financial goals, manage and streamline the company's operational processes, replace an existing ERP software system that is out of date or unable to handle a company's daily activities; or improve information management through better data accessibility, decreased data reduplication and optimal forecasting features [1]. Many business owners see ERP software systems to be critical to their business functions, as they allow companies to achieve absolute business process automation. While most companies use countless processes, activities and systems to run operations, workflows and procedures can go awry when it comes to today's highly competitive marketplace, thus hindering productivity, growth and profitability. As a result, the implementation of an ERP software application can result in increased productivity, reduced operating expenses, improved data flow, and optimal performance management. ERP software comes in many forms, including supply chain management, manufacturing, distribution, warehouse management, retail management, and point-of-sale software. ERP software (or enterprise resource planning software) is an integrated system used by businesses to combine, organize and maintain the data necessary for operations. ERP systems merge each of the company's key operations, including the manufacturing, distribution, financial, human resources and customer relations departments, into one software system. For many companies, the ERP software is the heart of their operations and the backbone of the organization. ERP software consists of many enterprise software modules that are individually purchased, based on what best meets the specific needs and technical capabilities of the organization. Each ERP module is focused on one area of business processes, such as product development or marketing. Some of the more common ERP modules include those for product planning, material purchasing, inventory control, distribution, accounting, marketing, finance and HR. As the ERP methodology has become more popular, applications have emerged to help business managers implement ERP in other business activities and may also incorporate modules for CRM and business intelligence and present them as a single unified package [2]. Configuring an ERP system is largely a matter of balancing the way the customer wants the system to work with the way it was designed to work. ERP systems typically build many changeable parameters that modify system operation. Data migration is the process of moving/copying and restructuring data from an existing system to the ERP system [3]. Migration is critical to implementation success and requires significant planning. Unfortunately, since migration is one of the final activities before the production phase, it often receives insufficient attention. Advantages: The fundamental advantage of ERP is that integrating the myriad processes by which businesses operate saves time and expense. Revenue and salary tracking, from invoice through cash receipt. They provide a comprehensive enterprise view (no "islands of information"). They make real–time information available to management anywhere, any time to make proper decisions. This article addresses the latter; rather than propose any new security architecture, we present a security characterization framework [4]. Our approach concerns the security functions of software components by exposing their required and ensured security properties. Through a compositional security contract between participating components, system integrators can reason about the security effect of one component on another. A CSC is based on the degree of conformity between the required security properties of one component and the ensured security properties of another. At the application level, such consent based trust perhaps works fine. But in a component-based development environment, universally shallow commitment regarding component security is dangerously illusive and can trigger costly consequences. Trust requirements in a development environment significantly differ from those of application

users. Component security— based on various nondeterministic elements such as the use domain, magnitude of the hostility in the use context, value of the data, and other related factors—is relative, particularly in a component-based development environment. Therefore, software engineers must be assured with more than just a component security or insecurity claim[10]. Whatever small role a component plays, the software engineer cannot rule out its possible security threats to the entire application. Component developers might not be aware of the security requirements of their products' potential operational contexts. Software engineers do not expect such knowledge from the component developer, but they do expect a clear specification of the component security requirements and assurances. 1 This information should be made available if queried at runtime. Developers must be able to do runtime tests with candidate components to find possible security matches and mismatches. The major concern—the disclosure of components' security properties and security mismatches of those properties—has received little attention from the security and software engineering research communities. Current practices and research for security of component-based software consists of several defensive lines such as firewalls, trusted operating systems, security wrappers, secure servers, and so on. Some significant work on component testing, component assurances and security certification has been done, particularly in the last two years. These efforts basically concentrated on how to make a component secure, how to assure security using digital certification, and how to maximize testing efforts to increase the quality of individual components. Undoubtedly, such work is important to inspire trust, but we must explore other possibilities that would let software engineers know and evaluate the actual security properties of a component for specific applications. If the developer doesn't know these attributes during system integration, the component might not be trustworthy [11]. In current practice, the trust-related attributes are often neither expressed nor communicated. Software developers are reluctant to trust a third-party software component that does not tell much about its security profile. Despite these shortcomings, software engineers are still inclined to use them to minimize development effort and time. Today, trust in an application system is based on consent—that is, the user is explicitly asked to consent or decline to use a system. At the application level, such consent-based trust perhaps works fine. But in a component-based development environment, universally shallow commitment regarding component security is dangerously illusive and can trigger costly consequences. Trust requirements in a development environment significantly differ from those of application users. Component security— based on various nondeterministic elements such as the use domain, magnitude of the hostility in the use context, value of the data, and other related factors—is relative, particularly in a component-based development environment. Therefore, software engineers must be assured with more than just a component security or insecurity claim. Whatever small role a component plays, the software engineer cannot rule out its possible security threats to the entire application. Component developers might not be aware of the security requirements of their products' potential operational contexts. Software engineers do not expect such knowledge from the component developer, but they do expect a clear specification of the component security requirements and assurances. These efforts basically concentrated on how to make a component secure, how to assure security using digital certification, and how to maximize testing efforts to increase the quality of individual components. Undoubtedly, such work is important to inspire trust, but we must explore other possibilities that would let software engineers know and evaluate the actual security properties of a component for specific applications. Since 1999, several seminal books have helped define the software security field. These books introduced the approach to building security in, which practitioners have since enhanced, expanded, and published in various technical articles; including the Building Security In series (see the sidebar).The core philosophy underlying this approach is that security, like dependability and reliability, can't be added onto a system after the fact through the addition of sets of features, nor can it be tested into a sys- tem. Instead, security must be designed and built into a system from the ground up. More than 90 percent of reported security incidents are the result of exploits against defects in the designer code of software, according to the CERT Coordination Center (CERT/CC) of the SEI. Although traditional security efforts attempt to retroactively bolt on devices that make it more difficult for those defects to be exploited, such devices simply aren't effective. Standard-issue software development lifecycle models—ranging from the process-heavy Capabilities Maturity Model (CMM) to the lightweight Extreme Programming (XP) approach—are not focused on creating secure systems. They all exhibit serious shortcomings when the goal is to develop systems with a high degree of The only way to develop systems with required functionality and performance that can also withstand malicious attacks is to design and implement them to be secure. Soft- ware security is thus a full lifecycle undertaking in which critical design decisions and trade-offs must be clearly and thoroughly under- stood. In addition, tools for supporting security engineering (for example, source code analysis tools) must be integrated into the software development environment. By treating software security risk explicitly throughout the soft- ware life cycle, we can properly identify and mitigate the consequences of security failure and successful security attack. For each lifecycle activity, a team made up of security analysts and developers must address security goals and incorporate best practices to assure security. In some situations, existing development methods can be used to enhance security [5]. Current research is also creating new methods that developers and analysts can apply as they build software; however, more research and experimentation are required before the goal of security can become a reality [6]. One way of illustrating a lifecycle approach that incorporates security

into each basic phase of software development has been intentionally created to be process agnostic. That is, the best practices and methods de- scribed are applicable to any and all development approaches as long as they result in the creation of software artifacts. Given this approach, software development processes as diverse as the waterfall model, Rational Unified Process (RUP), XP, Agile, spiral development, and CMM involve creating a common set of software artifacts (the most common artifact being code). In this way, we can apply software security best practices and their associated knowledge catalogs regardless of exactly which "base" software process is followed. Figure includes best practices (as does Figure A in the sidebar), knowledge, and tools, all organized ac- cording to software artifacts. The Build Security In (BSI) Software Assurance Initiative seeks to alter the way that software is developed so that it's less vulnerable to at- tack by building security in from the start. BSI is a project of the Strategic Initiatives Branch of the DHS's NCSD, which has sponsored the development and collection of software assurance and software security information that will help software developers and architects create secure systems. The effort is managed by Joe Jarzombek, the DHS director for soft- ware assurance. As part of the initiative, a BSI content catalog will be made available as a Web portal in October. This portal is intended for software developers and software development organizations that want in- formation and practical guidance on how to produce secure and reliable software. The catalog is based on the principle that software security is fundamentally a software engineering problem that we must address systematically throughout the software development life cycle. The catalog will contain links to a broad range of information about best practices, tools, and knowledge. Figure identifies aspects of software assurance covered in the catalog[9]. The BSI portal includes information about which tools developers and security analysts can use to detect and/or remove common vulnerabilities. Of particular interest are static analyses tools that help developers look for common security- critical problems in source code. The best current commercial tools support languages such as Java, CLR, C++, C, and PHP (see key BSI5 in the sidebar).Even with deep technical content, a business case is required to convince industry to adopt secure software development best practices and educate consumers about the need for software assurance. Therefore, each documented best practice addresses the business case for use of that practice. In addition, the portal will include overall business case framework dynamic navigation. The extent to which users will find the content accessible as well as useful will determine how this portal impacts real-world development practices and, thus, overall systems security. The BSI team is trying to make the content approachable in several different ways. For example, a soft- ware engineer might use the catalog to determine applicable security guidelines; an architect might use security principles to determine how to design an n-tier application in a secure fashion; and a development team leader might use the information to justify software assurance techniques to management by building a business case. Because the repository will be structured and designed to evolve as well as support usage by a variety of user types, it will include a dynamic navigation interface. Once practical guidance and reference materials are available forth day-to-day work most development organizations do, the BSI team plans to identify and organize content for practical guidance and reference materials for enterprise-level security concerns. To help ensure that this software assurance initiative is accepted and supported by the community of soft- ware development organizations, the team is seeking involvement from representatives from industry, academia, and government. Toward this goal, working groups to guide the creation of the BSI software assurance portal have been formed. The Software Technical Working Group (STWG) is composed of respected individuals in the technical community whose primary function is to re- view the portal content's technical veracity and identifies future content [7]. Although the portal is currently in a nascent stage, the BSI team welcomes feedback; prior to the site's launch, you can send it to Jan Philpot at the SEI (philpot@sei.cmu.edu). Community involvement and use is crucial to the portal's success, and we look forward to help from the community in improving software security worldwide. To the best of our knowledge, this paper is the first to experimentally examine the resistance of several security patterns to known categories of attacks. The main contribution of this paper is to propose a complete methodology for calculating the risk of STRIDE attacks on a software system composed of security patterns already from its design. Additionally, we make use of a fuzzy risk analysis framework. Using fuzzy terms is more appropriate when examining the design of a system for security. We cannot apply exact numbers due to the lack of exact information about the security of the system. We note here that we make use of nine levels of risk, which leads to better granularity compared to using fewer levels[8]. Additionally, our approach is security pattern centric. All security estimates are based on used and missing security patterns in places where they are needed. Finally, in this paper, we propose a new security pattern against an attack that we discovered during our experiments and that existing security patterns do not protect against. The rest of this paper is organized as follows: Section 2 describes the systems that we used to experimentally determine the resistance of several security patterns to known categories of attacks. Section 3 contains preliminaries on the fuzzy-set theory and calculations on fuzzy fault trees. In Section 4, the methodology for constructing fuzzy fault trees from UML-class diagrams is described. In Section 5, experimental results are presented, concerning the resistance of security patterns to known attacks, risk evaluation of a no secure and a secure system, and the risk evolution when patterns are introduced in different orders. In the Section, we propose and evaluate a new security pattern named "Secure GET Parameters." Finally, in the Section, we draw some final conclusions and propose future work. In order to experimentally examine the

robustness of various security patterns to known attacks, we have developed two systems. The first system, hereafter denoted as no secure application, is a typical e-commerce application with no usage of security patterns, except for Protected System, where various sources for attacks were deliberately included.. If no Secure Pipe pattern is present in the system, a factor to the fault trees for Spoofing Identity, Information Disclosure, and Elevation of Privilege is added, since information could be eavesdropped. Resistance of the Security Patterns Examined against STRIDE Attacks guard to dictionary attacks [7]. The authentication mechanism of a guard can still be marked as of high security. All authentication patterns and, consequently, the Protected System and the Secure Proxy pattern should be resistant to eavesdropping attacks to serve their purpose. Thus, they should always be used together with the Secure Pipe pattern that enforces the use of the SSL protocol. The Secure Pipe pattern offers protection from Information Disclosure attacks. Finally, the Secure Logger pattern offers a strong protection mechanism from reading/tampering the logs, preventing from Tampering-with-Data, Repudiation, and Information Disclosure attacks. Based on the above analysis, we can make conclusions about the resistance of the security patterns under consideration to known categories of attacks. The results are summarized in Table 3. Irrelevant entries to the specific security pattern are left blank. Since we have not considered security patterns that can confront Denial-of-Service attacks, the corresponding category has been eliminated from our analysis. Next, we perform a likelihood-exposure-consequences investigation for attacks that occur in cases where specific security patterns are missing and cases where the security patterns used do not offer total protection. Our investigation is based on the previous analysis, together with knowledge on possible attacks on Web Applications. We note that the likelihood and the exposure (ease) of an attack are the same, regardless of the application, whereas the consequences depend on the data affected and, thus, on the specific application. Although in our investigation, consequences for the specific applications could be considered, we examined the worst case scenario for the consequences, considering that all system data is of crucial importance. Regarding the authentication mechanism, the categories of attacks affected when the authentication mechanism is broken are Spoofing[7], Information Disclosure, and Elevation of Privilege (if someone gets administrator rights). The most trivial case is when no authentication is used at an application entry point. In this case, the likelihood of an attack is very high, the ease of performing an attack is very high, and the consequences are damaging (very high). When the Protected System pattern is used, the likelihood of successfully attacking a guard of this pattern is low, the ease (exposure) of a dictionary attack can be regarded high, and the consequences are very high. When the Secure Proxy pattern is used, two guards must be compromised for an attack to succeed. The likelihood and exposure of compromising the first guard are the same as in the case of a guard of Protected System. The consequences of attacking the first guard are very low, since the first guard only acts as a front end to the second guard, and no resources are compromised yet when the first guard is compromised. The likelihood, exposure, and consequences of attacking the second guard are the same as in the case of a guard of Protected System. The consequences of attacking the second guard of Secure Proxy are very high, because if the second guard is compromised, then all the protected resources are compromised. In case the Secure Logger pattern is not used in a place where logging is performed [6], the categories of attacks affected are Tampering with Data, Repudiation, and Information Disclosure [8]. If the server where the logs reside is compromised, the log data can be read and changed, letting a user deny having performed an action. The likelihood of such an attack and the ease of such an attack are low, since generally, it is not easy to compromise the server where the logs reside. The consequences regarding Tampering with Data and Information Disclosure are low, since the data kept in the logs is not usually of high importance [10]. The importance of the logs is, however, very high when considering Repudiation (someone could deny having performed an action that he/she performed, or conversely, someone could accuse someone else of having performed an action that he/she did not), and therefore, the consequences are also very high. When the Secure Pipe pattern is not used, the application may not be configured to work with an SSL connection. In this case, important data could be eavesdropped, leading to an Information Disclosure attack, and additionally, if the credentials are eavesdropped, this would lead to Spoofing and Elevation of Privilege[11]. The likelihood of an eavesdropping attack in this case can be considered high, the ease of such an attack is high, and the consequences for all categories affected are very high. When no intercepting validator is used in a path from a class where data is input to a class where this data is shown or a resource (for example, a database) is accessed, having this data as a parameter, then an SQL Injection and/or an XSS attack could occur.

Fig. 1. The Sonar Quality Dashboard for SecureCI. It displays integrated software vulnerability information.

Automated CI is often performed during Code check-ins—code checked into a source code control system can be automatically integrated and unit tested to assure its quality. CI done during code check-in typically doesn't test the application's entire feature set but quickly confirms that code enhancements compile and pass a set of unit tests [9]. Nightly builds—each night, software is automatically compiled and a full battery of regression tests are run to ensure the entire code base integrates and operates properly.

2. Methodology

Nightly builds also often automatically execute code analysis to ensure quality and compliance. Weekly builds—for tests that take too long to execute on a nightly basis, weekly builds are often established to compile and test software more fully to manage an automated CI process, CI servers have emerged. Methodology: Driven by these ideas and motivations, we propose a security characterization framework in this article. The framework addresses how to characterize the security properties of components, how to analyze at runtime the internal security properties of a system comprising several atomic components, how to characterize the entire system's security properties, and how to make these characterized properties available at runtime. To inspire trust in a particular composite system, a component's security contract with all the other components, the security provisions that each component requires from ensures to the others, and the ultimate global security profile of the entire federated system should be clear. Security properties and behaviors of a software system are categorized into 11 classes in ISO/IEC-15408 Common Criteria. These classes are made of members, called families, based on a set of security requirements. We will only discuss a subset of one such security class, user data protection, just to give a snapshot of our characterization framework. The publishable security properties related to user data protection of any atomic component can be categorized as required—a precondition that other interested parties must satisfy during development to access the ensured security services—or ensured—a post condition that guarantees the security services once the precondition is met. Security properties are typically derived from security functions—the implementation of security policies. And the security policies are defined to withstand security threats and risks. A simple security function consists of one or more principals (a principal can be a human, a component, or another application system, whoever uses the component), a resource such as data, security attributes such as keys or passwords, and security operations such as encryption. Based on these, three main elements characterize an ensured or required security property: security operations executed by the components to enforce security properties, security attributes required to perform the operation, and application data manipulated in a compositional contract. Using these elements, we can formulate a simple structure to characterize the security requirements and assurances of individual components'(O_i, K_j, D_k) where f represents a security objective formed with three associated arguments; O is the security-related operation performed by the principal i in a compositional contract; K is a set of security attributes used by the principal; subscript j contains additional information about K such as key type, the key's owner, and so on; D is an arbitrary set of data or information that is affected by the operation O; and the subscript k contains additional information regarding D such as whether a digital signature is used or not. The following examples represent a required security property R (protect_in_data) and an ensured security property E (protect_out_data) of a component P: In this example, component P's required property RP states that the data is to be encrypted by any component Q with component P's public key. A plus sign (+) after P denotes public key. The ensured property EP states that component P encrypts the data file with the public key of any component Q. The data is also digitally signed by P with its private key, denoted by the minus sign (−) after P. This format is specific to a particular type of security function related to user data protection. This notation, or a similar one, can be standardized for all components. However, alternative structure might need to be formulated to represent other security classes such as authentication, security audit, trusted path, privacy, and so on. A component that broadcasts an event to receive a service is called a focal component. Software components that respond to the event are usually called candidate components, and they might reside at different remote locations [9]. With

the security characterization structure of atomic components previously explained, a CSC between two components such as x and y can be modeled as existing CSC can be referred to as $Cx,y.Ry$ or $Cx,y.Ex$ respectively. The degree of conformity between the required security properties of one component and the ensured security properties of another is the ultimate CSC of the composite system. As is the case of atomic components, we also need to establish a global security characterization of a composite system, because it might be used in further composition as a component. In fact, developers often view this kind of system as a single entity or an atomic component, not as a collection of components in such further components. Current frameworks for software component models such as EJB, Corba, COM, and .Net are limited to the specification and matching of structural interface definitions. Interface description languages (IDLs) deal with the syntactic structure of the interface such as attributes, operations, and events. In our approach, an active interface not only contains the operations and attributes to serve a function but also embodies the security properties associated with a particular operation or functionality. An active interface supports a three-phase automatic negotiation model for component composition: A component publishes its security properties attached with functionality to the external world. The component negotiates for a possible CSC at runtime with other interested candidate components. If it succeeds, the negotiation results are used to configure and reconfigure the composition dynamically. An active interface consists of a component identity, a static interface signature, a static (read-only) security knowledge base of the component, and a (read–write) CSC base that is dynamic based on the information available from the security knowledge base. Before a component is available for use, a certifying authority must certify it. A certificate ensures that the implementation matches the published functionality and the exposed security properties. It is argued that software components can only be tested and certified individually—not within the context of the complete composite system. The certified assurances must be verifiable statically and dynamically. Figure 1 illustrates a skeleton of an active interface structure. The Component in the active interface includes a unique identity (UID) provided by a certifying authority, the component's current residing address (URL), details about the component developer, and the certification authority that certified the component: Component ID (uid, URL, developer_ID, certificate) A certifying authority will verify, certify, and digitally stamp all of this data. It can further reveal more identity information if queried about the certificate, certification stamp, validity period, and so on. All identity and certification information is read-only and public—only the certifying authority can alter it. An interface signature consists of operations and attributes for a particular functionality. These operations and attributes are used for structural plug-and-play matching. These properties are static— read-only properties. Components cannot make any modification to this. This interface is intended to make a structural match before two components are composed. A security knowledge base stores and makes available the security properties of a component in terms of $f(Oi, Kj, Dk)$. The required and ensured properties stored in this KB are specific to the functionality that the component offers. These properties must be based on the actual security functions that the component uses to accomplish a particular functionality. A component might offer various functions, so the exposed security properties can vary accordingly. Once the information is stored in a KB and certified, no other entities can alter its content. Any recompilation of the certified component would automatically erase all certification and identity information stored in Component [8]. If the component needs to alter its security properties, it requires a new certificate after the recompilation. A binary executable piece of code residing in the active interface of the focal component generates CSC conformity results between the focal component and a candidate component. If the system identifies nonconformance between the required and ensured properties it concludes with a security mismatch. The resulting CSC is automatically stored in the CSC base of the focal component, and remains there as long as the composition is valid. Also, a component can accept a partially or completely mismatched CSC, although this might have negative security effects on the global system. If a component becomes obsolete or is no longer needed in a dynamic composition, the associated obsolete CSC might be stored in a log belonging to the focal component for future audit purposes, but it would not be available to any of the participating components. We use a fictitious distributed-system topology as an example of how our proposed active interface would work in a distributed environment. Consider an e-health care system that regards all clinical information passing among the stakeholders, such as the general practitioners, specialists, patients, and pharmacists, as confidential. Assume a focal component Y running on a machine at a GP's office connects with a trusted candidate component S chosen from among many such systems running at various specialists' offices. Y provides a patient's diagnosis report to S to get a prescription. After receiving the prescription from S, Y sends it electronically to a candidate component P residing on a pharmacist's system for a price quotation. Developers would independently develop many such Ps and Ss and make them available from their various distributed sources, potentially able to deliver the functionality that Y wants. However, component Y not only is interested in specific functionality but also wants to know upfront the security properties that those components provide. Assume [3]. In return, Y requires that P digitally sign and encrypt the price data. Note that these security properties of Y are quite different from those for the specialist prescription. Now assume that in response to Y's broadcasting a request for a price quotation, remote components P1 and P3 have registered their interests in providing the functionality that wants. P1 and P3 are developed and serviced by two different development organizations and have their own security requirements and assurances [10]. Y now runs a security test with P1 to verify whether the component could deliver the

functionality as well as the security that Y requires. It also verifies whether Y by itself could The entire system scenario is shown in Figure. There are two CSCs in this system: one between Y and S2 (shown by the red dotted line) and the other between P3 and Y (shown by the larger blue dotted line).In the latter composition, S2 is transitively composed with P3 because P3's security requirements partly depend on S2's security assurances, although P3 does not have any direct composition with S2.With the previous examples, we have demonstrated that software components can know and reason about the actual security requirements and assurances of others before an actual composition takes place. The example also suggests that a security characterization is a mechanism to provide "informed consent."2 An informed consent gives the participating entities explicit opportunity to consent or decline to use components after assessing the candidate components' security properties.[A component can accept a partially or completely mismatched CSC, although this might have negative security effects on the global system. Our framework's main objective is to generate computational reflection to let components and their developers identify and capture the various security properties of the other components with which they cooperate [4]. In such a setting, components not only read the met description of others' security properties but also identify security mismatches between two components and evaluate compos ability realistically. Security characterization and third-party certification of components would mutually benefit each other: first, a security characterization would contribute significantly to the process of component security certification; second, certification would make the exposed security properties more creditable to software engineers. When required and ensured security properties are spelled out in simple, comprehensible terms, software engineers are better positioned to evaluate the strength of the security a component provides. They are also well informed about what to expect from and provide to the component to establish a viable composition. In a software engineering context, we must balance security against the other design goals of the entire component-based system. To achieve this, application developers must know about components' security properties. A trusting profile could be gradually built and inspired on the basis of the participating components' self-disclosure of their security properties. The security properties built into a component represent the efforts already put into place to withstand certain security threats. However, the real protection with the committed effort of the component from any security threat is beyond the control of the component. Whether the available resources disclosed by the component are sufficient to withstand a threat is outside the parameters of our framework. A trust-generating effort could only be viable by exposing actual certified security properties of interested parties in a composition as opposed to "secure or insecure" claims. We acknowledge that software engineers' trust in unfamiliar components is understandably difficult to cultivate and that complete trust is undoubtedly desirable, but we believe that our approach would at least contribute to such trust. One of the real challenges facing the emerging field of software security is the lack of an easily accessible common body of knowledge. Simply put, most software developers and architects—the very people who need to understand and practice software security—remain blithely unaware of their critical role. Without their direct participation, software security will languish. In this installment of Building Security In, we describe a software security portal that the US Department of Homeland Security (DHS) National Cyber Security Division (NCSD) is developing (along with the Carnegie Mellon Software Engineering Institute [SEI] and Digital). The launch of this portal is scheduled for October 2005 as part of the US-CERT Web site. The portal aims to provide a common, accessible, well-organized set of information for practitioners wishing to do software security. In this section, we summarize some of the limitations of the proposed methodology and suggest some extensions and improvements. Our methodology relies on the accuracy of function cycle count measurements. This is possible only if a sophisticated, cycle-accurate simulator is available for the system under consideration, which reports cycle counts for each function excluding the cycles spent by the processor in its descendants. Point your web browser to www.cucwings.com alternatively we can go to www.cucwings.com and click HR in Top Menu Bar. Initially basic data needs to be set up before getting benefitted and utilizing all the options in HR module. To go to Employee Basic Data Set-up page click on the HR Basic Data Set-up link at the Left Side Menu Bar in HR page.

Fig. 2. *Needs of basic data to be set up before getting benefitted and utilizing all the options in HR module*

To add an employee you need to click on the Add Employee button in the left side menu bar of Employee page and you will land in Add Employee page as shown above.

There are different ways to enter information in the system through different fields.

3. Entering Information

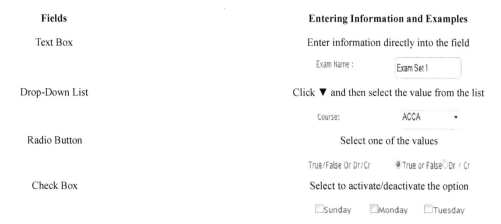

Fields	Entering Information and Examples
Text Box	Enter information directly into the field Exam Name : Exam Set 1
Drop-Down List	Click ▼ and then select the value from the list Course: ACCA
Radio Button	Select one of the values True/False Or Dr/Cr ● True or False ○ Dr / Cr
Check Box	Select to activate/deactivate the option ☐ Sunday ☐ Monday ☐ Tuesday

Fig. 3. *Different ways to to enter information in the system through different fields.*

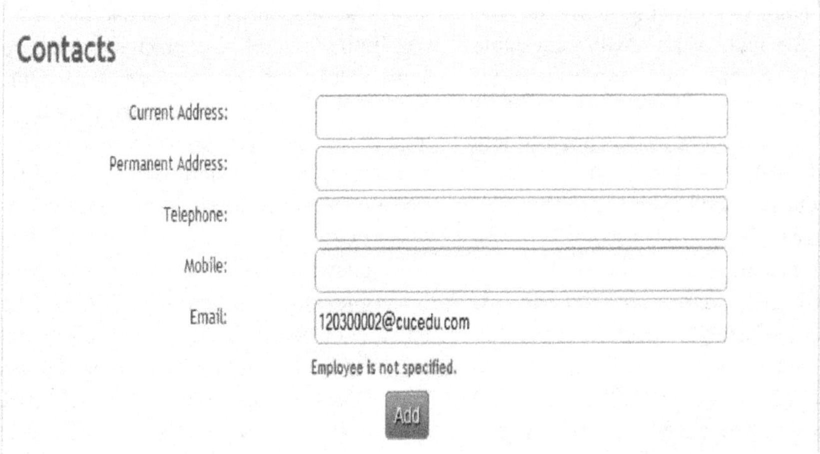

Fig. 4. Continuous Assessment of security hardening of the ERP software system.

The system also comes with a 'what you see is what you get editor', which allows user to easily enter and preview larger amount of information.Software-based protection systems are coming into common use, driven by their inherent advantages in both performance and portability. Software fault isolation, proof-carrying code, or language-based mechanisms can be used to guarantee memory-safety. Secure system services cannot be built without these mechanisms, but may require additional system support to work properly. We have described three designs which support interposition of security checks between entrusted code and important system resources. Each design has been implemented in Java and both extended stack introspection and name space management have been integrated in commercial Web browsers. All three designs have their strengths and weaknesses. For example, capability systems are implemented very naturally in Java. However, they are only suitable for applications where programs are not expecting to use the standard Java APIs, because capabilities require a stylistic departure in API design. Name space management offers good compatibility with existing Java applets but Java's libraries and newer Java mechanisms such as the reflection API may limit its use. Extended stack introspection also offers good compatibility with existing Java applets and has reasonable security properties, but its complexity is troubling and it relies on several artifacts of Sun's Java Virtual Machine implementation. Understanding how to create such a hybrid system is a main area for future research. Training throughout the company focused on architectural reviews, secure coding, and testing processes. The training materials were initially licensed from a major university, and have since been customized to their needs. H further customizes the training for product groups, to maximize relevance to the staff. While training is usually a one-time event, organizational turnover is high enough that the training is repeated in each location on a regular basis. In some cases, threat modeling as part of the design process. A company-wide license to use a source code analysis tool, along with training by the evangelist team on how to use the tool effectively[11]. An in-house penetration testing team, coupled with third-party penetration testing when the need

arises (e.g., because the in-house team is unavailable).Use of a third-party team to assess the security status of products being considered for OEM or acquisition, to minimize the risk of acquiring security vulnerabilities along with products. This review team currently operates after the OEM arrangement or acquisition has been completed. The evangelist team believes it would be more effective before the deal is signed, but that change has not occurred. Software testing is one of the most fundamental assurances for the high quality of a developed product [2]. Quality of software represents consumer satisfaction across the breadth of a products´ features, including assurances about safety, privacy and security. The commercial software industry typically employs Quality Assurance (QA) technicians through a dedicated QA department. The area of formal testing is identified as a major difference between the commercial and open source projects. The section is by no means arguing against system wide tests but is pointing out the interesting side effects that could result from abusing the system on the commercial side and the extra diligence for the lack of it on the free side. We believe that if QA abuse is true on the commercial side then abiding by good development practices like unit tests and developer diligence while reaping the benefit and the extra assurance of system testing could boost the quality and stress the competitive edge that it has in this area. Consumers can reap the benefits of all of this by having a super reliable system upon delivery that could be deployed with more confidence. Despite the claims by the open source proponents that open source is more secure, a more close examination of the OSS and IP development processes shows advantages and disadvantages on both sides. The claim of open source intrinsic advantage over "closed source" could not be verified from the examined perspectives.

4. Conclusions

Hackers are now targeting the organization's data, putting at great risk of organization and its stakeholders. A secure, formal and structured software development methodology, along with enforceable and pertinent policies was our main target on this project development. A stunning combination of software assurance is achieved when the above things are combined with a professional certification. In our view "openness", being the most controversial aspect discussed, may not have a big advantage in security. This is evident from the fact that expert "eyeballs" make the difference to the casual developer review. The openness of open source doesn't automatically make it more secure, but it creates an opportunity for motivated individuals to pool together security expertise to do code reviews, security auditing and create tools to help improve security. Two great examples of this are the Sardonyx project On the other hand, disclosing source code can be a slight advantage to the expert hacker in reducing the overhead of analyzing issued patches to produce an exploit for un-patched systems. Lack of formal testing may constitute a disadvantage to open source but produces an implicit advantage by making developers work in a more responsible manner. The numbers come in support of findings that both sides exhibit a mixed set of pros and cons. The record of problems found in OSS and IP don´t suggest the superiority of one over the other when it comes to security [1]. Both open source and IP software have suffered from an abysmal rate of security failures in the last few years. In both worlds the number and sophistication of attacks are on the rise. If software is to meet future needs of business, government and home users, there has to be an order of magnitude improvement in the resilience of software products to attack. Finally we believe that there is a slew of inherent potential on both sides that could be leveraged. There is also room for hybrid models reaping the advantages of both camps. This might be evident from the hybrid development model used with Mozilla Companies like Apple and Sun have taken the initiative to freely publish the source code of projects, indicating potentially closer steps toward a hybrid model. With increased software security incidents, regulatory and compliance requirements, and globalization all changing the landscape of security, one simply cannot take the chance of releasing vulnerable software. Hackers are now targeting your organization's data, putting at great risk your organization and its stakeholders. Damage to your reputation caused by a security breach, and the ensuing loss of customer trust and confidence, might prove irreparable. In today's business environment, software assurance is imperative. In addition to network perimeter security controls, organizations must ensure that software security controls are designed, developed, and deployed to protect their critical information assets. A secure, formal and structured software development methodology, along with enforceable and pertinent policies, must become a part of any organization's operations.

References

[1]   Voas, "Certifying Software for High-Assurance Environments," IEEE Software, vol. 16, no. 4, July/Aug.1999, pp. 48–54.

[2]   W. Councill, "Third-Party Testing and the Quality of Software Components," IEEE Software, vol. 16, no. 4, July/Aug. 1999, pp. 55–57.

[3]   A. Ghosh and G. McGraw, "An Approach for Certify- ing Security in Software Components," Proc. 21st Nat'l Information Systems Security Conf., Nat'l Inst. Stan- dards and Technology, Crystal city, Vir., 1998, pp.82–86.

[4]   ISO/IEC-15408 (1999), Common Criteria for Informa- tion Technology Security Evaluation, v2.0, Nat'l Inst. Standards and Technology, Washington, DC, June1999, http://csrc.nist.gov/cc. (current Dec. 2001)

[5]   K. Khan, J. Han, and Y. Zheng, "A Framework for an Active Interface to Characterize Compositional Security Contracts of Software Components," Proc. Australian Software Eng. Conf., IEEE CS Press, Los Alamitos, Calif., 2001, pp. 117–126.

[6]   C.A. Berry, J. Carnell, M.B. Juric, M.M. Kunnumpurath, N. Nashi, and S. Romanosky, J2EE Design Patterns Applied. Wrox Press, 2002.

[7]   Blakley, C. Heath, and Members of the Open Group SecurityForum, Security Design Patterns: Open Group Technical Guide, 2004.

[8]   Braga, C. Rubira, and R. Dahab, "Tropyc: A Pattern Language for Cryptographic Software," Proc. Fifth Conf. Pattern Languages of Programming (PLoP), 1998.

[9]   P.J. Brooke and R.F. Paige, "Fault Trees for Security SystemDesign and Analysis," Computers and Security, vol. 22, no. 3, pp. 256-264, Apr. 2003.

[10]   K.-Y. Cai, Introduction to Fuzzy Reliability. Kluwer AcademicPublishers, 1996.

[11]   K.-Y. Cai, "System Failure Engineering and Fuzzy Methodology: An Introductory Overview," Fuzzy Sets and Systems, vol. 83, no. 2,pp. 113-133, Oct. 1996.

3

Research on service reputation evaluation method based on cloud model

Tingwei Chen, Jing Lei

College of Information, Liaoning University, Shenyang, Liaoning, China

Email address:

twchen@lnu.edu.cn (Tingwei Chen), 478444577@qq.com (Jing Lei)

Abstract: With the increasingly evident advantages of service-oriented software architecture, Web service received widespread attention, and the numbers of Web Services are increasing constantly. It is more difficult to select high-quality Web service that meets user requirements. Because traditional service reputation evaluation approaches cannot ensure the authenticity and reliability of user ratings, this paper proposes a cloud-based reputation evaluation approach for assessing the history behavior of service consumers, and also takes into account the rating similarity to generate rating quality cloud. With the parameters of cloud model, we can measure the quality level and stability of rankings, which provide additional evidence for trust decision-making. The result of simulating experiments shows that the proposed approach can improve the accuracy of reputation evaluation and the quality of Web service selection, and defend against malicious attacks, so that the interests of service requesters and service providers can be protected.

Keywords: Web Services, Trust Model, Cloud Theory, Recommendation Trust

1. Introduction

Service Oriented Architecture (SOA) provides business with a competitive environment, for enterprise can shorten product cycles, save development costs and enhance enterprise competitiveness using SOA-based applications. And service consumers are even not concerned with how these services will execute their requests. Figure 1 shows the collaboration among the entities in a service-oriented architecture. The collaborations in SOA follow the "publish, find, bind and invoke" paradigm.

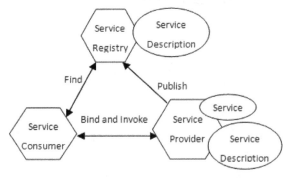

Figure 1. SOA's Publish-Find-Bind-Invoke Paradigm

Web services as a SOA implementation has begun to caught great attention of industry and academia. With the expansion and increasing number of Web services, it is inevitable that there will be a lot of the same or similar functions Web services. As a result, how to choose a high-quality Web services to help customers meet their requirements has become a hot issue in the field of service-oriented architecture.

Currently, there has been an extensive amount of research focused on reputation evaluation and computation, and many scholars have made a wide range of analysis and some achievements. In respect of calculation methods, there are weighted average method, trust model based method, fuzzy theoretical based method, QoS-aware method and so on. Meanwhile, there are distributed statistical model and centralized statistical model in respect of the statistical architecture of reputation evaluation [1-5].

Fu Xiao-Dong [2] designed a QoS-aware reputation mechanism to measure service reputation using the similarity of service QoS true value and declaration. However it only takes service QoS evaluation into account, ignoring customer experience and subjective feelings; Hien Trang Nguyen[3] designed a trust and reputation evaluation system based on Bayesian network. The system evaluated direct and indirect trust relationships among agents by analysis the past behavior of service. However it didn't take users' fake ratings into account, and the result deviates from the true value of the reputation evaluation; Sun Qiu-Jing [4] proposed a recommended trust computation approach based on similarity of users' ratings, which can reflect differences of assessing standards for the same service between different users, ignoring the uncertainty and ambiguity of some qualitative concepts.

Therefore, considering the fake ratings in network, it is necessary to measure the quality of customer ratings and its uncertainty during the evaluation of service reputation. Cloud model is an appropriate tool to describe uncertain concepts and transform quantitative expressions into qualitative concepts. The trust decision evidence will be more sufficient because Cloud model can give description and characteristics of a concept from multiple angles more than just one numerical value. With these research problems in mind, we develop a Cloud-based Reputation Evaluation Approach (CREA), which could be applied to Web service selection. The results of simulation-based experiments show that CREA can provide a high success rate of service transaction and resist fake ratings of malicious attacks.

2. Related Works

2.1. Trust Mechanism

"Trust" is a similar concept to another concept "reputation", and they are often confused because they are very close and share some common ground diversity and dynamics. There is no uniform standard of definition of the concept of "trust", since people have different views about trust and reputation. In this paper, we make the integration of other researches and give the following definition of trust, reputation and referential concepts [5]:

Definition 1: Trust is a subjective evaluation based on customers' experience. For instance, trust is a prediction of customer A according to his/her knowledge and network environment, which reflect the credibility of service B for its ability to perform a specific action or provide some function.

Definition 2: Reputation is a quality of service evaluation of the customer, which reflects the performance of service for fulfilling its quality standard declared and trust level evaluation of the service from other customers in network.

Customers' trust in service comes from two aspects, one is direct trust in service based on customers' using experience, and another is indirect trust based on recommend from other customers. Followings are definitions of direct trust and indirect trust in Beth model:

Definition 3: If customer A's trust in service B is got from direct experience, then the trust is called direct trust denoted as DT.

Definition 4: If customer A's trust in service B is got from other customers' recommend or rating, the trust is called indirect trust expressed as IT.

For a service never used before, a customer's trust and judgment most depend on indirect trust and reputation; when the frequency of use increase to some extent, customer's trust will depend on indirect trust from most part. Therefore, other customers' rating and reputation are very important for strange services.

Customer ratings play an important role in reputation calculation. However, there are many abnormal customers in network. They are driven by business benefit, for benefit-connection service, they give an extreme high rating; for competitive-connection service, they give an extreme low rating, as a result, reputation evaluation will be affected. One way to address this problem is to develop evaluation methods. In this paper, we develop a Cloud-based reputation evaluation mechanism for establishing rating quality cloud of customers that can eliminate or punish users' rating if its rating quality is under the benchmark. At the same time, the parameters from rating quality cloud reflect stability of user rating quality, so service reputation evaluation result will be more accurate.

2.2. Cloud Model

LI Deyi proposed the concept of cloud model [6] based on fuzzy theory and probability theory, focused on studying fuzziness and uncertainty of concepts. Cloud model not only can convert qualitative concepts into many quantitative values with certain distribution pattern and characteristic, but also can pick up significant information of qualitative concepts from quantitative value expressions.

Definition 5: Supposing U is quantitative discourse domain expressed by value, C is a concept in U. If quantitative value $x \in U$ and x is a random implementation of concept C, then x's certainty of C, $\mu(x) \in [0,1]$ is a random number $\mu(x) \in [0,1]$, $\forall x \in U, x \to \mu(x)$. The distribution of x in discourse domain U could be called cloud expressed as $C(X)$, and every x is called a cloud drop.

Expected value "Ex", entropy "En" and hyper entropy "He" are three most important digital characteristics of cloud model, which show major point of qualitative concept. In general, "Ex" reflects the center of cloud, which is the expected value of cloud drops in discourse domain, moreover, it is the most representative sample point; "En" reflects the dispersion of cloud drops, which is the measurement of uncertainty and fuzziness of qualitative concepts. For the graphic of cloud, "En" refer to the width of cloud; "He" is the measurement of uncertainty and fuzziness of entropy "En". In addition, the larger Cloud's width is, the bigger "He" is.

Cloud generator refer to generation algorithm for cloud model, including forward cloud generator, backward cloud generator, X conditions cloud generator, Y conditions cloud generator and so on. The most significant are forward and backward cloud generator. Forward cloud generator can be used for converting qualitative concept into quantitative value expression, and backward cloud generator can be used for building cloud to describe the characteristics of qualitative concept. The cloud model can be divided into several categories depending on its shape. There are normal distribution cloud, triangle cloud, echelon cloud, Γ cloud and so on. Normal cloud is the most important cloud model, because normal cloud can be applied to most fuzzy concepts in realistic environment. Li Xiong[11] stated the universality of normal cloud, and all of the cloud generators used in this paper are backward normal cloud generator. Following are its algorithm description:

Algorithm 1. Backward normal cloud generator

Input: data sample xi, i=1,2,3…n.

Output: digital characteristics of qualitative concept (Ex, En, He)

Calculate mean of data samples $\bar{x} \leftarrow \frac{1}{n}\sum_{i=1}^{n}x_i$ and sample

variance $S^2 \leftarrow \frac{1}{n-1}\sum_{i=1}^{n}\left(x_i - \bar{x}\right)^2$

Expected value $Ex \leftarrow \bar{x}$

Entropy $En \leftarrow \sqrt{\frac{\pi}{2}} \times \frac{1}{n}\sum_{i=1}^{n}|x_i - Ex|$

Hyper entropy $He \leftarrow \sqrt{S^2 - En^2}$

3. Cloud-based Reputation Evaluation Approach

3.1. Quantization of User Ratings

There are two different kinds of user ratings: explicit rating and implicit rating. Explicit rating comes from user feedbacks, which can be used after simple quantization. However, the major consumers of service are computers, and it is unrealistic to force clients submit their feedbacks every time when they used services. Therefore, this paper take only implicit ratings [7] into account, using Delphi[8] method to build rating index system and FAHP[9] to confirm weights of indexes from every level. Finally, user rating value will be got by collecting and statistics of bottom rating index.

Define user rating as vector $\vec{V}_{i,j}''' = (V_1''' , V_2''' , V_3''' , ...V_n''')$, and V_n''' denotes customer ID_i 's feedback value on n.th bottom index during his/her use of service j. following is the final expression of user rating :

$$EV_{i,j} = \sum_{s=1}^{m}\omega_s'' (\sum_{k=1}^{n}\omega_k''' \times V_k''') \tag{1}$$

Table 1. Implicit rating index system

Stair index	Secondary index	weight	Bottom index	weight
Implicit rating index	"Mark" behaviour	0.36	Adding to bookmark	0.21
			Login or entry	0.15
			Save the page	0.14
	"Conserve" behaviour	0.28	Open new page	0.10
			printing	0.04
			Clicking the cursor	0.09
	"Repeat" behaviour	0.25	Dragging the scroll bar	0.08
			Copying and pasting	0.08
			Opening a hyper link	0.70
	"Quote" behaviour	0.11	Copying a hyper link	0.40

3.2. Rating Quality Cloud Generation

Customers' feedbacks are curial, since service reputation relies on the comprehensive perspective and subjective feeling of customers. However, ratings in network are in chaos. If cannot distinguish noise and malicious feedback from all user feedback, the result of reputation evaluation will be inaccurate. It is necessary to measure the trustworthiness of every customer's rating. In another word, measurement of rating quality is needed.

Definition 5: Rating quality is the evaluation and prediction of customer's rating ability through assessing and quantifying history feedback behavior of customers. In this paper, rating quality denoted by ω_i , the larger ω_i is, the higher the user's rating quality could be, and his/her feedback will be more accurate and objective for showing the real performance of services.

The assessment of rating quality consists of two parts. The first part is customer feedback similarity for each customer. We designed a customer feedback similarity algorithm for assessing each customer's history rating set to quantify

customer's preference and rating ability. The customer's feedback similarity shows whether his/her rating accord with normal judgment standard. Malicious customer and customer with deficient rating ability have lower feedback similarity. Consequently, if a customer's feedback similarity is below benchmark, his/her rating should be eliminated for reputation evaluation. Following is definition of feedback similarity among customers:

Definition 6: Customer feedback similarity is the result of assessing customer's rating difference with other customers who come from the same user set by evaluating customer's history ratings, which reflects customers' rating quality from one aspect.

The process to calculate customer's feedback similarity: First, we need to collect and search service set that ever used by the given customer, such as Figure 2; Second, search user set and their rating information of each service as Figure 3, and compare the ratings with given customer's rating for feedback similarity calculation. The mentioned user set could be original user set in early days, when there are enough feedback and transactions, it could be user set clustered by customers' preference and interest [10], and the feedback similarity will have more worthiness.

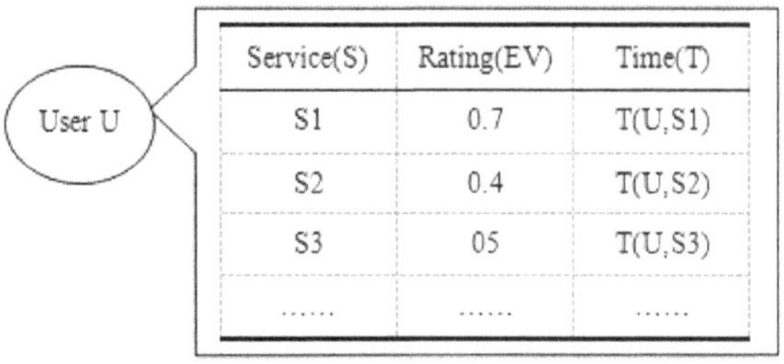

Figure 2. Given customer U's service rating set

Because of large amount of malicious customers in Web service environment, some of them tend to disguise their malicious behavior. For example, if an abnormal customer provide fake feedback to benefit-correlated services, and provide normal feedback to other uncorrelated services. As a result, their feedback similarity will keep at a high level for disguising their attack behavior. This behavior will lead to a more rating fluctuation than other normal customers. So the second part of assessment of rating quality is rating stability, is defined in definition 7. For customers with lower rating stability than benchmark, rating quality will be decrease, it means that they have attack or malicious tendency, and their feedback will be eliminated or punished for reputation evaluation.

Figure 3. User set and rating information of given service S1

Definition 7: Customer feedback stability is the concept shows that his/her rating ability won't change in a given time window by assessing customer's history rating information, which reflects customer's rating quality from another aspect besides feedback similarity.

Since cloud model is a good way to measure stability problem, we introduced it in this paper for converting quantitative value expression into qualitative concept with three important parameters, Ex, En and He. We applied cloud model to sketch fuzzy concept, rating quality, and evaluate its feedback similarity and stability. Following is an example for generating rating quality cloud of customer A, the algorithm is given in Algorithm 2.

Algorithm 2 Rating quality cloud generation of customer A
Input: Customer A and his/her history service rating set
Output: Rating quality cloud of A

$$Cld(User_a) = (Ex, En, He)$$

Set(si)←Search Services Set of Customer A in Given Time Window $win = [t_{start}, t_{now}]$

for i←1 to $N_a(s)$ do

  Search Customer Set Is of Given Service Si

for j ← 1 to $N_{si}(u)$ do

  Search Each Customer's rating for Service Si in User Set Is

  dv_s ← Compute Difference of Ratings between Each Customer in User Set Is

item [i,j]←Put Feedback Similarity $1-dv_s$ into Backward normal Cloud Generator

end for

end for

The expected value of customer A's rating quality cloud from algorithm 2 is denoted in (2):

$$Ex_{(a)} = \begin{cases} \dfrac{1}{N_{total}} \displaystyle\sum_{i=1}^{N_a(s)} \sum_{j=1}^{N_{si}(u)} \left(1-dv_s\right), & N_{total} \neq 0 \\ 0, & N_{total} = 0 \end{cases} \quad (2)$$

In formula (2), the sum of sample is denoted as N_{total} and

$$N_{total} = \sum_{i=1}^{N_a(s)} N_{si}(u)\,;$$ sum of customers in user set of service Si is denoted as $N_{si}(u)$. Cloud model uses three parameters to describe qualitative concept. Concretely, Ex reflects customer A's rating quality, which means trustworthiness level of his/her rating; Another two parameters En and He, reflects the stability of the rating, when the sum of sample is certain, the discrete level just rely on En and He, so we use $\lambda = \sqrt{En^2 + He^2}$ to measure the stability of rating quality.

3.3. Computation of Service Reputation

We have discussed the method to evaluate customer rating quality, but there remains another question that how to compute service reputation based on customer rating quality. Following is an example of service S to show the process to calculate service reputation.

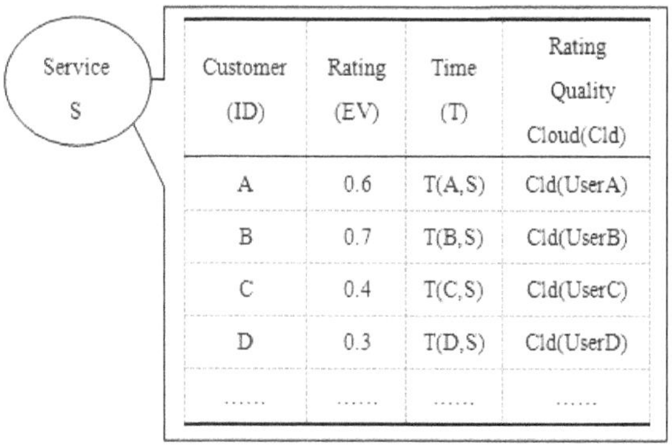

Figure 4. Customers' Rating Quality Information Set of Service S

Firstly, collect and search users who ever used service S in a given time window $win = [t_{start}, t_{now}]$, in other words, get the user set who have interacted with S in the past.

Secondly, generate each customer's rating quality cloud through algorithm2, as shown in Figure 4.

For picking up credible and high-quality customers' ratings due to evaluation for performance of Web services, we measure the parameters of rating quality cloud of each customer. On one hand, we set benchmark for parameter Ex for eliminating ratings of customers whose rating quality cloud parameter $Ex \leq Ex'$, which ensure that customers' feedback and judgment standard are similar for a given level of service performance, in addition, malicious and inexperienced customers' ratings are reduced.

We set the penalty factor α and fluctuation value limit $\varDelta$ for fluctuation factor $\lambda = \sqrt{En^2 + He^2}$. Customer ratings with low stability will be punished, and their rating quality, denoted as ω_i, will be applied to reputation calculation.

$$\omega_i = \begin{cases} Ex \times \alpha^{\Delta - \lambda} & \lambda > \Delta \\ Ex & otherwise \end{cases} \quad (3)$$

Service reputation calculation relies on customers' ratings and their rating quality. It equals to the weighted average of customer rating, and the weight factor is the revisions of Ex based on rating stability.

$$rep(s) = \frac{\sum_{i=1}^{n}(\omega_i \times EV_i)}{\sum_{i=1}^{n}\omega_i} \quad (4)$$

3.4. Service Comprehensive Trust

Customers' trust in services comes from two parts. First part is direct trust DT in service based on interacted experience in the past. Second part is indirect trust IT based on other users' experience and recommend of the given service. Along with the increase of interacted experience, the weight value of direct trust will grow larger. Following is formula(5) of comprehensive trust computation.

$$CT_{a,s} = c \times DT_{a,s} + (1-c) \times rep_s \quad (5)$$

In formula(5), c is weight factor of direct trust; rep_s is reputation of service S; $DT_{a,s}$ is direct Trust of customer A for service S, and it equals to the average of rating values in a given time window of customer A as shown in formula (6).

$$DT_{a,s} = \frac{1}{N_a} \sum_{i=1}^{N_a} ev_{a,s}^i \quad (6)$$

Customer's trust in a given service decides whether it will interact with the service. It is important that select service based on service reputation when there is no interacting experience avoiding blindness for service selection, so that transaction success rate can be guarantee.

4. Experimental Results and Analysis

4.1. Experiment Environment

We performed experiments to evaluate the effectiveness, robustness and accuracy of CREA. The experiments simulated by software QualNet, consists of 3 servers, 300 customers and 2000 services as shown in Figure 5. Each server equipped with a processor (Intel ® Xeon ® 3.0GHz), 1GB of memory, 2MB L2 cache, a 250GB SCSI disk, and an Intel Pro1000G NIC. We will test CREA in simulation experiment with different scenarios, and we will be comparing the result and performance of CREA with other approaches [14] to analyze and prove the superiority of CREA.

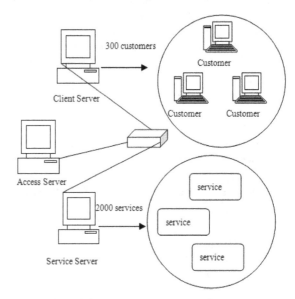

Figure 5. Simulation Environment Implementation

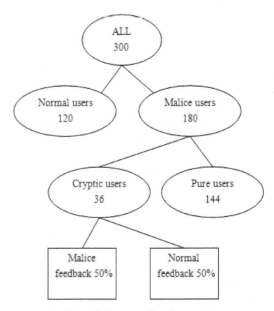

Figure 6. Customer Type Proportion

According to real circumstance in network, we set certain abnormal customers with proportion 0.4, and normal customers with proportion 0.6. There are two different patterns of abnormal customers. One type is pure malicious customers with proportion 0.8, who would always provide malicious ratings. If the service is profit-correlation, they provide extreme high rating to rise up the service reputation called speculation. If the service is competitive-correlation, they provide extreme low rating to debase the service reputation called slander. In contrast, disguise malicious customers provide normal ratings for services with proportion 0.5 to accumulate rating quality for concealing his malicious behavior.

4.2. Resistance against Malicious Customer Attack

In the first scenario, all of malicious customers provide extreme high ratings for profit-correlation services; we compared and analyze reputation change with other approaches in 10 recent time window to prove effectiveness for resisting malicious customer attack. The reference standard is ideal reputation, and it means that all customers provide the same rating for the same service in ideal circumstance. The more close to ideal reputation, the more accurate the reputation evaluation result is.

The results showed on figure 7. We can see that Beth and adaptive Beth[14] didn't test and resist the attack of malicious customers' speculation, service reputation deviate ideal reputation. Beth can't resist the speculation so that reputation will be rise up maliciously and deviate from ideal reputation, because Beth lacks of effective measure for abnormal ratings. Although adaptive Beth has taken actions to resist against fake ratings, it couldn't test the fluctuation of customer behavior. Because adaptive Beth is not available if disguise malicious customers provide fake ratings once in a while after they have accumulated a good rating quality. CREA could measure customers' rating quality and its stability through parameters Ex and λ of cloud model, so the fake ratings from abnormal customers will be eliminated. After 10 time window, the reputation evaluation result is 0.546, still close to ideal reputation.

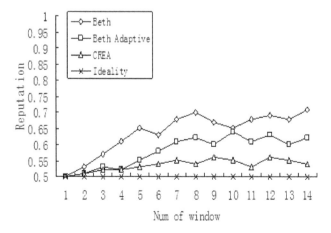

Figure 7. Resistance of Malicious Customers' speculation

In the second scenario, abnormal customers will debase competitive related services. Compare reputation change of CREA in 10 time window with other two approaches, as

shown in Figure 8.

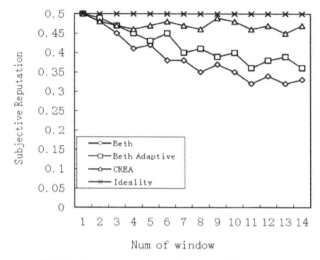

Figure 8. Resistance of Malicious Customers' Disparagement

Similar to first scenario, when abnormal customers provide disparaging ratings, Beth and adaptive Beth didn't test and resist these attacks. As a result, service reputation is debased and far away from ideal reputation. However, CREA could keep the reputation evaluation result at 0.472 after 10 time window, which is still close to ideal reputation.

4.3. Resistance Against Malicious Customer Attack

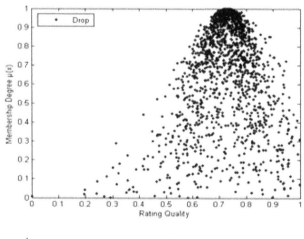

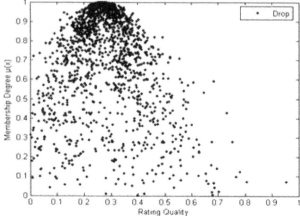

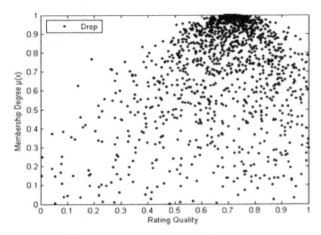

Figure 9. Different Types of Customers' Rating Quality Cloud Comparison

Abnormal customers' attack could be test easily, because CREA relies on cloud-based rating quality evaluation model. Following is an example of rating quality cloud comparison of three different types: a normal customer A, a pure malicious customer B and a disguise malicious customer C.

We can see that customer A's rating quality is kept at a high level (Cld_a(0.71,0.08,0.245)), because he/she always provided trustworthy ratings and the stability is good; Pure malicious customer B's rating (Cld_b (0.27,0.11,0.29)) is eliminated for reputation calculation, because B always provided fake ratings and Ex of the rating quality cloud is lower than benchmark Ex'(Ex'=0.64 in this paper). Disguise malicious customer C sometimes provided credible ratings, and sometimes provided fake ratings, so that the Ex of rating quality cloud could be kept at high level Ex=0.76. However, fluctuant behavior of C lead to a low stability and fluctuation factor $\lambda > \Delta$(Δ=0.38), so that C' ratings will be punished. Furthermore, customer C's influence for reputation evaluation will be less with low-weighted ratings.

4.4. Transaction Success Rate

In third scenario, we performed an experiment to prove the transaction success rate of CREA and its superiority. Transaction success rate (TSR), service selection success times to total service selection time's ratio, and reflects accuracy of service reputation computation in time window. We compared TSR of CREA with other approaches, and the formula of TSR is shown in (7).

$$TSR = \frac{1}{N}\sum_{i=1}^{N}k_i \times 100\%, \quad k_i = \begin{cases} 0, & if \ EV_{i,j} \geq 0.6 \\ 1, & otherwise \end{cases} \quad (7)$$

TSR is an important index to reflect the safety of reputation evaluation model. In this paper, transaction success means customer's rating value $EV_{i,j}$ is equal to or larger than 0.6.

For this experiment, CREA didn't show superiority at the beginning phase because of data sparseness, and there are not enough customer ratings. So TSR grew at lower speed than Beth and adaptive Beth. However, when time went by and transaction quantity accumulated to 400, CREA began to show its superiority and TSR grew at a stable speed. The

other two approaches, by contrast, TSR growth rate decreased, sometimes TSR even fell down or fluctuated when transaction quantity accumulated because of the influence of malicious customers' fake ratings. In comparison, CREA performed a credible and stable service selection, so that TSR could be kept at high level and grew continuous.

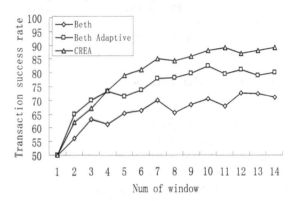

Figure 10. Transaction Success Rate Comparison

5. Conclusion

This paper proposes the approach and framework of cloud-based reputation evaluation when malicious customers provide fake ratings. This framework can generate rating quality cloud, and cloud parameters will reflect customer's rating ability and stability, so that malicious and disguise malicious customers could be distinguished from honest customers. The next step will be to study other trust mechanism, and to better improve reputation evaluation performance.

Acknowledgements

This work is supported by National Natural Science Foundation of China (No.60903008) and General scientific research project of the Education Department of Liaoning Province (No.L2011004).

References

[1] Min Luo, Mark Endrei, et al. Patterns: Service-Oriented Architecture and Web Services. International Technical Support Organization，Raleigh Center

[2] Fu Xiao-Dong, ZOU Ping, JIANG Ying. Web Service Reputation Measurement Based on Quality of Service Similarity. Computer Integrated Manufacturing Systems, Vol.14, No.3, March 2008, pp.0619-0624.

[3] Hien Trang Nguyen, Weiling Zhao, Jian Yang. A Trust and Reputation Model Based on Bayesian Network for Web Services[C] IEEE International Conference on Web Services,2010, pp.251-258

[4] Sun Qiu-Jing, Zeng Ping-Fan. Trust Model Based on Reputation and Cloud Model in P2P Environment. Journal of Chinese Computer Systems, Vol.31, No.7, July 2010, pp.1328-1332.

[5] Billhardt H, Hermoso R, Ossowski S, Centeno R. Trust-Based Service Provider Selection in Open Environments. In: Proc. of the22nd Annual ACM Symp. on Applied Computing. New York: ACM Press, 2007, pp. 1375-1380.

[6] Li DY, Du Y. Artificial Intelligence with Uncertainty. Beijing: National Defense Industry Press, 2005 (in Chinese).

[7] Claypool M et al. Implicit interest indicators[C]. In: Proceedings of ACM Intelligent User Interfaces Conference (IUI) , Santa Fe, New Mexico, ACM, 2001.

[8] Liu Xue-yi. Delphi Technique in the Assessment of Interdisciplinary Research. JOURNAL OF SOUTHWEST JIAOTONG UNIVERSITY, vol. 8, No. 2, 2007.

[9] Li Zhen, Yang Fang-Chun, Su Sen. Fuzzy Multi-Attribute Decision Making-Based Algorithm for Semantic Web Service Composition, Journal of Software, Vol.20, No.3, March 2009.

[10] Sun Ping, Jiang Chang-Jun. Using Service Clustering to Facilitate Process-Oriented Semantic Web Service Discovery. CHINESE JOURNAL OF COMPUTERS, Vol18, No.8, Aug. 2008

[11] Li Xiong, Liu Ling. Peer Trust supporting reputation-based trust for peer-to-peer electronic communities [J]. IEEE Transactions on Knowledge and Data Engineering, 2004, 16(7), pp.843-857.

[12] Li DY, Meng HJ, Shi XM. Membership cloud and membership cloud generator. Journal of Computer Research and Development, 1995, 32(6), pp.16-21 (in Chinese with English abstract).

[13] Wang Shang-Guang, Sun Qi-Bo, Yang Fang-Chang. Reputation Evaluation Approach in Web Service Selection. Journal of Software, 2012, 23(6), pp.1350-1367.

[14] Beth T, Borcherding M, Klein B. Valuation of Trust in OpenNetwork[C]//Proceedings of the European Symposium on Research in Security. Brighton: Springer-Verlag, 1994, pp. 3-18.

4

Assessment of health management information system implementation in Ayder referral hospital, Mekelle, Ethiopia

Kidane Tadesse[1, *], Ejigu Gebeye[2], Girma Tadesse[3]

[1]Biostatistics and Health Informatics, Department of Public Health, College of Health Sciences, Mekelle University, Mekelle, Ethiopia
[2]Department of Epidemiology and Biostatistics, Institute of Public Health, College of Medicine and Health Sciences, University of Gondar, Gondar, Ethiopia
[3]Health Informatics, Tulane University Technical Assistant Program to Ethiopia, Addis Ababa, Ethiopia

Email address:

Kiducs98@yahoo.com (K. Tadesse)

Abstract: Effective Health Management Information System (HMIS) is essential for setting priority for community based problems, for allocation of budget and human resource and decision making in general to managers and stakeholders. In Africa there are many problems in data management in the health sector in relation to missing of data in reports this leads to a picture which could not represent the country health information. A facility based cross sectional study was conducted in Ayder referral and teaching hospital. Six months reports have been assessed including all the data, which were registered in the six month. In addition the tally sheets generated during this six month were also included as part of the assessment. Out of the six-month data used 63.3% was accurate. More than 95% of the reviewed patient cards were complete. Out of the questioned 50 staffs (93%) have good attitude towards HMIS. Data consistency between register and the tally sheets was measured as 72.2% even though the value difference was not largely seen. There was 78.6% an average report completeness measure in the HMIS unit. There was no sign of using the information generated by the facility. Use of accurate data in the facility was low. In addition, information was not still used for action. The original HMIS tallies were not used in the hospital instead minimized and photocopied tallies were used. Refreshing training was not given to staff. Therefore; training should be given to the higher bodies and all staffs about the importance of HMIS and the value of health data in decision making. The performance monitoring team should have to be established. The HMIS unit staffs should have to be trained on basic indicators calculation.

Keywords: HMIS, Ethiopia, Ayder Referral Hospital, Data Quality

1. Background

Health management information system (HMIS) is a System that allows for the collection, storage, compilation, transmission, analysis and usage of health data that assist decision makers and stakeholders manage and plan resources at every level of health service. It also used to improve patient satisfaction with health services by tracking certain dimensions of service quality [1].

In most African countries, a country-wide health management information system compiles records about how many patients are being diagnosed with and treated for certain diseases. The actual data are meant to be collected and reported monthly by the individual health-care facilities. The HMIS compiles and analyzes these records, giving a picture of which patients are being treated across districts, regions, and the entire country [2].

In Ethiopia, like the service delivery instruments, there is little standardization of HMIS reporting forms. At the onset of health system decentralization as a primary health care strategy, which constituted a key feature of health sector reforms across the developing world, efficient and effective health management information systems were widely acknowledged and adopted as a critical element of district health management strengthening programs[3]. According to the Ethiopian context Health Management Information System and Monitoring and Evaluation (HMIS/M&E) was one of seven components of the Health Sector Development Program (HSDPIII) [5].

Health service-based sources generate data on outcome of

health-related administrative and operational activities. There are a wide variety of health service-based data: facility-based data on morbidity and mortality among those using services; types of services delivered, drugs and commodities provided; information on the availability and quality of services; financial and management information. Most health service-based data are generated "routinely" in the course of recording and reporting on services delivered [6]. At the health facility it is better for providers to know how to use the forms, and that HMIS can generate useful information for planning and managing health services. Over all they have to create a sense of ownership putting themselves in the health system hierarchy. Basically Performance of Routine Information System Management (PRISM) broadens the analysis of RHIS performance to include three key categories of determinants that affect performance: behavioral, technical and organizational determinants [7].

Although reliable and timely health information is the foundation of public health action, it is often unavailable due to under-investment in systems for data collection, analysis, dissemination and use. The rationale for HMIS has been that the availability of operational, effective and efficient health management information systems is an essential component of the required district management capacity [8, 9]. Many data elements critical to high quality care were not recorded completely or accurately at enrollment or follow-up [10]. In addition resistance to change, which comes in form of individual actors having certain viewpoints and understandings of the nature and purpose of the HMIS, based on their past experience is a problem [11].

2. Methods and Materials

The study was in one of the hospitals of Tigray i.e. Ayder Hospital. It is both service and teaching hospital and one of the referral hospitals of Ethiopia which is found in Mekelle (the capital city of Tigray region) in which the manual HMIS was already implemented and partially the Electronic Medical Record was in practice (in the card room). The Hospital starts offering health service phase by phase. It started the service first by giving outpatient service followed by inpatient service with the four major departments namely internal medicine, surgery, pediatrics and child health, and gynecology and obstetrics. This service has already expanded to give more services that one referral hospital is required to give. The hospital is serving as a referral hospital not only for Tigray region but also neighboring regions like Amhara and Afar. [4]. Facility based cross sectional study was conducted to view the data collection, processing and reporting health related information used to measure the health management performance of the hospital.

The source of data was Ayder Hospital's data collection tools filled by the clients which submit their data to the HMIS unit, registration books ,data processing mechanisms used to analyze the collected information base on the standards, and compiled reports made by the hospital HMIS unit and the data and information processing and sharing at all level. From the huge amount of health information data only those reported according to the evaluation format which was designed to evaluate the routine health information system based on the basic indicators were used. On the other hand other type of information which exists may have not included in the study.

Samples were purposively selected for different data types. The samples were six month tallies, registered data, 50 staffs, 50 individual patient cards and the two quarter hospital reports. Qualitative data were collected using Focus group discussion with those who were working on the HMIS unit to assess factors that influence the HMIS performance including the main attributes of information system such as timeliness, simplicity, accuracy, completeness and usefulness of data. Observation of daily registers, compiling tools and reporting formats for data quality, consistency and completeness was undertaken using an adapted check list. All the data collection tools have been seriously checked in relation to the data which were generated by clinicians, nurses and other users. In addition to this the analysis methods were evaluated by observing basic indicator value calculation. The use of the compiled data has been also assessed.

All the data collected, processed and prepared as a report were evaluated using check lists for their quality in relation to accuracy, timeliness, consistency, relevance and completeness. This data were entered into statistical software (spss v.16) and descriptive analysis was performed.

3. Results

3.1. Data Collection

The registers were available in each unit but some of the registers were worn out their pages. There were findings on using different naming for specific disease by violating the HMIS disease classification. The size of the register has also its own effect on filling data because the total size of the left and right sides of the registers. The full name area in almost all registers was not completely used because of shortage of space. Registers were not complete; the values which have to be calculated were not performed.

In the facility there was no shortage of tally sheets. To some extent the tally sheet format made also some data mismatch because of the un-relaxed (small size) cells nature and the disease names were not easily identifiable and all used sheets were photo copied. In addition the HMIS tally sheet do not have place for the number of beds, total admission in IPD, length of stay, total discharges of IPD. The original HMIS tallies were not used in the hospital. On the other hand there were units which don't even use the tally sheet but used a white flat A4 sheets by preparing their own tables. The facility used photocopy tally sheets but the list of diseases was not easily readable. In some other units there were also reversely printed pages. The staff motivation to fill daily tallies is low, they prepare at the end of the month.

3.2. Reporting

The HMIS unit receives monthly filled tally sheets from the hospital units but there were units which do not sent report to the unit with no known reason. There were also units which report quarterly and others say no data to be reported in words of mouth. In some other units even though they report monthly but there was no responsible body to make that report at the end of the month. Difficulties on indicator calculation due to the nature of reporting formats like the current number of ART users was the largest drawback seen in the HMIS reports. In addition the average length of stay number is 100% incorrectly reported. The HMIS unit used an average value every month in the reports for average length of stay. Except the weekly epidemic reporting format both the disease and service reporting formats were available in the facility.

3.3. Data Quality

3.3.1. Data Accuracy

Even though it was not at good level, the facility shows an increase in using accurate data from time to time.

The largest data in accuracy use was observed in the indicators PLWHA currently on ART, length of stay and TB case detection which measures 100%, 100% and 66.6% respectively from the data of six months. There was a significant increase of data accuracy from the data of six months and the average data accuracy measure of 62.9%. There was a serious problem on ART and length of stay data evaluation even there was no month without discrepancy (Figure-1).

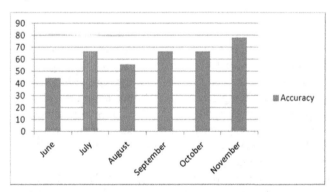

Figure 1. Trend of data accuracy use in Ayder referral hospital between June/2010 and November/2010

3.3.2. Consistency

Almost all the data were similar in both patient card and the register. But even though it was not much there was age registration difference observed. Consistency between register and the tally sheets measure showed 72.2% of the values were equal even though the difference was not largely seen. Insignificant value shows age miss match in counting individuals from the register to the tally sheet.

3.3.3. Completeness

In the facility there was no limited number of monthly reports expected by the HMIS unit. Many of the units report

monthly, some of the others report quarterly and others never send their report. We have checked data completeness on both patient card and registers by taking 50 individual cards. On the patient card more than 95% of the required data were included except some cards miss summery sheet information and insignificant ART cards type of HIV test and date confirmed were left free. On the other hand, except the grand fathers name missed full information was included in all 50 individual register records.

A maximum of 95.5% report completeness and a minimum score of 71.2%. The average report complexness' measure in the hospital from the reports of six month submitted to the HMIS unit was 78.6% (Figure-2).

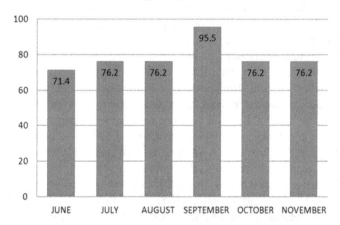

Figure 2. Monthly report completeness in Ayder referral hospital between June/2010 to November/2010.

3.3.4. Staff Attitude on HMIS

The result shows around 50(100%) of the respondents agreed that HMIS plays a great role for improving health of community and quality of decision making in the facility. Out of this respondents 30(40%) rated generally that HMIS is expensive. Ten (20%) of the respondents have doubt about its easy means of information communication to the higher bodies (Table-1).

Table 1. Response of staffs to measure HMIS attitude in Ayder Referral Hospital January, 2011

Questions	Agree N (%)
Facilitate information use	50(100)
Facilitate data standardization	50(100%)
Reduce data burden	46(92%)
Make reporting system simple	48(96%)
Data handling using HMIS is inexpensive	30(60%)
Improve early detection and solving of problem	48(96%)
Permit easy communication with RHB and WoHO	40(80%)

3.3.5. Training

A short training was given to majority of the workers before 2 years for five days on HMIS but there were no other trainings on HMIS as refreshment prepared in the hospital. Even new staffs do not have taken any training about HMIS. The HMIS unit staffs were not also well trained to accomplish the tasks and to play their role in the facility.

3.3.6. The HMIS Unit

It was before two years the facility implement HMIS. Currently there were two workers in the unit they have good skill on computer basics. There was no focal person and budget allocated for HMIS unit. The basic manuals of HMIS were not available in the facility HMIS unit. In addition there was no communication means like telephone, internet and printing device. The role of this unit was not clearly identified and understood by the higher officials out of submitting quarterly reports.

3.3.7. Information Use

In the hospital there was no known performance monitoring team but there was informal monthly performance made by the higher bodies' team which didn't include the HMIS unit as a part. This team doesn't evaluate the monthly data generated by the HMIS unit in relation to the regional or national level target instead using informal information from departments the team call meeting and take actions. The hospital also gets supportive supervision from RHB and frequent feedback made from different bodies at least four times per year. But there was no regularly monthly /quarterly data evaluation made with the alignment of the national and regional targets. In the facility there were no charts of target displayed at any of the higher officials. The catchment area map was not also available in the facility. There was no report displayed using a chart in the facility using the data of either quarterly or monthly.

3.3.8. HMIS Process

The hospital has a well established card room of size 111 m^2 with 4 windows, a total of 15 workers, 4 runners and total of six computers. There were 65 well established shelves. They made use of Medical Patient Index (MPI) card but MPI box and tracer card were not still in use. In the card room, cards were arranged according to the Medical Record Number (MRN) with in specified range.

4. Discussion

The use of accurate data in the facility on average was 63.3% which indicates significant percentage of data in accuracy. This value was low when we compare with the national HMIS guide line a minimum of 80% [15]. This was most probably due to counting error in the registers and lack of ability to calculate indicators. Data entry was also another problem that creates data in accuracy in the HMIS unit. In addition to this due to unreported values the HMIS unit uses average value of the reporting units every month for the non reporting units. On the other hand there was good measure of data accuracy improvement between months except one month shows a decrement. This improvement was due to the formation of good relationship between the HMIS unit and other departments which creates fine communication. In addition the HMIS staff motivation was increasing even they collect the monthly reports themselves.

In the hospital, 100% of the report of ART and length of stay were in accurate on the data of all six month. This could be due to some units don't submit the length of stay monthly because there was no space for this indicator in the tally sheet. As a consequence the compiled reports showed that a great discrepancy every month. For the ART, there was a significant number represented as other in the tally sheet. There was no space for such value in the HMIS unit reporting format so that this value was missed every month. This happened due to use of edited format of the HMIS ART tally sheet. In addition this might be due to lack of knowing what the basic indicators and lack of communication between the HMIS unit and the ART to identify with what values were reported [5, 13]

Like other previous studies there was a significant problem in data recording in registers observed in the facility [5, 11]. This could be due to the large size of the left and right sides of registers. The space provided to fill some data was not also enough which leads to incomplete or unreadable data on register. Like the space for Full name was not enough, some units use first name and middle name only and others used unreadable full names. Results showed, 73.3% the units do not fully calculate the number of admission, length of stay and sum of discharge at every completed page. This could be due to lack of knowledge about basic indicators and lack of supervision from the HMIS unit. Even since there were no cross checks made by the HMIS unit within the departments it gives them not to calculate these values.

Consistency of data value between registers and the tally sheets generated every month was measured as 72.2% which indicates significant difference. This could be due to use of different naming for a particular disease which causes counting error. In addition it could be category (age or sex) classification problem. Over the entire major problem was all units do not prepare daily tally rather they make it at the end of the month this leads to inn correct count. There was a slight data in consistency between the patient card and the register in some basic data values like the age.

Results showed that 46(93%) of have good attitude towards HMIS and 38(75%) of the respondents agree that their staff mates have good attitude towards HMIS. This value difference could be due to different reasons. Firs there were new staffs which do not have taken any training about HMIS. Secondly there could be resistant staffs which influence other staffs. On the other hand 12(24%) of the respondents have doubt about cost minimization by using HMIS. This could be due to lack of consecutive training to increase awareness and also staffs do not want to spent time in counting data every month even to follow every HMIS disease classification they think it kills their time[14].

There was no well established information-use culture in the facility. This might be mostly due to lack of knowledge on how to use HMIS data for allocation of resource and man power. In addition to this lack of strict supervision and follow up from the regional health bureau might be another reason. Lack of consecutive training to the higher bodies might be also another factor. Over all it looks the body who take responsibility for the implementation of this system was not doing follow up after the first training has been given.

The HMIS unit received many reports from the facility departments. The results showed completeness maximum 95.5%, minimum of 71.2%. An average of 78.6% report completeness was measured from the data of six month this has a small difference with the HMIS guide line minimum requirement that was 80% [15]. The difference between the maximum and minimum results was seen due to some units start reporting lately. In addition to this some of the units submit their report quarterly which creates value difference between the end month of the quarter and the rest two months.

In the HMIS unit there were no enough resources made available. This could be due to lack of allocated badge to that unit this aligned with the national survey made in 2006 by the HMIS Re-engineering team. The staffs members were both degree holders but not health professionals this was the maximum staff number in the survey of the 2006 composition measured by Tigray and SNNP [14].

The results showed that there were registers, tally sheets and reporting forms made available in the hospital. The IPD tallies do not have space for length of stay, bed occupancy and discharged variables. There were also units which do not use this tally sheets.

Majority of the departments do not submit their report at a specific time and they didn't write date of submission. There were also difficulties in indicator calculation .The hospital shows an increase in using accurate data from time to time. In the hospital both the number of PLWHA currently on ART and length of stay shows the largest data in accuracy in all six months.

Data completes measured from individual patient cards was good, on the contrary the average report completeness measure in the hospital was lower than the national minimum. The HMIS unit lacks resources and new staffs have not taken ant training on HMIS. In the facility there was no performance monitoring team formed according to the HMIS procedure and composition. Information generated by the facility was not used for action.

Health management information system is an essential tool for strengthening planning and management in the health facilities. But in developing countries due to resource limitation, HMIS implementation is at its infant age. Many of health professionals focus on treatment due to lack of training there is no awareness on the importance of patient record. Consequently, decision-makers cannot identify problems and needs, track progress, evaluate the impact of interventions and make evidence-based decisions on health policy, programmed design and resource allocation. Staff training, information use culture and strengthening the HMIS units are some of the major focus areas that developing countries should have to work on because this will help them to collect complete, accurate and timely data, therefore decisions will be efficient and effective. At the top of this health facility managers and district heath managers should have to have knowledge on the importance of quality data, strict follow up, supportive supervision and feedback mechanisms are very important to produce quality information at the higher level.

Author's Contributions

KT.: proposal writing, designing, recruitment and training of supervisors and data collectors, analysis and write-up of the paper. EG. and GT.: proposal writing, designing, recruitment and training of supervisors and data collectors.

Acknowledgement

The Authors are grateful to the Mekelle University, College of Health Sciences for sponsoring this research project. Also extend sincere appreciation to all health workers of Ayder referral and teaching hospital, who helped us during data collection. Last but not least, we are grateful to the supervisors and data collectors for carefully undertaking of their tasks.

Significance of the Work

We believe that this study is important to explore how HMIS is implementing in resource limited settings, Ethiopian. In this study it is illustrated what are the possible gaps during implementation. Not only for the Ethiopian setting, are findings in the study also useful for other developing countries.

References

[1] F. Rabbani, B.a (2005). health management information system: a tool to gauge patient satisfaction and quality of care. Easter Mediterranean health journal

[2] Gething PW, Noor AM, Gikandi PW, Ogara EAA, Hay SI, et al. (2006) Improving Imperfect Data from Health Management Information Systems in Africa Using Space–Time Geostatistics. PLoS Med 3(6): e271. doi:10.1371/journal.pmed.0030271

[3] HMIS reform, t. (2008). HMIS/M&E strategic plan for Ethiopia health sector. FMoH.

[4] MekelleUniversity. (2002). nine months performance report of 2002 fiscal year of Ayder referal hospital. Mekelle.

[5] Department, p.a (2005) Ethiopian sector strategic plane (HSDPIII) 2005/6-2009/2010.Addis Ababa: Federal Ministry of Health

[6] WHO, FMO, CSA, & HMN. (2007). Assessment of the Ethiopian national health informationsystem. Addis Ababa.

[7] Hotchkiss, D., Aqil, A., & Mukooyo, T. L. (2010). evalution ofperformance routine information system management(PRISM) framework:evidence from Uganda . BioMed central.

[8] World Health Organization. (2008). Framework and Standards for Country Health Information System.Geneva:WHO.

[9] MUTEMWA, R. I. (2005). HMIS and decision-making in Zambia: re-thinking. Oxford university.

[10] Peter Y. et al. Medical record completeness and accuracy at an HIV clinic in Mozambique. JHIDC.(2010)

[11] Murodillo Latifov A. Global standards and Local Applications: Case of Implementing ICD-10 Standard in HMIS Tajikistan..JHIDC.(2013).

[12] Garrib, N. Stoops, A.McKenzie, L.Dlamini, T.Govender, J.rohde, et al. (2008). An evaluation of District health informatio system Rural South Africa. south aafrican Medical jornal .

[13] Igira, F. T., Titlestad, O. H., Lungo, J. H., Makungu, A., & Khamis, M. M. (2006). Designing and Implementing Hospital Management Information Systems in developing countries: case study from Tanzania -Zanzibar.

[14] HMIS reform, t. (2006).HMIS Business Re-engineering Assessment Report. FMoH.

[15] HMIS Reform Team. (2007). Indicator definition: Area 1. Addis Ababa: FMoH.

5

E-Learning and Semantic Web

Ahmed Rashad Khalifa

Systems and Computers Engineering Dept., Faculty of Engineering, Al Azhar University, Cairo, Egypt

Email address:

khalifah2@hotmail.com

Abstract: Nowadays, e-learning systems are widely used for education and training in universities and companies because of their electronic course content access and virtual classroom participation. But not all learners learn in the same way and at the same rate, some prefer the traditional text-based or oral presentation of content, while others learn more easily in a visual or kinetic instruction style. The real value of e-Learning lies not in its ability to train just anyone, anytime, anywhere, but in our ability to deploy this attribute to train the right people to gain the right skills or knowledge at the right time. Learning objects and courses databases are syntactically structured text archives with powerful search engines. But, there is no semantic relationship between information needs of the user and the information content of documents. Because of many limitations using web 2.0 for creating E-learning management system, now-a-days we use Web 3.0 which is known as Semantic web. It is a platform to represent E-learning management system that recovers the limitations of Web 2.0. However, with the rapid increase of learning content on the Web, it is time-consuming for learners to find contents they really want to and need to study. "Making content machine-understandable" is a popular paraphrase of the fundamental prerequisite for the Semantic Web. This paper focuses on e-Learning, benefits and requirements of e-Learning and potential uses of semantic web technology in e-Learning.

Keywords: E-Learning, Semantic Web, RDF, Ontology

1. Introduction

The real value of e-Learning lies not in its ability to train just anyone, anytime, anywhere, but in our ability to deploy this attribute to train the right people to gain the right skills or knowledge at the right time [1].

E-learning is not just concerned with providing easy access to learning resources, anytime, anywhere, via a repository of learning resources, but is also concerned with supporting such features as the personal definition of learning goals, and the synchronous and asynchronous communication, and collaboration, between learners and between learners and instructors.

Not all learners learn in the same way and at the same rate. Learners' learning styles that reflect their cognitive abilities vary in known ways; some prefer the traditional text-based or oral presentation of content, while others learn more easily in a visual or kinetic instruction style. Simulation has been shown to be an effective way of teaching abstract concept, principle and process in many application domains.

Web-based e-learning systems are normally used by a wide variety of learners with different skills, background, preferences, and learning styles. Recent advances in Web-based and E-learning technology provide a wide range of learning materials and learning objects available to learner.

However, the increase of reachable material confuses a selection decision for most suitable learning objects. A support system based on learner demands, backgrounds, and users' preference is needed to help effectively search preferred materials [2]. The Semantic Web can offer more flexibility in e-learning systems through use of new Semantic Web technologies (SWT). Thus, it may advise a learner with most suitable learning objects

Unfortunately, the Web was built for human consumption, not for machine consumption, although everything on the Web is machine-readable, it is not machine-understandable. We need the Semantic Web to express information in a precise, machine interpretable form, ready for software agents to process, share, and reuse it, as well as to understand what the terms describing the data mean. This would enable web-based applications to interoperate both on the syntactic and semantic level.

One of the hottest topics in recent years in the Artificial Intelligence (AI) community, as well as in the Internet community, is the "Semantic Web". It is an evolving extension of the World Wide Web (WWW) in which the semantics of information and services on the web is defined, making it possible for the web to understand and satisfy the requests of people and machines to use the web content." It is about making the Web more understandable by machines. It is also about building an appropriate infrastructure for intelligent agents to run around the Web performing complex actions for their users. Furthermore, Semantic Web is about explicitly declaring the knowledge embedded in many web-based applications, integrating information in an intelligent way, providing semantic-based access to the Internet, and extracting information from texts. Ultimately, Semantic Web is about how to implement reliable, large-scale interoperation of Web services, to make such services computer interpretable, i.e., to create a Web of machine-understandable and interoperable services that intelligent agents can discover, execute, and compose automatically.

Semantic Web (http://www.semanticWeb.org/), it is the new-generation Web that makes it possible to express information in a precise, machine-interpretable form, ready for software agents to process, share, and reuse it, as well as to understand what the terms describing the data mean. It enables Web-based applications to interoperate both on the syntactic and semantic level [3].

Note that it is Tim Berners-Lee (inventor of the WWW, URIs, HTTP, and HTML) himself that pushes the idea of the Semantic Web forward. The father of the Web first envisioned a Semantic Web that provides automated information access based on machine-processable semantics of data and heuristics that use these metadata. The explicit representation of the semantics of data, accompanied with domain theories (Ontologies), it enables a Web that provides a qualitatively new level of service, such as: intelligent search engines, information brokers, and information filters. Researchers from the World Wide Web Consortium (W3C) already developed new technologies for web friendly data description. Moreover, AI researchers have already developed some useful applications and tools for the Semantic Web.

We introduce the implementation of Semantic Web concept on the e-Learning environment offered by our web-based E-learning. The facilities that the application will provide include allowing e-learning content to be created, annotated, shared and discussed, together with supplying resources such as lecture notes, course description, documents, announcements, student papers, useful URL links, exercises and quizzes for evaluation of the student knowledge [4].

The major industrial firms and academic and research institutions have started to think seriously about the use and applications of Semantic Web Technology (SWT) in which information in machine processable form can coexist and complement the current web with better enabling computers and people to work in co-operation [5].

This paper is organized as follows: Section (2) presents a brief overview about e-Learning benefits and requirements, section (3) gives a brief overview about the Semantic Web and discusses the common technologies used to construct the Semantic Web as well as the limitations of the conventional Web and how the Semantic Web overcomes those limitations. Section (4) presents an overview about layers of the Semantic Web architecture. In section (5), E-Learning, semantic Web and potential uses of semantic web technology in e-Learning, are discussed. Finally, section (6) concludes the paper.

2. E-Learning

Distance Learning is characterized by the fact that the student (learner) does not have to be present in a classroom (a given location) in order to participate in the instruction. Time and place parameters of an instruction can be variable. There is no face-to-face environment.

Although a number of definitions for distance learning (DL) have been proposed over the years, the majority seems to agree on the basic elements, which differentiate the method from conventional teaching and learning. Such elements include separation of the teacher from the learner in space and/or in time during at least a major part of each educational process, the use of special training material to unite teacher and learner and carry course content, the provision of two-way communication between them, and the control of learning by the student [6].

Distance learning can be a good method to transfer and learn new Knowledge and information, the student is a passive learner. Techniques for Distance learning include broadcast TV, audiotape and videotape; it is a one-to-many communication.

An e-learning system can be defined as a social and information technological system that supports learning processes [7].

E-learning is also called Web-based learning, online learning, distributed learning, computer-assisted instruction, or Internet-based learning. Historically, there have been two common e-learning modes: distance learning and computer assisted instruction.

Distance learning uses information technologies to deliver instruction to learners who are at remote locations from a central site.

Computer assisted instruction (also called computer-based learning and computer based training) uses computers to aid in the delivery of stand-alone multimedia packages for learning and teaching. These two modes are subsumed under e-learning as the Internet becomes the integrating technology [8].

E-learning is defined as "The delivery of individualized, comprehensive, dynamic learning content in real time, aiding the development of communities of knowledge, linking learners and practitioners with experts"[9].

Table 1 illustrates the benefits of E-Learning.

Table 1. Benefits of e-Learning.

Benefits of e-Learning	
Information is consistent or customised, depending on need	Everyone gets the same content, presented in the same way. Yet the programs can also be customised for different learning needs or different groups of people
Content is more timely and dependable	Because it is web-enabled, e-Learning can be updated instantaneously, making the information more accurate and useful for a longer period of time. The ability to upgrade e-Learning content easily and quickly, and then immediately distribute the new information to users is extremely time efficient.
Learning is 24/7	Students can access e-Learning anywhere and at any time of the day. It's "just in time – any time' approach makes the learning process ubiquitous.
Universality	e-Learning is web-enabled and takes advantage of the universal Internet protocols and browsers. Concern over differences in platforms and operating systems is rapidly fading. Everyone on the Web can receive virtually the same material in virtually the same time.
Scalability	e-Learning solutions are highly scalable. Programs can move 10 participants to 100 or even more participants with little effort or incremental cost (as long as the infrastructure is in place).
Builds communities	The Web enables students to build enduring communities of practice where they can come together to share knowledge and insight. This can be a tremendous motivator for learning.
e-Learning lowers costs	Despite outward appearances, e-Learning is often the most cost effective way to deliver instruction or information. It cuts travel expenses; it can also reduce teaching time, and significantly reduces the need for a classroom/teacher infrastructure.

Drucker [10] has defined e-Learning as "just-in-time education integrated with high velocity value chains. It is the delivery of individualized, comprehensive, dynamic learning content in real time, aiding the development of communities of knowledge, linking learners and practitioners with experts". E-Learning aims at replacing old-fashioned time/place/content/ predetermined learning with a just-in time/ at workplace/customized /on-demand process of learning [11].

Learning environment allows learners to access electronic course contents through the network and study them in virtual classrooms. It brings many benefits in comparison with conventional learning paradigm, e.g. learning can be taken at any time and at any place. However, with the rapid increase of learning content on the Web, it is time-consuming for learners to find contents they really want to and need to study. The challenge in an information-rich world is not only to make information available to people at any time, at any place, and in any form, but to offer the right thing to the right person in the right way [12].

Table 2 shows the characteristics (or pitfalls) of the standard learning scenario and the improvements achieved using the e-learning approach. These are the most important characteristics of e-learning.

Table 2. Difference Between Training and E-Learning [10].

Dimensions	Training	eLearning
Delivery	Push–Instructor determines agenda	Pull–Student determines agenda
Responsiveness	Anticipatory–Assumes to know the problem	Reactionary–Responds to problem at hand
Access	Linear–Has defined progression of knowledge	Non-linear–Allows direct access to knowledge in whatever sequence makes sense to the situation at hand
Symmetry	Asymmetric–Training occurs as a separate activity	Symmetric–Learning occurs as an integrated activity
Modality	Discrete–Training takes place in dedicated chunks with defined starts and stops	Continuous–Learning runs in the parallel to business tasks and never stops
Authority	Centralized–Content is selected from a library of materials developed by the educator	Distributed–Content comes from the interaction of the participants and the educators
Personalization	Mass produced–Content must satisfy the needs of many	Personalized–Content is determined by the individual user's needs and aims to satisfy the needs of every user
Adaptivity	Static–Content and organization/taxonomy remains in their originally authored form without regard to environmental changes	Dynamic–Content changes constantly through user input, experiences, new practices, business rules and heuristics

E-Learning and its technological basis: E-Learning environments - proved to be an appropriate tool which can support the learning process efficiently, effectively and satisfactorily. In the future, they will open up to us new dimensions in the world of learning we never experienced before. With their help, the right knowledge will be learnt at the right time, by the right person, in the right context – a lifelong [13]. Courses that never end, provide ongoing digital learning and performance support for the learner, making a number of perpetual courses [14].

Why ('life-long learning')

As mentioned before, there is a growing need for continuing, life-long learning in our society because:

- There is a rapid technological change.
- Training and education is an ongoing necessary in business.
- Workers have to remain current with required skills and knowledge.

- People change their carriers and jobs more frequently, six to seven changes as average.
- Increasing the skill and knowledge means to increase someone's marketability.

Learning Objectives is defined as the desired outcome of education. Three major learning objectives can be classified (information transfer- Skill Acquisition - Team-learning Experience), which should be taken into consideration when designing a course or a curriculum. It is important to ensure that all parts of skills-cycle have been learned (receive signal, perceive and interpret, decide on action, take action) [15].

The different types of E-learning are based on:
1. Means of communication.
2. Schedule.
3. E-learning class structure.
4. Technologies used.

Not all learners learn in the same way and at the same rate. Learners' learning styles that reflect their cognitive abilities vary in known ways; some prefer the traditional text-based or oral presentation of content, while others learn more easily in a visual or kinetic instruction style. E-Learning has been shown to be an effective way of teaching abstract concept, principle and process in many application domains [16].

Numerous research efforts on the effect of media on learning have shown that different media types have different efficiencies in terms of what a learner can recall. Especially the combination of media has very different efficiencies.

In general from 100 % of the learning material (facts) we can remember, figure 1 illustrates this percentage:

- 10 % through reading,
- 20 % through hearing,
- 30 % through seeing,
- 40 % through hearing and seeing,
- 80 % through hearing, seeing and doing (interacting).

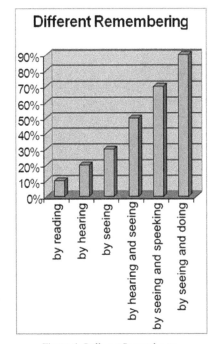

Figure 1. Different Remembering.

In addition to that, well prepared content is fun learning and thus motivates the learner which increases learning success.

To challenge and engage learners, the development team needed to produce courses that offered more than the average page-turner tutorials [17].

3. Semantic Web

In the beginning of the internet days, software programmers developed all Web pages. Today, the Web provides perhaps the simplest way to share information, and literally everyone writes Web pages, with the help of authoring tools, and a large number of organizations disseminate data coded in Web pages. The Hypertext Markup Language (HTML) is typically the language used to code information about renderization (font size, color, position on screen, etc.) and hyperlinks to other Webpages or resources on the Web (multimedia files, text, e-mail addresses, etc.).

The net result is that the Web keeps growing at an astounding pace, now having over eight billion Web pages. However, most Web pages are still designed for human consumption and cannot be processed by machines. Computers are used only to display the information. that is, to decode the color schema, headers. and links encoded in Web pages. Furthermore, web search engines, the most popular tools to help retrieve Web pages, do not offer Support to interpret the results. For this reason, human intervention is still required. This situation is progressively getting worse as the size of search results is becoming too large. Most users only browse through the top results, discarding the remaining ones. Some search engines are resorting to artifice to help control the situation, such as indexing the search result, or limiting the search space to a relevant subset of the Web (such as in Google Scholar). The conclusion is that the size of search results is often just too big for humans to interpret, and finding relevant information on the Web is not as easy as we would desire [18].

This traditional or current Web is sometimes called Web 1.0. Since its inception in 1990, the World Wide Web (www) has been visualized as a repository to store information as Web documents. The Web document has been mainly designed in Hyper Text Markup Language (HTML) which enables the document developer to link to other HTML documents. The improvement of technology helps in increasing the number and quality of images, movies and other media elements in the hyper document.

Many search engines are available to search this Web such as Google and Yahoo. These search engines are based on keyword matching. The user enters the keywords to search through the Internet; the search engine returns a list of the pages matching these keywords. The Web pages in the result list may be ranked according to its relevance to the keywords. The browsing, searching, and many other available services on this Web-1 represent "Client Server Model".

A next generation of the Web, called Web 2.0, has been introduced as a social networking where the user contributes to the Web content not just consumes. In Web 2.0, users basically make content of Websites, instead of the Webmasters.

Wikis, You Tube, and even Twitter are examples of such social Web. The Facebook is another example where users can build social connections with friends. While Web 1.0 has delivered the Internet and connected large numbers of people, Web 2.0 has demonstrated the technology to assemble and manage large global crowds with a common interest in social interaction. Web 2.0 is the current generation of Internet technology. In the context of the social Web, user data is composed of identity, social-graph data identifying the user, and content data. Accessibility to this huge amount of the Web content is still restricted to humans and not to machines and this restricted accessibility causes a lot of problems.

The Semantic Web (Web 3.0) is assumed to be the solution of such problems. It is an extension to the current traditional Web which helps humans and machines to work together and its information has a well defined meaning. In order to allow machines more actions, the Web data must be in a form that machines can understand. This is done by developing new technologies and languages to express the Web data in such forms.

The Semantic Web is the extension of the WWW. That allows people to share content beyond the boundaries of web sites and applications. There are many different ideas about what the Semantic Web is. Berners-Lee, Hendler and Lassila (2001) define the Semantic Web, also known as Web3.0, as "not a separate Web but an extension of the current one, in which information is given well-defined meaning, better enabling computers and people to work in cooperation"[19].

Berners-Lee hopes that eventually computers will be able to use the information on the Web, not just present the information. "Machines become capable of analyzing all the data on the Web. content, links, and transactions between people and computers" [20]. Based on his idea, the Semantic Web is a vision and is considered to be the next step in Web evolution. It is about having data as well as documents on the Web so that machines can process, transform, assemble, and even act on the data in useful ways. One of the great promises of the Semantic Web is flexibility in accessing and identifying information [21].

The Semantic Web is a mesh of information linked up in such a way, as to be easily processable by machines on a global scale. It is the new-generation Web that makes it possible to express information in a precise, machine interpretable form, ready for software agents to process, share, and reuse it, as well as to understand what the terms describing the data mean [22].

The Semantic Web offers new technologies to the developers of web based applications aiming at providing more intelligent access and management of the Web information and semantically richer modeling of the applications and their users. "Expressing meaning" is the main task of the Semantic Web. Semantic Web is not the separate web but it is the extension of the current web which makes possible information to share and reuse. Semantic Web Technology (SWT) provides such environment, so that machines can talk with each other to fulfill the needs of the user by providing the right information. To accomplish this task, SWT uses a number of techniques like Ontology, RDFs, XML and SPARQL.

4. The Semantic Web Architecture

"Expressing meaning" is the main task of the Semantic Web. In order to achieve that objective, several layers of representational structures are needed. They are illustrated in Figure 2 (Berners-Lee 2000), among which the following layers are the basic ones [23]:

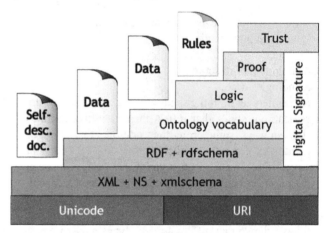

Figure 2. *Layers of the Semantic Web architecture.*

The term "Semantic Web" encompasses efforts to build a new WWW architecture that enhances content with formal semantics, means the content is made suitable for machine only, as opposed to content that is only intended for human. This will enable automated agents to reason about Web content, and produce an intelligent response to unexpected situations. "Expressing meaning" is the main task of the Semantic Web. In order to achieve that objective several layers of representational structures are needed [24].

The architecture can be divided into three parts which are [25]:
1. Knowledge representation (XML, XML schema and RDF, RDF schema layers).
2. Ontology (Ontology vocabulary layer).
3. Agents (Logic, Proof, Trust layers).

The important property of the Semantic Web architecture (i.e., common-shared-meaning and machine processable metadata), enabled by a set of suitable agents, establishes a powerful approach to satisfy the E-Learning requirements.

The process is based on semantic querying and navigation through learning materials, enabled by the ontological background. The Semantic Web can be exploited as a very suitable platform for implementing an E-learning system, because it provides all means for E-learning: ontology development, ontology-based annotation of learning materials, their composition in learning courses and active delivery of the learning materials through E-learning portals [26].

Tim Berners-Lee proposed four versions of Semantic Web architecture [27]. Such versions describe the languages needed for data interoperability between applications in the form of layering architecture, where each layer represents a language that provides services to the upper layer. However, layers described in such versions suffer from several deficiencies such as poor abstraction and rarely functional descriptions. Gerber in [28] avoided those deficiencies and designed a new architecture.

Additional layer called "Rules" layer was added although its functionality is already embedded inside other layers. The authors in [29] explored many layers compared to the Gerber's model. However, the overlapped functionalities among layers are more than overlapping in the Gerber's model and this increases the difficulty of the system engineering description and the layers integration. [30].

These versions describe the languages needed for data interoperability between applications in the form of layering architecture where each layer represents a language that provides services to the upper layer. The four versions (layered architectures) are composed mainly of seven functions. Each function is nearly represented by a layer. As we are talking about architecture concept, then there are some discrepancies and irregularities in Tim Berners-Lee's architectures considering the layered architecture evaluation criteria [31]. The layered architecture evaluation criteria are clearly defined context, an appropriate level of abstraction, hiding of unnecessary implementation details, clearly defined functional layers, appropriate layering, and Modularity. These criteria are used as an evaluation for any layering architecture.

The Semantic Web consists mainly of three components: the Extensible Markup Language (XML), the Resource Description Framework (RDF), and the ontologies.

Figure 2 shows the 9 layers architecture of semantic web in which the lowest layer starts from the bottom of the layer, followed by the highest layer, which is at the topmost position. The various layers and its challenges are described below.

UNICODE

Unicode is the basic universal number for every character, which works in multiple platforms. It is the basic notation, which is supported by top multinational companies like Motorola, IBM, Intel, etc. Unicode allows a single software, text or single character to be transported to other parts without corruption and re-engineering.

URI (Uniform Resource Identifier)

The URI is termed as Uniform Resource Identifier, which is a basic syntax for strings that is used to identify a resource. URI is the generic term of addresses and names of objects or resources in the WWW. A resource is any physical or abstract things in which each item has an identifier. The URI consists of two types: First is Uniform Resource locators (URL) which identifies a resource and how it can be accessed, and the second part is Uniform Resource Names (URN)that is used to create a universal and persistent name about a resource in its namespace. This namespace dictates the syntax of URN identifier [26].

It is used to identify resources on the web, in which every resource in the World Wide Web should be uniquely identified so we give it a URI. Resources could be anything such as a book, document, or video. There are different forms of the URIs. The most familiar form is the URL (Uniform Resource Locator) which is typed in the Web browser to locate its corresponding resource, so it has two functionalities which are identifying and locating the resources. There are other forms that only identify the resources but can't tell us their locations. Because the Web is too large to be controlled by only one person or organization [32], so creation of URIs is decentralized and anyone could create URI for his resources. It is clear that a problem of identifying the same resource with more than one URI may exist, but it is the cost of having such flexible and simple technique to identify resources on the Web [33].

XML (Extensible Mark-up Language)

The Extensible Markup Language (XML) is a W3C-recommended general-purpose markup language that supports a wide variety of applications. XML is also designed to be reasonably human-legible, and to this end, terseness is not considered essential in its structure [32]. XML is evolved from simplified subset of Standard Generalized Markup Language (SGML). Its main task is to facilitate the sharing of data across different information systems, particularly systems connected via the Internet. XML is the simplest way to send the document across the web to its specific format. It allows users to edit or modify it and again transfer it. These document formats can include mark up also to enhance the meaning of the document [34]. Scientifically, XML is built upon Unicode characters and URI's. The Unicode characters allow XML to be characterized using International characters [26], [35].

XML Schema

XML Schema is a document definition language that enables you to develop XML documents into a Specific vocabulary and a specific hierarchical structure. The things you want to define in your language are element types, attribute types, and the composition of both into composite types (called complex types). XML Schema is different to database schema, which defines the column names and data types in database tables. XML Schema has been approved by W3C consortium in the year 2001. XMLS allows the validation of instances to ensure the accuracy of field values and document structure at the time of creation. The accuracy of fields is checked against the type of the field; for example, a quantity typed as an integer or money typed as a decimal. The structure of a document is checked for things like legal element and attributes names, correct number of children, and required attributes. All XML documents should be checked for validity before they are transferred to another partner or system [26]. There are different types of XML Schema Languages [34]: Document Definition Markup Language (DDML), Document Schema Definition Languages (DSDL), Document Structure Description (DSD), Document Type Definition (DTD), Namespace Routing Language (NRL), RELAX NG and its predecessors RELAX and TREXSGML Schema for Object-Oriented XML (SOX), Schematron XML-Data Reduced (XDR), XML Schema (W3C) (WXS or XSD).

XML Namespaces

An XML namespace is the W3C recommendation for providing uniquely named elements and all of its attributes in an XML instance. An instance of an XML contains element or attribute names from more than one vocabulary. If each vocabulary is given a namespace, then the uncertainty or what is unexpected between identically named elements or attributes can be resolved. All elements which are within a namespace must be in unique component [36].

RDF and RDF Schema

Resource Description Framework (RDF) is a foundation of metadata processing. It provides interoperability between applications that exchange machine-understandable information on the Web. It defines the relationship between the resources on the web. There are different syntaxes that can represent the RDF, one of the most popular syntax is the XML where the RDF based on this syntax is called RDF/XML model.

The RDF statement is written in a triple form consisting of three parts which are the subject, the predicate and the object, so it seems like it is a natural phrase but its parts are URIs as they are resources on the Web.

RDF defines a simple, yet powerful model for describing resources. A syntax (which is XML) representing this model is required to store instances of this model into machine-readable files and to communicate these instances among applications. RDF imposes formal structure on XML to support the consistent representation of semantics [37], [38].

The RDF and RDF Schema layer is located above the XML layer, which provides more functions and capabilities than in XML and XML schema. The Resource Description Framework is an XML based language that is used to describe resources. Such a resource is identified via a uniform resource locator (URL). As compared to XML documents that attach the metadata of the document, RDF captures the metadata of the externals of the document such as author, creation, date, etc.

RDF is the machine processable language, unlike XML which is human process able and it is not understandable by humans i.e. it knows what the machine is doing in the way it does. So that it can store smart information back on the Web. [39].

RDF model is also called as triple, because it contains three parts viz. Subject, Predicate and Object. In Subject, there is none of phrase that is the source of action. In Predicate, which is a part of triple edit the subject and includes the verb phrase? And in the object, it is a noun phrase that is the source of action by the verb.

RDFS or RDF Schema is a knowledge representation language, providing basic elements for the description of ontologies [40], otherwise called RDF vocabularies, intended to structure RDF resources. The data model of RDF schema allows creating classes of data. A class is defined as group of things with common characteristics. An object in the RDF schema is the instance of the class.

Ontology Vocabulary

The term "ontology" can be defined as an explicit specification of conceptualization [41], [42]. The conceptualization means modeling certain domain and the

Ontology is used to describe important concepts of this domain, so it is the specification of this conceptualization. Ontology is the stage where the vocabularies related to a specific domain should be defined. It provides the capability to make analysis on the relationships between the vocabularies to discover problems such as the existence of two vocabularies of the same meaning. In this stage, the relationships between vocabularies of a specific domain are created in hierarchal form by using the inheritance and classes concepts.

Languages such as OWL (Web Ontology Language) which may be considered as a syntactic extension for RDF/RDFS, are provided at this stage. The main layer of semantic web architecture is Ontology vocabulary, which typically consists of hierarchical distribution of important concepts in a domain, along with descriptions of the properties of each concept.

Ontologies play a pivotal role in the semantic web by providing a source of shared and precisely defined terms that can be used in metadata.

OWL (Web Ontology Language): OWL is intended to be used when the information contained in documents needs to be processed by applications, as opposed to situations where the content only needs to be presented to humans. OWL can be used to explicitly represent the meaning of terms in vocabularies and the relationships between those terms. This representation of terms and their interrelationships is called ontology. OWL has more facilities for expressing meaning and semantics than XML, RDF, and RDF-S, and thus OWL goes beyond these languages in its ability to represent machine interpretable content on the Web. The OWL has been designed to meet the requirements of RDF, RDFS, XML Schema [43].

Logic Layer

The logic layer in the semantic web is the universal language of monotonic logic. In the logic layer of semantic web architecture, any rule can export the code but cannot import it. Any system in the logic layer can validate proofs. This layer functions on the basic principle of first order predicate logic, so the information is displayed accurately on the web. [44].

Proof

In this layer, the ultimate goal of semantic web is to create a much smarter content which could be understood by the machines. When the content is understood by machine, some assertions may come out of the content and new pieces of information are produced. Unfortunately, this layer has not been investigated enough, this lack of investigation is not yet sufficiently considered to be a crucial problem.

Trust

This is the top most layer of the semantic web architecture, in which the trustworthiness of information should be subjectively evaluated by each information consumers. The trust does not exclude information providers which have not been rated or do not publish trust relevant information in a specific way. The trust layer in semantic web architecture is analyzed into four parts: The Information integration layer handles aggregation of information from different sources and adds provenance metadata in the information. The Repository

Layer stores the aggregate information. The Query and Trust evaluation layer handles the actual trust decisions using query specific trust policies. The Application and explanation layer on which the retrieved information is used which an application context provides functionality to browse through explanations why data should be trusted.

Digital Signature

Digital signatures run horizontal to the RDF family up through the proof layer and support the notion of trust. Developments in the area of digital signatures are progressing, and could eventually help validate the integrity of metadata that an agent is using for reasoning and task completion. The main purpose of the digital signature is to digitally sign the document. Also encryption methods are used to run on digital signed documents to prevent against unauthorized access.

The semantic Web architectures show the main functionalities that should be provided to achieve the desired goals of the semantic Web. Each of these functionalities is associated with one of the layers of layered cake architecture of the semantic Web. Each function may be realized in several ways using any of the suitable available technologies.

5. Results and Benefits of Using Semantic Web

Limitation of current e-learning environments

E-Learning (Electronic-Learning) is just learning using technologies like computer system, internet, and network [45]. Current e-learning environments are developed in computer programming languages. It works according to how it is programmed well in advance. Sometimes it fails to supply learning resources according to the learner's needs, and produce irrelevant results which do not match the learner's query and interest. So that learner has to be involved and should spend time to categorize the web results, which he/she actually requires to learn [46].

The Semantic Web is used as a backbone for e-learning. Foremost, the objectives are to ease the contribution of and the efficient access to the information. But, in general, a Semantic Web-based learning process could be a personalized (user customized), relevant (problem-dependent), and an active (context-sensitive) [47].

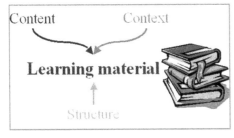

Figure 3. Learning Material Dimension.

From the student point of view, the most important criterions for searching learning materials are: what the learning material is about (content) and in which form this topic is presented (context). However, while learning material does not appear in isolation, another dimension (structure) is needed to encompass a set of learning materials in a learning course as shown in figure 3.

Learning object and courses databases are syntactically structured text archives with powerful search engines. But, search engines for Learning objects information retrieval do not include knowledge into their search strategies. These strategies include keyword and metadata search, but do not address the semantics of the keywords, which would allow, for instance, conceptual query expansion. In other words, there is no semantic relationship between information needs of the user and the information content of documents [48] [49].

Nowadays, e-learning systems are widely used for education and training in universities and companies because of their electronic course content access and virtual classroom participation. However, with the rapid increase of learning content on the Web, it is time-consuming for learners to find contents they really want to and need to study.

The e-learning material (course) may be decomposed into Learning Objects (LOs). The LOs may be considered as basic units (modules) of the e-learning material satisfying certain requirements. This mechanism enables reusability, in which the same LOs may be used to build different courses.

Decomposing the e-learning material into LOs and knowing the relationships between these learning objects is one of the main problems that face this approach. Improving the creation of the relationships between the LOs in an efficient way needs understanding of the context and the semantics of the learning objects. This is one of the main functionalities and roles of the semantic Web since the Semantic Web is an efficient mechanism to represent the semantics of the resources. It aims at providing a promising foundation for enriching resources, with well defined meanings.

If an e-learner needs to know about a specific course, then he/she may search using specific related keywords. The result of the search may include irrelevant data with respect to his/her preferences. One of the best approaches to overcome this issue is to use ontology for the e-learner. This e-learner ontology defines concepts about the e-learner and relationships between the concepts. It enables us to describe an e-learner profile that semantically relates the appropriate and relevant learning objects to the e-learner.

Retrieving information effectively on the Web is becoming a harder problem. Most current search engines are keyword based, so the retrieved documents match these submitted keywords. In traditional search, not all retrieved documents are relevant. Approximately one half is irrelevant regardless the user model; the same keywords always return the same documents. The users may not have similar interests, background, preferences, and goals, so the same keyword may have different meanings to different users. Personalized or customized retrieved document list is more helpful since it is more relevant. A user model is needed to allow customized responses to the user according to his/her model.

The semantic Web overcomes this limitation where structured meaning and annotation is attached to the navigational data of the current Web.

Semantic Web Technology (SWT) helps the learners for better e-learning by providing the most significant learning materials, which suit the individuals, like learner's profile,

needs and interest [45]. Semantic Web solves the limitation of current e-learning environment by providing most relevant learning resources to an e-learner quickly.

In Table 3, a summary view of the possibility to use the Semantic Web, for realizing the e-Learning requirements, is presented.

Table 3. Benefits of using Semantic Web as a technology for E-Learning.

Requirements	E-Learning	Semantic Web
Delivery	Pull – Student determines agenda	Knowledge items (learning materials) are distributed on the web, But they are linked to commonly agreed ontologie(s). This enables construction of a user-specific course, by semantic querying for Topics of interest.
Responsiveness	Reactionary – Responds to problem at hand	Software agents on the Semantic Web may use a commonly agreed service language, which enables co-ordination between agents and proactive delivery of learning materials in the context of actual problems. The vision is that each user has his own personalized agent that Communicates with other agents.
Access	Non-linear – Allows direct access to knowledge in whatever sequence makes sense to the situation at hand	User can describe the situation at hand (goal of learning, previous knowledge,...) and perform semantic querying for the suitable Learning material. The user profile is also accounted for. Access to Knowledge can be expanded by semantically defined navigation.
Symmetry	Symmetric – Learning occurs as an integrated activity	The Semantic Web (semantic intranet) offers the potential to become an integration platform for all business processes in an Organization, including learning activities.
Modality	Continuous – Learning runs in parallel to business tasks and never stops	Active delivery of information (based on personalized agents) creates a dynamic learning environment that is integrated in the Business processes.
Authority	Distributed – Content comes from the interaction of the participants and the educators	The Semantic Web will be as decentralized as possible. This Enables an effective co-operative content management.
Personalization	Personalized – Content is determined by the individual user's needs and aims to satisfy the needs of every user	A user (using its personalized agent) searches for learning material Customized for her/his needs. The ontology is the link between User needs and characteristics of the learning material.
Adaptively	Dynamic – Content changes constantly through user input, experiences, new practices, business rules and heuristics	The Semantic Web enables the use of distributed knowledge provided in various forms, enabled by semantically annotation of Content. Distributed nature of the Semantic Web enables Continuous improvement of learning materials.

6. Conclusions

The real value of e-Learning lies not in its ability to train just anyone, anytime, anywhere, but in our ability to deploy this attribute to train the right people to gain the right skills or knowledge, at the right time. This process reduces the cost of learning and adds a degree of freedom that enables the e-learner to control the activities and the courses that he/she is interested in.

Semantic Web Technology (SWT) in which information in machine-processable form, can coexist and complement the current web with better enabling computers and people to work in co-operation. Making the content machine-understandable is a popular paraphrase of the fundamental prerequisite for the semantic web. With the rapid increase of learning content on the Web, it will be time-consuming for learners to find contents they really want to and need to study. The Semantic Web Technology (SWT) has the potentiality to be applied in different areas.

E-Learning is one of the domains which may benefit from this new web technology. Semantic Web Technology helps to learners for better E-learning by providing the most significant learning materials, which suit to the individual like learner's profile, needs and interest.

This paper focuses on potential uses of Semantic Web Technology (SWT) in E-Learning, as well as advantages of using Ontology to describe learning materials. It is a great platform to represent the E-learning management system that recovers the limitations of Web 2.0.

In this paper, the limitations of the conventional Web and how the Semantic Web overcomes those limitations have been discussed. Then, the common technologies used to construct the E-learning and Semantic Web is presented.

The architecture of the Semantic Web is discussed, which introduces the essential components of the Semantic Web, such as eXtensible Mark-up language (XML), XML scheme, Resource Description Framework (RDF), RDF scheme, and Web Ontology language (OWL).

The purpose of this paper is to clarify possibilities of using the Semantic Web as a backbone for E-Learning, which provides flexible and personalized access to these learning materials.

References

[1]   T. Govindasamy, "Successful implementation of e-Learning Pedagogical considerations," *Internet and Higher Education,* vol. 4, p. 287–299, 2002.

[2]   K. S. Neepa, "E-Learning and Semantic Web," *International Journal of e-Education, e-Business, e-Management and e-Learning,* vol. 2, no. 2, April 2012.

[3]   J. Hendler, "Agents and the Semantic Web," *IEEE Intelligent Systems,* vol. 16, no. 2, pp. 30-37, 2001.

[4]   G. Fayed, D. Sameh, H. Ahmad, M. A. Jihad, A. E.-S. Samir and E.-S. Hosam, "E-Learning Model Based On Semantic Web Technology," *International Journal of Computing & Information Sciences,* vol. 4, no. 2, pp. 63 -71, 2006.

[5]   B. Dutta, "Semantic Web Based E-learning," [Online]. Available: https://www.researchgate.net/publication/242691487_Semantic_Web_Based_E-learning.

[6]   N. Kontodimopoulos, A. BOUKOUVALAS1, K. Savidakis and A. Gasparinatou, "Distance-Learning Educational Material in the Biomedical Engineering Degree Program," in *WSEAS Int. Conf. on ENGINEERING EDUCATION,* Venice, Italy, 2004.

[7]   Hoppe, G.; Breitner, M. H, "Business Models for E-Learning," in *E-learning,models,istrument,experiences,of the Multikonferenz Wirtschaftsinformatik,* Essen-Germany, 2004.

[8]   G. Jorge, M. Ruiz and J. Michael, "The Impact of E-Learning in Medical Education," in *Academic Medicine,* 2006.

[9]   "e-Learning- Introductions," [Online]. Available: http://agelesslearner.com/intros/elearning.html.

[10]   P. Drucker, "Need to Know Integrating e-Learning with High Velocity Value Chains," A Delphi Group White, 2000.

[11]   L. Stojanovic, S. Steffen and S. Rudi, "eLearning based on the Semantic Web," in *WebNet'2001 World Conference of the WWW and Internet. AACE (2001),* 2001.

[12]   Y. Zhiwen, N. Yuichi, J. Seiie and K. Shoji, "Ontology-Based Semantic Recommendation for Context-Aware E-Learning," in *Ubiquitous Intelligence and Computing,* Springer Berlin Heidelberg, 2007, pp. pp 898-907.

[13]   T. Dietinger, "ASPECTS OF E-LEARNING ENVIRONMENTS," Graz University of Technology, 2003.

[14]   A. Rossett, THE ASTD E-LEARNING HANDBOOK BEST PRACTICES, STRATEGIES, AND CASE STUDIES FOR AN EMERGING FIELD, New York: McGraw-Hill, 2002.

[15]   M. R. Charles and A. C.-C. Alison, Instructional-Design Theories and Models, New York: Taylor & Francis publishing, 2009.

[16]   M. Elazony, "master's thesis"Presentation Techniques for Distance Learning"," cairo, 2011.

[17]   J. Hofmann, "Blended Learning Case Study," 2001. [Online]. Available: http://www.astd.org/LC/2001/0401_hofmann.htm. [Accessed 13 January 2009].

[18]   B. Karin, C. M. Antonio and T. Walt, Semantic Web: Concepts, Technologies and Applications, Springer Science & Business Media, 2007.

[19]   T. Berners-Lee, J. Hendler and O. Lassila, "The Semantic Web: A new form of Web content that ismeaningful to computers will unleash a revolution of new possibilities.," *Scientific American.,* 2001.

[20]   "Semantic_Web," 2013. [Online]. Available: http://en.wikipedia.org/wiki/Semantic_Web. [Accessed 2013].

[21]   B. Ö. Czerkawski, "THE SEMANTIC WEB IN TEACHER EDUCATION," *TOJET: The Turkish Online Journal of Educational Technology,* vol. 13, no. 4, October 2014.

[22]   V. Devedžić, "Web Intelligence and Artificial Intelligence in Education," *Web Intelligence and Artificial Intelligence in Education. Educational Technology & Society,* vol. 4, no. 7, pp. 29-39, 2004.

[23]   T. Berners-Lee, "What the Semantic Web can represent," 17 09 1998. [Online]. Available: http://www.w3.org/DesignIssues/RDFnot.html. [Accessed 31 03 2013].

[24]   T. Berners-Lee, "Semantic Web Road map," 1998. [Online]. Available: http://www.w3.org/DesignIssues/Semantic.html..

[25]   M.-B. T, Everything Integrated: A Framework for Associative Writing in the Web, University of Southampton, 2004.

[26]   L. O. K. T. S. Michael Daconta, The Semantic web: the guide to future of XML,web services and knowledge management.

[27]   A. B. A. J. v. d. M. A. Gerber, "Functional Semantic Web Architecture,"," *Springer Berlin / Heidelberg, Lecture Notes in Computer Science,* Vols. Volume 5021/2008, ISBN:978-3-540-68233-2, pp. pages: 273-287, 2008.

[28]   A. B. A. J. v. d. M. A. Gerber, "Towards a Semantic Web Layered Architecture," in *Software Engineering Proceedings of the 25th conference on IASTED International Multi-Conference,* Innsbruck, Austria,, 2007.

[29]   M. A. a. H. S. H. Al-Feel, "Toward an Agreement on Semantic Web Architecture," in *World Academy of Science,Engineering and Technology,* 2009.

[30]   H. Pascal and J. Krzysztof, "Semantic Web Tools and Systems," *Semantic Web,* vol. 2, no. 1 / 2011, 2011.

[31]   B. P. P. P.-S. J. I. Horrocks, "Semantic Web Architecture: Stack or Two Towers?" "*Lecture Notes in Computer Science,* Vols. Volume 3703/2005,, no. ISBN: 978-3-540-, pp. Pages: 37-41,, 2005.

[32]   A. Swartz, "The Semantic Web in Breadth," 2002. [Online]. Available: http://logicerror.com/semanticWeb-long..

[33]   R. Pandey and S. Dwivedi, "Interoperability between Semantic Web Layers: A Communicating Agent Approach," *International Journal of Computer Applications,* vol. 12, no. 3, p. 0975 – 8887, November 2010.

[34]   "XML_schema," [Online]. Available: http://en.wikipedia.org/wiki/XML_schema.

[35]   T. Bray, "Extensible Markup Language (XML) 1.1 (Second Edition)," 2006. [Online]. Available: http://www.w3.org/TR/xml11/#sec-origin-goals.

[36]   "REC-xml-names," [Online]. Available: http://www.w3.org/TR/REC-xml-names.

[37]   D. Beckett, "RDF/XML Syntax Specification (Revised)," 2004. [Online]. Available: http://www.w3.org/TR/REC-rdf-syntax/. [Accessed 2013].

[38]   E. Miller, "An Introduction to the Resource Description Framework," *D-Lib Magazine,* 1998.

[39]   "Resource Description Framework," [Online]. Available: http://en.wikipedia.org/wiki/Resource_Description_Framework.

[40] "rdf-schema," [Online]. Available: http://www.w3.org/TR/rdf-schema.

[41] M. Obitko., "Introduction to Ontologies and Semantic Web," 2007. [Online]. Available: http://www.obitko.com/tutorials/ontologies-semantic-web/.

[42] S. S. A. Maedche, "Ontology Learning for the Semantic Web," *IEEE Intelligent Systems,* vol. 16, no. ISSN:1541-1672, pp. 72-9, 2001.

[43] "owl-features," [Online]. Available: http://www.w3.org/TR/owl-features.

[44] "Logic layer," [Online]. Available: http://www.w3.org/2002/Talks/04-sweb/slide20-0.html.

[45] S. K. Patel and B. H. B, "AUTOMATIC DISCOVERY AND PRESENTATION OF HIGHLY PERSONALIZED E-LEARNING RESOURCES: A SURVEY," *International Journal of Advanced Technology & Engineering Research (IJATER),* vol. 3, p. 25–29, 2013.

[46] L. T and R. S, "Information Portal of E-Learning System in Semantic Web Environment," in *The 6th IEEE International Conference on Intelligent Data Acquisition and Advanced Computing Systems: Technology and Applications*, 2011.

[47] L. Stojanovic, S. Staab and R. Studer, "eLearning based on the Semantic Web," in *WebNet'2001 World Conference of the WWW and Internet. AACE (2001)*, 2001.

[48] M. Frank and E. Miller, "RDF Primer:W3C Recommendation 10 February 2004," W3C, 10 February 2004. [Online]. Available: http://www.w3.org/TR/2004/REC-rdf-primer-20040210/. [Accessed 10 8 2015].

[49] M. Frank, M. Eric and M. Brian, "RDF 1.1 Primer:W3C Working Group Note 24 June 2014," W3C, 24 June 2014. [Online]. Available: http://www.w3.org/TR/2014/NOTE-rdf11-primer-20140624/. [Accessed 10 8 2015].

Development of Operating Instructional System Using AR Technology in Chemical Plants

Atsuko Nakai[1], Shun Motoyoshi[2], Fuminori Oomori[2], Kazuhiko Suzuki[1, 2]

[1]Centerfor Safe and Disaster-Resistant Society, Okayama University, Okayama, Japan
[2]Graduate School of Natural Science & Technology, Okayama University, Okayama, Japan

Email address:

fumoto@safelab.sys.okayama-u.ac.jp (A. Nakai), motoyoshi.shun@safelab.sys.okayama-u.ac.jp (S. Motoyoshi),
oomori.fuminori@safelab.sys.okayama-u.ac.jp (F. Oomori), kazu@sys.okayama-u.ac.jp (K. Suzuki)

Abstract: In recent years, Japan's industrial accident rate has shown an increasing trend. This is especially remarkable due to chemical industrial complexes. As is well-known, many kinds of hazardous materials are being controlled in chemical facilities. If a serious accident occurs, there is the potential for severe damage to employees and the residents of local communities. A primary factor in these accidents is the lack of safety awareness, safety knowledge, safety management system deficiencies, and insufficiency of safety ethics. In addition, industrial technology is highly diversified and complicated. As a result, operators cannot grasp the whole situation of the abnormalities and potential crises present. In other words, operators are unable to take the appropriate safety measures to prevent accidents. In some cases, equipment failure shave developed into serious accidents due to incorrect operation by the operator. This paper presents systems that provide information to operators by using augmented reality (AR) technology in chemical plants. AR can enhance real-world environments using virtual objects such as computer graphics. This system can help plant operators to confirm procedures in order to ensure proper operation. Furthermore, the operator can recognize the equipment to be operated properly using a tablet PC with a built-in camera. The proposed system can provide the plant information based on the dynamic simulator (DS). In an emergency, chemical plant operators are required to make quick decisions to prevent the escalation of an accident. To convey accurate indication information of the work, it is useful to recognize target equipment using AR marker in addition to the output information by individual voice from control room. Our developed systems can support chemical plant operators to make quick decisions and to follow correct operating procedures.

Keywords: Instructional System, AR, Operation Support, Human Error

1. Introduction

Improving the safety and reliability of large-scale industrial facilities is extremely important for the safety of workers and also for the local residents. Consequently, a number of activities, countermeasures, and assessment techniques have been proposed. There is a need for detecting potential risks before an accident or disaster occurs, taking preventative/reactionary measures, and organizing a management system that is compatible with the risks. In addition, a safe process design is necessary for preventing human error. Control problems are increasingly significant in both software and hardware as the economic situation changes over time [1].

In a chemical plant, operators must be responsible for their own areas in order to ensure the safe operation of all plant components. There are two types of operators: field operators and board operators. Field operators are responsible for operating equipment in the field. Board operators' control refineries from a control center or control room. In order to achieve smooth operation in a chemical plant, cooperative work is necessary [1]. There were human factors at play in the recent accident, including misjudgment and miscommunication.[2]Accidents also often occur in non-steady-state operation.[3][4]When an accident or disaster, including during non-steady-state operation, emergency response operation is needed. Operators must make accurate and quick decisions in spite of being in high pressure situations.[5][6]At present, operational guidelines and procedures for emergencies have not been fully developed.

Accurate judgment, and the corresponding operational steps, are very important in order to prevent the escalation of the accident.[6][7]However , with the retirement of skilled workers, opportunities for technology inheritance, training and education have decreased. We are concerned that the flexible response capability of workers has also reduced. In this study, we propose a system to provide instructional information for field operators by using augmented reality (AR) technology in chemical plants. AR can enhance real-world environments by using virtual objects such as computer graphics. [8]By using this system, operators can confirm the required operating procedures in the field. Furthermore, the operator can recognize the proper operating equipment by using a camera-equipped tablet PC. Our system has been designed to aid chemical plant operators in making quick decisions and in taking the correct operating steps. The concept of the proposed system is shown in Fig. 1.

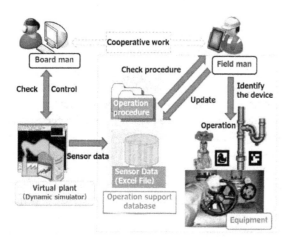

Fig. 1. Concept of the Proposed System.

2. Purpose and Approach

In chemical plants, a large amount of dangerous chemical materials of a very wide variety are controlled. Moreover, they are managed in high-temperature, high-pressure environments. The various chemical fluids that flow through into the pipe and the equipment (such as tanks or reactors) are arranged in close proximity. Based on the information from the distributed control system (DCS), board operators manage the plant process until the product from raw materials. Board operators instruct the field operators on the necessary operations by monitoring the conditions in plant. Field operators work according to instructions from the central control room. When an alarm is issued, field operators perform an emergency response in the facility. Operating instructions on the site is a qualitative indication, not a quantitative data, "Turn the valve to the right", such as radio contact (through the voice of the board operators).Also, due to the installation of similar aggregating devices, such as pipes and valves, there is a risk of serious accidents occurring due to operators operating the wrong device.

In recent years, workload shave increased due to labor-saving measures and cost reduction. Young, immature

plant operators are being forced to handle complicated facilities with fewer people due to the aging workforce situation. As a result, the potential for human error to occur has been increasing.

Human errors caused by field operators can be classified into the following types:[3]

1. *Misjudgment:* This involves a lack of understanding of the implications of the current situation and work

2. *Incorrect operation:* This includes mistakes made in operating procedures and operation details

3. *Cognition and verification mistakes:* This involves mistaking the operation target and omitting to give confirmation after completing an operation.

This study shows an information system that presents the relevant operating procedures and accurate equipment information to field operators. Using AR, the proposed system is created with additional information on the real image. The operators captured the equipment through camera; our system displays the name of equipment and operating information. The advantages of using AR include:

1. Virtual information is displayed simultaneously with real visual information

2. A real-time and interactive interface

3. Access to 3D representation

With advances in computer technology, AR technology has been implemented in various scenarios.AR can function in ways that enhance one's current perception of reality.[9]It does so by incorporating computer vision and object recognition, so that the information about the real world of the user becomes interactive and digitally alterable. Virtual information about the environment and its objects can be overlaid on the real world.[9][10][11]AR systems are effectively used for emergency management.[12] Also previous research for chemical industries operators are presented by companies.[13][14]As previous research for the safe operation of large-scale facilities, there is the wearable supervision system that can provide to support the on-site operator. Using the system, the on-site operator have the ability to do the same things as if he or she were in the control room.[15] In nuclear power plant, Augmented Reality is a promising technology that will improve the efficiency and safety of maintenance work. [16]

By enhancing the information available on the real-world environment, the proposed system is able to provide the correct procedures and identify the target equipment for the operators. This system is linked to the plant dynamic simulator, instead of a real chemical plant, to provide plant information. Actual chemical plant facilities are controlled by the DCS. The number of equipment operated by the field operator is managed by the board operator in the control room. We used a dynamic simulator (DS) as a virtual plant in this system. DS is a software tool for building a virtual plant on a computer by modeling an existing plant or a plant that is yet to be built.[17] With the DS, operators can be educated in various situations. This system can be implemented with the actual control and safety systems using plant data. [18]Field operators operate the plant on the basis of the procedures outlined in the plant information.

By using the AR markers, the proposed system makes it possible to accurately recognize the target device. Field operators can determine whether the correct operation has been performed by using the camera-equipped tablet PC. The AR marker presents an image of a set pattern, which is indicator for specifying the installation site and displaying additional information, the name of equipment and process value etc. The operator identifies an operation object with the camera, and can confirm the correct operating procedure on the tablet PC. First, the work information is displayed to the operator; after the task has been completed, the next work procedure is presented by updating the plant information. Human errors often occur when a field operator works alone or in a non-steady-state operation. [3][5]The purpose of this study is to support the work of young, immature operators and to reduce human error.

3. Operation Instructional System

3.1. Outline of Operation Instructional System

The proposed system consists of two subsystems: the operating procedure system, and the device recognition system. Plant information for the operating procedure is stored in the database and presented as required. Operators can confirm the procedures and recognize the target device using the system through the camera-equipped tablet PC. Fig. 2 shows an outline of the proposed system.

An approximate workflow utilizing the system is shown in Fig. 3.

This entails the following steps:

1. Check the displayed procedure on the tablet screen.
2. Operate the equipment based on the instructions of the system.
3. Recognize the operation target device.
4. Operate the target device.
5. Check the operation and proceed to the next task.

3.2. Operating Procedure System

Traditionally, the operating procedure manual is created on printed paper. Usually, operating procedures are displayed in the form of a list, with no detailed information provided on the timing and the operation. Operating manual slack is descriptions of operational targets and their location through photos or figures. The instructional information that is presented to workers is, therefore, not considered to be sufficient. Conventional operating procedures are hard to understand intuitively. In order for the operator to perform alone without a trainer, considerable money and time must be spent. Furthermore, the retirement of skillful workers is advancing in Japan, which is posing labor-related challenges.

These experts' knowledge and skills are not being sufficiently transferred to the younger generation. Moreover, skilled workers may not remember the procedures of non-steady-state work.

Operating procedure systems compensate for the gaps in knowledge of safe operation. First, work procedure is

indicated by the system. The field operator operates the equipment with reference to the work procedure outlined by the system. The virtual plant changes the process value by reflecting on the result of the work. After this, the next procedure can be displayed. The field operator then refers to the tablet PC and advances to the next task. In this study, we propose ways to present operators with the correct operating procedures that can be used in the field of chemical plants using AR.

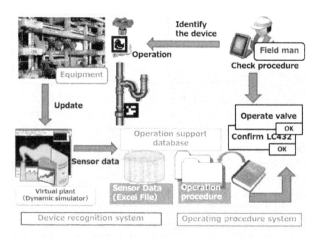

Fig. 2. Outline of the Operation Instructional System.

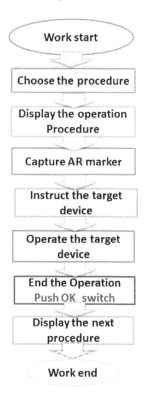

Fig. 3. Workflow Utilizing the System.

3.2.1. Divide Operating Procedures

Existing operating procedures are presented in a list. In order to systematize the operating procedures on paper, the contents of the procedure should be divided into steps. The standard operating procedures contain too much information.

Therefore, there is a need to clearly describe the role of the workers. Accordingly, we sorted the information by using the 6w2h method. 6w refers to "what", "who", "when", "where", "whom" and "why"; 2h refers to "how" and how many. The procedure of each operation is further divided and described in length it can be understood at once in the form of cards. The cards can be freely positioned on the display and be overlaid on real image using AR technology. Fig. 4 shows the image of the operating display.

3.2.2. XML Description of Operation Procedure

Operation procedures using this system are conveyed based on the progress of the work. Procedural information is written using Extensible Markup Language (XML). XML defines a set of rules for encoding documents and allows users to specify their own tags. It is possible for users to create their own meaning, structure and hierarchy in a unified manner. XML is also useful for creating files to store data [16].Fig. 5 shows the operating procedure written in XML.

The operating procedure to be used in this system, as shown in Fig. 5 is divided into steps<Step>, the ID information of each device <Target>,name <Name> and the associated markers <Marker>.Information such as the absolute coordinates of the markers are entered in the target space <X>·<Y>·<Z>. By using XML, documentation can be easily created, changed and appended.

3.3. Operation Support Database

Fig. 4. *Image of the Operating Display.*

The created procedures, plant conditions, and information of the equipment are stored in the database. Operating data of the dynamic simulator is stored in the Excel file in PC. The sensor data of the plant equipment from the DS is stored in Excel files on the database in this system. Exchange data with dynamic simulator by using the Excel file may be performed smoothly. Field operators can request procedures and equipment information from the database by operating the tablet PC. The information in this database is updated by

performing the operation of the plant in the simulator; this can be presented to the worker. The next procedure is updated for display in the system after the completion of the first procedure to prevent a slip in operation. The information in the database is thus capable of being modified when necessary. And it may be further expanded.

3.4. Device Recognition System

3.4.1. Device Recognition Using AR marker

The device recognition system identifies equipment using the camera on the tablet PC. AR markers are used to recognize the plant equipment; the system then presents the target device to the field operator. The AR marker, in an image recognition AR system, is an indicator for specifying a position to display additional information and the image of a set pattern. When the AR system recognizes the marker, it can display information that has been specified so as to overlap with the real image. Simple black-and-white graphics or QR codes are often used as AR markers. There are many similar equipment, such valves and pipes, in a chemical plant. When installing a marker on the operation target device, the system is able to identify and determine the correct operational target and the operating procedure is presented.

```
 1  <?xml version="1.0" encoding="utf-8" ?>
 2  <Manual>
 3    <Header>
 4      <Title>操作マニュアル</Title>
 5      <TargetList>                                    Operation Procedure
 6        <Target>
 7          <Name>バルブA</Name>
 8          <Marker>0</Marker>            Valve A
 9          <Size>77</Size>
10          <X>0</X>
11          <Y>0</Y>
12          <Z>0</Z>
13        </Target>
14        <Target>
15          <Name>バルブB</Name>
16          <Marker>20</Marker>            Valve B
17          <Size>77</Size>
18          <X>100</X>
19          <Y>-100</Y>
20          <Z>0</Z>
21        </Target>
22      </TargetList>
23    </Header>
24
25    <Body>
26      <Step>
27        <Text>バルブAを操作してください。</Text>
28      </Step>
29      <Step>                                          Operate Valve A
30        <Text>バルブBを操作してください。</Text>
31      </Step>                                          Operate Valve B
32    </Body>
33  </Manual>
```

Fig. 5. *Operation Procedure Written in XML.*

The field operator can perform the task by referring to the displayed procedure.

When the procedure is completed, the result of work is reflected on the plant information. The database, which stores the process value of the virtual plant, is also updated. This system links the DS as a virtual plant. According to the updated values, the next operating procedure is displayed.

3.4.2. Identify the Target Device

Workflow utilizing the system is performed based on the operating procedure to be accessed from the database. The operator checks the procedure in the field and identifies the AR marker of the target device with the help of the tablet PC camera. When the camera captures the correct target device, the device recognition system displays an orange object. If field operator tries to operate the wrong equipment, a blue object on the tablet PC indicates the direction of the target device. After the camera detects the target device, information on the device is displayed, followed by the operating procedure. The field operator can then perform along with the procedure displayed. If the operating instructions cannot be understood, the operator can refer to additional information in the system. In addition, it is possible to access device information from the plant, such as temperature and pressure.

3.5. Verification Experiment of the Device Recognition System

To check the operation of the system, experiments were carried out to identify the operation target device from a plurality of devices. Operating procedures were created using XML as follows:

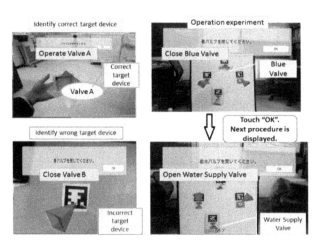

Fig. 6. *Verification Experiment of the Proposed System.*

1. Close blue valve
2. Open red valve
3. Check the increase in pressure
4. Open the water supply valve

When the camera recognizes the operation target device by the AR marker, the name of the target device is presented on an orange object. The system shows the correct device direction with a blue object, if the camera recognized a wrong device. When performing the operation of opening the water supply valve after the blue valve is closed, the system displays the screen shown in Fig. 6.

3.6. Conjunction with the Sensor Data

This system is linked with the dynamic simulator (DS). When the equipment is in operation, the system indicates the operating procedure. When field workers operate the target device, the fluctuant sensor data are updated in real time. Therefore, changes in the process values are reflected in the

virtual plant. The device recognition system compares the threshold, processes the value change of the DS, and displays the operating procedure. [18]When the process values meet the threshold, the operating procedure progresses and the system updates to display the next procedure. Fig. 7 shows the flow of the operation as it progresses in the system.

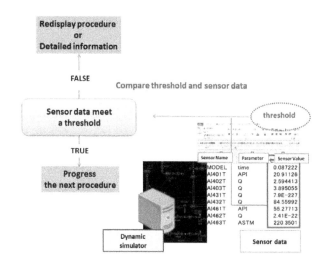

Fig. 7. *Flow of the Operation in Progress.*

4. Operating Experiment of the HDS Plant Procedure

4.1. Application of the Hydrodesulfurization (HDS) Process

This system is supposed to simulate the operating procedure of the HDS process. This process involves the reaction that comes with hydrogen separation and the removal of sulfur content from petroleum using the metal catalysts (such as nickel, cobalt, molybdenum, etc.) under high temperatures and high pressures; it also involves producing products with low kerosene and sulfur content and light oils. In this experiment, our system was applied to the field work. The Piping and Instrumentation Diagram (P&ID) of operating range is shown in Fig. 8.As the dynamic simulator is virtual; this experiment was carried out in our laboratory.

4.2. Making the Operation Procedures

In this paper, we referred to an operating procedure that had experienced Vacuum Gas Oil(VGO)charge pump failure trouble. The prerequisites for carrying out the HDS simulator training operations were as follows:

1. The time to activate a spare pump starts when the main pump is stopped in order to close the flow time of the real device. This takes about 3 or 5 minutes.

2. Aspects such as communication and reporting should reflect the training of the operators, and should protect what has been done within the department or company.

The outline of the corresponding operations is as follows:

1. The field operators need to switch from the main pump to the spare pump very quickly.

2. It is necessary to pay attention to the rising temperature of the furnace, due to the rise in temperature of the reactor.

3. A board operator should operate the DCS using caution, monitoring any change in the temperature of the inflow and outflow of the furnace.

4. A field operator should confirm the level of tanksD-402 and D-406 to prevent a rapid decrease liquid level.

In order to present the procedure on the system screen, the normal printed operating procedure should be divided into cards that clearly present individual steps, as follows:

Step1. Start a spare charge pump.

Step2. Adjust the temperature of the heating furnace.

Step3. Adjust the liquid level in the tank.

Step4. Open the main valve to 30% of the maximum value.

Step5.Resume the raw material supply to the heating furnace.

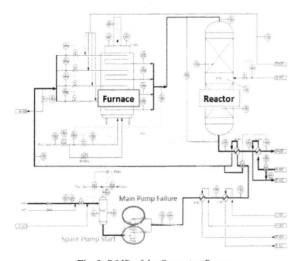

Fig. 8. *P&ID of the Operating Range.*

This procedure involves the cooperated work both field operator and board operator. The board operator control work flow from step1 to step5. Step 3, a required field operation, was applied to the operating experiment. It could be divided more finely. For storing information on the operating procedures in the system, we defined the parameters for this step as follows.

$$P_i = \{S_i, \ O_i, \ D_i, \ C_i\}$$

i: Number of the procedure

P_i: Procedure information

S_i: Start information

O_i: Operation information

D_i: Detailed information

C_i: Confirm information

Step 3 was divided into the following procedural cards:

Step 3: Adjust the liquid level in the tank

P_1: Adjust the level of the LGO (light gas oil).

S_1: Adjust the level of the tank.

O_1: Adjust the level of LGO.

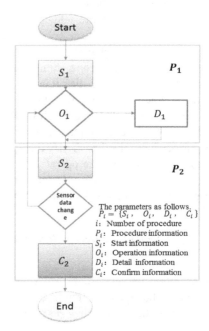

Fig. 9. *Model of Operation Procedures.*

D_1: Refer to LC432.

P_2: Check and adjust the level of LC432.

S_2: Adjust the level of LC432.

C_2: Confirm the level of D-402.

The operating procedure model for Step 3 is shown in Fig.9. Similarly, operating procedures were created for each step.

4.3. Operating Experiment

Using the operating procedure, the operating experiment of the proposed system was performed. Fig. 10 shows Procedure 1, and Fig. 11 shows Procedure 2. As a result, we confirmed that the developed system can perform as intended.

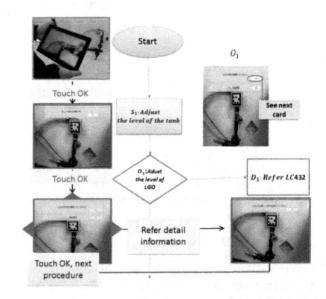

Fig. 10. *Result of Operating Experiment Procedure1.*

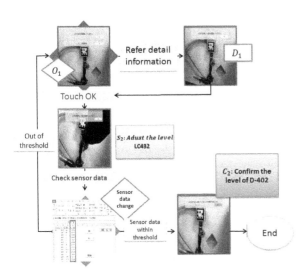

Fig. 11. Result of Operating Experiment Procedure2.

information system can indicate real-time operating procedures and accurate equipment information for field operators. In chemical plants in Japan, there have been rapid generational changes in the workforce. Technology and knowledge of the skilled workers is being gradually lost. Inherited technology and past accomplishments are essential factors in enhancing competitive production. Human errors often occur when a field operator works alone or performs non-steady-state operations. The proposed system tackles the issue of human error by recognizing correct equipment, presenting relevant information, and having a confirmation function to prevent erroneous operation. Moreover, when an accident occurs, the correct operation must be performed without any human error in order to prevent an escalation of the situation. The proposed system can help operators achieve this level of accuracy. Furthermore, the system can also be used for safety education and training. We especially hope that the proposed system can aid the next generation of operators in the field and also help clarify non-steady-state operations.

5. Results and Discussion

In this paper, we proposed a system to provide information for field operators by using AR technology in chemical plants. AR can enhance real-world environments through the use of virtual objects. By using AR markers, this system has made it possible to accurately recognize target devices. The operator can recognize the AR marker set for the target device with the help of a camera-equipped tablet PC. Field operators can detect the correct equipment to perform procedures on and more easily differentiate between similar aggregating devices, such as pipes and valves. Thus, the system can reduce the risk of serious accidents caused due to operators mistaking the device to be operated. In addition to identifying the correct equipment, the operator can confirm the correct operating procedure through the tablet PC. Operating procedures are displayed for the field operator, and after the procedure is completed, the next procedure is displayed by updating plant information. In order to systematize the operating procedure, we divided some steps to offer more clarity to operators. The system can then instruct operators on each operating procedure through cards on the tablet PC.

We used the dynamic simulator (DS) as a virtual plant in this system; actual chemical plant facilities are controlled by the DCS. The number of equipment operated by the field operator is managed by the board operator in the control room. In addition to presenting detailed plant information, the functionality of this system should expand to include presenting instructions to board operators as well. In future, this system can be implemented with the actual controls and systems, and by using real plant data. Now in the chemical plant, the field operator cannot confirm the real-time process value in the field.

6. Conclusion

In this study, we developed an operating instructional system using AR technology for chemical plants. This

References

[1]   A. Nakai, Y. Kaihata, K. Suzuki, 2014. "The Experience-Based Safety Training System   Using Vr Technology for Chemical Plant", International Journal of Advanced   Computer Science and Applications (IJACSA), Vol.5, No.11, pp.63-67.

[2]   K. Suzuki, Y. Munesawa, A. Nakai, 2013 "Recent Accidents and Safety Activities in JAPAN", AIChE Spring Meeting & 9th Global Congress on Process Safety, April.

[3]   A. Komatsubara, 2008."Human Error (second edition)", Maruzen Publishing, in Japanese.

[4]   Ministry of Health Labor and Welfare, 2003"Interim Report on Industrial Accident Survey", in Japanese.

[5]   S. Jürgen, 2013. "Process and Plant Safety – Research & Education Strategy to Keep Long Term Competences", Chemical Engineering Transactions, vol.31.

[6]   Norton, C., Cameron, I., Crosthwaite, C., Balliu, N., Tade, M., Shallcross, D., Hoadley, A., Barton, G., Kavanagh, J. 2008. "Development and deployment of an immersive learning environment for enhancing process systems engineering concepts", Education for Chemical Engineers, vol. 3, 2, December pp.75-83.

[7]   T Nakata, 2007. "Wisdom for Preventing Human Errors: Can all mistakes beeliminated ?",Kagaku-Dojin Publishing, 2007 in Japanese

[8]   Chen, Brian X, 2009. "IfYou're Not Seeing Data, You're Not Seeing", Wired, 25 August.

[9]   Nikkei Communications editorial office, 2009"AllAbout AR: Technology to innovate mobile phones and the Internet", Nikkei Business Publishing, in Japanese.

[10]   K. Oafish, Y. Sakurai, Y. Ishii, 2013. "An Adaptive AR Photographing Parameter Tuning for Industry Workspaces", SICE Annual Conference 2013, September.

[11]   T. Fabio,2013. "The HMI of the future will look very familiar," Control Engineering, Vol. 60, No. 7, pp. 26-29.

[12] G. Baron, 2009. "Augmented Reality--Emerging Technology for Emergency Management" [90]

[13] Y. Ishii, K. Ooishi, Y. Sakurai, 2013."Industrial Augmented Reality -Innovative operator assistance in collaboration with Augmented Reality-", Yokogawa Technical Report English Edition Vol.56 No.2.

[14] H. Hara, H. Kuwabara, 2015. " Innovation in Field Operations using Smart Devices with Augmented Reality Technology" FUJITUU,66,1 pp.11-17 (01 2015) in Japanese.

[15] O.Naef, P. Crausaz, 2006. " 6th Sense System Augmented Reality Chemical Plant Supervision System"International Journal of Online Engineering (iJOE), Vol.2, No.4.

[16] H. Ishii, Z. Bian, H. Fujino, T. Sekiyama, T. Nakai,A. Okamoto, H. Shimoda,M. Izumi, Y. Kanehira, and Y. Morishita, 2007. "Augmented Reality Applications forNuclear Power Plant Maintenance Work", International Symposium on Symbiotic Nuclear Power Systems for 21st Century (ISSNP).

[17] G. Fukano, K. Yokoyama, Y. Yahata, 2013. "MIRROR PLANT On-line Plant Simulator and its Applications", Yokogawa Technical Report English Edition, vol.56 No.1, pp. 11- 14.

[18] K. Yamamoto, A. Nakai, K. Suzuki, 2013. "Development of Experienced-based Training System combined with Process Dynamic Simulation" Asia Pacific Symposium on Safety 2013.

7

Hybrid techniques for Arabic letter recognition

Mohamed Hassine[1], Lotfi Boussaid[2], Hassani Massouad[1]

[1]LARATSI Lab, ENIM, University of Monastir, Monastir, Tunisia
[2]EµE Lab, FSM, University of Monastir, Monastir, Tunisia

Email address:

hassinemohamed60@yahoo.com (M. Hassine), lotfi.boussaid@enim.rnu.tn (L. Boussaid), hassani.massaoud@enim.rnu.tn (H. Messaoud)

Abstract: In this paper we investigate the use of the feed-forward back propagation neural networks (FFBPNN) for automatic speech recognition of Arabic letters with their four vowels (Fatha, dhamma, Kasra, Soukoun). This investigation will constitute a basically step for the recognition of continuous Speech. Features were extracted from recorded corpus by using a variety of conventional methods such as Linear Predictive Codes (LPC), Perceptual Linear Prediction (PLP), Relative Spectral Perceptual Linear Prediction (RASTA-PLP), Mel Frequency Cepstral Coefficients (MFCC), Continuous Wavelet Transform (CWT), etc. Here, several hybrid methods have been used too. Since the extracted features have large dimensionalities they were reduced by conserving the most discriminatory information with the Principal Component Analysis (PCA) technique. The recognition performance has been improved particularly when we use the PLP method followed by PCA technique.

Keywords: Speech Recognition, Arabic Letters, Hybrid Techniques, MFCC, PLP, LPCC, PCA and FFBPNN

1. Introduction

This template, Speech is a basic information vector that facilitates our daily life. It is the fact to translate the meanings in our minds into serial movements of our vocal tract in order to produce interconnected alphabets which form interconnected words that form sentences. Since Speech interests human life, a great part of researches in telecommunication domain has been concentrated during last decades on automatic speech recognition (ASR).

The automatic speech recognition is the fact to aid a computer interpreting a human voice. It consists in extracting oral messages included in speech signal and analyzing their sets of features. The latters will constitute inputs for recognition systems or classifiers which lead to different performances called the system performance.

Nowadays, the automatic speech recognition attracts the attentions of researchers due to the development of communication tools (computers, mobiles, internet, etc.). Compared to other languages such as English, French, Japanese, Spanish, etc., the research in Arabic speech recognition is poor due to the complexity of such language in different levels: Phonetic, linguistic, semantic, contextual, morpho-syntactic, etc.

Moreover, in Arabic language there are three classes: Standard or Classical Arabic (CA) which is the language of the Quran, Modern standard Arabic (MSA) which is used in media and studied in schools, and finally the dialect which is the spoken language that varies from one country to another or even from one region to other in the same country.

Our approach is motivated by this complexity and the lack of researches available in Arabic language speech recognition, that's why in this paper we focus on Arabic alphabet letters the joining of which generates words and consequently sentences.

A phoneme is a minimal unit that serves to distinguish between meanings in words.

In Arabic, there are 34 phonemes six of them are vowels and 28 are consonants [28]. We distinguish two classes of phonemes: pharyngeal and emphatic which characterize the Semitic language such as Arabic and Hebrew [15].

Arabic alphabets are used in many other languages beside Arabic such as Persian and Urdu. The allowed syllables in Arabic are: CV, CVC, and CVCC [21]. C represents a consonant and V represents a long or a short vowel [28]. In spoken Arabic, consonants are followed by four short vowels: "fatha": it represents the /a/ sound and is an oblique dash over a letter, "dhamma": it represents the /u/ sound and has the shape of a comma over a letter, "kasra": it represents the /i/ sound and is an oblique dash under a letter and "soukoon" which has the shape of a little circle over a letter [28].

Besides, these characteristics that make the recognition hard, the speech signal has a property to be non-stationary.

A normal speaker never pronounces the same alphabet two times identically because the speed and the period of uttering can vary from one time to another. Moreover, when the vocal tract is altered, the speech signal changes, the inter-speaker variability is evident, the same thing for the pitch, intonation and accent that vary with sexes, social, regional and national origins [7, 9, 12, 18].

The paper is organized as follows:

In section 2, we present some related works while in section 3 we describe different features extraction methods. In section 4, we present our proposed speech recognition system. Finally, the section 5 illustrates the experimental results and interpretation followed by conclusion.

2. Relates Works

Various methods and subjects were treated in Arabic speech recognition. Some researchers were interested in speaker identification with mono-speaker or multi-speaker recognition, independent or dependent speaker recognition. Some others were concerned by isolated words or continuous speech.

Due to advanced techniques, Speech recognition becomes an active research area. Satori H. and al. [24] have proposed a spoken Arabic recognition system, where Arabic alphabets were investigated to form the ten Arabic digits (from zero to nine). The proposed system consists of two steps:
- Mel Frequency Cepstral Coefficients (MFCC) features extraction;
- Classification and recognition conducted by CMU Sphinx4 which is a speaker independent system based on hidden Markov model.

The mean performance results reached, when realizing three tests, were between 83.33% and 96.67%.

Al Azzawi Kh. and al. [2] have proposed a hybrid method for automatic recognition of Arabic vowels. Feature extraction was realized by Wavelet Transform (WT) with Linear Prediction Coding (LPC). In the classification phase Feed-Forward Back Propagation Neural Network (FFBPNN) is used which performance obtained was 82.47%.

El-Mashed Sh. Y. and al. [14] have been interested in their paper on connected Arabic digits (numbers) where speaker independent Arabic speech recognition is used in order to recognize Colloquial Egyptian dialect. The proposed approach is divided into four stages: segmentation of each pronounced number in ten digits, MFCC features extraction of these digits, application of K-means clustering algorithm for the latter features in order to extract the relevant information and finally Support Vector Machine (SVM) is used where it yields to 94% accuracy.

Another work on the recognition of Arabic alphabets based on telephony Arabic corpus is realized by [5], these alphabets were recognized from a corpus developed by King Abdulaziz City for Science and Technology (KACST). The system is based on Hidden Markov Model (HMM) strategy carried out by Hidden Markov Toolkit (HTK); the performance obtained was 64.06%.

In [3], a system of automatic Arabic word recognition is proposed where the effectiveness of discrete wavelet transform is experienced. It was proved that neural network embedded with wavelet yields a good recognition result with 77% accuracy.

Arabic speech recognition (ASR) has attracted also the attention of [6] that introduced a genetic algorithm for Arabic handwriting character recognition and then Hopfield artificial neural network is applied. The recognition is divided in four phases: segmentation of the word into characters, pre-processing of each character, extraction and selection of character features and then word recognition. This research reached promising results with accuracies 99%; 92.13% and 90.52% respectively for the training, the validation and the testing sets.

A statically analysis of Arabic phonemes for continuous Arabic speech recognition using a widely used Arabic corpus is a work realized by [22] based on the (HMM). He showed that phonemes, which are based on statistical information, can be clustered in groups. An Arabic alpha digit recognizer was established by [13] where three subsets were used. When using a digit subset, the system recognized Arabic digits with 94.13% accuracy. In the case of alpha subset, alpha recognition is 64.06%, but when mixing alphas and digits subsets the recognition jumps to 76.06%.

Previously, Ganoun A. and al. [17] have developed a system for recognizing spoken Arabic digits from zero to nine based on three feature extraction techniques: Yule-Walker spectrum feature, Walsh spectrum feature and Mel Frequency Cepstral Coefficients. It was found that the MFCC provides the best recognition rate, while the worst rate was that of Yule-Walker. In [8], mono-speaker speech recognition of 11 Arabic words is realized. The authors used the MFCC followed by Bionic Wavelet Transform (BWT) for feature extraction. In the classification phase Feed-Forward Back Propagation Neural Network (FFBPNN) is used. With this system the recognition rate reached 89.09% with MFCC followed by BWT and 99.39 % with the second derivative of MFCC followed by BWT ($\Delta\Delta$MFCC+BWT).

Recently, Daqrouq K. and al. [11] have been interested in automatic recognition of Arabic digits from zero to nine uttered by 24 speakers in three Arabic dialects: Egyptian, Jordanian and Palestinian. The feature extraction has been realized by combining wavelet transform with the linear prediction coding and the classification by probabilistic neural network (PNN). The average recognition rate reached 93%, also the recognition performance in noisy environment has been investigated and the obtained results were very promising.

3. Theoretical Background

To realize our system, two phases are required:

3.1. Parameterization Phase

3.1.1. Cepstral Coefficients

The speech signal varies permanently in time according to the movement of the vocal tract; consequently analysis must be processed on short slide overlapped windows as a speech signal which is considered to be stationary in a short time interval. The speech signal is the result of the convolution in time domain of the source and the vocal tract (filter) [23]:

$$s(n) = e(n) \times h(n) \qquad (1)$$

Where s(n) is the filter output, e(n) is the excitation signal and h(n) is the impulse response of the filter. In order to replace the convolution by an addition operation, one passes to the log-spectral domain by the following equation:

$$\log(S(f)) = \log(E(f)) + \log(H(f)) \qquad (2)$$

Where S(f), E(f) and H(f) are the Fourier transform of s(n), e(n) and h(n) respectively.

The real Cepster of the speech signal is obtained by applying the inverse of discrete Fourier transform (IDFT) to equation (2), then separation of the source (excitation signal) and the vocal tract (Transfert function) is realized by a time windowing called 'Liftrage' resulting to Cepsral Coefficients. This stage is also called 'homomorphic analyses and it's widely spread in automatic speech recognition domain.

3.1.2. Mel Frequency Cepstral Coefficients (MFCC)

The MFCC are computed by discrete cosine transform of the power spectrum of the speech signal. It is based on the Mel scale which models the perception of the speech by the human ear.

The Mel scale behaves linearly between zero and 1000 Hz and logarithmically above, so it spaces small values and approaches large values: the main advantage of MFCC coefficients is that they are uncorrelated.

To extract MFCC coefficients five steps are employed:

The first step is to pre-emphasis the speech signal by applying a high pass filter in order to increase the high frequency contribution. In fact, when spreading via air, the magnitude of speech signal reduces as the frequency rises. In order to compensate the attenuated speech signal, it is passed through a high-pass filter (finite impulse filter) to recover the signal.

In practice, we use simply a finite impulse filter (1,-0.97). If s(n) is the speech signal and $S_p(n)$ is the pre-emphasized signal then:

$$s_p(n) = s(n) - 0.97s(n-1) \qquad (3)$$

The second step is to window the speech signal by overlapped Hamming windows. These windows are of little sizes (about 25 ms) and are used to reduce the discontinuity and to avoid the leakage effect and consequently to improve the analysis of the speech. The Hamming window is given by:

$$h_1(n) = \begin{cases} 0.54 - 0.46 \times \cos(2\pi n/N-1) & if\ 0 \le n \le N \\ 0\ otherwise \end{cases} \qquad (4)$$

Where N is the size of the window.

This window was chosen since it generates lesser oscillations than other windows and has reasonable side lobe and main lobe characteristics which are required for the DFT computation. The hamming window has effectively better selectivity for large signals and is commonly used is speech processing.

The third one is to compute the Discrete Fourier Transform of each windowed frame resulting in Short Time Discrete Fourier Transform (STDFT). The values derived from here are then grouped together in critical bands and weighted by a triangular filter bank counting M filters called 'Mel-Spaced filter bank'.

The Mel scale is given by the following equation:

$$f_{Mel} = 2595 \times \log(1 + f_{HZ}/700) \qquad (5)$$

Where f_{Hz} is the frequency in Hz.

In the fourth step, the logarithm of the band passed frequency response is computed. Finally, the Discrete Cosine Transform (DCT) is applied on the found data which results in Mel Frequency Cepstral Coefficients [27].

Assume that $H_m(k)$ is the frequency magnitude response of the mth filter of Mel filter bank, where k is the discrete frequency index in the digital domain. The filter output of the mth filter, X_m, can be expressed by:

$$X_m = \sum_{k=0}^{\frac{N}{2}-1} |S(k)|^2 |H_m(k)| \quad 1 \le m \le M \qquad (6)$$

The Mel Frequency Cepstral Coefficients of the filtered information by the mth filter are represented by $c(m)$ as:

$$c(m) = DCT(\log(X_m) \qquad (7)$$

3.1.3. Linear Predictive Cepstral Coefficients: LPCC

The LPCC feature extraction is based on the LPC analysis which computes the Linear Predictive Coefficients, so the LPCC are calculated from the autoregressive modeling of the speech signal. They are very simple and well used since they allow a good representation of speech overlap vowels.

Each frame is represented by static coefficients: In our work thirteen or sixteen coefficients are used in one hand. In the other hand we have increased the dimensionality of the MLP input vector which represents a letter by concatenating two or more vectors in order to form one vector to improve the recognition task.

After pre-emphasizing and windowing the signal, the autocorrelation features are extracted then the Levinson Durbin is used for computing linear predictive coefficients (LPC) since the vocal tract is modeled by a digital all-pole filter. Finally the linear predictive Cepstral Coefficients (LPCC) for a speech frame are calculated by using the following formula:

$$\hat{v}[n] = \ln(G) \quad for \quad n = 0 \qquad (8)$$

Where G is the gain of the all-pole filter (the vocal tract);

$$\hat{v}[n] = a_n + \sum_{k=1}^{n-1} (k/n) \; \hat{v}[k]a_{n-k} \qquad (9)$$

$$for \; 1 \le n \le p \quad [10].$$

Where $\hat{v}[n]$ is the nth linear predictive Cepstral Coefficient; p is the order of the LPC desirable analysis and a_n is the nth linear predictive coding coefficient computed with the Levinson-Durbin algorithm.

3.1.4. The Perceptually Based Linear Prediction Analysis: PLP and Rasta-PLP

The PLP technique uses several operations inspired of perceptual data: that's to produce a hearing spectrum with the integration of few critical bands in the Bark scale, taking into account the isotone curve, compression of the spectrum in sound intensity and it is based on that of the LPCC.

We just add three steps such as:
* Integration of critical bands;
* Equal loudness pre-emphasis;
* Intensity-loudness conversion to simulate the power low of hearing.

The Rasta-PLP is based on the PLP method. It applies a regressive filter for analyzing and reducing noise [20].

Rasta-PLP is performed in few steps as shown in Figure 1.

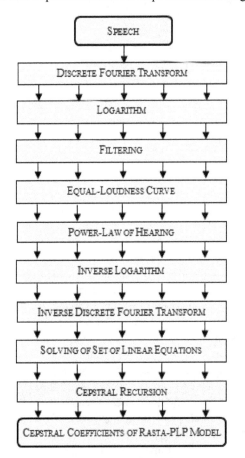

Figure 1. *Steps of Rasta-PLP*

* Compute the critical-band spectrum (as in the PLP) and take its logarithm;
* Apply a regressive filter for analyzing and reducing noise ;
* In accord with the conventional PLP, add the equal loudness curve and multiply by 0.33 to simulate the power low of hearing;
* Take the inverse logarithm of this relative log spectrum, yielding a relative auditory spectrum;
* Compute an all-pole model of this spectrum, following the conventional PLP technique [16].

3.1.5. Principal Component Analysis (PCA)

The principal component analysis technique is used for reducing dimensionality of the obtained features by conserving the intrinsic original information. We used PCA as a modeling tool of the extracted features because it is a simple, non-parametric method of extracting relevant information from confusing data sets. Here our purpose of using PCA is to facilitate the recognition since this technique allows us to represent each letter by a minimum number of vectors [25]. In practice and to apply PCA, we follow the steps below:
* Calculate the covariance matrix of the features on which we will apply PCA;
* Find the eigenvectors of the obtained covariance matrix;
* Extract diagonal of matrix as vector;
* Sort the variances in decreasing order;
* Project the original data set.

3.2. Recognition Phase

In the recognition phase, we have used the Multilayer Perceptron (MLP) Feed-Forward Back Propagation Neural Networks which is known as the most popular Multilayer architecture. It is formed by an input layer (Xi), one intermediary or hidden layer (HL) and an output layer (Y). A weight matrix (W) can be defined for each of these layers.

This artificial neuronal network topology can solve classification problems involving non-linearly separable patterns and can be used as a universal function generator [19]. Important issues in MLP design include specification of the number of hidden layers and the number of units in these layers. The number of input and output units is defined by the problem (there may be some uncertainty about precisely which inputs to use) [26].

In our work, the neural network has been trained in supervised mode, we used a binary code of 7 bits as a Target, we choose a number of neurons between 50 to 130 and the "TanSig" activation function for the hidden layer. For the output layer, we choose seven neurons and the "LogSig" activation function, the learning algorithm was stochastic gradient descent, the used epochs have been varied between 17 and 500. The performance function is mean square error (MSE) and the training function is 'Trainlm'. The remaining parameters are taken by default.

4. The Proposed Speech Recognition System

The proposed speech recognition system consists of three modules according to their functionalities.

The first module concerns the recording phase which is followed by an enhancement procedure in order to obtain a best and intelligible quality of signal.

In the second module features are extracted and transformed on reduced data variables keeping the most discriminatory information.

The last module is used in the recognizing phase which includes training and testing processes.

The used corpus of experimentation is based on all Arabic letters with their four vowels pronounced by four speakers. The main features were extracted by using separately different known techniques in speech analyzing domain (MFCC, PLP, etc.) and transformed to a reduced data with the principal component analysis (PCA) procedure. The obtained data is used to train a neural network (Feed Forward Back Propagation Neural Network). In this work, we have changed the feature extraction techniques applied in [1]. In fact, several hybrid techniques have been experienced such as MFCC combined to PCA, PLP followed by continuous wavelet transform (CWT) and PCA. In this work, the corpus of test is composed of sequences completely different from the training corpus.

4.1. Corpus Preparation

The corpus is interested in automatic recognition of Arabic letters. Four speakers (two males and two females) were participated to build it by uttering all Arabic letters (28) with their four vowels three times each one firstly and secondly five times.

For the first case (three trials): the number of utterances of each speaker is equal to: $28 \times 4 \times 3 = 336$ utterances, then the total number of utterances for the four speakers was equal to 1344. Each utterance is put in a separate wave file and each trial of each speaker is put in a separate sub corpus.

Suppose for example that Sal, AFi, Fat and Sou are the four speakers, so Sal corpus is composed of three sub corpora of 112 utterances each.

The training corpus is composed of the two first trials of the four speakers (Sal_1, Sal_2, Afi_1, Afi_2, Fat_1, Fat_2, Sou_1, Sou_2), so the number of files used here is equal to 896 files.

The validation corpus is composed of the second trial of Afi (Afi_2 =112files) and the first trial of Fat (Fat_1=112files). So the total number of files in validation corpus is equal to 224 files.

The test corpus is composed of the third trial of Sal (Sal_3) and the third trial of Sou (Sou_3). So the total number of files in test corpus is equal to 224 files.

Thereby, the train corpus is composed of 80% of the total corpus and we choose to construct the test corpus by 20% of the total corpus from who hasn't been included in the train corpus. The validation corpus is composed of 20% of the total corpus from that has been included in the train corpus.

4.2. Data Acquisition

The recording of the speech has been occurred in a suitable environment, with professional materials in a professional acoustic studio: A digital mixing console (Studer 2000M2) and a dynamic microphone MD421. The speech signal of each letter is recorded and digitized with a sound card of a computer equipped by "Sound Forge" software. The parameters of the recordings were: Mono wave files, a sampling rate of 44100 Hz and a 16 bits resolution. During all the recording sessions, each utterance was played back to ensure that the entire signal of each letter was recorded then stored as a Mono wave file in a corresponding sub corpus.

4.3. Feature Extraction

For all the whole work, feature extraction and recognition were implemented in Matlab7.1 platform language. Each speech signal corresponding to any letter is put in a specific file. The stages of analysis have been occurred in the following steps.

- Extract each file corresponding to each letter from its sub corpus and read it by using the corresponding Matlab command;
- Remove Silence and reduce noise in the signal obtained in the first step in order to improve quality and enhance the speech signal by applying the algorithm of "Minimum Mean Square Error Short Time Spectral Amplitude Estimator" (MMSE-STSA);
- Apply one of the feature extraction techniques which have been already mentioned above to the signal obtained in step 2;
- Apply PCA to the extracted features resulting from step3, in order to represent the letter with the minimum number of vectors;
- Concatenate the obtained vectors in order to obtain one vector which will represent the speech signal for one letter. Our purpose from concatenating these vectors is to simplify computing and improve recognition performance.
- Do the same steps for all Arabic letters;
- Put all the final total vectors (these represent the total letters) obtained in step5 in one matrix. Each column in this matrix represents one letter;
- Select from the matrix obtained in step7 the number of vectors which are designed to build the different corpora (training, validation and test) taking into account the size of each one. On the one hand, we have chosen 80% of vectors obtained in the latter matrix to construct the train corpus. On the other hand, 20% are selected for the test corpus and 20% among that of the train corpus to build the validation corpus.

Each corpus will be put in a matrix and constitute an input for the feed-forward back propagation neural networks.

5. Experimental Results and Discussion

The features extraction techniques mentioned above (such

as MFCC, PLP, etc.) have been applied to speech signal corresponding to each letter to provide Matrices. The PCA technique is then applied to these matrices to reduce the dimensions. In order to represent each letter with one vector, vectors of each Matrix were concatenated. All obtained vectors which represent the total letters are grouped in one matrix. The final matrix is provided to Multilayer Perceptron MLP as inputs. The number of neurons in the hidden layer has been varied between 50 and 130, the goal was G=0.01. We let the Matlab program prepared for our recognition system running until one of the known MLP stop criterions is reached, and we note each time the corresponding error rates.

Another independent stage has been done when we conserved the same parameters already used and we increased the trial number. Instead of uttering three times each letter, each speaker is invited to utter each letter five times. This latter operation has significantly improved the recognition performance.

It is found that when we concatenate feature vectors which represent the speech signal of any letter in one vector, we obtain a better result for speech recognition. In addition, the choice of the number of vectors to concatenate and the convenient parameters for the neural network are very interesting. The extension of the trials number of uttering letters from three to five times and consequently the extension of speech corpus has improved the recognition performance with all feature extraction techniques.

Compared to all used feature extraction methods tested in this work, the Perceptual Linear Prediction Technique (PLP) occupies the first order in term of recognition performance and in term of computing time.

After different experiments, we have reached the following error rates as presented in tables I and II.

Table II shows that performance is far better improved when the number of trials or recordings per person was increased.

The best performance was obtained by using the PLP technique combined with PCA. This outperformance can be interpreted by the fact that the PLP technique adopts three essential properties which are: The integration of critical bands, the equal loudness pre-emphasis, and the intensity-loudness conversion. With these aspects the PLP becomes nearer to the human hearing than other techniques and consequently it allows obtaining robust and discriminatory parameters.

The same feature vectors (PLP and PCA), already used, were also computed as inputs for RBF neural networks. The obtained results show that RBF neural networks respond poorly when using large training vectors. The reached performances were respectively 587.056e-030%, 261.71e-030 % and 27.98% for training, validation and test. These results prove that FFBPNN is more efficient than RBF neural networks.

Finally, the use of several hybrid techniques for feature extraction phase, the concatenation of input vectors and the Feed-Forward Back Propagation Neural Network has significantly improved the recognition systems. However, in order to obtain more efficient results, the experimental corpus should necessary be extended in terms of speaker numbers and different Arabic dialects.

Table 1. Recognition performance by using three trials per person

Method	Training Error in %	Validation Error in %	Testing Error in %	# of Epochs
MFCC + PCA	1.187189	0.897189	18.3939	930
ΔΔMFCC + PCA	0.991074	0.860687	30.4044	177
MFCC + ΔMFCC + ΔΔMFCC + PCA	8.29687	9.33385	23.5392	232
PLP + PCA	0.978391	1.20843	12.6183	27
Rasta PLP + PCA	0.732753	0.715146	17.5906	17
LPCC + PCA	0.99792	1.02594	23.8582	83
CWT + PCA	3.30559	3.09105	26.1099	490
CWT + PLP + PCA	0.961214	0.783404	24.8872	36
PLP + CWT + PCA	7.48001	7.10607	21.6927	72
CWT + MFCC + PCA	0.987389	0.837862	27.5388	41
MFCC + CWT + PCA	4.48791	4.95848	23.2967	146
CWT + LPCC + PCA	1.40306	1.21173	32.2703	91

Table 2. Recognition performance with five trials per person

Method	Training Error in %	Validation Error in %	Testing Error in %	# of Epochs
PLP + PCA	0.992308	0.814672	*11.7432*	179
MFCC + PCA	0.890573	0.664166	13.1609	53
Rasta PLP + PCA	0.936744	0.819379	16.9822	30
LPCC+PCA	1.73818	1.72194	18.4507	271
MFCC + ΔMFCC + ΔΔMFCC + PCA	6.93287	6.8629	20.0726	78

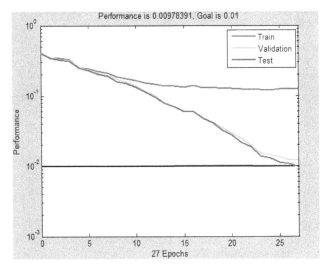

Figure 2. Performance curves by using three trials with PLP and FFBPNN techniques.

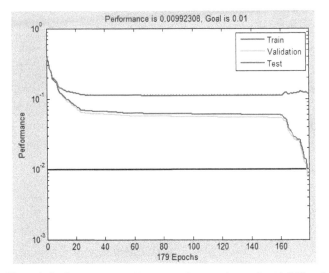

Figure 3. Performance recognition curves by using five trials with PLP and FFBPNN techniques

6. Conclusion

In this paper, a variety of feature extraction techniques and a feed forward back-propagation neural network (FFBPNN) have been tested for automatic speech recognition system of Arabic letters. For this purpose, a proper corpus was prepared involving recordings of four speakers.

In the first set of experiments, each speaker was invited to utter the total letters three times. Obtained data were performed with a variety of approaches and hybrid techniques. In this case PLP technique associated to PCA algorithm have presented the best performance with a testing error equals to 12.6183%.

In the second set of experiments, the corpus was improved by increasing the number of trials of each speaker to five. In this second case, recognition performances were far better with all used approaches. However, the PLP technique still the best one and presented a testing error of 11.7432%.

Compared to RBF neural networks, FFBPNN has given more satisfactory results in terms of training, validation and test performances.

In the future work, we plan to extend the experimental corpus and to develop a new system based on some other advanced techniques such as Bionic Wavelet Transform (BWT) for the feature extraction and Support Vector Machines (SVM) for the recognition phase. This research can be used in order to improve isolated word recognition and Arabic dialect recognition.

References

[1]   Abdulfattah Ahmad M. and El Awady R. M., "Phonetic Recognition of Arabic Alphabet Letters Using Neural Networks," International Journal of Electric & Computer Sciences IJECS-IJENS, Vol. 11, No. 01, 112501-3434 IJECS-IJENS ©, February 2011.

[2]   Al Azzawi Kh. Y. and Daqrouq Kh., "Feedforward Backpropagation Neural Network Method for Arabic Vowel Recognition Based on Wavlet Linear Prediction Coding," International Journal of Advances in Engeneering & Technologiy", Ijalet ISSN:2231-1963, Sept. 2011.

[3]   Al-Irhaim Y. F. and Saeed E. Gh., "Arabic Word Recognition Using Wavelet Neural Network," Third Science Conference in Information Technology, November 2010.

[4]   Alkhouli M., "Alaswaat Alaghawaiyah," Daar Alfalah, Jordan, 1990.

[5]   Alotaibi Y. A., Alghamdi M. and Alotaiby F., Computer Engineering Department, King Saud University, Riyadh, A. Elmoataz et al. (Eds.): ICISP 2010, LNCS 6134, pp. 122–129, 2010. © Springer-Verlag Berlin Heidelberg, 2010.

[6]   Al-zoubaidy L. M., "Efficient Genetic Algorithm for Arabic Handwritten Characters Recognition," Raf. J. of comp. & Math's, vol.6, No.2, 2009, received on:29/4/2008,Accepted on :3/9/2008.

[7]   Barras C., "Reconnaissance de la Parole Continue : Adaptation du Locuteur et Contrôle Temporel dans les Modèles de Markov Cachés," Thesis, Université de Paris IV, 1996.

[8]   Ben Nasr M., Talbi M. and Cherif A., "Arabic Speech Recognition by MFCC and Bionic Wavelet Transform using a Multi-Layer Perceptron for Voice Control," CiiT International Journal of Software Engineering, Vol. 4, No 3, March 2012.

[9]   Boite R., Kunt M., "Traitement de la parole," Presse polytechnique romandes, 1987.

[10]   Cheng O., Abdulla W. and Sacic Z., "Performance Evaluation of Front-end Processing for Speech Recognition Systems," Electrical and computer Engineering Department School of Engineering, University of Auckland, School of Engineering Report No.621, 2005.

[11]   Daqrouq K., Alfaouri M., Alkhateeb A., Khalaf E. and Morfeq A., "Wavelet LPC with Neural Network for Spoken Arabic Digits Recognition System", British Journal of Applied Science & Technology, 1238-1255, 2014.

[12] Deroo O., " Modèles Dépendants du contexte et Méthodes de Fusion de données Appliquées à la reconnaissance de la Parole par Modèles Hybrides HMM/MPL ", Thesis, Faculté Polytechnique de Mons, 1998.

[13] El-Ghazi A., Daoui C. and Idrissi N. "Automatic Speech Recognition System Concerning the Maroccan Dialecte (Darija and Tamazight)," International Journal of Engineering Science and Technology (IJEST), ISSN: 0975-5462 Vol. 4 No.03 March 2012.

[14] EL-Mashed Sh. Y., Sharway M. I., Zayed H. H., "Speaker Independent Arabic Speech Recognition Using Support Vector Machine," ICI-11 Conference and Exhibition on Information technology and Instruction technology, Hungary 2011.

[15] Elshafei M. "Toward an Arabic Text-to-Speech System," vol. 4B no. 16, pp 565–583, Octobre 1991.

[16] Furui S., "Speaker-Independent Isolated Word Recognition Based on Enphasized Spectral Dynamics," Procs. IEEE Intl. Conf. on Acoustic, Speech & Signal Processing, pp.1991-1994, Tokyo, Japan 1986.

[17] Ganoun A. and Almerhag I. "Performance Analysis of Spoken Arabic Digits Recognition Techniques," Journal of Electronic Science and Technology, Vol. 10, No. 2, June 2012.

[18] Génin J., "La parole et son traitement automatique Calliope," Annales des Télécommunications, vol. 45, Issue 7-8, pp 457-458, August 1990.

[19] Haykin S., "Neural Networks and Learning Machines", Prentice Hall, USA, 2009.

[20] Hermansky H., Morgan N., Bayya A. and Kohn Ph., "Rasta-PLP Speech Analysis", TR-91-069, Decembre 1991.

[21] Kouloughli D. E., "Sur la Structure Interne des Syllabes «lourdes» en Arabe Classique," vol. 16, numéro 1, pp 129-154, 1986.

[22] Nahar K. M.O, Elshafei M., Al-Khatib W. G. and Al-Muhtaseb H., "Statistical Analysis of Arabic Phonemes for Continuous Speech Recognition," International Journal of Computer and Information Technology, ISSN: 2279 – 0764 Vol. 01, Issue 02, November 2012.

[23] Rabine L. and Schafer, R., "Digital Processing of Speech signals", Prentice Hall, 1978.

[24] Satori H., Hiyassat H., Harti M. and Chenfour N., "Investigation Arabic Speech Recognition Using CMU Sphinx System," The International Arab Journal of Information Technology, Vol. 6, No. 2, April 2009.

[25] Shlens J., "A TUTORIAL ON PRINCIPAL COMPONENT ANALYSIS," Derivation, Discussion and Singular Value Decomposition, March 2003.

[26] Venkateswarlu R.L.K., Kumari R. V. and Vani Jayasri G., "Speech Recognition Using Radial Basis Function Neural Network", IEEE, 2011.

[27] Zabidi A., Mansor W., Khuan L. Y., Sahak R. and Rahman F. Y. A., "Mel-Frequency Cepstrum Coefficient Analysis of Infant Cry with Hypothyroidism," 5th Int. Colloquium on Signal Processing & Its Applications, Kuala Lumpur, Malaysia, 2009.

[28] Zitouni I., Sarikaya R., "Arabic Diacritic Restoration Approach Based on Maximum Entropy Models," Computer Speech and Language, vol. 23 pp 257–276, july 2009.

8

Relationship between human characteristics and adoption of project management information system in non-governmental organizations' projects in Nakuru Town (Kenya)

Oyugi Tobias, Maina Kairu

Department of Education and External studies, University of Nairobi, Nairobi, Kenya

Email address:

koyugibft@gmail.com (T. Oyugi), mainakairu@yahoo.com (K. Maina)

Abstract: The purpose of this study was to determine the relationship between human characteristics and adoption of project management information system (PMIS) in non-governmental organizations' projects in Nakuru Town. The independent variable (Human characteristics) was conceptualized into; resistance to change, project management skills, user's skills and awareness, power struggles and perfectionism. These indicators were individually related with adoption of project management information system. This study adopted both descriptive and correlational design. It was a survey and primary data was collected through structured questionnaires and interviews. Both descriptive and inferential analysis was employed in this study. The research findings were presented through tables. The research findings revealed that one's competence level in using PMIS, level of training received, willingness to adapt to using PMIS, attitude towards technology and own expectation when using PMIS are positively related with adoption of project management information system. Attitudinal change and support in using the system also appeared to hugely influence adoption of PMIS. The study underscored the analogy that before the management puts pressure on using the system, they must first adopt its usage then spiral it down to subordinates. The study recommended that mentorship and training are critical drivers to successful implementation of PMIS. Training not only should be at the initiation phase of the system but embedded as a continuous skill enhancement and as part of professional development in the organization. A part from training, employees must be motivated and involved at all stages of the implementation process.

Keywords: Human Characteristics, Project Management Information System, Non-governmental Organizations

1. Introduction

1.1. Background of the Study

Advances in information technology are affecting most segments of business, society, and governments today in every part of the world (Hundley, 2004). The changes that IT is bringing about in various aspects of life are often collectively called the "information revolution (Hundley, 2004)." The current project manager must bring on board suitable technological tools and integrate such with the project practices.

PMIS as a part of IS refers to the tools and techniques used to gather, integrate, and disseminate the outputs of project management processes. It is used to support all aspects of the project from initiation through closing, and can include both manual and automated systems (PMI, 2008). In line with information systems experts and already existing body of knowledge and in the description of MIS technology; emphasis is put explicitly on organizational/firms characteristic and individual/user behavior (Huber 1990, Orlikowski and Lacono 2000). This research thus focused specifically on the influence of human characteristics on PMIS adoption by NGO's. To this end considerations were based on traditional PMIS studies and in particular the concept of task/technology fit as developed by Goodhue and Thompson (1995) and Zigurs and Buckland (1998).

To develop the theory further, a review of different

organizational tasks and typical MIS support was sought, and then focus on PMIS. Putting the theory into perspective and appreciating that it cannot be used entirely in supporting MIS adoption on its own, other proposed theories were as well evaluated and factors that can support positive PMIS adoption unpacked by further research in redefining a framework for TTF's project successful..

Drawing from the Project management Maturity Model (PMMM); organizations vary on their maturity hierarchy based on their specific goals, strategies, resource capabilities, scope and needs. TTF theory by its design assumes that the technology will take care of the diverse needs of the system but does not capture in its three tenets the social characteristics of the ever changing existing project team. At whichever level of the PMMM i.e. awareness, understanding or adoption social aspects are very key in full use and integration of the system into the organizational processes. As aforementioned, the gap in operation of the TTF model to successful use of a PMIS informs this study by acknowledging that system implementation must be a dynamic exercise that takes into cognizance an integrated approach to the myriad of IS theories. Further, the information required by management for their decision making are more summarized and requires off-line interpretation which cannot be generated by the PMIS yet this dimension has been left out in the TTF theoretical framework. Appreciating dynamism in theories, the study further redefines TTF to capture management decision making in the context of the social dimension.

1.2. Research Objectives

This study was guided by two objectives:
- To establish the influence of resistance to change on adoption of project management information system in non-governmental organizations' projects
- To establish the influence of project management skills on adoption of project management information system in non-governmental organizations' projects
- To establish the influence of user's skills and awareness on adoption of project management information system in non-governmental organizations' projects
- To establish the influence power struggles and perfectionism on adoption of project management information system in non-governmental organizations' projects

1.3. Research Hypothesis

Ho1: Resistance to change negatively influence adoption of PMIS in non-governmental organizations' projects

Ho2: Project management skills negatively influence adoption of PMIS in non-governmental organizations' projects

Ho3: User's skills and awareness negatively influence adoption of PMIS in non-governmental organizations' projects

Ho4: Power struggles and perfectionism negatively influence adoption of PMIS in non-governmental

organizations' projects

1.4. Conceptual Framework

The design of the conceptual framework outlines the independent and dependent variables in the study. The independent variable (organizational factors) is conceptualized into operational factors and human characteristics and related with implementation of project management information system. Three intervening and four moderating variables are also captured in the framework to ensure reliability of making generalizations after data analysis.

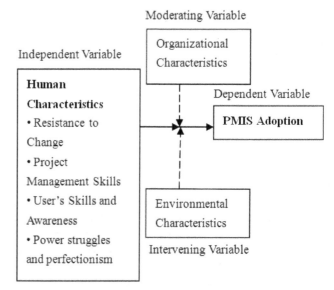

Figure 1. Conceptual Framework

2. Literature Review

2.1. Human Characteristics

These relate to the interpersonal skills of the individuals involved with the project. Burke et al (2001) suggests that human issues have the biggest impact on the process as they argue that when implementation and adoption of information systems is successful, it is because a focused attention was paid to the human issues. This prompts discussion into the following areas:

2.1.1. Poor Project Management

Out of the many organizations that have adopted PMIS, very few have had the experience in running such systems especially on a large scale front. Most organizations will involve consulting firms in the process from design to implementation, this poses a challenge for if the senior management is not fully involved their information expectation from the system will not be in synch with what would be users will be generating. Implementation of projects thus needs very close working ties between the executive management, the middle management and the hands on workers to ensure that the right participation mix of business and IT is done and to resolve later conflicts (Turbit, 2005).

Top management support is therefore a critical organizational factor for the success of PMIS adoption and diffusion (Omware et al., 2014).

2.1.2. Lack of User's Skills and Awareness

Burke et al (2001) identified poor skill sets among users as an issue. This view is supported by research by META Group (2004) that indicated that more than 75% of organizations identified lack of user awareness as a challenging factor. Furthermore, in the same study, 66% of organizations identified lack of executive awareness as having a similar effect. Martin Harvey, the director of IT user skills at e-skills UK, states that lack of user skills is "a major problem" which is supported by a recent study showing that 7.6 million employees needed improved IT skills out of the 21.5million IT-using work forces (Murray, 2007). It is also suggested by Turbit (2005) that when upgrading from old technology, the skills of the staff need to be upgraded as well.

The upgrade will place significant demands on the team who are geared to maintain an old but stable environment; usually this effort is underestimated by most organizations. Fear of technological changes often is attributed to user's lack of confidence in articulating tasks which therefore means the challenge to be locked out in the implementation of a PMIS. In keeping in line with imminent change in organizations, a continuous professional development approach must be rooted at the organizational policy level so as to guarantee success when systems change.

2.1.3. Resistance to Change

This refers to the refusal by individuals to reap the benefits of a new system. Burke et al, (2001) posits that as long as what the individuals are comfortable with works for them, there is no need trying what they are jittery might not work even before trialing its' usage. A case study based on Hayward Gordon Ltd. (HGL) in 2004 revealed that one of their major human issues was that people can become lazy and copy electronic records. A study by Gupta (2000) revealed that the main hurdle faced by most companies was resistance to change. He expanded on this by explaining that resistance was due to employees being reluctant to change due to its attachment to the product. Employees play an important role as Muguire (2000) identifies that the "vast majority of IS's used by staff within the organizations". Moguire (2000) also notes that there are still too many examples of IS projects that have failed due to increasing problems of rising costs and the misuse of IS rather than acceptance and use of the system. PMIS seen by many as a good thing still has its challenges of user's resisting usage for a myriad reasons that are more personal; research thus must delve into the causes of user resistance and out wittingly expose such factors.

2.1.4. Benign Neglect

Ignoring the situation and refusing to stay on track or fulfill responsibilities (Burke et al, 2001) means there is lack of focus on the project which indicates that the organization is not very inclined to seeing the implementation of the IS a success. Benign neglect is mostly displayed by the users as if they are against the implementation of the PMIS. They may refuse to take part in making the system successful (Magutu,et al.2010). Benign neglect is synonymous with resistance to change but it is seen as its key component. Non participatory consultation in the implementation of systems is disastrous to organizations which therefore demand an all-inclusive approach through the entire project lifecycle if success is to be realized.

2.1.5. Power Struggles and Perfectionism

Synonymous with all organizations, power struggles and hierarchical perception of positions is usually a recipe for chaos. Who is responsible for what? Who owns what information? Are questions that must be addressed for the success of the smooth running of IS's. Power struggles and employee relations often occur leading to implementation challenges (Burke et al, 2001). Perfectionism occurs when certain users refuse to use the ISs because it is not working exactly as specified. In information systems project implementation, a huge amount of work requires the analysis and interpretation of data and input from many people. Inadequacies in such a process could have significant consequences later on in the project, causing even something dramatic as redesign and re-implementation (Burke et al, 2001). It is therefore quite prudent for the project team to work harmoniously at each stage not only to accomplish the tasks at hand but to guarantee integrity and security of the data and information that is in the system

2.2. Project Management Information System

Project management has historically been considered an important characteristic of successful companies; this analogy has been supported by the need for improved efficiency and effectiveness in managing projects (Wesonga et al., 2014). Several PMIS's have been developed and adopted by many organizations both in the private and public sector with a sole objective of making significant contribution to enhancing project management. Just like other IS, a successful PMIS should have individual impacts evident in user satisfaction and effective use. A successful PMIS must also have organizational impacts, that is, impacts on project success in terms of respecting budget, schedule and specifications. While projects increasingly procure PMIS, not much is known on the characteristics of these systems that contribute to adoption and project success; empirical analysis of adoption models and what constitutes a PMIS is aimed at unlocking this relationship.

Maredith and Mantel (2006) found that utilizing IT has a major impact in solving all difficulties that may appear during the project's lifecycle. This is achieved through the various applications that constitute a PMIS; in procuring a PMIS it is prudent to evaluate such functionalities and even further seek to know if value adds components such as project risk management module and knowledge management are integrated (Ahlemann, 2007). Monitoring and evaluation being very essential components of projects; their inclusion as part and parcel of the standard modules of a

PMIS is quite fundamental.

Essentially, the task of PMIS has been described as subservient to the attainment of project goals and the implementation of project strategies; it provides project managers with essential information on the cost-time performance parameters of a project and on the interrelationship of these parameters (Raymond l., 1987). In the IT industry today, Gartner research estimates that 75% of projects managed with PMIS support will succeed while 75% of projects without such support will fail (Light M., et.al., 2005). In light of this, research also cautions that only a small number of projects utilize all PMIS tools during the project management life cycle such as planning, scheduling, risk management, cost estimates, document management, communicating, and reporting (Herroelen,2005; Love & Irani 2003).

2.3. Theoretical Framework

There are many theories used in MIS research (Wade 2009). This study is interested only in theories about PMIS technology adoption. The most used theories are Technology Acceptance Model, Theory of Planned Behavior, and Unified Theory of Acceptance to Use Technology, Task Technology Fit, Diffusion of Innovation and Expectancy Confirmation Theory. In reviewing these theories of MIS adoption, the study puts into perspective the two tenets that dictate how well MIS is acceptable and adopted by an organization i.e. the firm level and the individual level based on DOI model.

2.3.1. Innovation Theory

Individuals are seen as possessing different degrees of willingness to adopt technology, and thus it is generally observed that the portion of the population adopting an innovation is approximately normally distributed over time (Rogers 1995). Breaking this normal distribution into segments leads to the segregation of individuals in to the following five categories of individual innovativeness (from earliest to latest adopters): innovators, early adopters, early majority, late majority and laggards (Rogers 1995).

At the firm level (Rogers 1995), technology adoption is related to such independent variables as individual (leader) characteristics, internal organizational structural characteristics, and external characteristics of the organization. Individual characteristics describe the leader attitude towards change and internal characteristics of organizational structure include observations according to Rogers (1995) whereby: "centralization is the degree to which power and control in a system are concentrated in the hands of a relatively few individuals", "complexity is the degree to which an organization's members possess a relatively high level of knowledge and expertise"; "formalization is the degree to which an organization emphasizes its members' following rules and procedures"; "interconnectedness is the degree to which the units in a social system are linked by interpersonal networks"; organizational slack is the degree to which uncommitted resources are available to an organization", "size is the

number of employees of the organization". External characteristics of an organization refer to the system openness.

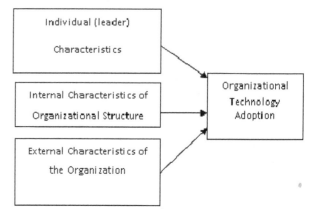

Figure 2. *Innovations theory*

Source: Rogers (1995).

2.3.2. Technology Acceptance Theory

The Technology Acceptance theory (TAT) also referred to Technology acceptance model (TAM) (Davis 1985, Davis et al. 1998) is a specific adaptation of the Theory of Reasoned Action (TRA) model (Ajzen and Fishbein 1980) to the study of IT usage. The TRA and its successor, the Theory of Planned Behavior (TPB) (Ajzen 1985), are well known, and have been widely employed in the study of specific behaviors (Ajzen and Fishbein 1980). In general, these theories (TRA, TAM) state that a behavior is determined by intention to perform the behavior. Actual behavior and intention have been found to be highly correlated (Davis 1985, Fishbein and Ajzen 1980). Intention, itself, is determined by attitude towards behavior.

Davis' research, in essence examines the external variables that determine or influence attitude towards IT use. The TAM identifies Perceived Ease of Use and Perceived Usefulness as key independent variables (Davis 1989). Perceived Ease of Use also influences Perceived Usefulness. The TAM includes the very important assumption that behavior is volitional, which is to say voluntary or at the discretion of the user. The TAM has been tested in several studies of IT use (Adams et al. 1992, Davis et al.1989, Mathieson, 1991, Straub et al. 1997).

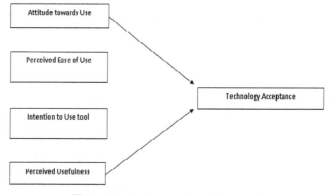

Figure 3. *Technology Acceptance Framework*

Source: Davis et al. (1998)

2.3.3. Theory of Acceptance and Use of Technology

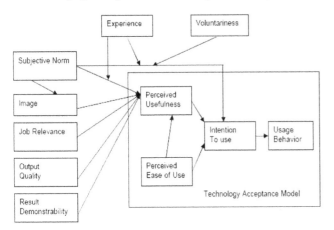

Figure 4. *Theory of Acceptance and Use of Technology*

Source: Venkatesh et al. (2003).

Recently, Venkatesh et al. (2003) reviewed the eight most prominent models/theories (Theory of Reasoned Action (TRA), Technology Acceptance Model (TAM), Motivational Model (MM), Theory of Planned Behavior (TPB), Combined TAM and TPB (C-TAMTPB), Model of PC Utilization (MPCU), Innovation Diffusion Theory (IDT), Social Cognitive Theory (SCT)) that predict behavioral intentions and/or usage, developed a unified model that incorporates elements of the previous eight models, and empirically validated the resulting model. This new model, known as the Unified Theory of Acceptance and Use of Technology (UTAUT) is depicted in Figure 1. Venkatesh et al. (2003) report their model explains up to seventy percent of variance in intention to use technology, outperforming previous models.

2.3.4. Planned Behavior Theory

Ajzen and Fishbein formulated in 1980 the theory of reasoned action (TRA). This resulted from attitude research from the Expectancy Value Models. Ajzen and Fishbein formulated the TRA after trying to estimate the discrepancy between attitude and behavior. This TRA was related to voluntary behavior. Later on behavior appeared not to be 100% voluntary and under control, this resulted in the addition of perceived behavioral control. With this addition the theory was called the theory of planned behavior (TpB). The theory of planned behavior is a theory which predicts deliberate behavior, because behavior can be deliberative and planned.

The theory of planned behavior holds that only specific attitudes toward the behavior in question can be expected to predict that behavior. In addition to measuring attitudes toward the behavior, we also need to measure people's subjective norms – their beliefs about how people they care about will view the behavior in question. To predict someone's intentions, knowing these beliefs can be as important as knowing the person's attitudes. Finally, perceived behavioral control influences intentions. Perceived behavioral control refers to people's perceptions of their ability to perform a given behavior. These predictors lead to intention. A general rule, the more favorable the attitude and the subjective norm, and the greater the perceived control the stronger should the person's intention to perform the behavior in question.

2.3.5. Expectation Confirmation Theory

Expectation-confirmation theory (ECT) is widely used in the consumer behavior literature to study consumer satisfaction, post-purchase behavior, and service marketing in general (Anderson and Sullivan 1993; Dabholkar et al. 2002; Oliver 1980, 1993; Patterson et al. 1997; Tse and Wilton 1988). The predictive ability of this theory has been demonstrated over a wide range of product repurchase and service continuance contexts, including automobile repurchase (Oliver 1993), camcorder repurchase (Spreng et al. 1996), institutional repurchase of photographic products (Dabholkar et al. 2002), restaurant service (Swan and Trawick 1981), and business professional services (Patterson et al. 1997). Figure 10 illustrates key constructs and relationships in ECT. The process by which consumers reach repurchase intentions in an ECT framework is as follows (Oliver 1980).

First, consumers form an initial expectation of a specific product or service prior to purchase. Second, they accept and use that product or service. Following a period of initial consumption, they form perceptions about its performance. Third, they assess its perceived performance vis-à-vis their original expectation and determine the extent to which their expectation is confirmed (confirmation). Fourth, they form a satisfaction, or affect, based on their confirmation level and expectation on which that confirmation was based. Finally, satisfied consumers form a repurchase intention, while dissatisfied users discontinue its subsequent use.

ECT holds that consumer's intention to repurchase a product or continue service use is determined primarily by their satisfaction with prior use of that product or service (Anderson and Sullivan 1993; Oliver 1980, 1993). Satisfaction is viewed as the key to building and retaining a loyal base of long term consumer's .Investing in customer satisfaction is like taking out an insurance policy. If some temporary hardship befalls the firm, customers will be more likely to remain loyal. (Anderson and Sullivan 1993). Satisfaction was initially defined by Locke (1976) in the context of job performance as a pleasurable or positive emotional state resulting from the appraisal of one's job.

3. Research Methodology

3.1. Research Design

This study adopted a descriptive research design. It was a survey and both qualitative and quantitative approaches were employed. According to Garson (2008), survey research is suitable in the case researcher wants to establish more variables relevant to the study which can then be used to inform application or interventions in other similar contexts.

3.2. The Target Population

The target population for this study was the non-governmental organizations within Nakuru town, mainly that have operations outside the town that requires remote linkage with the main offices in Nakuru for local NGO's and international headquarters for those that are international. Within these NGO's, the study focused on Project managers and the functional project coordinators in each of their project areas. Currently there are 1195 NGO' in Nakuru Town (NGO coordination board 2012) with 145 having operations outside Nakuru town and with linkages in other towns both local and international.

3.3. Sampling Procedure

The determination of the sample size was done using Cochran's (1977) formulas. Cochran's sample size for categorical data is:

$$n = t2pq/d2$$

$$(1.96)2\ (.50)(.50)/(.50)2$$

n thus = 384
Where: n = desired sample size
t = value of selected alpha level of 0.25 in each tail = 1.96 (the alpha level of 0.5 indicates the level of risk the researcher is willing to take; the true margin of error may exceed the margin of acceptable margin of error.
pq = estimate of variance =0.25 (maximum possible proportion (.50) producing maximum possible sample size)
d = acceptable margin of error
Therefore for a population of 90 NGO's (270) with PMIS the required sample size is calculated as follows:
nf = N/(1+n/population)
nf = 384/(1+(384/270)
nf = 160
The study used a sample size of 159 respondents comprising project managers and coordinators distributed across all selected 53 NGO's which mathematically fit within the 1:2 ratio though not 160 as above.

3.4. Data Collection

Structure questionnaires were used to collect primary data. The questionnaires were given to the respondents after which they were picked for analysis. To ensure the qualitative data is obtained, In-depth Interviews was used based on the duties and responsibilities of the respondents.

3.5. Validity and Reliability Test

Mugenda and Mugenda (2003) assets that validity has everything to do with how accurately the data obtained in the study represents the variables therein; if such data is a true reflection of the variables, then inferences based on such data will be accurate and meaningful. It is noted also that, a non-random error which is unidirectional dissuades the research findings to a specific conclusion when instrument

validity is taken for granted. In this study, existing hypothetical connotations in MIS research were used in developing the research tools; in a pre-test administration of these tools a close eye was kept on the inclination of the findings to the proposed hypotheses.

Muma et al. (2014) define reliability as the measure of the degree to which a research instrument yields consistent results or data after repeated trials. The pretest method was used to provide the researcher to refine the final questionnaire to be used in the actual study area. Also, the dummy questionnaire is essential when conducting a peer review with colleagues and the supervisor. Correlating the scores obtained from the selected NGO's should inform the researcher on the acceptable level of reliability; if the coefficient is high, the instrument will be said to yield data that has a high equivalent reliability. Another approach that was employed in checking for reliability is the use of the split-half reliability procedure where the researcher administers the entire instrument to a sample of respondents during the pilot test and calculates the total score for each randomly divided half i.e. odd and even numbered items of the questionnaire.

3.6. Data Analysis

In order to facilitate data analysis the filled up questionnaires were checked for completeness, consistency and clarity. The responses were coded by assigning a numerical value to each; this was to make them quantitative for ease of possible capture by the computer in SPSS for Windows Version 19 analysis. In order to clean up the data averages like mean and median as well as distributions like standard deviations were performed on the data sets in order to discover any anomalies and appropriate corrections done. Descriptive statistics such as frequencies, percentages, median and mode were used for quantitative analysis of the data.

For establishing the extent to which several NGO have adopted use of PMIS, a Pearson product correlation moment coefficient of selected variables were generated to obtain a general view of the respondents' opinions on the influence on PMIS adoption. The choice of these statistical tests was guided by the nature of the data as presented in the questionnaire which were mainly ordinal and nominal. To establish the magnitude of relationships as captured by the hypotheses, a cross tab chi-square coefficient guided the acceptance on non –acceptance of p -values based on a statistical standard of measure at (0.05) 95% confidence level. Finally to help predict if a given independent variable predicts a given dependent variable the study used regression analysis.

4. Discussion

4.1. Years the Organization has been in Existence

The below figure show the length of time an organization has existed. It further correlates how old the organization is and the current situation regarding PMIS usage.

Table 1. Years the organization has been in existence

Range of Years	Frequency	Percent
Below 5	11	27.5
Between 5 and 10	18	45.0
Between 11 and 25	6	15.0
>25	5	12.5
Total	40	100.0

The above figures show that majority of the NGO's have existed for over 10 years (45%) with a minority of 12.5% having existed for more than 25 years.

Comparing the length of their existence and driven by an analogy of growth and adoption of technology reveals that there is very minimal positive correlation (r (40) = 0.081) between years of existence and usage of PMIS. These results

imply that the existence of an organization and full adoption of PMIS are not in any way significantly related.

Table 2. Correlation between Years the organization has been in existence and PMIS usage

		Existence of organization	PMIS Use at present
Existence of organization	Pearson Correlation	1	.081
	Sig. (2-tailed)		.618
	N	40	40
PMIS Use at present	Pearson Correlation	.081	1
	Sig. (2-tailed)	.618	
	N	40	40

4.2. Current Adoption PMIS in the NGOs

The findings in respect to current level of usage of PMIS among the organizations are as shown in the table below.

Table 3. Current Adoption of PMIS in NGOs

PMIS Use at present * Perception on PMIS Cross tabulation

			Perception on PMIS		Total
			Y	N	
PMIS Use at present	Extensively used	Count	26	0	26
		% within Perception on PMIS	66.7%	.0%	65.0%
	Quite used	Count	7	0	7
		% within Perception on PMIS	17.9%	.0%	17.5%
	Slightly used	Count	1	1	2
		% within Perception on PMIS	2.6%	100.0%	5.0%
	Not sure	Count	5	0	5
		% within Perception on PMIS	12.8%	.0%	12.5%
Total		Count	39	1	40
		% within Perception on PMIS	100.0%	100.0%	100.0%

4.3. The Influence of Individual Characteristics in Ascertaining Adoption of PMIS by NGO's

This section presents the findings related to the influence of

individual characteristic in ascertaining PMIS adoption and usage.

Table 4. Individual Characteristics Indicators

Individual characteristic indicator	Respondent	Category	Freq.	Percent
Agreement PMIS is good	Project managers	Y	39	97.50
		N	1	2.50
	Project coordinators	Y	80	100.00
Training on PMIS	Project coordinators	Y	64	80.00
		N	16	20.00
Willingness to use PMIS	Project coordinators	Extremely Likely	46	57.50
		Quite Likely	16	20.00
		Slightly Likely	8	10.00
		Not Likely	3	3.80
		Not Sure	7	8.80
Competency in PMIS usage	Project coordinators	Extensively high	44	55.00
		Quite high	22	27.50
		Slightly high	6	7.50
		Not high	5	6.30
		Not sure	3	3.80

4.4. Agreement that PMIS is a Good Thing in Organizations

The results show a massive unanimity at 97.5% that PMIS is a good thing with a paltry 2.5% in the contrary. The facts as they are presented do give a perception on the management

that using PMIS has far reaching advantages to the organization. Despite the disagreement at a minimum 2.5%, personal mindset to the positive therefore gives the implication that using a PMIS is a good thing and that the increased adoption and use of a PMIS starts with the conviction that the benefits outweigh the failures.

4.5. Training on PMIS Use

Training is an essential step in adoption of PMIS use. Before the deployment of PMIS within any NGO training is presumed to have been done; in some cases, prior experience in using the PMIS enables some respondents to easily use the PMIS without any formal training. The study sought from the respondents if they had received any training on using the PMIS and the results show that 80% of users have received training on PMIS which justifies how lack of it could negatively affect adoption of PMIS. The 20% of users are of the opinion that they have not received any training which is then hypothetically tested as shown in Table 5 to show if there is reason to believe if training improves ones competence level. The results are that training does improve one's competency level and thus implying the key role it does in PMIS usage and adoption.

P< 0.05 at 0.001 thus accepting the alternative hypothesis that training indeed does enhance PMIS use competency level.

Table 5. Chi-square test on Training in PMIS use and competency level

Chi-Square Tests			
	Value	df	Asymp. Sig. (2-sided)
Pearson Chi-Square	23.864ᵃ	4	.000
Likelihood Ratio	22.041	4	.000
Linear-by-Linear Association	9.292	1	.002
N of Valid Cases	80		

a. 7 cells (70.0%) have expected count less than 5. The minimum expected count is .60.

4.6. Competency in PMIS Usage

The Table show five levels of competency with extensively high 55%, quite high 27.5%, slightly high at 7.5%, not high at 6.3% and 3.8% of the respondents not sure of their competency level. System usage being mandatory in most of the NGO's under the study; indicates that for maximum adoption and usage the users must have a very high competency level. The implied understanding from these figures is that whatever approach is used to boost competency level of the users, it must be such that every user is confident in using the system. Table 7 presents a correlation between PMIS competency level and training; it is evident that there is

very significant moderate positive correlation at r (80) = 0.343 indicating that indeed training to some degree does enhance ones competency level in PMIS use and by extension building ones confidence to adopting PMIS.

4.7. Correlation between Competency in Using PMIS and Training

Table 6 correlates competency level in PMIS usage against level of training. A Pearson correlation is used in establishing the nature of the relationship.

Table 6. Correlation between competency in Using PMIS and Training

Correlations			
		PMIS Use competence	Training on PMIS use
PMIS Use competence	Pearson Correlation	1	.343**
	Sig. (2-tailed)		.002
	N	80	80
Training on PMIS use	Pearson Correlation	.343**	1
	Sig. (2-tailed)	.002	
	N	80	80

**. Correlation is significant at the 0.01 level (2-tailed).

4.8. Willingness to Use PMIS Now and in the Future

The results show 57.5% extremely likely to use PMIS in future, 20% quite likely, 10% slightly likely 3.8 not likely and 8.8 not sure of continued use of PMIS if it still part and parcel of an organizations systems. The implied argument here was that there are certain hiccups that are likely to influence someone's continued usage of the system in the future, as presented above a huge number has a positive mindset and attitude to continued usage meaning there is willingness to patiently accommodate challenges that the system portends and that despite such challenges the belief of PMIS being a good thing cannot be whisked away.

4.9. The Influence of Management Type and PMIS Expectations by Project Managers in Ascertaining Adoption of PMIS by NGO's

This section presents the findings related to the influence of management type and PMIS expectations by project managers ascertaining adoption of PMIS by NGO's.

Table 7. Management characteristic indicators

Management characteristic indicator	Respondent	Category	Frequency	Percent
Pressure on PMIS usage	Project manager	Y	52	65.0
		N	28	35.0
Attitude of towards PMIS usage	Project coordinator	Y	39	97.5
		N	1	2.5
Expectation on PMIS usage	Project coordinator	Mandatory	75	93.8
		Discretionary	5	6.3
Reasons for pressure in PMIS use	Project coordinator	Skill level	28	35.0
		Too much work	22	27.5
		Attitude	24	30.0
		Others	6	7.5

5. Conclusions and Recommendations

The Human factors which in an organization constitutes both the management and the functional unit(s) personal attributes, skills and attitudes affects greatly PMIS adoption. Burke et al (2001) suggests that human issues have the biggest impact on the process as they argue that when implementation and adoption of information systems is successful, it is because a focused attention was paid to the human issues. This study thus concurs with current literature on the effect of human factors in influencing adoption, it however goes deep into not just establishing why their characteristic nature influences adoption but further seeks to obtain from the respondents own conviction as to what works best in their interest.

Management being the drivers of implementation in any organization was found to play not only a leadership role in PMIS usage but also was meant to inspire and instill a love for usage of the system. The study sought to find out what level in an organization the usage of the PMIS was at its high and it did indicate a fair balance at all levels. This therefore underscored the analogy that before the management puts pressure on using the system, they must first adopt its usage then spiral it down to subordinates.

Increased knowledge on ICT systems and the latest of technology was realized as a key enabler in bringing on board systems that are robust and those that are expansible into the future. Organizations planning to fully embrace PMIS must thus be in the fore front in keeping in touch with the latest in the market not only to cut a niche in their service delivery but to make informed choices that are cost effective and acceptable seamlessly across other organizations of interest.

References

[1] Ackerman, M. S. (2000). The intellectual challenge of CSCW; The gap between social requirements and technical feasibility. Human-Computer Interaction,15 (2),179-203.

[2] Adams, D. A., Nelson, R. R. & Todd, P. A. (1992). Perceived usefulness, ease of use, and usage of information technology: A replication. *MIS Quarterly*. 16(2), 227-248.

[3] Ahlemann F. (2008), Project management Software Systems Requirements, Selection Processes and Products, 5th edition. Wurzburg: BARC.

[4] Ajzen, I. (1985). From intentions to actions: A theory of planned behavior. In J. Kuhl & J. Beckman (Eds.), *Action-control: From cognition to behavior* (pp. 11-39). Heidelberg: Springer Press.

[5] Ajzen, I.; and Fishbein, M. *Understanding Attitudes and Predicting Social Behavior.* Englewood Cliffs, NJ: Prentice-Hall, 1980.

[6] Anderson, Eugene W. and Mary W. Sullivan (1993), "The Antecedents and Consequences of Customer Satisfaction for Firms," *Marketing Science*, 16 (2), 129-45.

[7] Baccarini, D 1999, 'The Logical Framework Method for Defining Project Success', *Project Management Journal*, vol. 30, no. 4, pp. 25-32.

[8] Bergeron, F., Raymond, L., Rivard, S. & Gara, M. F. (1995). Determinants of EIS use: testing a behavioral model. *Decision Support System*, 14 (1), 131-146.

[9] Brandon, D. (2002). Issues in the globalization of electronic commerce. In V. K. Murthy & N. Shi (Eds.), *Architectural issues of Web-enabled electronic business.* Hershey, PA: Idea Group Publishing.

[10] Brandon, D. (2004). Project performance measurement. In P. Morris & J. Pinto (Eds.), *The Wiley guide to managing projects.* New York: Wiley.

[11] Burgelman R.A., Maidique M.A. and Wheelwright S.C. 1996. 'Strategic Management of Technology and Innovation'. Irwin. Chicago. USA. Second Edition.

[12] Burke, R. J. 2001a, 'Spence and Robbins' Measures of Workaholism Components: Test-Retest Stability', *Psychological Reports*, Vol. 88, no. pp. 882-888.

[13] Caldwell, R. (2004). *Project Management Information System: Guidlines for Planning, Implementing, and Managing a DME Project Information System.* New York: CARE Press.

[14] Cleland, D. I. (2004a). *Field Guide to Project Management* (2nd ed.). New York: McGraw-Hill Press.

[15] Cleland, D. I. (2004b). *Project Management Information System in Project Management: Strategic Design and Implementation* (5th ed.). New York: McGraw-Hill Press.

[16] Clements, J. P. & Gido, J. (2006). *Effective Project Management.* Canada: Thomson South-Western.

[17] Cochran WG. Sampling Techniques. John Wiley & Sons:New York, 1977. pp.74-76.

[18] Cragg, P. B. and King, M. (1993). Small-Firm Computing: Motivators and Inhibitors. *MIS Quarterly*, 17 (1): 47-60.

[19] Dabholkar, P. A. and Bagozzi, R. (2002) *An Attitudinal Model of Technology-Based Self-Service: Moderating Effects of Consumer Traits and Situational Factors*, Journal of the Academy of Marketing Science, 30 (3), pp. 184-201.

[20] Davis, F. D. (1989). Perceived usefulness, perceived ease of use, and user acceptance of Information technology. *MIS Quarterly*. 13(3), 319-339.

[21] Davis, F.D., Bagozzi, R.P. & Warshaw, P.R. 1989, " User acceptance of computer technology: a comparison of two theoretical models.", *Management Science*, vol. 35, no. 8, pp. 982–1003.

[22] DeLone, W.H., and Mclean, E.R. (1992), Information Systems Success: The Quest for the Dependent Variable, Information Systems Research, 3(1), 6095.

[23] DeLone, W.H., and Mclean, E.R. (2003), The DeLone and McLean Model of Information Systems Success: A TenYear Update, Journal of Management Information Systems, 19(4), 930.

[24] Dishaw, M. T. & Strong, D. M. (1998a). Experience as a Moderating Variable in a Task-Technology Fit Model Presented at the Fourth Americas Conference on Information Systems. Baltimore.

[25] Dishaw, M.T. & Strong, D. M. (1998b). Supporting Software Maintenance with Software Engineering Tools: A Computed Task-Technology Fit Analysis. *Journal of Systems and Software*, 44, 107-120.

[26] Fenech, T. (1998).Using Perceived Ease of Use and Perceived Usefulness to Predict Acceptance of the World Wide Web. *Computer Networks and ISDN Systems*, 30 (7), 629-630.

[27] Gabber, E., The Case Against User-level NetworkingProceedings of the Third Annual Workshop on System-Area Networks (SAN-3), February 2004, Madrid Spain.

[28] Garson, G. D. (2008). Multiple regression. Retrieved January 28, 2008, from http://www2.chass.ncsu.edu/garson/pa765/regress.htm

[29] GoK (2004b). Nakuru district strategic plan. Nakuru. Government of Kenya.

[30] Goodhue, D. L. & Thompson, R. L. (1995). Task-Technology Fit and Individual Performance. *MIS Quarterly*, 19 (2), 213-236.

[31] Goodhue, D. L. (1995). Understanding User Evaluations of Information Systems. *Management Science*, 41(12), 1827-1844.

[32] Gupta, A. (2000) Enterprise resource planning: the emerging organizational value systems, Industrial Management & Data Systems, April, 2000, Volume 100, Issue 3, p114-118.

[33] Havelka, D., & Rajkumar, T.M. (2006), Using the troubled project recovery framework: Problem recognition and decision to recover. eService.Journal, 5(1), 4373.

[34] Herroelen W. (2005), Project scheduling theory and practice. Prod Oper Manage, 14(4):41332.

[35] Huber, G. P. (1990) „A Theory of the Effects of Advanced Information Technologies on Organizational Design, Intelligence, and Decision Making", *The Academy of Management Review* 15 (1), pp. 47-71.

[36] Hundley, R., et al. (2004). The global course of the information revolution: recurring themes and regional variations. Retrieved from www.rand.org/publications/MR/ MR1680/

[37] Information Technology: Toward a Unified View. *MIS Quarterly*. 27(3), 425-478.

[38] Kothari, C.R.,1985, Research Methodology- Methods and Techniques, New Delhi, Wiley Eastern Limited.

[39] Kwon, T. H.; and Zmud, R. W. "Unifying the Fragmented Models of Information Systems Implementation." In J. R. Boland, and R. Hirshheim (eds.), *Critical Issues in Information Systems Research*, New York: John Wiley, 1987, pp. 227-251.

[40] Laudon, K., & Laudon, J. P. (2009). *Management Information Systems* (11th ed.). New York: Pearson press.

[41] Light M, Rosser B, Hayward S. (2005), Realizing the benefits of projects and portfolio management. Gartner, Research ID G00125673, 131.

[42] Maciaszek, L. A. (2001). *Requirements analysis and system design: Developing information systems with UML*. Harlow: Addison-Wesley Press.

[43] Maguire, S. (2000) Towards a "business-led" approach to Information Systems development, Information Management & Computer Security, December, 2000, retrieved May 10th 2006, from: http://www.emeraldinsight.com.

[44] Magutu et.al (2010), "Management Through Effective Information Quality Management (IQM) in Banking Services",AJBUMA Vol.1pp.96-111.

[45] Mathieson, K. (1991). Predicting user intentions: Comparing the Technology Acceptance Model with the Theory of Planned Behavior. *Information Systems Research*. 2(3), 173-191.

[46] Meredith, J. R., & Mantel, S. J. (2006). Project management: A managerial approach (6th ed.). New York: Wiley.

[47] Mgaya, R. J. (1999). *Adoption and diffusion of group support systems in Tanzania*. Netherlands: Delft University of Technology Press.

[48] Model with the Theory of Planned Behavior. *Information Systems Research*. 2(3), 173-191.

[49] Moran, C. R. (1998). *Strategic information technology planning in higher education: A new roadmap to the 21st century academy*. Bolton: Anker Publishing Press.

[50] Mugenda, O. & Mugenda. A. (2003). Research methods Quantitative and Qualitative Approaches. Nairobi acts Press.

[51] Mugonyi, D. (2003). *US queries new computer deal*. General format. Retrieved from http://www.nationaudio.com/News/DailyNation/03092003/Ne ws/News81.html

[52] Muma, B. O., Nyaoga, B. R., Matwere, B. R. and Nyambega, E. K. (2014). Green Supply Chain Management and Environmental Performance among Tea Processing Firms in Kericho County, Kenya. *International Journal of Economics, Finance and Management Science 2(5) 270-276*

[53] Muma, B. O., Nyaoga, R. B., Matwere, R. B. and Onyango J. O. (2014). Green Supply Chain Management and Economic Performance: A Review of Tea Processing Firms in Kericho and Bomet Counties, Kenya. *International Journal of Science and Research, 3 (11), 2319-7064*

[54] Ndou, V. (2004). *E-Government for developing countries: Opportunities and challenges*. General format. Retrieved from http://www.is.cityu.edu.hk/research/ejisdc/vol18/v18r1.pdf edn.

[55] Odedra, M. (1993). *Information technology policies and applications in the commonwealth countries*. London: Commonwealth secretariat.

[56] Oliver, Richard L. (1980), "A Cognitive Model of the Antecedents and Consequences of Satisfaction Decisions," *Journal of Marketing Research*, 17 (3), 460-469.

[57] Oliver, Richard L. (1993), "Cognitive, Affective, and Attribute Bases of the Satisfaction Response," *Journal of Consumer Research*, 20 (3), 418-430.

[58] Oruma, B. W., Mironga, J. M. and Muma, B. O. (2014). Top Management Commitment Towards Implementation of Total Quality Management (TQM) in Construction Companies in Nakuru County-Kenya. *International Journal of Economics, Finance and Management Sciences. Vol. 2, (6),332-338*

[59] Peter Drucker (2004, January). What makes an effective Executive. *Harvard Business review*

[60] Pinkerton, WJ 2003, *Project management: achieving project bottom-line success*, McGraw-Hill, New York.

[61] PMI (2008). *A Guide to the Project Management Body of Knowledge: PMBOK Guide* (3rd ed.). Pennsylvania: Project Management Institute Press.

[62] Omware Q., Nyonje, R. and Muma B. (2014). Determinants of Quality Management Practices in Kenyan Sugar Processing Industry: A Case of Chemelil Sugar Company, Kisumu County, Kenya. *International Journal of Economics, Finance and Management Science.*

[63] Support System Effectiveness", *MIS Quarterly* 22 (3), pp. 313-334.

[64] Tuman, J. J. (1988). Development and Implementation of Project Management systems. New York: Van Nostrand Reinhold Press.

[65] Turner, J. R. (1999). *The Handbook of Project Based Management* 2nd ed.). Maidenhead Berkshire: McGraw-Hill.

[66] Van der Meijden, M. J., Tange, H. J., Troost, J. & Hasman, A. (2003). Determinants of success of inpatient clinical information systems: a literature review. *Med inform Associate,* 10 (3), 235-243.

[67] Van Der Westhuizen, D. & Fitzgerald, E.P. (2005). Defining and measuring project success. Proceedings of the European Conference on IS Management, Leadership and Governance. Reading, UK.

[68] Venkatesh, V.; Morris, M. G.; Davis, G. B. & Davis F. D. (2003). User Acceptance of Information Technology: Toward a Unified View. *MIS Quarterly*. 27(3), 425-478.

[69] World Bank report (2008) World poverty index (Revised), Ministry of planning and Development (GoK).

[70] Yates, J. (2000, August). Origins of project management. Knowledge Magazine.

[71] Zigurs, I., and B. K. Buckland (1998) "A Theory of Task-Technology Fit and Group Support System Effectiveness", *MIS Quarterly* 22 (3), pp. 313-334.

9

Information Accessibility and Utilization: The Panacea to Job Performance and Productivity of Academic StaffIn the Faculties of Agricultural Sciences

Familusi E. B., N. A. Ajayi

University Library, Ekiti-State University, Ado-Ekiti, Ekiti-State, Nigeria

Email address:

familusiezekiel@gmail.com (Familusi E. B.), nathajayi@yahoo.com.uk (N. A. Ajayi)

Abstract: This study probes into accessibility and utilization of information resources by academic staff in the Faculties of Agricultural Sciences of selected universities in the Southwest, Nigeria. The objectives of this study were to determine the level of information access and utilization, identify the factors responsible for low productivity, and investigate challenges confronting information access and utilization. This study adopted a descriptive survey design to describe information accessibility and utilization. The researchers made use of questionnaires which were administered among two hundred (200) out of which 182 (91.9percent) were found useful Academic Staff randomly selected from Faculties of Agricultural Sciences. The study found that majority of the respondents (51.3%), frequently used virtually all the resources, and e-resources most especially internet/CD-ROM and databases were perceived to be most accessible of all the resources (index of 3.9), followed by textbook (index of 3.7), while the least accessible information resources was electronic board. Low productivity was caused by high no of students assigned to each academic staff for teaching and supervision (11.8%) followed by lack of internet facilities (11.1%), while inadequate workspace did not significantly contribute to their low productivity (6%). Challenges faced by academic staff in information resources accessibility and utilization include epileptic power supply, poor ICT maintenance, poor funding, internet connectivity and, computer illiteracy. It was recommended that the Federal government of Nigeria should collaborate with the universities administrators to accord priority to Nigerian Universities in financial commitment, provision of regular supply of electricity in campuses and others to enhance high productivity of the university academic staff.

Keywords: Information Resources, E-Resources, ICTs, Accessibility, Utilization, Job Performance, Productivity, Academic Staff, Agricultural Sciences

1. Introduction

Information has become a critical economic resource globally, even in the most remote villages. People including illiterates cannot do but need information for their day to day livelihood. Amogu, (2010) asserted that, information is the processed data that could be converted into more meaningful format which is the end product of data processing. Information accessibility and utilization has multiplying effects on individual's positive tendencies. Information access and utilization will make people to understand their environment better, learn new skills and be able to make well informed decisions about their lives. The onus rest on the university management in collaborating with Librarians to use professional's skills to facilitate access to useful and relevant information, which will enable people to develop their full potentials and live productive lives. It is therefore, imperative that libraries must provide relevant literature to academic communities for the realization of research and academic excellence.

With the information explosion being experienced all over the world and the demand for quick and relevant information by library users, librarians are constantly challenged to provide accurate, complete and timely information for research and development. Information access is the gateway to information utilization and consequently high productivity is easily achievable. Aina, *et.al.* (2010) argued that, the evolving information and knowledge-based economy has resulted in a climate of transition and change especially in academic libraries around the world, including Nigeria as universities, polytechnics and colleges make the transformation to higher institutions. Adebowale(2007) observed that, globally education is seen as the bedrock of a nation; hence its quality should be well enhanced and ascertained. However, Ileboya(2010) emphasized that, productivity is considered as key source of economic growth and competiveness and as such, it is a basic statistical information for many international comparisons and country performance assessment.

1.1. Literature Review

Information had become an all-embracing factor with which man can effectively cope with the challenges of the present dynamic world posed daily by science and technology as a result of industrial revolution cutting across all sphere of human endeavour. Popoola(2009)viewed information as a critical economic resource when utilized is capable of increasing the knowledge state of an individual in taking the right decision. Aina(2004)opined that information is a process which involves transmitting information from the source to a recipient. It is knowledge when is performing the role of imparting knowledge to an individual, where it reduces uncertainty.

Lawal and Taofeek(2009)identified information in the new world order that there is every reason to believe that information has become ubiquitous and therefore can be obtained at any time, and in any location no matter the distance, as long as necessary infrastructural devices and the skill to retrieve information from global networks are available. Information access and utilization play dominant roles in teaching, learning and research process. Popoola (2009) asserted that information enables the user to take the right decision which positively affects productivity. Also, organizations are made up of people working together to achieve common goals. Edom(2010) posited that, beside teaching, learning, and research, ICTs are also used in the performance of other tasks in the universities. Edom(2010) cited Ebijuwa (2005) that ICT could be used for administration, information management, teaching and learning, research and national networking, library and information services.

Nwokedi (2007) opined that the internet has broken down the barriers of communication access from anywhere in the world. It is fast, reliable, and does not have restrictions on content formats. Tibenderana (2010) also asserted that, with the introduction of new technologies in the last quarter of the past century such as ICT and other services can be automated such that end users can access them by means of networked computers through the web (internet/intranet) or a Local Area Network (LAN). Convincingly, access to information is a motivator that naturally encourages the three domains of learning and teaching to maximally utilize information. Abdullahi and Haeuna (2008) argued that, Librarians as information managers should be up to the task by being familiar with this digital era so as to give the clients the services required. Ogundeji, et.al.(2009) also stressed the

importance of the Internet on learning, research and teaching process. Danjuma, (2011) opined that, information utilization goes beyond research and service delivery, and the users outlook as well. The advent of Information Communication Technology (ICT) has brought along stress-free academic and research delivery.

The impact of ICT on Nigerian universities teaching and learning processes are enormous. Information access, dissemination, utilization, teaching and learning processes passes through other ICT mediums unlike the verbal and manual delivery of lectures. Such media include the use of computers and its software, overhead projectors, laptops, PowerPoint lecture delivery, teleconferencing -mail messages, facsimile, Hotmail, newsgroup, etc. Kumar et.al (2011) advocated that the effect of computer simulation supported learning on the conceptual understanding of elementary and secondary teachers were presented. Khan(2011) corroborated Kumar et.al.(1997) that Technological Pedagogical Content Knowledge (TPACK) is an emerging theoretical framework on teaching that articulates a tri-partite relationship among teacher's knowledge, technology pedagogy, and content. Aina (2004) in her own view submitted that modern technologies in libraries create a new forum for global information access. Rajput and Gautam (2010) stated that modern society is characterized by an increasing need for specialized information in various fields of activities for the performance of their day to day functions as well as research consultancy services to handle the vast amount of information and for providing faster, accurate precise, efficient and effective information dissemination. Bwalya(2013) advanced the significance of access and utilization of information that most of the contemporary socio-economic value chains can be amassed by appropriate and efficient utilization of ICTs.

Oyekunleand Majebi (2013) upheld Bwalya(2013)that, rapid development of the World Wide Web offers universities unparalleled possibilities for communication with internal and external audiences. Nigerian universities, like those in developed countries, have more and more adopted the Internet as a communication and information tool. Oyekunle et.al.. (2011) agreed that, the birth, creation, planning, implementation, appraisal and amendment of the universities' curriculum is now much more universally uniform, accessible and easily utilized with the advent of the Internet. Much more could be archived in job performance and productivity. The ICT has finally removed the stress, time wastage, passive participation of the teacher-student interactions in lectures and enhanced productivity.

1.2. Statement of the Problem

Information access and utilization is very significant to the rapid economic transformation of any nation in the world. It is very imperative that uninterrupted access and utilization of information in our citadels of learning is an indicator to rapid production and growth of human and material resources. Continuous access and utilization of information is a correlate of high level of productivity. Accessibility and utilization of information by academics in higher institutions will go a long way to make teaching and learning process easier, meaningful, and effective, result oriented and productive. Availability of the relevant information and access to internet deserve utmost attention by the university management. Accessibility to exploit the seamless information via the internet is lacking in most universities which can lead to low productivity. This study is set to investigate and determine the level of accessibility and the utilization of information by the academic staff of the Faculties of Agricultural Sciences in selected universities in Nigeria.

1.3. Objectives of the Study

The objectives of this study are to:
i.   Find out the level of accessibility and the utilization of information by the lecturers in the Faculties of Agricultural Sciences.
ii. Identify the factors responsible for low productivity if any
iii. Investigate challenges confronting accessibility and utilization of information by the university lecturers, and recommend possible solutions.
iv. Suggest possible solutions to identified problem

1.4. Research Questions

i.   What is the level of accessibility of information resources?
ii. What is the frequency of use of information resources?
iii. What are the challenges confronting accessibility and utilization of information?
iv. What are the factors responsible for low productivity?

2. Methodology

In carrying out the study, the advice of Quinsee and McDonald (1991) and Obiagwu (1992) that the views of academic staff are the most revealing on issues like this in academic libraries was utilized. Using a structured questionnaire the information elicited from the respondents included accessibility of information resources, use of available resources, challenges of information availability and factors responsible for low productivity. The data also included the demographic background and academic status.

A total of 200 academic staff randomly selected from 5 Faculties of Agriculture in Federal, State and private universities who were users of their University Libraries were sampled, using a systematic random sampling technique to distribute the questionnaire. Focus group discussions (FGD) were also conducted to clarify some of the perceptions that were indicated in the responses. A total of 198 completed questionnaires were returned of which 182 were found useful. Of the 182 respondents, considering the gender of the respondents 99(54.5 percent) were male, while 83(45.5 percent) were female. Also, the academic

qualifications of the respondents revealed that, 83(45.5 percent) were PhD holders, 62(34.1percent) holds Masters Degree while the remaining 37(20.3 percent) were First degree holders. 25(13.6 percent) were Professors, 33(18.2percent) were Readers, 59(32.4 percent) were Senior Lecturers and 65(35,7percent) were Lecturer 1 and below.

3. Results and Discussion

3.1. Use of Information Resources

The respondents were asked to indicate the frequency use of Information Resources. They were to choose from options given like {MF} most frequently,{F}frequently, {LF}less frequently, and {NF} not frequently. Fig.1. below shows that fifty one (51.3%) percent of them frequently used virtually all the resources available to them. Almost thirty three {32.9%} percent less frequently used the resources. Just 6.9percent did not use any of the resources meaning that they were not library users. From the above research result, information utilization is the key to effective learning, teaching, and research delivery. Popoola {2009} opined that, information utilization increases the knowledge state of an individual which enables him to solve a problem and take the right decision. Also, Hussain and Kumar {2013} suggested that there should be no restriction in the utilization of information resources including photocopying from remains encyclopedias because it is beyond financial reach of scholars/ researchers.

3.2. Use of Electronic Resources

The respondents were asked explicitly about their use of e-resources and printed resources and how they felt this had changed the relationship between the use of library resources and the support of research. Researchers saw many conveniences of electronic resources. There was a perception, true or not that almost all resources were available "It has certainly affected the way I work, simply by being able to access libraries". "I get a lot of empirical data from the Internet".

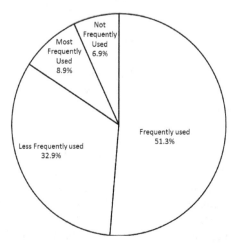

Fig. 1. Use of Information Resources.

3.3. Accessibility to Information Resources

The respondents were asked how accessible are the information resources listed below in table 1. The table shows that 3.9 index indicated their accessibility to the Internet/ Database .Access to textbooks was 3.7 and 3.5 index for references sources. The least of the resources is electronic board with 2.5. Ode and Ape (2013} stated that,

information literacy sometimes referred to as information competency as the ability to access, evaluate, organize and use information from a variety of sources. In the same vein, Nwokedi (2007) corroborated that, the Internet has broken down barriers of communication access from anywhere in the world. It can be inferred that lecturers had access to most resources available to them.

Table 1. Accessibility to Information Resources.

Information Resources	Very Easily Accessible	Easily Accessible	Occasionally Accessible	Not Accessible	Total	Index
	{5}	{4}	{3}	{2}		
Internet/CDRom Databases	370	340	-	46	756	3.9
Textbook	250	336	75	46	707	3.7
Reference Materials	45	408	213	-	666	3.5
Abstracts	-	500	102	46	648	3.4
Statistical Publications	-	500	102	46	648	3.4
Conferences Proceedings	-	420	195	24	639	3.3
Technical reports	150	216	225	46	637	3.3
Journals	-	336	225	46	607	3.2
These/ Dissertation	-	400	87	106	593	3.1
Government Document	-	216	348	24	538	3.1
Newspapers/Magazines	-	220	225	104	549	2.9
Project/Electronic Board	-	120	147	206	473	2.5

3.4. Factors Responsible for Low Productivity

This study was out to identify the factors responsible for academic staff low productivity. Table 2.below revealed that high number of students assigned to an academic staff were the bane of low productivity (11.8%), in the same vein, lack of internet facilities (11.1%) was the cause of low productivity. The least cited cause of low productivity was inadequate workstations (6.6%). It is true that in most faculties, lecturers shared offices. This becomes complicated with the existing poor working environment in terms of inadequate offices accommodation, furniture and insufficient working materials. Akinyemi and Bassey (2012)emphasized that students enrolment in Nigerian public universities yearly was outrageous by outnumber the available spaces, infrastructure and the few lecturers were overstretched with teaching activities.

Table 2. Factors Responsible for Low Productivity.

Causes of Low Productivity	Responses	Percentage%
High number of Students Assigned to lecturers	176	11.8
Lack of internet facilities	166	11.1
Inadequate space	150	10.1
Computer illiteracy	140	9.4
Poor maintenance of ICT facilities	137	9.2
Poor library services	136	9.1
Low bandwidth	136	9.1
Obsolete print materials	133	8.9
Expensive costs of internet connection	166	7.8
Epileptic power supply	104	7.0
Inadequate workstation	98	6

3.5. Challenges Confronting Accessibility of Information

The respondents were requested to prioritize the challenges faced in the utilization of information resources. Fig. 2.below shows that twenty-two (22.1%) percent

indicated that poor funding of the universities was their major constraints, while epileptic power supply (16.6%) and inadequate workstation and space respectively ranked second. The least of the challenges was computer illiteracy (5.1%). Akinyemi and Bassey (2012) lamented that higher institutions have experienced increase in enrolments; therefore Nigeria is faced with the challenges of high demand for admission leading to escalated enrolment, insufficient funds and physical facilities. In addition, Kpolovie and Obilor (2013) reported that Nigeria's annual budgetary allocation to education was (5.57%) which was significantly lower than the UNESCO recommended minimum of 26% for developing countries.

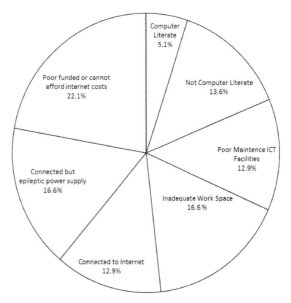

Fig. 2. Challenges.

3.6. Summary

The study reveals that e-resources remain the most accessible information resource while books and journals, were also considered moderately. One may identify citations in indexes, but may not have access to the sources containing the relevant articles. The more accessible information sources are, the more likely they are to be used. One reason why library-held resources (electronic and print) are of importance to the research-teaching relationship is that they are both the tools and the product of scholarship and enquiry. As one of the Zamdock(2002) put it every book you pick up, every journal article and resources you look at is based on somebody's research. Dictionaries were the most frequently reference resources used followed by Journals, Abstracts and Textbooks. This is corroborated by Korobili, et. al. (n.d.) who conducted a research on the use of library resources by the members of the faculty of a higher educational institute in Thessaloniki, Greece found that the great majority of the faculties of TEI uses printed sources more than e-sources, but they also used e-sources quite frequently. There were many challenges confronting information accessibility, the greatest challenge militating against easy access to information was the epileptic power supply in all the universities surveyed in this study, poor maintenance, inadequate work stations and space were also cited. It was equally revealed that the problem of easy access to information were peculiar to all the universities, this was corroborated by Oyewusi, & Oyeboade (2009), Ugah (2007) & Ogunsola (2004).

Information accessibility and utilization by academic staff of Agricultural Sciences in the selected universities leaves much to be desired because the respondents' access to the Internet acccelerate the rate and success of learning, teaching and research in higher institutions of learning. Ofori-Dwumfuo&Ado (2012) Hussain& Kumar (2013) emphasized that the Internet services must be improved to help access information and added that information is acquired, processed and disseminated through the university library and there should no restriction in the utilization of information resources. Also, student's overpopulation admission syndrome in tertiary institutions with few academic staff, lack of ICT facilities due to poor funding and maintenance culture were contributory factors. It was not therefore a surprised that Ayo-Shonibare (2011) stated that the problem of funding and financing of our universities in Nigeria has become a recurring decimal, oftentimes resulting into strikes and closure of the ivory towers.

4. Conclusion

Information accessibility and utilization unarguably has multiplying effects on individual's positive tendencies and a key to effective learning, teaching and research delivery. The libraries provide relevant literature to academic communities for research and academic excellence. It is established through this study that although researchers found it more convenient with electronic resources but efforts to optimize utilization resulted in low productivity as a result of many challenges. This includes inadequate workstations, poor working environment, and outrageous enrolment of students above available spaces resulting into lecturers being overstretched with academic activities. Others include poor funding of libraries, epileptic power supply and computer illiteracy. All contributed to academic low productivity. Fixing-up of all the above challenges with training and re-training of lecturers on ICTs and government adequate intervention are among the remedies that would enhance job performance of university lecturers.

Recommendations

The roles that access to information and utilization play in the learning, teaching and research process in any higher institution especially the universities in Nigeria are enormous. The Federal government of Nigeria in collaboration with the university administrators should attach greater importance to teaching resources that can enhance job performance of the lecturers. Regular distribution of electricity power to campuses is very important, but as a palliative, powerful generators could be provided to keep the ICT facilities functioning when there is power failure.

Funding in any organisation/ institutions determine the success or failure of the goals and objectives of the parent organisation. It was clearly revealed that Faculties of Agricultural Sciences in the selected Universities were inadequatelyfunded; improved funding will bring about high job performance and productivity.University lecturers should also be exposed to continuous training and retraining on ICT education so that information utilization and accessibility could be friendlier to use.

References

[1]   Abdullahi, Z. M., & Haeunna, I. (2008). Public Library Boards, Information andCommunication Technology: Imposed Challenges in Adamawa State, Library Boards;. *The Research Librarian Journal of the Nigerian Library Association, Abia State Chapter, 3*, 19.

[2]   Adebowale, T. A. (2007). Marital Conflict As Determinant of Poor Academic PerformanceAmong Some Selected Secondary Schools in Ibadan, Oyo-State, Nigeria. *International Journal of Applied Psychology and Human Performance, 2*, 386-394.

[3]   Aina, A. (2010). A Panacea for Effective Technical Services in Nigerian Academic Libraries. *International Journal of Creativity &Technical Development, 2* (1-3): 51-60.

[4]   Aina, L. O. (2004). *Library and Information Science Text for Africa, Gaboron: University of Botswana, xi.* 1-365.

[5]   Akinyemi,S& Bassey, O. I. (2012). Planning and Funding of Higher Education in Nigeria: The Challenges. *International Journal Education Studies, 1* (4): 1-86.

[6]   Amogu, U. (2010). Availability of Information and Communication Technology and Users Patronage of

Academic Libraries in Abia State of Nigeria. *in the Librarian Information Journal, Journal of the Nigerian Library Association, Akwa-Ibom State Chapter, 3* (1):28-43.

[7]   Anunobi,C.V. (2013)Human Capacity Building in Nigerian University Libraries: An Imperative for Academic Reference. African Journal of Library, Archival & Information Science, 23(1): 33-44.

[8]   Ayo-Shoibare, M. (2011). Funding Strategies for Quality Education in Nigeria;The Principles of Fiscal Justice. *Journal of Studies in Education, 1* (1): 14-19.

[9]   Brady, E. E., & Galbraith. (2006). Print Versus Electronic Journal Use in Three Science/Technology Discipline:The Cultural Shift Process. *College and Research Libraries, 67* (4): 354-363.

[10]   Bwalya, K. J. (2013). Towards ICT Mainstreaming in Zambia and Botswana: Issues and Policy. *International Journal of Information Processing and Communication.(IJIPC), 1* (1): 1-15.

[11]   Danjuma,P.(2011).Business Environment Scanning for Effective Productivity. International Journal of Business and Common Market Studies,8 (1&2):25-36.

[12]   Edom, B. (2010). Personal Characteristics and Academic Staff Utilization of Information andCommunication Technology (ICT) in Evan Ekwerem. *Nigerian Libraries, Journal of the Nigerian Library Association* (43): 87-106.

[13]   Ileboya, I.R. (2010). The Role of Productivity in Achieving Vision 2020. In Nigeria;. *International Journal of Labour and Organizational Psychology, 4* (1&2): 15-35.

[14]   Korobili- Stella, T. I. (2014). Factors that Influence the Use of Library Resources by Faculty Members. Retrieved from http://eureka.lib.teithe.gr:8080/bitstream/handle/10184/1172/koro_01.pdf?sequence=1.

[15]   Kpolovie, P. J., & Obilor, I. E. (2013). Adequacy- Inadequacy: Education Funding in Nigeria. *Universal Jnr. of Education and General Studies, 2* (8):239-254.

[16]   Kumar, D. D. (2011). Effect of Current Electricity Stimulation Supported Learning on the Conceptual Understanding of Elementary Secondary Teachers. *Journal of Science Education and Technology, Massachusetts- USA, 20* (3): 215-231.

[17]   Lawal, W. O., & Taofeek, B. (2009). Survey of Information and Communication Technology (I.C.T) Availability and use in selected private secondary school Libraries in Ibadan Township, Oyo-State. *Journal of Library Education, Media and Information Studies, 1*: 86-98.

[18]   Nwokedi, V. C. (2007). Impact of Internet Use on Teaching and Research Activities of The Academic Staff of Faculty of Medical Sciences, UNI JOS: A Case Study. *Gateway Library Journal, 10* (1): 13-22.

[19]   Ode, M.I. & Ape,R.(2013) Developing Information Literacy Skills in Students of Nigeria Tertiary Institutions: Impetus for Information Services in the Era of Globalization. Ibadan :Waltodammy Visual Concepts. 169-185.

[20]   Ofori-Dwumfuo, G. O., & Ado, L. (2013). Utilization of Information and ICT Resources by Parliamentarians in Ghana. *Current Research Journals of Social Sciences, 4* (3): 213-221.

[21]   Ogundeji, V. A., Oluwatomilola, B. O., & Olatunji, O. (2009). Internet Use and Librarian Productivity in Two University Libraries. *Journal of Library, Educational Media and Information Studies, 1*: 13-24

[22]   Oyekunle, R. A., & Majebi, O. V. (2013). An Evaluation of the Websites of Nigerian Universities. *International Journal of Information Processing and Communication.(IJIPC)., 1*: 60-72.

[23]   Oyewusi, F. O., & Oyeboade, S. A. (2009). An Empirical Study of Accessibility and Use of Library Resources by Undergraduates in a Nigerian State University of Technology.Library Philosophy and Practice. Retrived from http/www.webpages.uidaho.edu/moblin/oyewusi-oyeboade.htm on November 2014.

[24]   Popoola, S. O. (2009). Self efficacy, Information Acquisition and Utilization as Correlates of Effective Decision Making among Managers in Insurance Companies in Nigeria. *Malaysian Journal of Library and Information Science., 14* (1): 1-15.

[25]   Rajput, P. S. (2010). Automation and Problems in their Implementation: An Investigation of Special Libraries, in Indore, India. *International Journal of Library and Information Science, 2* (7): 143-147.

[26]   Tunde, O., & Issa,A (2013). The Quality of Nigerian Higher Education and The Funding of the Library Resources. *Ozean Journal of Social Sciences, 6* (2): 1-25.

[27]   Ugah, A. D. (2007). Obstacles to Information Access and Use in Developing Countries. *Library Philosophy and Practice, retrieved   from http://www.webpages.uidaho.edu/~mbolin/ugah3.htm on 24th November, 2014.*

10

Weak Amplitude Modulated (AM) Signal Detection Algorithm for Software-Defined Radio Receivers

Thomas Kokumo Yesufu[1], Abimbola Oyewole Atijosan[2]

[1]Department of Electronic and Electrical Engineering, Obafemi Awolowo University, Ile-Ife, Nigeria
[2]Cooperative Information Network, Obafemi Awolowo University, Ile-Ife, Nigeria

Email address:

thomas_yesufu@yahoo.com (T. K. Yesufu), bimbo06wole@yahoo.com (A. O. Atijosan)

Abstract: In this paper a software implementation of a reconfigurable Amplitude Modulated (AM) receiver for weak AM signals detection with reduced processing latency is presented. The Stochastic Resonance (SR) algorithm, which is a technique for weak signal detection was developed for software defined, AM receiver. The performance of the SR based AM receiver was evaluated in terms of its output Signal to Noise (SNR) Ratio, and processing latency. From the results from our simulations, this approach provides better performance and lesser processing latency requirement than conventional signal processing methods for detecting AM signals.

Keywords: Weak Signal Detection, Reconfigurable Receivers, Amplitude Modulation Receivers, Signal Processing

1. Introduction

Traditional communication systems have typically been implemented using custom hardware solutions (Iancu et al 2004). The shift away from hard-wired communication terminals towards software defined and reconfigurable communication devices will introduce new and efficient ways for existing and future technologies to implement radio communication devices. The phrase "software radio" refers to the class of reconfigurable radios in which the physical layer behavior can be significantly altered without the change in the hardware (Shajedul Hasan et al, 2005).

Software radios are fundamentally different from hardware radios, and new algorithmic ideas are needed to make them viable (Matteo, 2002). Challenges confronting software defined AM receivers include signal degradation which militates against the effective use of the AM band (Yesufu, 1995). Other challenges stem from the poor signal to noise ratio of weak AM stations (Oliver et al., 2003), and the latency requirements of signal processing algorithms for AM receivers and other emerging applications (Anthony, 2012); latency can be described as the amount of time it takes the input signal to pass through the system, and reach the output, and it plays a vital role in the design of software radios.

Recovery of a signal of interest that is obscured by noise is becoming the limiting process in many applications particularly since modern data acquisition techniques make capture and processing of the final signal of interest quite straightforward (White and Williams, 2012). Developments of signal processing algorithms are needed (CSDR, 2007), to advance the frontiers of software defined AM receivers, improve performance and confront the challenges of latency and buffer sizes that arise in using Digital Signal Processing (DSP) platforms for radio detection.

2. Theoretical Development

Amplitude modulated signals can be represented mathematically as

$$s(t) = A[1 + k_a m(t)]cosw_c t \qquad (1)$$

Where $m(t) = Acos\omega_m t$ is the baseband or message signal with a bandwidth of W and amplitude A, c(t) = $cos(w_c t)$ is the carrier wave, The parameter k_a is a positive constant called the amplitude sensitivity of the modulator.

In a coherent receiver the input AM radio signal $s(t)$ is multiplied by a copy of the carrier wave c(t) and the result is passed through a lowpass filter (LPF) with a cut-off frequency W. The signal at the output of the multiplier can be

represented as

$$y(t) = s(t) * c(t) \qquad (2)$$

The lowpass filter completely suppresses those spectral components of signal $y(t)$. At the output of the filter, a signal proportional to the original signal $m(t)$ can be obtained. For a non-coherent detector (based on a square law device), the output of the detector can be described as

$$y(t) = s(t) * s(t) \qquad (3)$$

The output of the detector is then lowpass filtered and the square root obtained to produce an output proportional to m(t) with a DC offset.

Stochastic resonance (SR) is a phenomenon in which a nonlinear system is subjected to a periodic modulated signal so weak as to be normally undetectable, but it becomes detectable due to resonance between the weak deterministic signal and stochastic noise (Weinstein, 2008).

Consider a one-dimensional nonlinear stochastic system which is defined by the nonlinear langenvin equation:

$$\frac{\partial x(t)}{\partial t} = -V'(x) + \xi(t) \qquad (4)$$

Where $x(t)$ is the state of the SR system, $\xi(t)$ represents bandlimited Gaussian white noise with zero mean. $V(x)$ is a double-well potential with positive parameters b and a characterizing the system. $V(x)$ is represented as:

$$V(x) = \frac{1}{4}bx^4 - \frac{1}{2}ax^2 \qquad (5)$$

Applying $y(t)$ to (4), the equation can then be written as

$$\frac{\partial x(t)}{\partial t} = -V'(x) + p(t) = ax - bx^3 + p(t) \qquad (6)$$

where $p(t) = y(t) + \xi(t)$

Equation (6) is a first order differential equation and can be approximately solved using the Runge-Kutta method.

The Runge-Kutta method for solving differential equations is a more accurate method of great practical importance. The method is well suited for computers because it needs no special starting procedure, makes light demand on storage and repeatedly uses the same straight forward computational procedure. It is also numerically stable (Kreyszig, 2006).

For $y' = f(x, y), y(x_0) = y_0$, we generate approximations y_n to $y(x_0 + nh)$ for h fixed and for $n = 0,1,2, ... n - 1$ using the recursion formula

$$y_{n+1} = y_n + \frac{1}{6}(k_1 + 2k_2 + 2k_3 + k_4) \qquad (7)$$

Where

$$k_1 = hf(x_n, y_n)$$

$$k_2 = hf(x_n + \frac{h}{2}, y_n + \frac{1}{2}k_1)$$

$$k_3 = hf(x_n + \frac{h}{2}, y_n + \frac{1}{2}k_2)$$

$$k_4 = hf(x_n + h, y_n + k_3)$$

The algorithm steps can be described as follows:

$$x_{n+1} = x_n + \frac{1}{6}(k_1 + 2k_2 + 2k_3 + k_4) \qquad (8)$$

$$n = 0, 1, ... N - 1, x(0) = x_0$$

$$k_1 = h[ax_n - bx_n^3 + pr_n]$$

$$k_2 = h[a\left(x_n + \frac{k1}{2}\right) - b\left(x_n + \frac{k1}{2}\right)^3 + pr_{n+1}]$$

$$k_3 = h[a\left(x_n + \frac{k2}{2}\right) - b\left(x_n + \frac{k2}{2}\right)^3 + pr_{n+1}$$

$$k_4 = h[a(x_n + k3) - b(x_n + k3)^3 + pr_{n+1}]$$

x_n and pr_n denote the nth sample of $x(t)$ and $p(t)$, respectively, h denotes time step, N is the total number of sampling points. The developed system is as shown in Fig. 1 (Atijosan, 2010).

Fig. 1. *Block Diagram of the Improved AM Receiver Using Stochastic Resonance (SR).*

3. Simulation

The simulation was carried out using Matlab 7.1. The corresponding simulation examples are given to validate the effect of SR on detection of weak AM signals. A modulation index of 0.6 was used. A cosine wave with centre frequency of 20 Hz was used as the baseband signal, carrier and sampling frequencies were set at 1kHz and 10kHz, respectively. Fig. 2 shows the baseband signal after amplitude modulation in time and frequency domain. The weak AM signal was simulated by adding additive white Gaussian noise (AWGN) signal, at various levels of signal-to-noise ratio (SNR), to the AM signal at the input to the demodulator.

4. Results and Discussion

The performance comparison of a SR based product detector and a product detector at input SNR of 10dB is shown in Fig. 3. The time domain plot shows that the SR based coherent detector performed better than the product detector. Fig. 4 compares the performance of SR based product detector, SR based square law detector, square law and product detector based on their input SNR and output SNR.

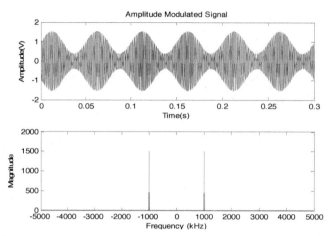

Fig. 2. *(a) Baseband signal after Amplitude Modulation in time domain. (b) Baseband signal in frequency domain after Amplitude Modulation*

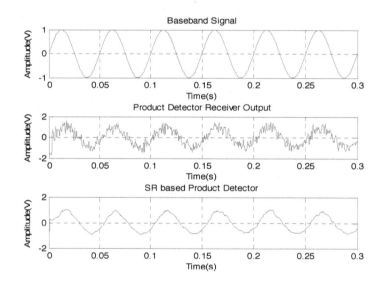

Fig. 3. *Performance Comparison of SR based product detector and product detector at input SNR of 10dB.*

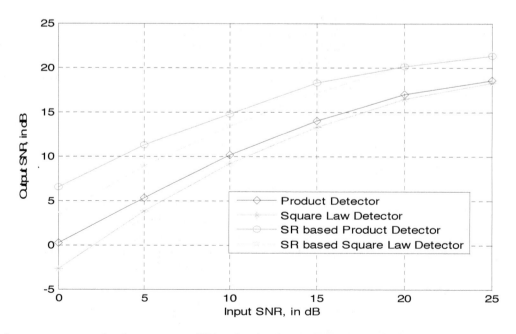

Fig. 4. *Performance comparison of stochastic resonance (SR) based product detector, SR based square law detector, square law and product detector.*

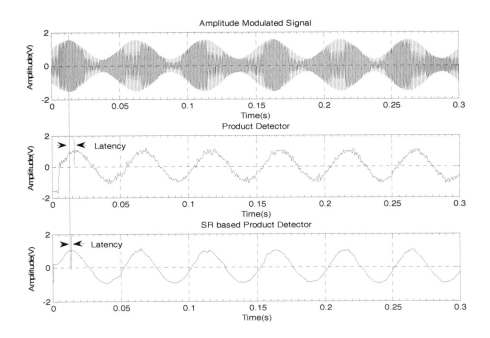

Fig. 5. *Latency and Performance Comparison of a product detector (Lowpass filter length of 100) and an SR based product detector (Lowpass filter length of 10) at input SNR of 20dB.*

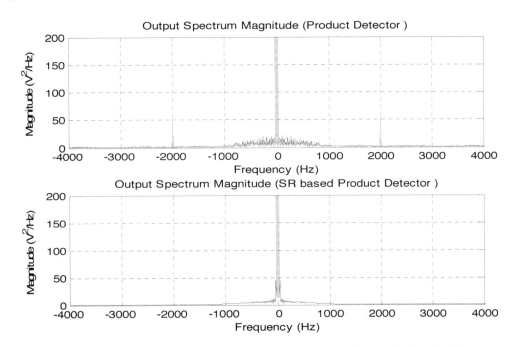

Fig. 6. *Spectral comparison of product detector and SR based product detector at the same low pass filter length of 10 and input SNR of 20dB.*

Fig. 5 shows the latency and performance comparison of a product detector, with low pass filter length of 100 and an SR based product detector with a low pass filter length of 10, at input SNR of 20dB. The SR based product detector has a processing latency of 1.4 ms while the product detector has a processing latency of 4 ms. Fig. 6 compares the performance of a product detector and an SR based product detector using the same low pass filter length of 10 at an input SNR of 20dB. The spectral plot (Fig. 6) shows that the product detector has a higher noise floor when compared with that of the SR based product detector, the output quality of the product detector can be increased by using a longer filter length but at a cost of increasing the latency time, as shown in Fig. 5.

5. Conclusion

In this paper, an efficient algorithm for weak signal detection in software defined AM receiver based on the stochastic resonance model for extracting weak signals was developed. From the results, this approach provides a better performance and lower latency than some conventional signal processing methods for detecting AM signals.

References

[1] Anthony, S. (2012): Increasing Wireless Network Speed by 1000%, by Replacing Packets with Algebra, Available Online: http://www.extremetech.com/ computing/138424- increasing-wireless-network-speed-by-1000-by-replacing-packets-with-algebra.

[2] Atijosan, A.O. (2010): Development of a Reconfigurable Amplitude Modulation Receiver, An M.Sc. Thesis Submitted to the Department of Electronic and Electrical Engineering, Obafemi Awolowo University, Ile-Ife, Nigeria.

[3] Centre for Software Defined Radio (CSDR), (2007). "Software Defined Radio: Terms, Trends and Perspectives". Aalborg Universitet, Aalborg, Denmark. January 2007, pp. 6.

[4] Iancu, D., Glossner, J., Ye, H., Abdelila, Y., Stuart S. (2003), "Software AM Radio Implementation". Sandbridge Technologies Inc, 1 N Lexington Avennue, 10th Floor, White Plains, New York 10601.

[5] Kreyszig, E. (2006). " Advanced Engineering Mathematics ", 8th Edition. John Wiley and Sons, Inc, pp. 947 – 948.

[6] Olivier, R., Denby, B. and Sid-Ahmed, H. (2003). "A Real Time Software Radio for the AM Long Wave Band". Laboratoire des Instruments et Systemes d'Ile de France (LISI6F), Universite Pierre et Marie Curie, B.C. 252, 4 PLACE Jussieu, 75252 Paris Cedex 05, France, pp. 1-4.

[7] Matteo, F. (2002). 'Algorithmic advances for software radios', Vanu Inc, porter square, suite 18, Cambridge, MA 02140, pp.1.

[8] Shajedul Hasan S.M. and Balister P. (2005): "Prototyping a Software Defined Radio Receiver Based on USRP and OSSIE". Chameleonic Radio Technical Memo No. 1.

[9] Weisstein, E. (2008). "Stochastic Resonance." From MathWorld – A Wolfram WEB Resource, Available Online: http://mathworld.wolfram.com/ StochasticResonance.html.

[10] White, A. and Williams, A. (2012): Systems, Methods and Computer-Readable Media for Configuring Receiver Latency, Available Online: Http://www.google.com.ng/patents/ US 8966109 B2.

[11] Yesufu, T.K. (1995). "The Dynamics of a Regenerative Receiver". Proceedings of the Regional Workshop on Radio Communication in Africa, (Radio Africa 1995) held at Obafemi Awolowo University Ile-Ife, Nigeria, pp. 185.

11

"Soft" system of coordinates in regular simplexes

Tomas Georgievich Petrov

St. Petersburg State University, Institute of Earth Science, St. Petersburg, Russia

Email address:

tomas_petrov@rambler.ru, tgpnever@gmail.com

Abstract: In different areas of knowledge, there are common problems of coding and ordering of multicomponent compositions of objects as well as representation of their processes of change. These problems are solved by the language-method RHAT. It can be considered as a coordinate system of regions in space limited by regular simplex. Here R is a sequence of composition components by decrease – names of sectors in the simplex distinguished by hypermedians, a semiquantitative substantial characteristic of compositions, "word" of a new type; H – Shannon information entropy – entropy of mixing; A – anentropy – entropy of separation; T – tolerance. The arrangement of coordinates allows obtaining an alphabetical hierarchical periodic system of compositions (HPSC) of objects of different nature, in particular, the Hierarchical Periodic System of Chemical Compositions (HPSCC) that uses the Periodic System of Elements (PSE) as an alphabet, as well as the Hierarchical Periodic System of Molecular Compositions (HPSMC) that uses HPSCC as an alphabet. Diagrams HA or HT are designed to display random and ordered sets of compositions of any nature as the most appropriate means of studying the processes of separation and mixing. The applicability of the method has been tested on analytical materials in natural and social science fields.

Keywords: Regular Simplex, Coordinate System of Region, Information Entropy, Entropy of Separation, Anentropy, Ultrapurification, Tolerance, Information Language, Hypermedian, Hierarchical Periodic System

1. Introduction

Background of the method, common for the natural sciences, is presented in [3, 9, 10]. Mostly it relates to the multicomponent nature of objects (cenoses, communities, mixtures), namely: uncertainty of boundaries between compositions of such objects, which is significant in nature and in all areas of human activity, including dispensing medicines and food, choice of winner, study of isomorphism in crystals, financial capacity determination, military solutions, etc.) and uncertainty of naming what is inside the boundaries, difficulties in visibility and ordering of object compositions, diversity of content measurement units and disproportionality of large and small in the same composition, difficulty in identifying the general direction of the evolution of compositions under multi-directional changes in individual components. To reduce the complexity of solving these problems, information language method, or rank-entropy method (hereinafter - way or method) for displaying, particularly, coding of compositions *RHAT* has been proposed. Here *R* is a sequence of symbols of composition components by reduction of their contents; *H* is C. Shannon

information entropy as entropy of mixing; A – anentropy [6-13, 15, 20, 21,], as entropy of separation [13, 15]; T – tolerance [10, 15] - as "entropy of purification". The method has been repeatedly described in [6 9-13; 17], and will be outlined briefly here. Details are presented in [21].

Method wasinitially proposed particularly for convolution of chemical compositions of rocks and minerals, but later its usefulness has been shown in solving conceptual tasks in various fields of knowledge [4, 13, 15,16, 19, 25; 26].

Method is usually set out in terms of algebra, information theory. Here, we present it at the elementary level as a *way of describing – coordination – coding of an area in space limited by a regular simplex* with equal distances from the center to all vertices, and distances between all vertices. Of all simplexes, triangle has long been a "sacred cow" of mineralogists, petrologists, and many other geologists, at the same time becoming a dead end in the representation of multicomponent systems on paper. Background demand of visibility at preservation of the traditional approach has not enabled to pass into the volume and work in it, since even imaging of tetrahedron content is problematic. Representation of 5-10-50-component analysis without a radical convolution of analysis is impossible, and, at the same time, chemical analyses with 50 or more elements have become quite common. On the other hand, actively working "naturalists" and "humanitarians" accumulate thousands of chemical, mineral, biospecies, age, linguistic "analyses". There are problems in putting them in order, discovering duplicates, defects, seeing the material as a whole (rather than its individual components, or the relations between two or three of them), seeing the relationship between compositions, concentrations and rarefactions, banality and originality of individual analyses, identifying the direction of change and path length of the evolution of composition, and, amid all this, in detecting a law or prohibition of a certain already formed hypothesis: all that was worth of the efforts spent on the method development and is worth of the work to become acquainted with it.

The method can be considered both as a way of coding, and as a "soft" system of coordinates, meaning by its "softness" lack of an exact solution of the inverse problem with the number of variables exceeding the number of equations. Thus, 40-element composition analysis of a complex mineral, tourmaline, contains 50 unknowns convolved in 4 equations: H, A, T and $\mathrm{Sum}p_i=1$.

Under "soft" coordinate system we mean description of area position (and not point, as in a "hard" one of some space, in this case, space of a regular simplex).

Purpose of the article is to pay attention to the universal encoding method of multicomponent compositions *RHAT*, as well as to the problems in mathematics arising from the use of the method in different fields of knowledge.

2. *R, H, A, T as* Coordinates in a Simplex Space

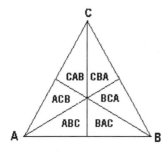

Figure 1. *Simplex with names of sectors distinguished by medians*

First coordinate: R, rank formula of composition, rating, is a sequence of symbols (or names) of n components (selected from the total possible in this branch of knowledge number N) by reduction of their contents p, when $\mathrm{Sum}p_i$ =1. This series (e.g. "quartz-feldspar-mica", a sequence by reduction of contents of principal rock minerals – granite) is a sector name in a regular simplex having three vertices when split by medians in a triangle (Fig. 1). Rating R, a semiquantitative while substantial characteristic of composition, is regarded as the major semantic part of the composition convolution in the form of *RHAT* code. Four-component composition

requires a tetrahedron when split by median planes, and further – an unthinkable regular polyhedron with median hyperplanes. In the simplex vertices all $p = 1$, that is, here are absolutely pure components (not present in nature, but more on that below). In the simplex center $p_1 = p_2 = p_3 == \ldots . p_n =1/n$. In volume of a simplex with n vertices, the number of sectors $K= n!$ An elementary example of sector naming is shown in Fig. 1.

Contents of the first component are in the range $1/n$-1. In other ranks, 0-$1/n$.

Besides the said role, R is a means of component selection if the sample contains analyses of different lengths, which is critical for subsequent calculations of composition characteristics. Namely, for comparability of the processing results of analyses with varying n detail, after ranking of the initial data, further computing includes the amount of components not greater than n of the shortest analysis. This does not eliminate the possibility to find in the analysis a component, the content of which is smaller than would be in the case of a more complete analysis. Therefore, there is a choice: increasing of details and reduction of confidence in the correctness of the result, or increasing of confidence at reduction of analysis details.

2.1. Information Entropy H or En

The second coordinate: H, Shannon information entropy up to a constant is an analog of the thermodynamic *entropy of mixing* [2] and the measure of complexity, diversity of system composition. (The diversity problem is discussed in [26]). Evaluation by formula $H = - \mathrm{Sum}p_i\ln p_i$. To reduce to the interval 0-1 we use $En = H/\ln n$, where $\ln n=H\mathrm{max}$. Maximum value of contribution of one component in entropy $-p_i\ln p_i$ for logarithms with any base is at $p =0.368\ldots$. In a simplex-triangleisolines of entropy normalized to 1 are shown in Fig. 4. In accordance with isoline appearance, entropy can be regarded as a *generalized distance from simplex vertices to the composition point.*

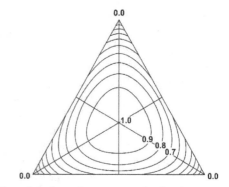

Figure 2. *Isolines of entropy normalized to the interval 0-1.*

2.2. Anentropy A or An

The third coordinate, anentropy [6, p.34; 9, p.17] is regarded as a measure of smallness of small components and calculated by formula $A = -1/n*\mathrm{Sum}\ln p_i- \ln n$. According to the formula, A exists in the range 0-+∞. To reduce to the interval 0-1, convenient for many applications diagrammaticform (in combination with entropy), A of a real composition is divided by anentropy of a "simple analytically perfectly clean" system[9, p.18]. This is necessary, since zero in composition responds to the logarithm of minus infinity. For maximum pure composition is taken composition, in which $p_1 = 1-(n-1)^*$, $p_2 = p_3 = ... = p_n =$, where are contents equal to half sensitivity of the analysis method. This trick is dictated by V.I. Vernadsky "ubiquity principle" (as it is called, slightly reinforcing the position of its author) [1. p.518-527], according to which any macroobject contains all elements of the Periodic System. Let us add: tricks are useful as well (with their) when considering compositions of any real systems, whether mineral, national, age etc., in which the smallest contents are almost always underestimated - to the detriment of the meaning of quantitative estimates.

Anentropy isolines in a regular triangle are shown in Fig. 5. In accordance with their nature, anentropy can be considered a *generalized distance from the simplex center to the composition point.*

Anentropy is regarded as *entropy of separation*, since many observations of trajectories of processes of separation, for example, by grain size in sedimentary rocks, population age, during mineral processing, show its increase [13, p.24; 22].

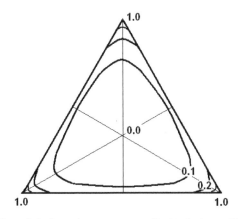

Figure 3. Isolines of anentropy normalized to the interval 0-1.

2.3. Tolerance – T

Tolerance as a coordinate [10, p.30; 13, p.24], the contribution to which is $1/p$, is calculated by formula $T = \ln[1/n^* \mathrm{Sum}(1/p_i)] - \ln n$. We do not show isolines of normalized tolerance because they are pressed to the simplex vertices even in a greater extent than anentropy isolines. This characteristic is most applicable for estimating the degree of composition closeness to the simplex vertex, to a state of perfect purity of composition.

To distinguish it from the entropy of separation (as a means to display widely used methods of relatively coarse separation), tolerance, the means to show processes of extremely pure substances, can be called *entropy of purification.*

From the viewpoint of information theory, the value of tolerance is the logarithm of average signal waiting time at their uniform arrival.

Contributions of three quantitativecomposition coordinates are shown in Fig. 6.

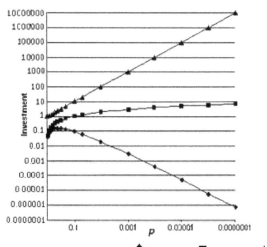

Figure 4. Contribution into entropy ◆, anentropy - ■, tolerance - ▲.

Contributions into A and T are functionally dependent on the contribution into entropy. If we take the contribution into entropy $(-p\ln p)$ for a primitive function, its first derivative with respect to p minus one will be contribution into anentropy $(-\ln p)$, contribution into tolerance – the second derivative with respect to contribution into entropy and the first one with respect to contribution into anentropy $(1/p)$. Thus, both anentropy and tolerance are natural outcomes, subsequent development stages of the ideology embedded in C. Shannon information entropy. The transition from the widely applicable one-dimensional data representation of the complexity of systems to the two-dimensional, diagrammatic and three-dimensional, spatial, that is to the means more filled (or richer) in content is implemented this way.

3. Systematics – Ordering of Composition Codes

RHAT composition coordinates (with descriptions of specific objects) are recorded in a row and arranged in a column, as shown in Table 1. For this a set, series of *RHAT* coordinates is taken as a word that uses three alphabets. One is letter, for rank formulas playing the role of "roots", semantic meaning of a word, and two numerical: for entropy ("suffix") –by reduction of H values and for A and T – by their increase ("inflexions"). Ordering is done according to the known linguistic principle, consistently. First roots are ordered, then suffixes, and further inflexions.

In general, it is desirable to use any "intensional" alphabets as symbols in rank formula R[25, 28]. They are understood as alphabets which have semantic links between adjacent symbols (entities), as opposed to "natural" alphabets, in which such links either do not exist or are very weak [28]. It is known that dictionaries using "natural" alphabets usually put close words and form groups having similarity in inscription (alt, altar, alter, altimeter, altruism...) and rare with a similar sense. Unlike the latter, when using the most famous *intensional* alphabet in encoding chemical compositions of geological objects, the Periodic Table of Elements, groups of rank formulas OSiAlH..OSiAlNa… OSiAlK contain different, but related in chemical composition objects. They have a common name - "alumosilicates"; some of them are presented in Tab. 1. When rank formula length increases, certainty of allocating a portion of space, to which the composition belongs, and, on the other hand, the degree of generalization at its reduction are growing.

In case of equal R, ordering of composition coordinates is made by reduction of H, the preferential direction of entropy change during separation [29]. (Separation is understood as formation of two or more systems from one that differ in composition. Mixing is the opposite process of forming a relatively homogeneous system of two or more differing in composition). In case of equal H, ordering of coordinate lines is made in the usually opposite direction of A and T changes, i.e. by their increase.

Such ordering results in a Hierarchical Linear Periodic System of Compositions, in particular, chemical, when coordinates of chemical compositions of objects are ordered [12]. Table repeated from [12] shows a sample of code coordinates from the existing Database of Chemical Compositions that contains more than 80 000 entries. This is a negligible part of a full table (probably impossible to construct), given the number of stable elements (88?) and taking into account $n= 10$ elements in R. Horizontal lines in the table are dividers revealing the hierarchical structure of the system. Equal signs mean that $p_n/p_{n+1} \leq 1.15$, i.e. indicate the proximity of contents of the adjacent components in a rank formula.

Table 1. *Sample from the "Chemical Compositions of the Universe" Database*

Rank formula										En	An	Object
H	O	C	N	Ca=	P	K=	S	Na	Cl	0.428	0.434	human body
H	O	N	Cl	Si	Li	B =	S	C	Ca	0.278	0.980	water, geyser, Kamchatka
O	C	Ca	Mg	Fe	Si	P	Al	Mn	K	0.561	0.210	carbonatite, Sallanlatva
O	Mg	Si	Fe	Al	Ca	Na	K =	Cr	Ti	0.542	0.301	Mars
O	Mg	Si	Fe	Al	Ca	Na	Cr	K	Ti	0.511	0.305	The Earth, mantle+crust
O	Si	H	Al	C=	Ca=	Mg=	Fe=	K	Na	0.578	0.166	Quaternary clay
O	Si	H=	Al	Fe	K	Mg	C=	Ca	Ti	0.361	0.401	sandstones, Kazakhstan
O	Si	Na	Mg	Al=	Ca	Fe	Mn	W	Ti	0.286	0.804	quartz, Transbaikalia
O	Si	Mg	Al	Ca=	Fe	Cr	Ti	Mn	Na	0.554	0.274	pyrope, Urals
O	Si	Mg	Fe	Al	Ca	Na	Mn	S	K	0.567	0.193	meteorite, Zhmerinka
O	Si	Al	Na	K	H	Fe	Ca	Mg	Ti	0.488	0.247	granite, average of 2,485 an.
O	Si	Al	Ca=	Fe	Mg	Ti	Na	K	Mn	0.552	0.236	basalt, Moon
O	Si=	Ca	C	H=	Fe	P	F=	K	Al	0.617	0.138	carbonatite, Malawi
O	Ca=	C	Fe	Mg	P	Si	Al	Sr	Na	0.519	0.278	carbonatite, Kovdor
O	Ca	Fe	P	Mg	Si	Al	Na	Mn	Ti	0.569	0.268	phoscorite, Kovdor
F	Ca	Ba=	Ti	Zr	O	Be=	Al	Bi	Mn	0.281	0.962	fluorite, Transbaikalia
S	Fe	As	Sb	Zn	Pb	Co=	Ni	Bi	Se	0.282	0.967	pyrite, Sibay
Cu	Sn	As	Fe	Sb	Pb	Ni=	Ag	Bi=	Co	0.069	0.526	bronze, knife, Alekseevka

The database of object descriptions contains a reference to the source, the number of table and analysis in it, as well as other specific information about the object.

4. Properties of Databases Systematized Using RHAT Method

Database, a sample of which is shown in Table, has the following properties:

Versatility – with respect to the possible diversity of chemical compositions (hence the database name), since there is no chemical (let us add: and any other) composition, which would be impossible to imagine in *RHA(T)* form;

Linearity - has no branching and therefore is extremely simple;

Algorithmicity – when constructing;

Openness – to expand the list of components;

Stability, i.e., the system allows for the removal and inclusion of new records without changing the order of the others;

Countability – the maximum number of rank formulas

U(from Universum) can be defined as the number of permutations without repetitions of N possible components of this alphabet by n, i.e. $U=N!/(N–n)!$. For $N=88$ and $n=10$ we have $U= 1.64E+19$. The chemical Universe can be placed in this catalog.

Completeness – for a certain alphabet length and a certain length of rank formula there are no and cannot be other rank formulas over the number of permutations, as defined above. Therefore, for these N and n the sequence is a Universum of existing, possible and impossible compositions in this field of knowledge;

Hierarchicity– ordering, as in alphabetical dictionaries, is primarily done by the first, the highest rank (first letter). Further, inside the rank formulas with the same first rank ordering takes place by the second, lower rank (second letter), etc. As a result, we have a hierarchical ordering of codes.Rank formula with length n is an ordered list of all higher taxa;

Periodicity – rank formulas of objects with similar composition are arranged in table in groups, between which there are other, much different ones; thus, in Table 1 rank formulas OCCa...OCaC... located at opposite ends of the table belong to rocks of the same facies – these are carbonate varieties.

Arrangement of objects in a system manifests connection with the procedure of changing some properties of object ordering in the original alphabet (here, in the Periodic Table). Thus, for chemical compositions, from the classification beginning to its end, average atomic masses of objects, their densities grow statistically, occurrence in nature decreases statistically.

5. Entropy diagrams *HA* and *HT*

Values of all three numeric coordinates *H,A,T* depend on the number of components. Therefore, if desired to deal with full analyses, very often having different *n*, their comparison will be either difficult, or impossible, or this fact can be used (but at a sufficiently large amount of data) to identify the structure of the information space. Specifically, to image variety of materials by their detail (analyses length), that is clearly manifested in *HA* diagram of age distributions of population in countries of the world [14].

Bearing in mind great importance of the issue let us partially repeat. For comparability of data, *R* lengths are standardized on some general level and, after renormalization of sums of truncated analyses to the unity, *HAT* is calculated. To account for the fullest possible information, standard should be brought into proximity with the length of the shortest analysis in the sample. It should be borne in mind that the shorter the analysis, the greater the chance to lose underestimated components and include in the calculation lower values than would have been at a more complete analysis, respectively, the higher anentropy can be [21, p.68]. There is reason to believe that the delay in the use of entropy in some branches of knowledge, particularly in geology, is associated with ignoring the need to standardize the analysis details before computations.

Field of allowable *EnAn* values for a 10-component system is shown in Fig. 5. The upper limit was obtained by mixing of compositions described in detail in [9, p.17]. Figures near the points along the upper curve correspond to the number of components with equal contents, assuming that the remaining ones (10 minus "figure"), supplementing the analysis to ten components, had contents of half sensitivity of the analysis method taken for 0.00005. (This value corresponds approximately to the sensitivity of "wet" analyses that have been ubiquitous until recently and did not lose value with the advent of new technologies). The lower curve meets the condition: $p_1 = 1 - (p_2 + p_3 + ... + p_{10})$, thereby: $p_2 = p_3 = p_4 = ... = p_{10}$.

Abbreviations S denote point of original compositions (Start), F (Final) - final product compositions. The diagram shows the typical directions of composition change during separation (two S-F patterns on the left) and mixing processes (two patterns on the right), found in tracing the evolution trajectories of compositions in dozens of real processes of change in composition of rocks and minerals.

Featured direction ratios during mixing – combination of two different compositions into one, and during separation – formation of two or more different compositions from one illustrate Yu.V. Shurubor's theorems of preferred directions of entropy change during mixing and separation [29].

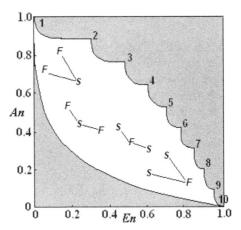

Figure 5. *Limits of EnAn field and typical directions of composition evolution during separation and mixing (explanation in the text).*

Separation and mixing processes shown in Figure 5, "pull" points of compositions to vertex No.1, if content of one component is growing in composition (native elements, or close to mono-ethnic community); to No.2, if, except for two components with equal contents, the remaining components are removed (purification of rock salt NaCl); to No.3, if a three-element compound of KOH, NaOH type is purified, and so on. Reverse movement, towards the simplex center (No. 10 in the diagram) corresponds to mixing processes. Neither simplex center nor its vertices contain real (or at least chemical) compositions, since to achieve these points, non-existent in nature and in laboratory ideal pure substances are required. Everything happens between these two extremes in a cyclic implementation of separations and mixings. For example, in geology, formation of granite is separation, then hydration of certain minerals, mixing, further disintegration of rock with removal of having become mobile solutions and clays – separation, entering of granite degradation products in streams and soil–mixing and so on, for each preserved chemical element of the primary system, an eternal change of participation in mixing and separation processes. In biocenoses, birth and death of organisms is imposed on separation-mixing processes, but the reciprocating motion of a point noting the seasonal cycles in *HA* diagram will occur monotonically as long as the ecosystem is not "sick" or starts to disintegrate.

According to the data published in [5] and calculations conducted by the author, it is known that the scatter in *EnAn* data in the middle of the diagram when using standard chemical analysis in geology for *n*=10 is approximately ±0.005 in both axes.

Description of the diagram is presented in [9, 13] and in most detail in [21]. Model of the separation-mixing process in qualitative presentation is given in [15].

6. Unresolved Problems

Development of the method has mainly taken place "broadwise", towards the testing of opportunities and meaningfulness of results when using the method in various areas of knowledge, which are already about 20. At the same time, the mathematical aspect has been apparently developed insufficiently.

Exceeding the number of unknowns on the number of equations implies uncertainty when solving the inverse problem, inability to determine p_i for *HA* or *HT* data. However, in each triple combination: R_i, *H*, *A*, (or R_i, *H*, *T*), p_i range is not unlimited. There is a task to find a way for calculating p_{min} and p_{max} *for each* R_i of the system with cardinal *n* for the set *HA*, *HT*, *EnAn* at $p_{min}=$. In other words, what are shapes of "bodies of R_i contents" in projections on the fields of *EnAn*, *HA*, and *HT* diagrams?

Another question is very important in the practice of studying evolution of compositions. All mathematically made mixings (interpolations) of compositions, that is when signs of change are preserved, and the vast majority of the examined processes of evolution of compositions of natural objects give arcs convex downward or downward – to the right (such as given in [13] in Fig. 7). [3] describes the process, which has a curve of the opposite form: bulge upward – to the left. As has been well established, it took place in two stages: the first one, with the normal trend of separation – decrease of *H*, growth of *A*, and the second one with the opposite trend, mixing. There was a task to determine whether this type of curve may correspond to a "one-way" ("monotonic") process, that is, without changing the signs of change in content? If we prove that this is impossible, there will be confidence that the processes of this type are not monotonic.

7. Some Results and Prospects

RHAT is a universal method for describing compositions, one of the methods along with the principal component analysis, cluster analysis, and others that may be included in generalizing discipline "Composistics" enabling to work with compositions, intensities, weights, values of components of any complex systems [8 p.271]. The method provides a wide range of possibilities; alternatives for applying it are described in [11]. The same publication lists three types of work, namely: with primarily disordered analytical materials, with a database, and with materials ordered in space and time.

Proposed in 1971, the method can be said to lie long, it was not properly claimed in geology due to several reasons, among them probably the most important: a) unconventional measurement units – atomic fractions accepted by the author for a universal approach – for chemical composition (instead of remaining since the 19th century oxides such as SiO_2, Al_2O_3, FeO...); b) integrated approach to complex compositions at prevailing in diagrams consideration of only 2-3 components of composition, c) more than once mentioned logarithmic curve. It is also very likely: d) distrust

of a geologist-crystallographer who encroached on the solution of problems that appeared to be insoluble in the 70-ies: uniform ordering of all chemical and mineral compositions, and placing in a single diagram, having a genetic interpretation, compositions of objects of any nature, and thus being able to *display and study the evolution of the whole world of multicomponent compositions in diagrams, and not using one-dimensional sequences of information entropy.* The proposed method for construction of a two-parameter alphabet was the first step to address the issue of *content encoding of crystal-chemical structural formulas of minerals* [16] (and not only them), in combination with the *R*-dictionary-catalog of chemical compositions of minerals [18]; it *offered an opportunity to create a unified structural-chemical classification of real minerals* and to develop on its basis the looming *"RHAT dictionary-catalog of crystal-chemical compositions of minerals".*

Work on the method and several others is supported by original Petros3 software enabling to deal with 100 alphabets, to form databases, including bibliographic one, to perform calculations of correlation coefficients and distances of several kinds, convolutions of large amounts of information in the form of "generalized rank formulas" etc. [10].

8. Conclusion

The author will consider his mission accomplished, if he draws attention to the fields of mathematics, that enable a consistent encoding of compositions of objects of any nature and development of an algorithm for constructing rank-entropy alphabetically ordered Hierarchical Periodic Systems of *Compositions*, in contrast to the original Periodic System of *Elements*, in addition, showing the processes of composition change, revealing common in disparate at first glance processes in stagnating, living and social, in particular, regarding them as separation and mixing – implementation of differentiation and integration, recognized fundamental by Herbert Spencer.

Acknowledgements

The author thanks his long-time collaborator N.I. Krasnova for dedicated efforts to disseminate the method, S.V. Moshkin for programming and implementation of the endless requests to add another method in the software, to explain how-to, A.G. Bulakh, Yu.L. Voytekhovsky, and recently deceased V.V. Gordienko for deep understanding and high public estimation of the method, S.V. Chebanov for continued support and strengthening methodological fundamentals of the method, A.A. Andriyanets-Buyko, V.A. Glebovitsky, V.Ya. Vasiliev, V.N. Dech, I.S. Sedova, P.B. Sokolov, O.I. Farafonova, V.V. Khaustov, A.V. Shuisky who contributed to the author in his work towards formation and development of the method, and all others who resisted the method development in different ways, prompting the author to a more thorough understanding and description of his work. Special thanks to O.Yu. Bogdanova, whose translation of the papers promoted their publication in the multidisciplinary scientific environment.

References

[1] Vernadsky V.I. On the scattering of chemical elements. Selected works. V.1. AS USSR Press. 1954. - Pp. 517-527

[2] Moelwyn-Hughes E.A. Physical chemistry. Mon. In 2 v. M. IIL, 1962 - 1148 p.

[3] Gordienko V.V., Petrov T.G. Studying of rare-metal pegmatites using RHA language. // RMS Proceedings. – Part 110. – Iss.5 – 1981 Pp. 546-558

[4] Kramarenko S.S. Features of using entropy information analysis for quantitative criteria of biological objects // Bull. Samara Sci. Centre of RAS. – 2005

[5] Kukharenko A.A., Ilyinsky G.A., Ivanova T.N. et al. Clarkes of the Khibiny alkaline massif // RMS Proceedings 1968. – Part 97. Iss. 2. – Pp.133-149

[6] Petrov T.G. Substantiation of a version of general classification of geochemical systems. // LSU Bulletin. No. 18. – 1971. – Pp. 30-38.

[7] Petrov T.G. A problem of separation and mixing in inorganic systems. In: Geology. Ed by V.T. Trofimov, v.2. – Moscow State University. – 1995. – Pp.181-186.

[8] Petrov T.G. Language-method RHA for describing, systematizing, and studying changes in compositions of any nature. // In: Cenological studies. Ed. B.I. Kudrin. Iss. 1 Mathematical description of cenoses and technetical laws. Abakan: SRC – 1996. – Pp.256-273

[9] Petrov T.G. Information language for description of multi-component objects composition // Scientific and technical information. Ser. 2. – 2001. – No. 3. – Pp. 8-18.

[10] Petrov T.G. Rank-entropy approach to description of compositions of geological objects and their changes (exemplified by geological cenology). // General and applied cenology. 2007. – No.5. – Pp.27-33

[11] Petrov T.G. RHA method as a solution of systematization problem of analytical data on the material composition of geological objects. Otechestvennaja geology. 2008. – No.4. – Pp.98-105.

[12] Petrov T.G. Hierarchical periodical system of chemical compositions and its association with the periodical system of elements. // SPbSU Bulletin. Ser. 7. 2009. – Iss. 2. Pp. 21-28.

[13] Petrov T.G. Graphic Representation of Evolutionary Processes of Compositions of Multicomponent Objects of Any Nature // Automatic Documentation and Mathematical Linguistics. 2012. – V. 46. – No. 2. – pp. 79–93. © Allerton Press, Inc., DOI: 10.3103/S0005105512020045

[14] Petrov T.G. RHA method for coding, systematizing, and displaying the changes in age compositions of population. // Coll. dedicated to the 60th anniversary of S.V. Chebanov (in press)

[15] Petrov T.G. Separation-Mixing as a Model of Composition Evolution of any Nature. // J. Systemics, Cybernetics and Informatics V. 12. – N 1 – 2014. – Pp. 76-81.

[16] Petrov T.G., Andriyanets-Buyko A.A., Moshkin S.V. A Two-Parameter Alphabet for Coding Structural-Chemical Information and its Systematization (Using the Example of Tourmaline).// Automatic Documentation and Mathematical Linguistics. 2012. – V. 46 –.No. 1. – pp. 40–49. SpringerLink Online– DOI 10.3103/S0005105512010086

[17] Petrov T.G., Moshkin Sergey V. RHA(T)-System for Coding of Discrete Distributions and Their Alteration Processes. // Proc. The 3rd International Multi-Conference on Complexity, Informatics and Cybernetics IMCIC 2012. – 2012. – Pp. 12-16.

[18] Petrov T.G., Krasnova N.I. R-dictionary-catalogue of mineral chemical compositions. Mon. St. Petersburg, – "Nauka". – 2010. – 150 p.

[19] Petrov T.G., Krasnova N.I. RHA-coding of mineral composition of crystalline rocks and method of their systematization. // Modern problems of magmatism and metamorphism. Mon. Vol.2 – St. Petersburg – 2012 – Pp. 120-123

[20] Petrov T.G., Moshkin S.V. RHA method and its implementation in Petros-3 software system. Calculations in geology. 2011. – No.1. – Pp. 50-53.

[21] Petrov T.G., Farafonova O.I. Information-component analysis. RHA method. Study guide. St. Petersburg – 2005. – 168 p.

[22] Petrov T.G., Farafonova O.I., Sokolov P.B. Informational-entropic characteristics of composition of minerals and rocks as a reflection of crystallization process stress: RMS Proceedings – 2003. – No.2. – Pp. 33-40.

[23] Khaustov V.V. Role of deep geodynamics in hydrolithosphere formation (exemplified by the Caspian-Caucasus segment of the Alpine-Himalayan mobile belt. Abstract of Doc. Thes. St. Petersburg – 2011 – 40 p.

[24] Khaustov V.V. Towards the problem of mud volcano water formation in the South Caspian basin // "Space and Time" Almanac. T. 1. – Iss. 1 – 2012.

[25] Chebanov S.V. Logical fundamentals of linguistic typology. Mon. Vilnius. VLANI. 1996. – 92 p.

[26] Chebanov S.V. Optimality and extremality in culture, zipfiades and Lotman's law. // In: Technogenic self-organization and mathematical apparatus of cenologic studies. M SRC. – Iss. 28. – 2005 – Pp.411-428

[27] Chebanov S.V. Dynamics of cultural forms.// In: Fundamental problems of cultural studies in 4 vol. Cultural dynamics v.3. St. Petersburg. Aletheia. 2008. – Pp. 184-197

[28] Chebanov S.V., Petrov T.G. Intensionality, intensional alphabets, intensional words and dictionaries // In: Actual problems of modern cognitive science. Ivanovo. – 2013. – Pp.239-266

[29] Shurubor Yu.V. On one property of complexity measure of geochemical systems.// Proceedings of the AS USSR. – 1972. – V. 205. – No.2. – Pp. 453-456

12

Segmentation of cells from 3-D confocal images of live embryo

Ali Zeynali Aaq Qaleh[1, *], Seyyed Mahdi Haji Mirahmadi[2]

[1]Faculty of Engineering, Islamic Azad University, Qom, Iran
[2]Software Engineer, Young Researchers and Elite Club, Qazvin Branch, Islamic Azad University, Qazvin, Iran

Email address:
a.zaynali.a@mail.com (A. Z. A. Qaleh), Caspiansys@gmail.com (S. M. H. Mirahmadi)

Abstract: Partial-differential-equation- based segmentation has been employed to accurately extract the shapes of membranes and nuclei from time lapse confocal microscopy images, taken throughout early Zebrafish embryogenesis. This strategy is a prerequisite for an accurate quantitative analysis of cell shape and morphodynamics during organogenesis and is the basis for an integrated understanding of biological processes. This data will also serve for the measurement of the variability between individuals in a population. The segmentation of cellular structures is achieved by first using an edge-preserving image filtering method for noise reduction and then applying an algorithm for cell shape reconstruction based on the Subjective Surfaces technique.

Keywords: Partial Differential Equations, Segmentation, Confocal Images, Morphodynamics

1. Introduction

The extraction and segmentation of true 3-D shapes is a crucial task in the analysis of morphodynamical patterns in biology. The shape reconstruction of nuclei and membranes during embryogenesis is the basis for a strategy of automated measurements of the cell proliferation rate in the embryonic tissues that will be used for designing low-cost methods for the pre-clinical evaluation of anti-cancer drug effects in vivo. Prior and during cell division, the cell shape undergoes characteristic changes. Thus, shape analysis of nuclei and membranes is essential for the detection of cell division which is necessary to get a measurement of the cell proliferation rate in living tissues. Furthermore, the reconstruction of the cellular shape will provide relevant parameters to mea- sure the variability between different individuals of the same species, opening the way for understanding the individual susceptibility to genetic diseases or response to treatments.

Our aim is to design an algorithm providing in an automated way the correct segmentation of nucl ei and membranes in live embryos. We expect to avoid the need for any manual intervention which is in any case completely unrealistic when dealing with thousands of objects. A similar study can be found in a previous work by Sarti et al. [1], where confocal microscopy images were processed to extract the shape of nuclei. However, in that case, the analyzed volumes were not acquired from a living organism but from pieces of fixed tissues.

2. Imaging Acquisition

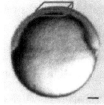

Fig1. Image of the Embryo.(Left) Start point (about 3 hours post fertilization).(Right) End point (about 7 hours post fertilization).

$$\Phi_t =_g H|\nabla\Phi| + \nabla_g . \nabla\Phi; \qquad H = \nabla . \left(\frac{\nabla\Phi}{|\nabla\Phi|}\right) \qquad (1)$$

First To obtain accurate measurements of 3-D features at the cellular level in living embryos, it is necessary to use an acquisition technique with micrometrical resolution and to reconstruct volumetric information. To fulfil these requirements, the analyzed images have been acquired by confocal microscopy with the best compromise in terms of spatial and temporal resolution [2].

In order to produce high contrast images, the specimen has been labeled through the expression of fluorescent proteins, the eGFP (Green Fluorescent Protein, targeted to the nuclei) and the mcherry (Red Fluorescent Protein, addressed to membranes). The two channels were acquired separately but simultaneously, as the emission spectrum of the two proteins are sufficiently distinct.

The x,y size of the acquired images is 512 x 512 pixels; the temporal resolution is about 5 minutes. The voxel size is not uniform in space: 0.584793 μm in x and y directions and 1.04892 μm in z. The overall volume submitted to optical sectioning is 30 microns thick. The embryo has been imaged from 3, 5 hours post fertilization (development at 28o C) for 4 hours (25o C under the microscope) [3].

3. Image Denoising

The noise present in the image can disrupt the shape information, therefore the de-noising process is an essential preliminary task in images segmentation. Different sources of noise can be identified: the non-homogeneous concentration of the fluorescent proteins in the labelled structures and the electronic noise from the instrument. In order to accurately reconstruct the object shape, the de-noising process has to improve the signal-to-noise ratio, faithfully preserving the edges position and definition. The geodesic curvature filtering [1, 4] is able to achieve this task. In the uniform regions, it moves the iso-intensity surfaces in the normal direction with a curvature-dependent speed, smoothing the superimposed noise, whereas near the edges it attracts the image levels towards the local contours, sharpening the edges and working to preserve the objects dimensions.

4. Segmentation

4.1. Theoretical Background

Beside the Subjective Surfaces technique [5,6] is particularly useful for the segmentation of incomplete contours, because it allows the reconstruction and the integration of lacking information. The analyzed images, especially the membranes images, are characterized by a signal which is almost undetectable or even absent in some regions. In such situations, the Subjective Surfaces technique should allow the completion of lacking-portions of objects.

Consider a 3-D image I : (x, y, z) → I (x, y, z) as a real positive function defined in some domain M ⊂ R3 .

One initial task in image segmentation is to build an edge indicator g, which is a representation of the local structures of the image. An expression of g can be [7].

Where Gσ (x, y, z) is a Gaussian kernel with standard deviation σ, (∗) denotes the convolution and n is 1 or 2. The value of g is close to 1 in flat areas ($|\nabla I| \to 0$) and close to 0 where the image gradient is high (edges). Thus, the minima of g denote the position of edges and its gradient is a force field

that can be used to drive the evolution, because it always points in the local edge direction. The second step is the selection of a reference point, approximately in the center of the object to be segmented. The initial hypersuface Si (Si : (x, y, z) → (x, y, z, Φ0)) is defined in the same domain M of the image I starting from an initial function Φ0 . There are some alternative forms for Φ0 , for example Φ0 = −αD or Φ0 = α/D, where D is the 3-D distance function from the reference point. The motion equation, which drives the hypersurface evolution, is the flow which ensures the steepest descent of the hypersurface volume:

where H is the Euclidean mean curvature. This equation is exactly the same of that defined in the well-known Geodesic Active Contours technique (GAC) [8], except for a parameter introduced in H expression to weigh the matching of level curves. The entire hypersurface is driven under a speed law dependent on the image gradient, whereas in classical formulation of Level Set methods, as in GAC, the evolution affects only a particular front or level. The first term on the right side of equation (1) is a parabolic motion that evolves the hypersurface in normal direction with a velocity weighted by the mean curvature and by the edge indicator g, slowing down near the edges (where g → 0). The second term on the right is a pure passive advection along the velocity field $-\nabla g$ whose direction and strength depend on its position. This term attracts the hypersurface in the direction of the image edges. In regions with subjective contours, continuation of existing edge fragments is negligible and equation (1) can be approximated by a geodesic flow, allowing the boundary completion with curves of minimal length (i.e. straight lines).

4.2. Numerical Approximation

After The partial derivatives in equation (1) are approximated with finite differences [5, 6, and 9]. Let us consider a uniform grid in space-time (t, x, y, z), then the grid consists of the points (tn , xi , yj , zk) = (nΔt, iΔx, jΔy, kΔz).

$\Phi_{i,j,k}^n$ We denote with the value of the function Φ at the grid point (tn , xi , yj , zk). Time derivatives are discretized with first order forward differences, the parabolic term with central differences and the advective term with upwind schemes, where the direction of the one-sided difference used in a point depends on the direction of the velocity field $-\nabla g$ in the same point.

4.3. Modification to the Algorithm for Cells Segmentation

In this section, we briefly introduce the segmentation algorithm based on the Subjective Surfaces technique. It allows the extraction of all the membranes and nuclei in the acquired volumes, processing the two channels separately. The focus point for the segmentation of hundreds of cells is to achieve a fully automated procedure; therefore the algorithm has been implemented to completely avoid the user intervention.

Every object is segmented separately from the others, limiting the computation to subvolumes containing only one cell. A different function Φ0 is defined for every cell, starting from a reference point automatically detected and located roughly in the center of the object. The hypersurface evolves under the flow equation (1) and, at the end of every partial computation, all the segmented surfaces are collected in a single total result.

Membranes segmentation requires an additional pre-processing: membranes images are corrupted by a weak nuclei signal, more intense during mitosis, which has to be removed because it can cause a wrong interpretation of the edges. This is due to overlapping between nuclei and membranes emission range during acquisition. A preliminary thresholding of nuclei images separates the nuclei signal from the background, then the interfering signal is removed from membranes images.

The algorithm has been implemented using the programming language C++ and libraries ITK [10] and VTK [11]. The final version has been integrated in a framework de- signed for managing series of 3-D biological images [12].

4.4. Edge Detection

The analyzed images (membranes versus nuclei) behave in a completely different way in terms of edge detection: The thickness of membranes signal is of about 3 or 4 voxels, whereas nuclei are solid objects. These specific features require using different functions for the detection of edges position in nuclei and membranes images.

In nuclei images, the contours to be segmented are located in the regions where image gradient is higher and the minima of (1) denote the position of the edges (Fig. 2(a)). On the contrary, the function (1) can't be applied on membranes images because it reveals a double contour, on the internal and the external side of the cell. An alternative edge indicator has been defined using the image itself (not its gradient) as contours detector. We can use the intensity information to locate the position of the edges, because the membranes images contain high intensity regions, where the labeled membrane structure has been acquired, versus low intensity background regions. The edge indicator we used is:

$$g(x,y,z) = \left(\frac{1}{1+(|G_\sigma(x,y,z)*I(x,y,z)|/\beta)^2}\right) \quad (2)$$

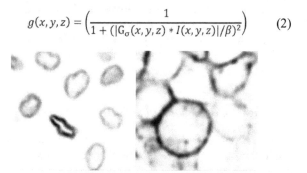

Fig 2. *Images of the edge indicators: membranes (a) and nuclei (b).*

As we expected, its minima locate the contours in the middle of the membranes thickness (Fig. 2(b)).

4.5. Cells Recognition and Location

A typical image contains a large number of cells, therefore the segmentation approach has to require minimal user

intervention. It means that the interactive step of the Subjective Surfaces technique, that is the choice of the reference point inside the object to segment, should be automated. This goal is achieved with the generalized 3-D Hough Transform [13] that allows detecting specific shapes in the image. Approximating the nucleus as a spherical object, the Hough Transform is able to recognize every nucleus, returning its center [14]. This point, which is roughly the cell center in early embryonic cells, is the initial condition for the segmentation of nucleus and membrane belonging to the same cell.

5. Results and Discussion

We obtained good results assigning different weighting factors to the curvature and the advective motions, respectively first and second term on the right side of equation (1). The same expression of Si can be employed both for nuclei and membranes segmentation. We used the initial function $\Phi 0 = \alpha/D$, instead of $\Phi 0 = -\alpha D$, to have an higher contrast in the processed image. After segmentation, the intensity distribution of the function Φ is typically associated to a bimodal histogram with a values range between 0 and 255, because of a linear rescaling. The higher intensity peak (near to 255) corresponds to the segmented object, the lower one to the background. Therefore, the segmented surfaces can be extracted as the iso surfaces corresponding to the intermediate value 128.

Fig. 3 shows the effect of boundary completion on membranes images: the missing contour, underlined by the red circle, is completed by a straight line. The algorithm shows the same behaviour for dividing membranes during telophase (Fig. 4), where there are two different nuclei inside the same cell and the membrane presents a constriction along the division plane. In this case, the algorithm segments two cells, because the Hough Transform detects two centers, and their contours are completed by straight lines.

The eye inspection of the resulting surfaces reveals some problems in the segmentation of the epithelial cells membranes. These cells surrounding the embryo are very flat.

This feature impairs membrane completion by the Subjective Surfaces 3-D technique, because the small extension in depth stops the evaluative process.

Before undergoing division, cells become spherical, whereas nuclei staining elongates as the chromosomes arrange in the future cell division plane (Fig. 5). It should be noted that the nucleus size is underestimated in the last two parts.

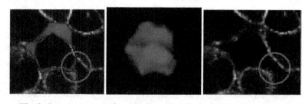

Fig 3. *Segmentation of a membrane with an uncomplete contour.*

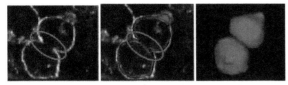

Fig 4. Segmentation of a dividing cell.

Fig 5. Segmentation of a dividing cell.

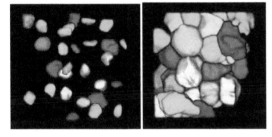

Fig 6. Segmentation of an entire subvolume.

This is due to the parabolic regularization term in the motion equation (1), which prevents the segmented surface to reach the contour if it is concave and with high curvature. However, the nuclei of not dividing cells are correctly segmented, as confirmed by visual inspection. Finally, in Fig. 6 we show the segmentation of two subvolumes of nuclei and membranes.

Visual inspection of the results has shown the ability of the algorithm to complete the missing contours, especially in membranes images, and to correctly reproduce the objects shape. The precision seems to decrease for elongated and flat shapes (epithelial cells and dividing nuclei).

The algorithm can be improved by integrating the segmentation of membranes and nuclei in the same process. An ad hoc method can be designed for the segmentation of the epithelial cells that have to be localized, prior segmentation, using a discriminating factor. Our segmentation procedure will now be tested on larger image data sets encompassing ten times of cells for a period of time at least twice as long. This should bring us close to an automated segmentation procedure for the whole zebrafish early embryogenesis.

References

[1]   A. Sarti, C. O. de Solo´rzano, S. Lockett and R. Malladi, "A Geometric Model for 3-D Confocal Image Analysis", *IEEE Transactions on Biomedical Engineering*, vol. 47, pp. 1600-1609, 2000.

[2]   S. Megason and S. Fraser,"Digitizing life at the level of the cell: high-performance laser-scanning microscopy and image analysis for in toto imaging of development," *Mech. Dev*, vol. 120, pp. 1407-1420, 2003.

[3]   C. B. Kimmel, W. W. Ballard, S. R. Kimmel, B. Ullmann, and Th. F. Schilling, "Stages of embryonic development of the zebrafish," *Dev. Dyn.*, vol. 203 , pp. 253-310, 1995.

[4]   B. Rizzi., "3D Zebra Fish Embryo Images Filtering by Nonlinear Partial Differential Equations," *29th Annual International Conference of the IEEE Engineering in Medicine and Biology Society.*

[5]   A. Sarti, R. Malladi, and J. A. Sethian, "Subjective Surfaces: A Method for Completing Missing Boundaries," *Proceedings of the National Academy of Sciences of the United States of America*, vol. 12, pp.6258-6263, 2000.

[6]   A. Sarti, R. Malladi, and J. A. Sethian,"Subjective Surfaces: A Geometric Model for Boundary Completion," *International Journal of Computer Vision*, vol. 46, pp. 201-221, 2002.

[7]   P. Perona and J. Malik,"Scale-space and edge detection using anisotropic diffusion," *IEEE Trans. Pattern Anal. Mach. Intell.*, vol. 12, pp. 629-639, 1990.

[8]   V. Caselles, R. Kimmel, and G. Sapiro, "Geodesic Active Contours," *International Journal of Computer Vision*, vol. 22, pp. 61-79, 1997.

[9]   S. Osher and J. A. Sethian,"Front propagating with curvature dependent speed: Algorithms based on Hamilton Jacobi formulation," *Journal of Computational Physics*, vol. 79, pp. 1249, 1988.

[10] L. Ibánez, W. Schroeder, L. Ng, and B. J. Cates, *The ITK Software Guide*, 2nd ed, 2005.

[11] W. Schroeder, K. Martin, and B. Lorensen, *The Visualization Toolkit: An Object-Oriented Approach To 3D Graphics*, 2nd ed., Prentice Hall, 1997.

[12] M. Campana., "A Framework for 4D-Biomedical Image Process- ing, Visualization and Analysis," *29th Annual International Confer- ence of the IEEE Engineering in Medicine and Biology Society.*

[13] J. D. Ballard,"Generalizing the Hough Transform to Detect Arbitrary Shapes," *Pattern Recognition*, vol. 13, pp. 111-122, 1981.

[14] C. Melani.,"Tracking cells in a live zebrafish embryo," 29th Annual International Conference of the IEEE Engineering in Medicine and Biology Society.

13

Malware detection using data mining techniques

Sara Najari, Iman Lotfi

Computer Department, Payam Noor University, Tehran, Iran

Email address:

Najari.sara@yahoo.com (S. Najari), Lotfi_iman@yahoo.com(I. Lotfi)

Abstract: Nowadays, malicious software attacks and threats against data and information security has become a complex process. The variety and number of these attacks and threats has resulted in providing various type of defending ways against them, but unfortunately current detection technologies are ineffective to cope with new techniques of malware designers which use them to escape from anti-malwares. In current research, we present a combination of static and dynamic methods to accelerate and improve malware detection process and to enable malware detection systems to detect malware with high precision, in less time and help network security experts to react well since time detection of security threats has a high importance in dealing with attacks.

Keywords: Malware, Malware Detection, Escape Techniques, Data Mining

1. Introduction

The Continues growth of malwares, has resulted in creating enormous threats in information and security points so that cyber defense centers have high importance in many countries. Like country boundaries which could be attacked from different aspects such as contraband and thieves, virtual space also suffer from these attacks [1].

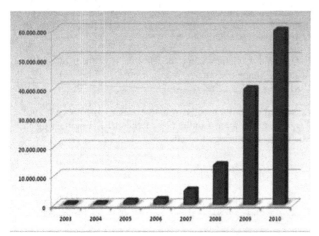

Figure 1. Ncreased volume of malware from 2003 to 2010.

Experiences have shown that most of these attacks are from malwares. On time detection of virtual space security attacks has a significant importance in protecting resources. In order to detect such malwares, before the advent of malicious effects, we should employ methods for detecting good and bad software behaviors to be able to detect which software is problematic and which ones are not. For this means, we should investigate both type of software in order to not face with a problem in detection process [2].

Figure 1 indicates increased volume of malware from 2003 to 2010 which has reported by Panda laboratory and it is predicted that this increasing trend of attack would continue in the next few years with a much faster speed so that the mean number of new threats per day exceeds from 55000 attacks per day. These attack are usually done to computer networks of sensitive agencies such as security entities, banks, economic centers, information storage centers, computer networks and etc.

2. Malware Definition and Analysis

Computer applications which have a destructive content and apply to system from invader, are called malware and the systems which apply on it is called victim system [3]. The malware word is assigned to virus, worm, Trojan and any other program which is created for distractive goals and abusing of users' privacy.

But what is the difference between a virus and a worm? What is the difference between these two and Trojan? Do antivirus programs apply against worms and Trojans or only against the viruses? All of these questions originate from one source and it's the complex and complicated world of destructive codes [1].

Enormous numbers of available destructive codes have made their classification difficult. Generally, malwares are classified into several kind based on behavior, attack method: For example, some kind of malware classification is as follow: virus, worm, spyware, rootkit, each one has a special behavior which are described below:

2.1. Virus

A code which includes itself to other programs such as operating systems and needs to run within the host program [4].

2.2. Worm

Malwares which transform themselves from one system to other using self-publishing in a network which include some connected computers. Generally, viruses try to publish themselves via a program, while worms unlike viruses put themselves only in one computer, and try to pollute a computer network [1].

2.3. Trojan Horse

A type of malware that appears in the form of pieces of software code and are intended for useful purposes. It runs up desired functions for users but hiddenly runs a series of actions beside it. It even can destroy the integration of a system [3].

2.4. Logic Bomb

A Logic bomb does not publish itself, but is installed on a system and waits until an external event such as data input, reaches to a special date, creating, deleting or even modify a special file leading to damaging the system [2].

2.5. Backdoors

Backdoor is a kind of software which enters the computer system without authorization and achieves its goals without normal entering to system [1].

2.6. Spy

A term for a collection of software that collects user personal information such as most visited pages, email addresses, keys pressed by the user [5].

2.7. Rootkit

Rootkit is a malware that has the ability to hide itself and its activities on the target system. Owner of rootkit is capable to run file and settings on the victim system without the owner of system being aware of it. It usually attaches itself to original files of operating system core and run with it.

Rootkits try targeting original structures and programs of the operating system and the integrity of their contents in order to change performance trend and the result of their running. Rootkits can hide themselves from users through the

following methods:

a) Rootkit integrate its codes with operating system codes which are at low-levels and accordingly can access all system requests such as reading files, running processes and etc.

b) Rootkit transfers its malicious codes into healthy processes and by doing so, it can use the memory that and do its malicious programs [6].

The base of traditional and usual methods to detect malware is using signature in which part of malware code is hold as the signature in the database and malware detection is carried out using signatures available in the database. Due to the failure of old methods in detecting new and unrecognized malwares or polymorphic malwares in recent years, researchers have tried to present more reliable methods for malware detection using unchanging characteristics of the malwares [6].

Nowadays, signature for antiviruses is a tool which is created manually. Before writing a signature, the analyst should identify how to deal with the unknown sample as a threat for users.

The process of searching malware is called analyzing. The more analysis tool and techniques, the more attackers try in using hidden making techniques and generating dynamic hidden codes from user's perspective. Analysts use two type of analysis to detect malware: static analysis and Dynamic analysis.

2.8. Static Analysis

Software analysis without execution, is called static analysis which without running the program, investigates the code and can detect malicious code and put it in one of the available groups based on different learning methods [7].

Since such methods deal with real codes, they can be used in the conditions in which there are polymorphic malwares. One of the problems of static analysis is that source code of the program isn't usually available which this reduces using of static analysis techniques that results in analyzing their binary codes which in turn is very complicated.

In the static method, binary codes are checked and viruses are detected based on binary codes. In fact this is the key part of static method. It is worth mentioning that extracting binary codes is a relatively complex work [5].

3. Dynamic Analysis

To overcome these shortcomings, several dynamic detection methods have been proposed. Unlike the static method which relies on malware binary codes, there is a completely different method without using the codes but according to the runtime behavior [3].

Although promising, but unfortunately this method is too slow as real time detectors on the end host and often need virtual machine technology [1]. In fact, program analyzing, while it is running, is called dynamic analysis which also referred to as behaviors analyzing and include software running and watching its behavior, system interaction and its effects on host system [6]. Dynamic analysis method need to run polluted files in a virtual environment like a virtual machine, a simulator, sand box, etc to analyze it in virtual environment [2].

To analyze programs by dynamic methods, different techniques have been applied.

So far which the most common method and techniques include [8]:

- Checking recalled functions.
- Following the flow of information.
- Following the order of running functions.

4. Malware Detection Techniques

There are different methods to detect malwares but considering that malware have become more complicated using hidden techniques; we need more advanced methods to detect them.

Generally, common malware detection techniques are divided into two categories:

- Detection methods based on signature
- Detection methods based on behavior

4.1. Signature- Based Detection

The main goal of this method is to extract the unique bytes sequence of codes as the signature. Searching for a signature in the suspicious files is a part of the task [8].

Most of today's commercial anti-malwares use a set of signatures to detect malicious programs which these suspicious codes are compared with a unique sequence of structures of programs or bytes [7].

If the signature is not available in the dataset, it means that the file is begin other than malicious [9].

The main problem of such approaches is that the anti-malwares experts should wait until new malware harm several computers, order to define a signature for it [8].

Usage of polymorphic model in cryptography has led to neutralize the signature based method which makes these polymorphic malwares undetectable through this method.

In order to overcome these problems, the behavior based method is used.

4.2. Behavior-Based Detection

Behavioral parameters include many factors such as source or destination of malware, kinds of attachments and other statistical properties [8]. Dynamic behaviors are directly used in evaluating the damage to the system and also help us to detect and classify new malwares. Malware clustering based on dynamic analysis is based on running the malware in a real controlled environment [7].

4.3. Comparison between Detection Methods

Given the polymorphism and transformation techniques which currently are used by malware designers, the signature based methods are inherently prone to errors [9].

Signature based methods are unable to detect more complex malwares and can hardly detect malwares which use polymorphism and transformation methods. In addition, one of the limitations of signature-based detection methods is that they require human knowledge to update the signature database by new signatures [8].

Furthermore, a number of research studies have shown that some of polymorphic software's writers can easily defeat signature based method by obfuscation methods [9].

Given the mentioned problems, it is better to use analysis method at runtime. However, the behavior based methods also have a major problem since this method is to slow as the real-time detectors on the final host and they often need virtual machine technologies.

5. Methods used for Escaping from Anti Malwares

Since signature-based antivirus systems try to find viral codes by searching for a character sequence string in the executive file, virus programmers apply various techniques to hide malwares and such sequences some of which are described below.

5.1. Cryptography

Virus code encryption by different encryption key would result in creating different texts.

As a result, it could be ensured that signature based scanners can't detect this virus. To run the virus, these texts should initially be decoded.

Detailed analysis of decoding algorithm is only possible if we know these keys [10].

5.2. Polymorphic Generator

Malwares use a polymorphic generator to change codes while the original algorithm remains intact. However, we should know that, at the end, all samples generated from a malware do the same work.

This is performed by combining many commands that have no impact on the execution mode and its effects. For example, each copy of the virus may be neutral group of commands such as increasing and then decreasing over the same operand or left ship and then right shift or push a value and pop it again.

All these methods will effectively hide virus codes from the signature based anti viruses [10].

5.3. Obfuscation

In malwares there are different evasion approaches to evade the malcodes from external anti malware scanners such as Code obfuscation, decrypting encryption and etc.

In code obfuscation the main goal is to hide the underlying logic of the program so as to prevent the others from having any related knowledge of the code[8].

The malicious code remains incomprehensible and all its harmful functionality whenever activated. When we apply some obfuscation transformations to a code, then it results in a kind of self-decrypting encryption.

But Packing refers to encrypt or compress the executable file. In Packing, original code remains hidden till the runtime or the unpacking process of executable codes which results in the immunity of code for static analysis [7].

Packed malware codes can be treated as subset of obfuscated codes which are compressed and cannot be analyzed so, consequently unpacking phase is necessary to reveal the overall semantic of the code [9].

6. Problem Definition

One the most important and most serious problems which the internet world is faced with is the existence of malwares like.

According to studies conducted in this field, we have concluded that 80 percent of damages to systems have been from malwares and only 20 percent of it has been from other factors [9].

However, unfortunately, most of the works has been on the 20% and the malwares have received less attention and thus we're facing many security problems every day [5].

In the early days of virus emergence, there were only static and simple viruses in the world [3].

Therefore, simple signature based methods were able to overcome them. But these methods were only useful as long as there weren't so many variations in the types of malwares and malwares writers didn't use obfuscation techniques to sophisticate them [5].

However, rapid developments in malwares activities convinced researchers to explore new methods, so that after some time, researchers were forced to use data-mining methods to detect malwares by employing data mining, they could add a lot of malware to anti-malware and hence they didn't have to investigate all malwares, because checking all of them require enormous time and cost [2].

One of such works was a method called n-grams. At that time, Geraldn et al. [3] developed n-grams analysis method to detect boot sector viruses using neural networks.

The base of n-grams detection method was the occurrence frequencies in the benign and malicious programs [3].

After that, Hofmeyr [10] used a simple sequence of system calls as a guide to evaluate malicious codes. This API CALLs sequence showed the hidden dependencies between code sequences.

Thereafter, Shultz, al. [7] tried to use the name of DLLs as a useful feature in the file categorization. However, in the recent work by Ye [7], a system (IMDS) was generated in which the system calls pattern has been used. Then data mining process has been applied on these patterns. The study includes 12214 healthy files and 17366 malicious files which they have only used 200 files to test the system [7].

Although the accuracy and learning rate of this method is relatively good, but there is a fundamental problem that is Unbalancing of the test data versus the balancing of learning data.

What we do in this study consists of a very large data set which involve various types of bengin and malicious softwares which generally, the number of extracted calls is about 5000 different features of 420 different files from 890 libraries which includes different types of malwares such as Trojan, Backdoor, Worm, Exploit, Flooder, Sniffer, Spoofer and viruses.

7. Research Methodology

This research has been performed by some basic steps:
- data collection
- data processing
- analysis of results

In the following, we will discuss each of these steps.

7.1. Data Collection

In order to collect data related to malwares. We examine the Anubis database [11].

Each sample of this set provides us its executive's code. These codes are used to learn the proposed model. In order to evaluate and test, a set of 3131 collected malware were tested which more than 90% of them include rootkits.

We selected this malwares set because in this study, our goal is detection rates of malwares especially rootkits.

7.2. Data Processing and Preparation

In this section, we deal with data processing using 3 reverse engineering tools namely: HDasm [12], Ida pro [13] and W32dsm89 [14] as well as Peid anti-packing tool [15].

First we process the Peid tool (which is the malware executive file) but with the understanding that the file has been packed by Packing tool. Otherwise, there is no need to apply this tool on it.

In fact by unpacking task, the packing task will be removed if it has been applied on it because otherwise, the file isn't executable by reverse engineering tool and thus we can't see the called system functions in it.

Afterwards, we give the file as input to three above-mentioned disassembler and they get the assembly code of these fields and return the called system functions list from these assembly codes. Then we save the list as an Xml file. Later, we apply our algorithm on this stored file to detect whether it is a malware or not and finally we obtain our success rate in detecting malwares using Weka data-minig tool.

7.3. Analysis of Results

Malwares of the same category usually have the samegeneral patterns, for example a number of system functions names are common in all members of this family.

We aim to analyze and detect malwares by examining the shared pattern using machine learning techniques among malwares.

In fact, we want to use so called Api calls in malware to overcome the limitations of traditional signature based methods and to cope with techniques used by malwares writers as well as to increase malware detection rate.

This method, which is based on called system functions in malware executive code, uses reverse engineering tool and monitoring tool for static and dynamic analysis, respectively. This means, that we obtain their assembly code by disassembling them and then extract called system function in it and obtain the API CALLs list of malware executive file by monitoring the file using monitoring tool.

Finally, with respect to the shared sequence of maleware which is common among them and could be used to detect and identify them as the signature, we deal with the detection of malwares.

The advantages of this method include its high success rate in malwares detection because it is directly in contact with malware binary codes and also there is no need to run them and we can understand whether it is a malware or not only using their code and obtaining the shared sequence of called system functions.

Furthermore, we apply the prepared algorithm on the log file of each file to obtain our database.

After that, we transform the information of this database to a data mining tool (here we used Weka tool) to obtain the success rate of detection task. Figure 2 shows a graph of data mining operation results using Weka tool on database. As shown above, the success rate of this method in rootkit detection is over than 97% which is a remarkable rate.

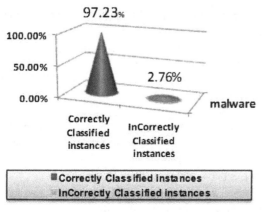

Figure 2. Success rate of our method in rootkit detection.

8. Discussion and Conclusion

Malwares are becoming widespread and more complex every day. As examples of their complexity, we can note the need of using polymorphism techniques, transformation and encryption, The traditional methods such as matching some code string of malwares signatures do not have enough efficiency.

However, there are also some problems in dynamic methods which their slowness is the most important one.

This is why we need a more intelligent detection method.

This type of detection (which is based on static method) is based on called system functions in each executive code of the malware and its goal is to detect versions of malware which haven't seen yet or are a new version of old malware families.

References

[1]   Ravi, C & Manoharan, R. Malware Detection using Windows Api Sequence and Machine Learning. International Journal of Computer Application, Vol.43, No.17, 2012.

[2]   Ravi, C & Chetia, G. Malware Threats And Mitigation Strategies: A Survey, Journal of Theoretical and Applied Information Technology, Vol. 29, No. 2, pp. 69-73, 2011.

[3]   Egele, M. S, A Survey on Automated Dynamic Malware-Analysis. ACM Computing Surveys, Vol. 44, No. 2, 2012.

[4]   Herath, H. M. P. S., & Wijayanayake, W. M. J. I. Computer Misuse in the Workplace. Journal of Business Continuity & Emergency Planning, Vol.3, No.3, P.P 259–270, 2009.

[5]   Mathur, K., and Saroj H. A Survey on Techniques in Detection and Analyzing Malware Executables. International Journal of Advanced Research in Computer Science and Software Engineering, Vol. 44, No. 2, 2012.

[6]   Doherty, N. F., Anastasakis, L., & Fulford, H, The Information Security Policy Unpacked: A Critical Study of the Content of University Policies. International Journal of Information Management, Vol.29, No.6, pp. 449–457, 2009.

[7]   G. Tahan, L.R.Y. Automatic Malware Detection Using Common Segment Analysis and Meta-Features. Journal of Machine Learning Research, 131, pp. 949-979, 2012.

[8]   I. Gurrutxaga , Evaluation of Malware clustering based on its dynamic behaviour. Seventh Australasian Data Mining conference, Australia, pp. 163–170, 2008.

[9]   Rieck. K, Willems.T, D¨ussel. P and Laskov. p, Learning and classification of malware behavior, 5th international conference on Detection of Intrusions and Malware, and Vulnerability Assessment. Berlin, Heidelberg: Springer-Verlag, pp. 108–125, 2008.

[10] Patel, S. C., Graham, J. H., & Ralston, P. A, Qualitatively Assessing the Vulnerability of Critical Information Systems: A New Method for Evaluating Security Eenhancements. International Journal of Information Management, Vol.28, pp. 483–491, 2008.

[11] http:// www.anubis.org

[12] http://hdasm.software.informer.com

[13] www.hex-rays.com

[14] processchecker.com/file/W32dsm89.exe.html

[15] https://boveda.banamex.com.mx/englishdir/ayudas/masinfoahnlab.htm

Measuring the qualitative feature of combined services

Aalia Hemmati, Sima Emadi

Computer Engineering department, Islamic Azad university of Meybod, Yazd, Iran

Email address:

Aaliahemmati64@gmail.com(A. Hemmati), au_emadi@yahoo.com (S. Emadi)

Abstract: The combination of web services is the result of complex and increasing needs of the users and disability of single web services in resolving the user's needs. One of the important challenges in the field of web 2.0 is the combination of web services based on their qualitative features. Since it is probable that there would be several different combinations of services for achieving a specific goal, choosing the service is based on some qualitative features like combining, availability, acceptability, service cost and security. One of the important issues is the quantitative survey of combining rate of the two services shared on the combination so that they have the ability to combine with each other, correctly. In order to measure the combining ability of services, in the first stage, the more number of effective factors on combining features of services are surveyed in comparison with the present methods. In the second stage, metric is introduced for the effective factors, and in the third stage, an appropriate weight for each factor is found and finally, based on their relationships with each other, a more accurate rate of combining is obtained.

Keywords: Web Service, Qualitative Feature of Service, Combining, Metric

1. Introduction

Service-oriented systems have special importance because of the possibility of working in heterogeneous distributed environments. The users of such systems use the web services that provide system components. In some cases, the needs of the users are not met with the single web service. However, each combination of services is not always the best possible solution and some criteria and features of the new combined service such as the quality of the new service can be a criterion for choosing the appropriate service. In fact, one of the important challenges in the field of web services is the combination of web services considering their quality. The need to combine web services is the result of complex and increasing requirements of users and disability of web services in responding to the goals of the users. Since it is likely that there would be several different combinations of services in achieving to a specific goal, choosing the service is based on some qualitative features like combining, availability, acceptability, service cost and security. One of the important issues that has been noted less is the accuracy quantitative survey of combination rate of the two services shared on the combined platform.

This feature brings the ability of a service for combining with other services in the runtime so that the combinations work out successfully. In fact, the rate of services' adaptation with each other for combination without facing problems in the runtime is a desired goal. After that the user applies for the required service, the component identifies the basic services with the combination of which it can get to the desired service and search for them inside the service store. Because of the diversity of different producers and services, it's likely that several candidate services be found for each desired request.

Considering the quality rate of combination that the candidate services have, the optimum service is selected. Combining two services that are combined in series is affected by some factors such as similarities of input and output, observing the preconditions, reusability, adaptability, loose coupling, etc. In [1], a framework is presented for choosing the service in terms of qualitative features in which the combination rate of services is focused. In [9], the combining feature is surveyed absolutely, in the way that the two services are combining with each other or not.

In this article, by surveying the available weaknesses in the presented method in [9], by surveying the more number of effective factors and the importance level of them and presenting a metric for each, a more accurate rate would be obtained for the combining feature. Some existing methods have more focused on similarities of services' input and output for surveying the combining rate of the two services and in cases that the other effective factors on combining is surveyed, no metric has been presented for its measuring. This article has evaluated various number of effective factors on combining feature such as the reusability and adaptability in comparison with other methods and finally a more accurate rate of combining has been obtained for each service. The structure of the article is in this way that in the second section, the effective factors on combining feature of services would be surveyed and metrics would be introduced for each. In the third section, based on the obtained values of the effective factors, the combining rate would be measured. In the fourth section, conclusion and future activities would be discussed.

2. Effective Factors on Combining Feature

In this study, web service is considered as a black box and there is access only to its interface. When the service is implemented as a web service, WSDL descriptions are the most common documents of service description. Since the available web services use WSDL, a semantic description in OWL-S language. OWL-S description of service comes in three part of service profile, service model and service support [9].

The service profile part includes input, output, name and service description and service support which includes transfer protocol and web service address are considered in our study. Also, it is supposed that services based on SOAP protocol communicate with each other [9].

Effective factors on combining are in two groups. One of them are the factors that are obtained from the communication between the desired candidate service with the previous existing service of the combination, like the surveying parameters of the similarity level of input and output parameters, effects and preconditions and the other are the factors surveyed on candidate atomic service. Table 1 shows the effective factors on combining with this condition that the importance level and the two qualitative parameters of reusability and adaptability are added, in order that a more accurate rate of combining is obtained. Furthermore, the effective factors on combining feature would be surveyed.

Table 1. Effective factors on combining, adopted from [9]

Effective Factors on Combining in Atomic Terms _ Importance level	Effective Factors on Combining in Combining Services' Aspect
Granularity	The similarity level of input- output
Reusability _ medium	The observing level of preconditions and effects
Adaptability_ high	The similarity level of input- output
Availability	The observing level of preconditions and effects
Well-defined interfaces_ high	The similarity level of input- output
Loosely-coupled _ medium	The observing level of preconditions and effects
Surveying the quality level of service	

2.1. Surveying the Similarity Level of Input and Output Parameters

When two services are combined with each other , the output of the first service is usually considered as the inputs of the second service. The input and output show the message interactions in services. Here, the two services have been showed as S_1 and S_2. The major purpose is surveying the similarity level of input and output parameters in the two services, considering that the m input s_2 corresponds with the n output s_1. Equation 1 has been defined for surveying the similarity level of input and output type in the two services [9]:

$$\lambda 1(S1,S2) = \sum_{i=1}^{n} \frac{P_i}{m} \qquad (1)$$

Equation 1: The similarity level of input- output parameters

$$p_i = \begin{cases} 1, \text{ifType}(\text{Output}(s1.i) = \text{Type}(\text{Input}(s2.i))) \\ \text{orType}(\text{Output}(s1.i)) \subset \text{Type}(\text{Input}(s2.i)) \\ \in, \text{Type}(\text{Input}(s2.i)) \subset \text{Type}(\text{Output}(s1.i)) \\ 0, \text{otherwise} \end{cases} \qquad (2)$$

Equation 2: input- output parameters
If 's_2' service input is exactly equal to s_1 service output or

's_1' service output is a subset of 's_2' service inputs, the amount 1 would be returned as result. But when 's_1' service outputs is a subset of s_2 service input, it is probable that some problems would be created in runtime for compatibility between two services.

2.2. Similarity Level of Preconditions and Effects

Preconditions show logical conditions that must be supplied before replying to the service. Effects are events that happen by the successful performance of a service. For example, "having more than 1000 dollar credits" is a precondition for the service of buying a book and "I'm the owner of a book" is the effect of performing this service.

According to relation 3, for measuring the effects and preconditions, suppose that k component is proposed as precondition in the second service that can be covered by the first service as its effects. According to Equation 4, the similarity level of preconditions and effects would be measured and also the number of all preconditions of the second service is equal to m [9].

$$Ki = \begin{cases} 1, if\ PC(S2) \cap ET(S1) \neq \emptyset \\ 0, otherwise \end{cases} \qquad (3)$$

Equation 3: preconditions and effects

$$\lambda 2(S1,S2) = \begin{cases} if PC(S_2) \neq \emptyset, & \sum_m^{i=1} Ki/m \\ if PC(S_2) = \emptyset, & 1 \end{cases} \quad (4)$$

Equation 4: Similarity level of preconditions and effects

2.3. Service Granularity

One of the measuring criteria of service granularity is service size and the other is the number of operations that service operates. The number of operations is shown by the word "operation" in WSDL file and "process" in OWLS file. The measuring criterion of this feature is stated as Equation 5 [5]:

$$\lambda_3(S_1,S_2) = 1/\text{number of "atomic process" in owls file} \quad (5)$$

Equation 5: Service granularity

In [5], a metric is presented for computing granularity rate which measures the level in which a service is independent of other services. Equation 6 measures this metric.

$$\lambda_3(S_1,S_2) = 1 - (\text{Num}_{\text{SRVOpWithDependency}}/\text{Num}_{\text{TotalSRVQp}}) \quad (6)$$

Equation 6: Service granularity

That in relation 6, $\text{Num}_{\text{SRVOpWithDependency}}$ is the number of operations dependent to other services and $\text{Num}_{\text{TotalSRVOp}}$ is the whole number of service operations and their amount interval is between 0 to 1.

2.4. Availability

This feature measures the availability rate of a service when the user applies for it. The reason why we use this feature is that the service availability is the first condition of a successful performance of a service. So, if only one service of the combination is not available, the whole combination would be considered unavailable [2].

Availability is defined as a level of a system or its component's being operational and available exactly when the user needs it. Services' availability is a concern for the success of service-oriented architecture from the aspect of both the user and the producer. In user's viewpoint, availability means that a service set becomes available for doing the functional needs of a system. Now, if one of these services become unavailable (even temporarily), it is because of the disorder success of service-oriented systems. From the service producer's aspect, the services must be available when needed, otherwise, the producer's capital and popularity would be affected. (Especially when the service is unavailable, he must pay the damages). This metric is computed by the Equation 7 [2]:

$$\lambda_4(S_1,S_2) = \text{WSOT}/(\text{WSOT}+\text{WSRT}) \quad (7)$$

Equation 7: Availability

Where WSOT is the time of service availability and WSRT is the time of repairing the system. We can also obtain the availability from the treaty file of the service level. Since in the existing format, no independent place is forecasted for index and definition of all variables, it's necessary that all the variables be defined immediately after its proposal in the article.

2.5. Loosely-Coupled Factor

The word coupling is a part of the information technology's dictionary. Whatever that communicates, has the coupling and whatever that has the coupling can be dependent to each other [8]. One of the common methods of defining the coupling is comparing it to the dependence. The level of coupling between two things is equal to the dependence level that exists between the two. For example, the relationship between a software program with others shows its coupling level or the relationship between the technical contract of the program with the logic of the solution it shows, measures the coupling level [11].

Whatever the coupling between the services be looser, the rate of service intelligibility, reusability and flexibility increases. With increase in service's reusability, the capability of service' combining increases either.

Assume that the metric ISCI be the number of services that are called by the desired service and let SOCI be the number of operations that are called by the service [4], Equation 8 is used for computing the loose coupling:

$$\text{Loose coupling} = \text{ISCI} + \text{SICI} \quad (8)$$

Equation 8: loosely-coupled

In [8], loose coupling has been defined as a concept that is related to scalability, flexibility and fault tolerance and has stated different types for loose coupling. One of these types is the dependence of data model or the data types in which the services that use the complex data types have the strong coupling and the services that use the simple data types have a loose coupling. In this research, the number of complex data types that have been introduced in interfaces, have a reverse relation with loose coupling. The rate of loose coupling is computed according to Equation 9:

$$\lambda_5(S_1,S_2) = 1/(\alpha_x \text{ Number of Complex data types} + \beta_x \text{ Number of service calls}) \quad (9)$$

Equation 9: loosely-coupled

β, α are the factors the amounts of which are obtained experimentally.

2.6. Reusability

In Equation 10, a formula is presented for reusability according to the rate of qualitative parameters of modularity, the rate of adaptability and universality in profession, ability to detect and alignment with standard SC [5]:

$$\lambda_4(S_1) = \text{BCM}*(\text{MD}*W_{\text{MD}}+\text{AD}*W_{\text{AD}}+\text{SC}*W_{\text{SC}}+\text{DC}*W_{\text{DC}}) \quad (10)$$

Equation 10: Reusability

Metric W is a weight that gives an assessor to each metric and the total weights is equal to 1. Whatever the amount of the weight be more, it shows that the reusability is higher.

In Equation 11, a formula is presented for the reusability feature according to qualitative criteria of loose coupling and the rate and parameters of granularity [6]:

$$\lambda_6(S_1, S_2) = -0.5 * Coupling + 0.61 * Service\ Granularity + 0.61 * Parameter\ Granularity \quad (11)$$

Equation 11: Reusability

In relation 11, parameters of loose coupling and the rate of granularity and the number of granularity parameters are measured based on the number of used messages, the number of simultaneous and asynchronous operations.

2.7. Adaptability

In [5], the adaptability of a service is measured by the internal adaptability. The internal adaptability would be measured if the internal variable of service can be adapted to the user's needs well. Assume 'n' be the number of change points in a service. For each change point, it's probable that the difference the service user expects be provided or not. If the default amount of a change point meet the expectations of the user, it is considered as a present change point. As it goes on, Equation 12 computes the adaptability of this case that how many change point can be adapted as the needs of the users:

$$\lambda_7(S_1, S_2) = Num_{Consumers\ Satisfied\ Variants}/ Num_{TotalApplicableConsumer} \quad (12)$$

Equation 12: Adaptability

The numerator is the number of the users that the default change points meet their needs and the denominator is the number of all the users that are dependent to change points. The computed amount is in intervals of 0 and 1 and whatever the amount is more, the adaptability is higher as well.

2.8. Well-Defined Interfaces

When the service is implemented, it has the documents of service description. The service can have a document in addition to the mentioned documents that is readable by human, like the treaty file of service that includes the additional descriptions about the qualitative capabilities, limitations and behavior of the service. Although the service contract is well-defined, it makes the user have a more accurate and convenient perception of the service and as a result, using the service will be easier. Since the services would be at the disposal of the users as a black box component, the service contract is the only solution by which you can have an accurate perception of the service [9].

By well-defined interfaces, we mean the surveying of the fields such as conditions, effects, input, output, service categorizing and describing service performance in file WSDL in terms of being available completely. When the semantic web is used, the service interface is OWL-S that again the mentioned cases are proposed for the way of filling the semantic web field and the accuracy of them. The ontology profile determines the following feature for referring to IOPE: (hasParameter, hasInput, hasOutput, hasPrecondition , hasResult)

Naturally, whatever the service contract has a higher standard, using and working with the service is easier and the

success is higher in that combination. This metric is computed by Equation 13 [9]:

$$\lambda_8(S_1, S_2) = \sum_{i=0}^{4} Xi \quad x_i \in \{0, 0.2\} \quad (13)$$

Equation 13: Well-defined interfaces

$$xi = \begin{cases} 0.2, hasparameter \\ 0, no\ parameter \end{cases} \quad (14)$$

$$x_0 = input,\ x_1 = output,\ x_2 = precondition,\ x_3 = result,\ x_4 = category \quad (15)$$

Equation 15: Well-defined interfaces parameters

2.9. Surveying the Quality Level of the Service

Generally, service quality is of great importance. Service applicant states limitations such as replying time, cost and so on for service (As stating limitations for service efficiency). If the quality limitations are not observed, the service is not appropriate for performing. Quality features that are proposed by the applicant are usually determined as a range (by determining the minimum and maximum of the feature amount). In this level of the combining, we can survey that how much of the user's quality features are supplied by the candidate service [9]. This metric is computed by the Equation 16:

$$\lambda_9(S_1, S_2) = \left(\sum_{Qi \in neg} W_i \frac{Q_i^{max} - Q_i}{Q_i^{max} - Q_i^{min}} + \sum_{Qi \in pos} W_i \frac{Q_i - Q_i^{min}}{Q_i^{max} - Q_i^{min}} \right) \quad (16)$$

Equation 16: quality level of the service

In Equation 16, the amount of Q_i is equal to the measure of quality feature of I th that is presented by the service. Q_i^{max} is equal to maximum amount of quality feature of I that is presented by the user and Q_i^{min} the minimum amount of quality feature of I that is presented by the user.

3. Metric for Measuring the Combining Feature

This metric is presented for measuring the combining rate of the two continuous services that are combined with each other. The input of the issue is a workflow including some duties that are to be performed by the real services. These services are shown as S_1 S_2.

Assume that for the duty x_1 a real service called s_1 has been found. Now, the issue is that among the candidate services for the duty x_2, which real service is better to be selected. The choosing criterion is the service that would have a higher combining capability with the real service s_1. This metric is computed by Equation 18 [9]:

$$Composability(S_1) = \lambda(S_1) \quad (17)$$

Equation 17: Composability

$$\lambda(S1, S2) = \begin{cases} 0, if \ \prod_i \lambda_i(S_1) = 0 \\ \sum a_i \lambda_i(S_1), if \ \prod_i \lambda_i(S_1) \neq 0 \end{cases} \quad (18)$$

Equation 18: Composability

In which, I is the number of effective factors, i ={1...9}, ai is the weight allocated to each criteria (between 0 and 1).

Finally, the obtained amount for combining is divided into the number of effective factors in formula so that the obtained number be normal. λ_i (S1) shows the amount of each mentioned parameters for service combining. $\lambda(S1) \in [0,1]$ is the combining rate of the desired candidate service. In order to normalize the acquired amount for combining, $\lambda(S1)$ is divided into $\sum_{i=1}^{n} ai$.

And finally, from among the candidate services, the service is selected that the combining rate of it be more than the defined threshold for combining. The combining threshold is the minimum amount that a service must have in order to face no problem in runtime when combining with other services. In this research, the combining threshold has determined 0.6 in the normal situation.

4. Discussion, Conclusion and Future Work

In this article, by surveying the available weaknesses in Rokni method [9], the two effective factors of adaptability and reusability were added to the other effective factors on combining feature and a more accurate rate of combining was obtained. Each of these features is effective on combining feature with a weight. Here, the weight of all cases is the same and equal to 1. Finally, by computing the combining metric for a candidate service, you can obtain its rate of combining. While in Rokni method [9], without considering the effective factors of adaptability and reusability, the rate of combining is obtained. Also, in most similar tasks, the time is spent on surveying the only effective factor on combining and no metric is presented for them. In line with this research, it's possible that in future, the effective qualitative parameters of autonomy on the rate of combining be estimated and a metric be presented for it. A more accurate surveying of the allocated weights to each combining parameters is another task that can be surveyed in the future.

References

[1] Q. Yu, M. Rege, A. Bouguettaya,B. Medjahed, M. Quzzani , A Two-Phase Framework For Quality-Aware Web Service Selection, Service Oriented Computing and Applications Journal, Vol 4, No.2, pp. 63-79, 2010.

[2] S. Choi, S. Jin Sun and S. D. Kim, QoS Metrics for Evaluating Services from the Perspective of Service Providers, in IEEE International Conference, e-Business Engineering, ICEBE, pp. 622-625, 2007.

[3] J. Fang, S. Hu and Y. Han, A Service Interoperability Assessment Model for Service Composition, in Proceedings of the 2004 IEEE International Conference on Services Computing, IEEE Computer Society, pp. 153-158, 2004.

[4] R. Sindhgatta, B. Sengupta and K. Ponnalagu, Measuring the Quality of Service Oriented Design, in Proceedings of the 7th International Joint Conference on Service-Oriented Computing, Springer-Verlag: Stockholm, pp. 485-499, 2009.

[5] S. Choi and S. Kim, A Quality Model for Evaluating Reusability of services in SOA, 10th IEEE Conference on E-commerce Technology and the Fifth IEEE Conference on Enterprise Computing, E-Commerce and EServices,2008.

[6] B. Shim, S. Choue, S. Kim and S .Park, A Design Quality Model for Service Oriented Architecture, 15th Asia Pacific Software Engineering Conference, pp.403-410, 2008.

[7] G. Feuerlicht, Design of Composable Services, in Service-Oriented Computing, ICSOC Workshops, 2009.

[8] N.M. josuttis, SOA in practice the Art of distributed system design, oreilly: united states. pp. 35-46, 2007.

[9] Z. Rokni, " choosing the service in service-based architecture based on qualitative features" MA thesis, Shahid Beheshti university, 2011

[10] A. Kazemi, "logical phase application in selection, evaluation and combination of services in service-based architecture", MA seminar, Shahid Beheshti university, 2010.

[11] A. Rostam Pour, "surveying the methods of service evaluation in service-based architecture", MA thesis, Shahid Beheshti university, spring 2010.

.

15

An efficient approach toward increasing wireless sensor networks lifetime using novel clustering in fuzzy logic

Morteza Asghari Reykandeh[1, *], Ismaeil Asghari Reykandeh[2]

[1]Department of Computer Engineering, Islamic Azad University Khoy Branch, Khoy, Iran
[2]Department of Computer Engineering, Islamic Azad University Sari Branch, Sari, Iran

Email address:
Asghari_stu@yahoo.com (M. Asghari. R), ismaeil.asghari@gmail.com (I. Asghari. R)

Abstract: Wireless sensor network (WSN) is composed of a large number of sensor nodes that are connected to each other. In order to collect more efficient information, wireless sensor networks are classified into groups. Classification is an efficient way to increase the lifetime of wireless sensor networks. In this network, devices have limited power processing and memory. Due to limited resources in wireless sensor networks, increasing lifetime was always of attention. An efficient routing method is called clustering based routing that finds optimum cluster heads and finding the correct number of them in each cluster remains a challenge. In this paper, we propose a novel and efficient method for clustering using fuzzy logic with four appropriate inputs and combine it with the good features of Low-Energy Adaptive Clustering Hierarchy (LEACH). Simulation results show that our method is more efficient compared to other distributed algorithms, because the proposed method if fully distributed. The result show that compared to centralized, the speed is more and its energy consumption is less.

Keywords: Wireless Sensor Networks, Clustering, Cluster Head, Fuzzy Logic, Lifetime

1. Introduction

In the past years, increasing improvements in digital electronics, semi-conductors building technology, and wireless communication, have led to develop tools with small size, low price and high power with communicating, computing and tracking capabilities. Wireless Sensor Networks (WSN) consists of hundreds or even thousands of such sensor tools that use radio frequencies to perform its tracking task [1-6]. A WSN consists of a large number of sensor nodes and a Base Station (BS). These sensors collect data and send them to the BS via radio transmitter. They have limited power and computational capacity. WSNs can be used in many applications such as military, biomedical, and environmental applications.

There are various challenges in wireless sensor networks because of its special features. One of these challenges is the nodes limited power supply. In most cases the power supply is irreplaceable and non-rechargeable. So WSNs must use methods that reduce energy consumption of nodes [1, 2 and 3].

The data that are sensed by nodes should be transferred to a station for processing and decision making. This station is called base-station or sink.

If each node sends its data directly to the sink a lot of energy is consumed. Since the sensed values by the close nodes are a little different, there is a possibility of redundancy in the transmitted data.

As mentioned before, a lot of energy is consumed for sending data to the sink. As a result, cluster head nodes are faced with the challenge of fast reducing energy. As soon as the cluster head off a part or the entire network falls of work. To avoid this issue a method is to cluster head nodes equipped with replaceable and rechargeable energy source. Another way is continuously change cluster heads among the nodes within the network to decrease the distributed energy consumption in the network [5].

We use the second method in which the nodes are homogeneous. In the proposed method cluster head is selected first. Each node selects then the nearest cluster head to its own. Thus clusters are produced.

Our method is similar to Low-Energy Adaptive Clustering Hierarchy (LEACH) [2].

Two periods of time are repeated alternately until the end of the network: Stage of cluster formation and stage of stability.

In this structure, similar to LEACH, each node itself decides to be cluster head and makes other nodes aware of this issue. Selecting cluster heads in LEACH are stochastic. While in our, method a cluster head is selected based on several parameters and a fuzzy system.

Because LEACH selects cluster head only with stochastic and does not care to other parameters such as residual energy and location of nodes, it does not necessarily make the best clusters.

For example, a node may be cluster head that have little energy may be turned off or if an isolated node becomes cluster head, other nodes must spend a lot of energy for sending data to this cluster head. Nevertheless, LEACH provides well uniform distribution of cluster heads and has high performance.

We use a fuzzy system with appropriate inputs to overcome the weakness of LEACH. The inputs that we consider in the fuzzy system are: number of neighbors, centrality, energy remaining, frequencies of signals received from neighbors and the number of round that the node wasn't cluster head. These parameters are not so closely related and can easily work with these heterogeneous parameters by using fuzzy logic. Also a fuzzy system does not need much computational complexity, consequently it is suitable for WSN.

The rest of this paper is organized as follows. In the next section, we give an overview of related work and some shortcomings of stochastically selecting cluster-heads. In section 3 we give an overview of fuzzy logic. In section 4 we describe our proposed method. Simulation results are presented in section 5. Finally, section 6 concludes the paper.

2. Related Works

A typical WSN architecture is shown in Figure 1. The nodes send data to the respective cluster-heads, which in turn compresses the aggregated data and transmits it to the base station. For a WSN we make the following assumptions:

- The base station is located far from the sensor nodes and is immobile.
- All nodes in the network are homogeneous and energy constrained.
- Symmetric propagation channel.
- Base station performs the cluster-head election.
- Nodes have little or no mobility.

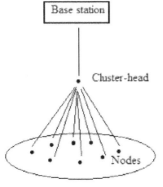

Figure 1. WSN Architecture.

One of the most popular cluster based routing protocol is Low Energy Adaptive Clustering Hierarchy protocol (LEACH) that is proposed in [4]. The operation of LEACH is divided into rounds and each round consists of setup phase and the steady state phase. In the setup phase, the clusters are organized and Cluster Heads (CHs) are selected. Each sensor n generates a random number between 0 and 1. If this number is less than T(n) defined by Equation 1, then sensor n would be selected as a cluster head.

$$T(n) = \begin{cases} \frac{p}{1-p\times(r \bmod \frac{1}{p})} & if\ n \in G \\ 0 & if\ n \notin G \end{cases} \qquad (1)$$

In this equation, 'p' is the desired percentage of CHs, 'r' specifies the current round and 'G' is the set of nodes which have not been selected as cluster head in the past 1/P rounds. Optimal number of cluster heads is estimated to be 5% of the total number of nodes. After cluster head election, the CHs broadcast an advertisement message and other nodes select the closest CHs based on the received signal strength. Although LEACH is able to increase the network lifetime, but it has two main weaknesses:

- It is possible that no or many of CHs are selected.
- It is possible that too many CHs are located in a specific area. This means that CHs are not selected in a distributed manner.

Gupta [6] used fuzzy logic to find cluster heads. In this algorithm three fuzzy variables is used for cluster head selection. Node's energy, node's concentration and node's centrality are these parameters. In this approach, the base station primarily collects the necessary information from all nodes and then selects a node as a cluster head according to the fuzzy rules. In this approach there is only one selected CH for each round, whereas more CHs are needed for balancing energy consumption and improving network lifetime.

In [7], Kim offers CHEF in which, the same as Gupta [6], the CHs are selected based on a fuzzy logic. The difference is that in this approach more than one cluster head is selected locally in each round. The fuzzy set includes nodes' energy and their local distances. CHEF also generates a random number for each sensor and if it is less than a predefined threshold, P_{opt}, then the node's chance is determined. Thus, there may be some qualified nodes that lose their chance on a random manner [7].

The method that is presented in [8] is a fuzzy approach to select cluster heads. This method is centralized and the network is aware of nodes coordinates. The decision for selecting a node as cluster head is done by the sink. This method is based on three variables, node energy remaining, node concentration and centrality which decides about being a node cluster head.

Heinzelman et, al. [9] introduced a method called LEACH-FL. The method uses a fuzzy system with three input battery level, node density and distance from the sink, for selecting cluster heads. This method is introduced with the assumption that the network coordinates is available.

Both of these two methods are centralized. Therefore they

are not suitable for the environments that required real-time processing. Also a lot of energy is spent for sending nodes situation such as energy remaining to the sink. These methods assumed that the network coordinates is available. For this issue, nodes need to be equipped with additional hardware such as Global Positioning System (GPS), which is not possible in all environments. Another issue is that we can use inputs for fuzzy system more efficient than inputs of these methods fuzzy systems [10].

Based on this discussion, we propose a distributed method where each node itself makes decision about being cluster head or not. This method works in all environments and therefore does not need the coordinates of nodes. This method by choosing suitable inputs for fuzzy system, is more efficient than the existence method and better clusters will be made.

3. Fuzzy Logic

Fuzzy logic (FL) is defined as the logic of human thought, which is much less rigid than the calculations computers generally perform. Fuzzy Logic offers several unique features that make it a particularly good alternative for many control problems. It is inherently robust since it does not require precise, noise-free inputs and can be programmed to fail safely [11, 12].

Fuzzy sets are described by the range of real values over which the set is mapped, called domain, and the membership function. A membership function assigns a truth (crisp) value between 0 and 1 to each point in the fuzzy set's domain. Depending upon the shape of the membership function, various types of fuzzy sets can be used such as triangular, beta, PI, Gaussian, sigmoid, etc. The trapezoidal and triangular membership functions suitable for real-time operation because they don't make complex computations and also have enough accuracy.

A Fuzzy system basically consists of three parts: fuzzification, inference engine, and defuzzification. Fig. 1 shows the fuzzy system components that we use in this paper. The fuzzifier maps each crisp input value to the corresponding fuzzy sets and thus assigns it a truth value or degree of membership for each fuzzy set. The fuzzified values are processed by the inference engine, which consists of a rule base and various methods for inferring the rules.

The rule base is simply a series of IF-THEN rules that relate the input fuzzy variables with the output fuzzy variables using linguistic variables, each of which is described by a fuzzy set, and fuzzy implication operators such as AND, OR, etc.

The defuzzifier performs defuzzification on the fuzzy solution space. It finds a single crisp output value from the solution fuzzy space. Some of common defuzzification techniques are: Center of Area (COA)[14], Center Of Gravity (COG)[15], Extended Center of Area (ECOA)[14], Mean of Maxima (MeOM)[16]. In this paper we use COA method for defuzzification which is one of the simplest and most widely used methods, The method is fast, because only simple oper tions are used in it, it gives continual change of defuzzification value, hence it is convenient to be used in fuzzy controllers. [17].

4. Proposed Method

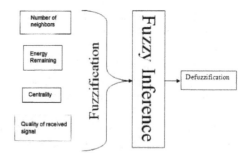

Figure 2. *Fuzzy system components*

Figure2 depicts the fuzzy system that is used by our method.

The fuzzy system inputs are crisp numbers converted to fuzzy values by membership functions. The nodes simply determine these input values. The nodes are aware of neighbor nodes and the distance to them, as soon as one sends and receiving data. We suppose here, the number of head clusters is 5 percent of total number of sensors in each round.

Parameters that have important role in selecting the head cluster and forming cluster are:

4.1. Number of Neighbors

If a node is in center of attention which means many signals pass through its order to reach a cluster head, then it is better that this node becomes cluster head.

$$Max\ number\ of\ neighbors = n - 1 \qquad (2)$$

4.2. Remaining Energy

A sensor that has maximum energy level; because the overhead of head cluster is more than other nodes.

$$E_{TX}(l,d) = \begin{cases} l * E_{elec}^{TX} + l * \varepsilon_{fs} * d^2, d < d_0 \\ l * E_{elec}^{TX} + l * \varepsilon_{mp} * d^4, d \geq d_0 \end{cases} \qquad (3)$$

$$E_{RX}(l) = l * E_{elec}^{RX}$$

4.3. Centrality

The closest sensor to gravity center of the cluster. Indeed, it is a node that average distance of other nodes in the cluster from it is minimum. Centrality of head cluster, leads to reducing energy consumption for communicating intra-cluster (between member nodes and head cluster).

4.4. Quality of Received Signals

This criterion is indeed based on which node receives more signal power; as many signals pass from this node, so it can be a good head cluster.

This operation is done easily by using of Received Signal Strength Indication (RSSI) technique [11].

Membership functions that convert crisp input values to fuzzy values are shown by fig. 3.

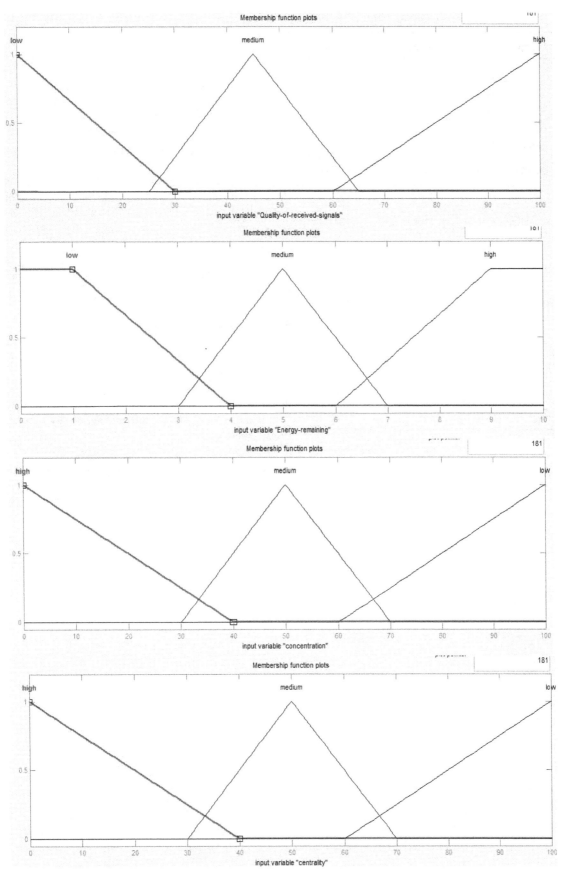

Figure 3. *Fuzzy set for fuzzy input variable Number of Neighbors ,Remaining Energy, Centrality and Quality of Received Signals*

In this stage (fuzzy inference) we use mamdani inference method to determine output from inputs [18]. Some rules that mamdani method employs are listed in Table 1.

Table 1. *Some of the existence rules.*

Concentration	Energy	Centrality	Quality Signal	Chance
low	low	low	low	worth
low	low	low	medium	v-low
low	low	high	high	low
low	medium	low	low	v-low
low	medium	high	high	medium
low	high	low	low	low
medium	medium	high	high	high
medium	high	low	low	medium
medium	high	high	high	v-high
high	low	low	low	medium
high	medium	medium	low	high
high	medium	medium	medium	high
high	medium	medium	high	v-high
high	medium	high	low	v-high
high	high	high	high	best

We need a membership function to convert the obtained output from fuzzy to crisp in the fuzzification stage. This function is shown in fig. 4.

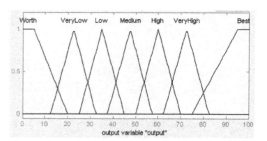

Figure 4. *Output membership function.*

In this paper, we use the Center of Area (COA) method to deffuzificate output. Threshold (α) in this measure is obtained from Equation 4.

$$\alpha = \frac{\int_z \mu A(x)z dz}{\int_z \mu A(z) dz} \qquad (4)$$

Where α is the non-fuzzy output for the fuzzy system (z) and μA(Z) is aggregated output membership function.

5. Results and Discussion

We have used of Matlab [11] for simulations. Fig. 6 shows influence of some fuzzy inputs on the output (α).

To compare with LEACH and LEACH-FL, the networks that have an area of 100*100 with 20 nodes are selected. The coordinate of the BS is (50,200) and the energy parameters are shown in table 2.

Table 2. *Energy parameters*

Initiate energy	0.5 J	Eelect	50nj/bit
εfs	10pj/(bit*m2)	εamp	0.0013pj/(bit*m4)

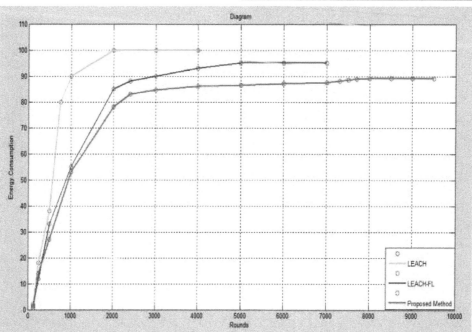

Figure 5. *Distribution of energy consumption according to the number of rounds for each algorithm*

Fig. 5 shows difference between proposed method and LEACH and LEACH-FL in energy consumption.

Residual energy of network in each round can be a good metric to measure the energy efficiency of the algorithms. The

less steep the figure is the more clearness is the energy utilization balance and fairer distribution of energy on the nodes would be.

Consider that the proposed method consumes less energy

than other two methods and thus the network lifetime increases.

Fig. 6 shows alive nodes in sense of number of rounds in these methods.

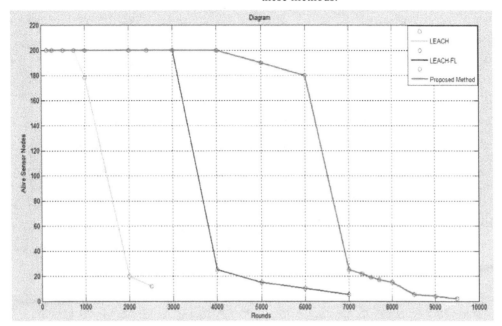

Figure 6. Distribution of alive sensor nodes according to the number of rounds for each algorithm

Unless there are six authors or more give all authors' names; do not use "et al.". Papers that have not been published, even if they have been submitted for publication, should be cited as "unpublished" [4]. Papers that have been accepted for publication should be cited as "in press" [5]. Capitalize only the first word in a paper title, except for proper nouns and element symbols.

For papers published in translation journals, please give the English citation first, followed by the original foreign-language citation [6].

6. Conclusion

Our aim of doing this research is to achieve an optimal approach for clustering in Low-Energy Adaptive Clustering Hierarchy (LEACH). Since all operations for cluster formation are done locally a large amount of energy is saved and speed of cluster formation is increased. We proposed an efficient clustering approach by combining good features of LEACH approach and fuzzy logic (with little computation overhead).

We compared our method with three similar methods, LEACH and LEACH-FL in lifetime, energy consumption and number of death of nodes. Simulation output with Matlab shows that our method saves more energy, thus increases lifetime of WSNs.

References

[1] K. Akkaya, M. Younis, "A Survey of Routing Protocols in Wireless Sensor Networks," Ad Hoc Network Journal, Vol. 3/3, pp. 325-349, 2005.

[2] J. N. Al-Karak and A. E.Kamal, "Routing techniques in wireless sensor network: A survey," IEEE wireless communications, Vol. 11, pp. 6-28, 2004.

[3] I. F. Akyildiz, W. Su, Y. Sankarasubramaniam, and E. Cayirci, "Wireless sensor networks: a survey," Computer Networks, Vol. 38, pp. 393- 422, 2002.

[4] J. Breckling, Ed., The Analysis of Directional Time Series: Applications to Wind Speed and Direction, ser. Lecture Notes in Statistics. Berlin, Germany: Springer, vol. 61, 1989.

[5] Seyyed Jalaleddin Dastgheib, Hamed Oulia, Mohammad Reza Sadeqi Ghassami, An Efficient Approach for Clustering in Wireless Sensor Network Using Fuzzy Logic, International Conference on Computer Science and Network Technology, Harbin, China 24-26, IEEE, 2011

[6] I. Gupta, D. Riordan and S. Sampalli, "Cluster-head Election using Fuzzy Logic for Wireless Sensor Networks," In Proceedings of the 3rd Annual Communication Networks and Services Research Conference, Washington, DC, USA, pp.255-260, 2005.

[7] J. Myoung Kim, S. Park, Y. Han and T. Chung, "CHEF: Cluster Head Election mechanism using Fuzzy logic in Wireless Sensor Networks," 10th International Conference on Advanced Communication Technology (ICACT),Gangwon-Do,South_Korea, pp.654-659, 2008.

[8] D. De, A Distributed Algorithm for Localization Error Detection-Correction, Use in In-network Faulty Reading Detection:Applicability in Long-Thin Wireless Sensor Networks, in Conference IEEE 2009.

[9] Heinzelman, A. Chandrakasan and H. Balakrishnan, An application-specific protocol architecture for wireless microsensor networks, in IEEE Transactions on Wireless communications, pp. 660 - 670, 2002.

[10] G. W. Nurcahyo, Selection of Defuzzification Method to Obtain Crisp Value for Representing Uncertain Data in a Modified Sweep Algorithm, Journal of Computer Science & Technology (JCS&T), Vol. 3 No. 2, October 2003.

[11] F. Vanheel, J. Verhaevert, "Automated Linear Regression Tools Improve RSSI WSN Localization in Multipath Indoor Environment," EURASIP Journal on Wireless Communications and Networking, vol.2011/2011,pp.1-27, 2011.

[12] http://www.mathworks.com/FuzzyLogic Toolbox user's guide.

[13] Z. Qin, M. Bai and D. Ralescu, A fuzzy control system with application to production planning problems, Information Sciences Elsevier Volume 181, Issue 5, Pages 1018-1027, 2011

[14] G. C. D. Sousa and B. K. Bose. "A FUZZY Set Theory Based Control of a Phase-Controlled Converter DC Machine Drive", 1991 IEEE hi.App. Sot. Annu. Meeting, pp.854-861, 1991.

[15] D. Z. Šaletić, D. Velašević: The formal description of a rule based fuzzy expert system, Proceedings of Symposium on Computer Scences and Information Technologies, Kopaonik 27-31. III 2000, pp. 251 –220, YUiNFO 2000

[16] W. Van Leekwijck, E.E. Kerre:Defuzzification: criteria and cla sification, Fuzzy Sets and Systems, 108, pp. 159-178,1999

[17] Dragan Z. Saletic, Dusan M. Velasevic, Nikos E. Mastorakis, "Analysis of Basic Defuzzification Techniques" inRecent Advances in Computers, Computing and Communications , pp. 247-252, WSEAS Press, 2002.

[18] E. H. Mamdani, "Application of fuzzy logic to approximate reasoning using linguistic synthesis," IEEE Transactions on Computers, Vols. C-26, pp. 1182-1191, 1977.

16

Applied research of RFID middleware system based on hierarchical structure

Zhengxi Wei

School of Computer Science, Sichuan University of Science & Engineering, Zigong Sichuan 643000, PR China

Email address:
413789256@qq.com

Abstract: RFID middleware system, as the nerve center of many RFID systems, is being more and more concerned on by the people. It plays a key role in the development of the entire RFID industry. Firstly, this paper briefly introduces the present situation of RFID middleware, and then focuses on data filtering, data aggregation and information transmission three important technologies. According to the function demand, the next section introduces the hierarchical design idea for RFID middleware system. Based on the layered design idea, we construct a hierarchy structure of RFID middleware and present a kind of enterprise class applied model, in which RFID event manager module is responsible for processing data streams and RFID information service module is responsible for system integration. This applied model is easy to build a new RFID middleware system provides a kind of reference. Simulation and practical tests prove that the middleware system can real-time reads the important information of tracked objects such as goods in storehouse, achieve a more efficient management and facilitate practical application for Internet of things technology.

Keywords: RFID Middleware System, Structure Design, Applied model, Data Processing, Middleware Application

1. Introduction

Being contributed to Internet of things technology, a high degree of information sharing enables enterprises to optimize business processes and resource allocation, strengthening detail management and process management, promotes that enterprises have to continuously adapt to changes in the external environment, and improves the core competitiveness and innovation ability. For example, Lockheed Martin military company, which uses advanced management information system (MIS), during the development of JSF aircraft, tooling reduces 90%, production time reduces 66% and manufacturing costs reduce 50%.

With the rapid development of Internet of Things, RFID middleware technology [1] is integrated with other information technology, forming the core technology during the informatization procedure of manufacturing and services industry, driving its informatization extent to a new level, and promoting its sustainable development. RFID technology can be used to significantly improve the efficiency of business processes by providing the capability of automatic identification and data capture. This technology poses many new challenges on current data management systems. RFID

data are time-dependent, dynamically changing, in large volumes, and carry implicit semantics. RFID data management systems need to support effectively such large-scale temporal data created by RFID applications. These systems need to have an explicit temporal data model for RFID data to support tracking and monitoring queries [2]. In addition, they need to have an automatic method to transform the primitive observations from RFID readers into derived data used in RFID-enabled applications.

RFID middleware is a kind of intermediate program, which achieves data transmission between the RFID hardware devices and software applications, filtering and converting data format. It reads the data from readers through the middleware extraction, decryption, filtered as well as format conversion, importing into enterprise information system to apply. Thus, it solves the problem that enterprises adopt RFID technology in the most time-consuming, labor-intensive highest complexity and difficulty, to ensure the reader to read the data correctly and import the data enterprise into the information systems according to the needs. In addition, RFID as a the key technology is also used in the field of manufacturing, assembly, postal services, warehousing and asset management, to build a smart RFID middleware system will make these applications become more convenient and efficient. In this paper, we present an integrated RFID middleware system based on hierarchical design idea and enterprise class applied model. Our system enables redundant RFID data filtering and automatic data transformation based on specific rules, provides powerful query support of RFID object tracking and management, and can be used to different RFID applications.

2. Important Functions

RFID middleware process data streams by distributed, hierarchical approach, with data collection, filtering, integration, delivery and other functions, so it is able to send information to the enterprise back-end applications, or other information systems. Thus, the following issues may occur in the course of information exchange. RFID device reading the data does not necessarily only use a particular application, so it may use multiple applications. Each application may also need many different sets of data, require data corresponding processing (such as redundant data filtering, etc.). This article next focuses on three key issues: data filtering [3], data aggregation[4] and transmission of information.

2.1. Data Filtering

Middleware receives massive EPC (Electronic Product Code) data from RFID readers, there is too much redundant information, and there exists a lot misread information. Therefore, it needs to filter the data and eliminate redundant data, and filter out unwanted information as well as send the useful information to the application. Redundant data includes: (1) in the short term the same reader repeat to report the same data. (2) More than one near reader may report the same data in the different time.

The solution for redundancy data is to set the various filter processing. The typical filter has four categories: product filter, time filter, EPC filters and smoothing filter. Product filter transmits only the product information related to a product or the manufacturer, that is, the filter transmits only a certain range of EPC data. Time filter can filter events based on time records, for example, a time filter may only send events that happened within the last 10 minutes. EPC code filter can send only to meet certain rules EPC code. Smoothing filter can handle those cases of error, including leakage read and misread. According to actual needs, the filter can be like assembling toys, like stitching together one by one, in order to obtain the desired event. For example, a smoothing filter can combine with a product filter. It leads events to separate to an application.

2.2. Data Aggregation

Because source RFID data stream received from the reader are simple single fragmented information, for giving applications or other RFID middleware to provide meaningful information, it needs for RFID data aggregation processing. CEP (complex event processing) technology can be taken into consider. Complex event processing is an emerging technology, used to handle a large number of simple events and sort out valuable event. It can help people through the analysis of complex events, change the simple event into a valuable event and derive actionable information.

Through data aggregation, source RFID data is simplified into meaningful complex events, such as a RFID tag firstly emerged in the range of a reader detecting, then disappeared. By virtue of a number of simple data analysis, it can determine the tag into the event and leave the event. The aggregation can solve a problem caused by a temporary error reading data, making data smooth.

2.3. Information Transmission

After filtering and aggregation processing, RFID data need reach those entities interested in it, such as enterprise applications, information service system or other RFID middleware, that leads a messaging services mechanism to transmit RFID information.In the form of information-to-information, a message is transferred from one program to another program or programs. Information can transmit in an asynchronous manner, so the sender does not have to wait for a response. Message-oriented middleware functionality includes not only the transmission of information, but also include an explaining data, data security, data broadcasting, error recovery, locating network resources, computing the path cost, message priorities as well as excluding error and other services.

Under J2EE platform, JMS (Java Message Service[5]) can implement interacting messaging between RFID middleware and enterprise applications. Using JMS publish / subscribe model, RFID middleware publish a topic messages so that enterprise applications can order the subject of the message. Here the message is the specific language of things - PML (Physical Mark-up Language) format. Even though the database software to change information or increase RFID reader types, it does not need to modify the front-side application to perform data processing, eliminating the need for multi to multi complex maintenance.

3. Layered Design

The next discussion will start from functionality requirement, structural design of RFID middleware, and subsequently present an enterprise-level application solution based on RFID middleware.

3.1. Functionality Analysis

Required functionality: (1) RFID devices access: make the different RFID reader with RJ-45 Ethernet port, RS232 serial, USB and other interfaces access to the middleware system. (2) Data filtering: remove and filter the redundant data of RFID tags. (3) Reliable transmission of real-time data: requires the RFID terminal equipment to gather information in order to ensure a good communication between devices with the reliability of data source. (4) Software Human Interface: view real-time status of each RFID equipment running, also manage the tagged data, the interface should be simple and easy to operate.

3.2. Middleware Hierarchy

The design uses layered approach to achieve the above functions, the system is by the device management, data filtering layer and the service layer to handle different tasks, as shown in Fig. 1. Moreover, the various parts are as follows.

(1) Device management layer: create the physical connection between the main provider of middleware and RFID devices, and process the related services of monitoring equipment.

(2) Data filter layer: mainly filter raw RFID events, providing specific semantic information messages to the upper application systems.

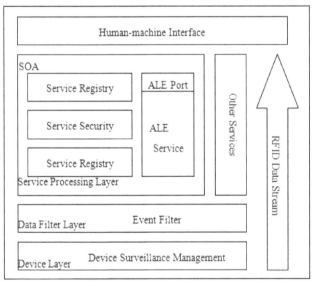

Figure 1. Middleware hierarchy

(3) Service processing layer: provide services to other applications through ALE (Application Level Events) interface. Service registration is used to define new services; security services provide secure transmission of messages; service management is to view a variety of services, reserved or revoked.

(4) Human-machine interface: real-time update RFID device information and achieve service inquiry.

(5) Other services: provide services for the enterprise ERP system and other management systems.

4. Applied Model

Based on the layered design idea, we construct a hierarchy structure of RFID middleware and present a kind of enterprise class applied model, in which RFID event manager module is responsible for processing data streams and RFID information service module is responsible for system integration.

4.1. Application Framework

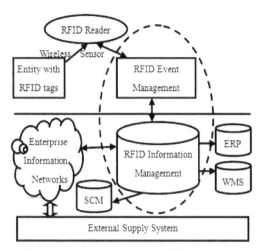

Figure 2. Application framework of RFID middleware

RFID middleware is essentially a service program that directly interacts with tag reader device. Its main functions include the RFID reader data extraction, filtering, processing and integration with other application interfaces, and the application framework is as shown in Figure 2.

In Figure2, the imaginary part of the coil is the RFID middleware. Reading continuously a large number of tags, the RFID reader transfers data to RFID middleware to process. Our design adopts SOA [6] (service-oriented architecture) architecture and divides the middleware into RFID event manager module and information-service module.

4.2. RFID Event Manager Module

This module is responsible for processing data streams from one or more RFID reader. Before data is sent to the relevant application, the data should be filtered and integrated pre-treatment. Therefore, it should set filtering mechanism in the module, discarding the redundant data that produces when the goods are not moving. The goods only when the state has changed, really triggers an action or event. The Event Manager module can also define additional filtering mechanism, through customized way to implement specific business logic, so that other software can continuously use relevant data.

RFID Event Manager Module involves: (1) device adapter sub-modules: use RFID air interface protocol to allow devices from different vendors can communicate and interact. (2) Filter sub-modules: customize semantic information and design of complex event processing mechanism to filter redundant data provided by RFID readers. (3) System connection: the underlying data can be sent to the file system, message queues and other places, to deliver RFID-related events and data to the upper application system.

4.3. RFID Information Service Module

The module connects to EIS (Enterprise Information System) which includes ERP (Enterprise Resource Plan), WMS (Warehouse Management System), SCM (Supply

Chain Management) and other systems that hope to use the RFID tag information, as shown in Fig. 2 lower right. In fact, this module can be thought as the integration layer of enterprise-level application system, which provides a connection channel between RFID data base and high-layer business applications.

This module obtains data include: (1) the reader's type and other data. (2) The key data labelled by tags, such as weight, manufacturing date, the upstream enterprise and so on. The RFID information service module is set between the RFID event management module and other enterprise applications, so it can provide maximum flexibility according to the change of the business needs or enterprise applications, and reflect the superiority of SOA software architecture.

5. Experiment Results

In the detailed design stage, we select the java language and MS Access database as development tool, programming to implement RFID middleware for identifying the different hardware and redundant data filtering. The experiment uses an open-source software Rifidi [7] for simulation testing. The Rifidi can create a kind of software simulation environment of the RFID system. Its software toolkit can be based on the realities of RFID applications to simulate RFID reader/tag hardware's access and achieve the interaction between middleware and virtual devices.

5.1. Simulation Testing

Experimental scene simulates goods entering and leaving the warehouse. Goods are inspected at an entrance or outlet equipped with RFID reader. First, create two components in the simulation software: Dock Door-1 and DockDoor-2 (both with a certain type of reader), defines two-batch testing: The first batch test group has three tags; the second batch test group has four tags. Define entrance or exit two scenes, each with a defined reader. Run middleware and test RFID reader how to read batch tags. The experimental results test two tag group behaviors, that is, whether the first group behaviors match the scene 1 and batch 1, and whether the second group match the scene 2 and batch 2.

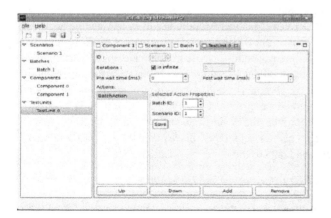

Figure 3. *Simulation result*

The console displays the matching results and the filtered tag data. After testing, successful identification-rate of RFID middleware reaches 100% and according to the results of the console displays, data-filtering module effectively filters many redundant data in tags. The simulation test interface is shown in Figure 3.

5.2. Practical Testing

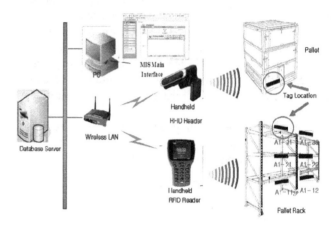

Figure 4. *Detection to goods out of storage.*

We apply our RFID middleware system to a logistics enterprise for detecting and tracking the goods out of storage, shown in Figure 4.

Practical results show that our system can display the physical location of goods in real time and enable redundant RFID data filtering and automatic data transformation. All the information on the items can be collected and tracked in real time, and provide a strong support to goods out of storage for its effective management and control.

6. Conclusions

The simulation and practical tests prove our RFID middleware system whose recognition rate, redundant data filtering capability and other performance indicators have reached the preset requirements. Moreover, device management layer can configure, operate and monitor the device; data management layer can process data and filtering tag data redundancy well; Event management can convert raw tag data into business events; application software can put easily the system at all levels into practice through application program interface.

From the application level, on this basis of the applied model of RFID middle system based on Internet of things, people can further research to establish general information processing custom rules, and enhance constructing efficiency. This is certainly conducive to facilitate practical application for Internet of things technology.

Acknowledgements

The research was supported by Artificial Intelligence Key Laboratory of Sichuan Province (No. 2013RYY04) and the

Sichuan Provincial Education Department's Key Project (No.14ZA0210).

Our work was also supported by university Key Laboratory of Sichuan Province (No. 2013WYY09) and Fund Project of Sichuan Provincial Academician (Experts) Workstation (No.2014YSGZZ02).

References

[1] Hoag J E, Thompson C W. Architecting RFID middleware[J]. Internet Computing, IEEE, 2006, 10(5): 88-92.

[2] Kim G, Ryu W, Hong B, et al. Real-Time Quantity Inspection Method for Moving Tags in RFID Middleware[M]//Secure and Trust Computing, Data Management, and Applications. Springer Berlin Heidelberg, 2011: 77-83.

[3] Zhang M Z,et al. Research of data filtering model in embedded RFID middleware. Computer Engineering and Design, 31(17), pp. 3743-3746,2011.

[4] Tan H O, Korpeoglu I, Stojmenovic I, Computing localized power-efficient data aggregation trees for sensor networks. Parallel and Distributed Systems, IEEE Transactions on, 22(3), pp.489-500, 2011.

[5] Kuehnhausen M, Frost V S, Application of the Java Message Service in mobile monitoring environments. Journal of Network and Computer Applications, 34(5), pp. 1707-1716, 2011.

[6] Seinturier Lionel, et al. A component‑based middleware platform for reconfigurable service‑oriented architectures. Software: Practice and Experience, 42(5), pp. 559-583, 2012.

[7] Huebner A, Facchi C, Janicke H. Rifidi Toolkit: Virtuality for Testing RFID[C]//ICSNC 2012, The Seventh International Conference on Systems and Networks Communications. 2012: 1-6.

17

Framework model on enterprise information system based on Internet of things

Zhengxi Wei

School of Computer Science, Sichuan University of Science & Engineering, Zigong Sichuan 643000, PR China

Email address:
413789256@qq.com

Abstract: A high degree of information sharing can enable manufacturing and services industry to optimize business processes and improve the core competitiveness and innovation ability. This paper aims to explore a framework model to build a kind of management information system based on Internet of things. Starting from the demand and functions of the system, we firstly outline a conceptual model based on sensing networks. Next, we construct the systemic framework and illustrate its running procedure in detail. Finally, we give experimental schemes designed for each module under J2EE platform. Practical application proves that our system can display the important information of tracking object in real time and achieve a more efficient management. Based on this model, people can further research and establish custom rules used to general information processing, make manufacturing and services enterprises build a modern information system more efficiently and faster, and facilitate practical application for Internet of things technology.

Keywords: Intelligent System, RFID Middleware, Framework Design, Enterprise Information System, Conceptual Model

1. Introduction

With the rapid development of cloud computing and RFID middleware [1] technology, etc., they are integrated with manufacturing technology, forming the core technology during the informatization procedure of manufacturing and services industry, driving its informatization extent to a new level, and promoting its sustainable development. Smart manufacturing [2] and services supported by sensing networks, database technology, business intelligence, virtual simulation, modelling technology and so on, makes the product intelligence, manufacturing process automation, and provides applications for aided management decision.

Thus, the informatization procedure of manufacturing and services industry combines information technology, automation technology, modern management techniques with manufacturing technology, and becomes a system engineering that improves manufacturing and service industries integrity, sustainability and service ability. Internet of things [3] through comprehensive perception, reliable delivery and intelligent processing makes the information reach different destinations so as to achieve "things - things" connected and information sharing. Manufacturing and services industries are required to achieve the informatization management from product design

and manufacturing to sales and service during the entire life cycle, while Internet of things technology can fitly help them gain this advantage.

Based on Internet of things technology, a high degree of information sharing enables enterprises to optimize business processes and resource allocation, strengthening detail management and process management, promotes that enterprises have to continuously adapt to changes in the external environment, and improves the core competitiveness and innovation ability. For example, Lockheed Martin military company, which uses advanced management information system (MIS), during the development of JSF aircraft, tooling reduces 90%, production time reduces 66% and manufacturing costs reduce 50%. This paper aims to explore and establish a framework model used to build MIS based on Internet of things. Based on this model, people can further research and establish custom rules used to general information processing, make manufacturing and service enterprises more efficiently build a modern information system, and facilitate practical application for Internet of things technology

2. System Analysis

2.1. Design Aim

In traditional manufacturing and services industries, the informatization plays an important role for supporting its development, such as bar code technology [4], infrared scanning and RFID technology having been widely used. However, the current extent of information sharing is still a lot of distances away from the level of Internet of things. For example, the bar code of goods is merely passive, which exists only in the process of recording and processing production line, warehouse and sales network, and is still lack of mechanisms for real-time tracking it. If we can effectively introduce mechanisms of Internet of things that can help enterprises grasp the real-time sales situation, combined with production or customer information, location information, transportation and warehouse information, etc., it can help companies more real-time, scientifically arrange procurement, production, storage, distribution, allocation and sales work.

Results of our study will contribute to enhance the informatization extent to traditional manufacturing and services enterprises. If there are many companies to carry out various forms of cooperation, it cannot only help them improve production efficiency, but also gain the good economic benefits for themselves.

2.2. Demand and Function

In most existing MIS in manufacturing and services enterprises, data entry and management are mainly by manual inputs or management approach. This mode may result in inefficient management and information lag and other issues. Our study is designed to change the traditional data-management mode in information system by Internet of things, and make information management of enterprises more automatically and intelligent.

Required functions of our MIS are as follow.

1) Information collection, which can non-stop gather various information to ensure manufacturing and services enterprises to perform real-time data management.

2) Intelligent processing algorithms, which can automatically call a specific event that information systems define and achieve intelligent processing to system data.

3) Developing system interfaces, which intelligent processing algorithms can call and implement specific data processing in the system.

2.3. Conceptual Model

Combined with the construction model based on Internet of things [5], we have seen a product system that contains sensing, storage, data processing, and decision capabilities at four intelligence levels. Address the above functional requirements, we outline a conceptual model of MIS used to manufacturing and services enterprises, shown in Figure 1, which mainly includes perception layer, control layer and information processing layer three layers.

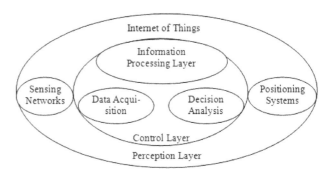

Figure 1. Conceptual model of MIS.

The perception layer is mainly used to sense data, while the control layer is mainly for data processing and information interface call. In the conceptual model, we takes sensing networks in Internet of things and positioning systems as perception layer, which gain relevant entity information such as the coding information and physical location information. The acquired data transports to the control layer of the system through a particular protocol, and the control layer is for data analysis. The latter analyzes subsequent operations that the decision system may request, and calls corresponding interfaces in information processing layer for data processing to ensure the automatic operation of MIS.

3. System Design

3.1. Structure Design

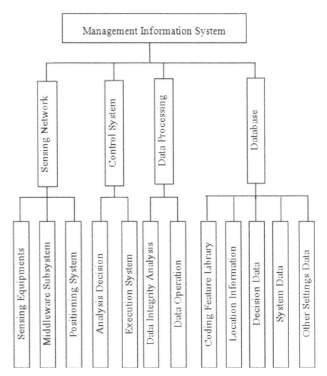

Figure 2. MIS framework.

MIS is mainly used to automatically and intelligently process data from manufacturing and services enterprises, while the database as data warehouse is also bound to be a key part of it. Combined systematic conceptual model presented in

Figure 1, we construct an MIS framework of manufacturing and service enterprise, shown in Figure 2.

MIS is composed of sensing network, control system, data processing module and database four parts, and its composition and function of each part is as follows.

3.1.1. Sensing Networks

It is primarily responsible for gathering entity information in manufacturing and services enterprises such as the feature and the physical location, and this part is mainly composed of information sensing equipment, intelligent signal processing and smart positioning system.

1) Signal sensing equipments are mainly responsible for obtaining enterprise entities' unique encoding or characteristics.

2) RFID middleware subsystem is mainly responsible for intelligent signal processing to convert and unify data format and interpret specific information used to the required operation. We will explain in detail this subsystem in section 4.

3) Positioning system is mainly responsible for gaining enterprise entities' physical location information, which will be stored in the database later.

3.1.2. Control System [6]

It can analyze and make decision by calling information system interface, and it is mainly composed of decision system and execution system. Decision system is as a core connected to sensing networks, which includes sensing-data acquisition module, data comparison and analysis module as well as sensing-network control module. Execution system includes enterprise-information interface calling module, information analysis and execution module. The components and functions of the two systems are as follows.

1) Sensing data module is mainly used to obtain sensing data received from sensing networks.

2) Data analysis module is mainly responsible for analyzing the sensing data from networks, comparing their feature information and location information with the same items in background database, so as to find the corresponding information system interface to perform system call.

3) Interface call module is mainly responsible for calling information interface and saving sensing data to the appropriate module of information system.

4) Data tracking module is mainly responsible for analyzing completeness and accuracy of sensing data, returning data entry to the decision system, and then control-sensing network starts a new round of data collection.

3.1.3. Data Processing Module

This module is mainly responsible for analyzing the data coming from the interface and performing informatization processing, which includes data integrity analysis and the operation such as data format check, data modify, data add or delete.

Database: it is mainly responsible for the data storage and retrieval operations. Stored information includes coding library and feature library, location information, analysis and decision data, system data, and other settings parameters.

Functions of each part are as follows.

1) Coding library and feature library are used to establish enterprises entity information. A unique entity code represents an individual entity, firstly written into coding library. Subsequently, the other information such as entity name, entity material and entity size, is also written into feature library. By querying entity code, it can obtain its feature information.

2) Location information is mainly used to save position-encoding information of each entity, by which people can obtain entity location name through the position encoder. The location name is usually corresponding to a work phase or other specific meaning.

3) Analysis and decision data mainly saves interface information that is sourced to entity code and entity location, and provides analysis data for decision systems.

4) System data is mainly used for system data storage.

5) Other parameters setup is used for setting parameters for other module in MIS.

3.2. System Running

Only when mutual coordination and mutual convergence among the various modules in MIS exists, it can ensure information system to work effectively and stably. System running procedure is as shown in Figure 3.

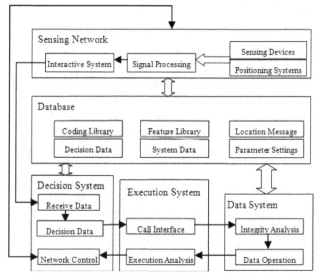

Figure 3. *System running procedure.*

3.2.1. Sensing Networks

It collects business entity information, which includes unique encoding or features message and location coding, by information-sensing devices and smart positioning systems.

And then it performs intelligent processing to provide data that the analysis and decision system can identify. Subsequently, the sensing networks through intelligent interactive system deliver sensing data to the decision system.

3.2.2. Decision System [7]

It receives business entities' messages coming from sensing network, including the only coding information or features and physical location information, and then executes data analysis.

On the one hand, by comparing the analysis and decision data in database, it can find the informatization interfaces that the system will pre-call; on the other hand, information system can find out correspondingly specific meaning by querying entity physical location or unique encoding from the database, such as a name corresponding to a working stage. Analysis and decision system will finally transfer the decision data to the execution system.

3.2.3. Execution System

It receives data from the decision system, calls corresponding interfaces in MIS, and transmits sensing data to the data system interface.

3.2.4. Data System [8]

It is called and then executes the corresponding informatization operations. First, data integrity analysis should be done to ensure the accuracy of sensing data, then performs the corresponding database operation and feedback, and output the results. By control system and decision system, the further action in sensing network will be controlled better so as to ensure the repeatedly effective operation of MIS.

During intelligent processing information, specific data stored in the database plays a fundamental role, for example, calling up information interface from the database according to entity information and its physical location information. This information is the predefined parameter stored in the database when information system is established. Data will be timely read as the system is running. As long as there are changes in enterprise business, it will be modified.

Effective operation of information systems mostly depends on accurately obtaining the entity information and physical location information. The analysis and decision system decide to call which information interface, and the execution system by interface call ensures the effective operation of the system.

4. RFID Middleware Subsystem

As the nerve center of Internet of things, RFID middleware can connect tag readers and enterprise application, eliminating the complexity maintenance, reducing the cost of enterprise integration. However, RFID middleware is also a complex and important system, needing further promote the use, progressively improve and perfect.

RFID middleware subsystems in our framework model shown in Figure 1 are mainly responsible for data format conversion in sensing network, which is essentially a service program that directly interacts with tag reader device. Its main functions include the RFID reader data extraction, filtering, processing and integration with other application interfaces, and the application framework is as shown in Figure 4.

In Figure 4, the imaginary part of the coil is the RFID middleware. Reading continuously a large number of tags, the RFID reader transfers data to RFID middleware to process. RFID as a key technology is also used in the field of

manufacturing, assembly, postal services, warehousing and asset management, to use a smart RFID middleware system will make these applications become more convenient and efficient.

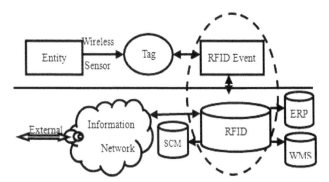

Figure 4. *Application framework of RFID middleware.*

5. Experimental Scheme

Our designed MIS can be tested on J2EE platform [9], using a combination of Struts, Spring, Hibernate, Servlet, HTML, JavaScript and other technology to develop a software and prepare for its application to logistics company.

5.1. System Construction

1) Sensing networks

This module uses common collection devices with microcontroller to gather information. Processing algorithms integrated in the device chip is used to complete the intelligent processing during information acquisition. The only identification and other information that is collected from sensing networks every time, will store in the temporary table of database, and analysis and decision system obtains data source by reading the data in the temporary table.

2) Decision system

Through the Servlet technology and database technology, analysis and decision system is built, which defines the interaction with the sensing network Servlet, and our MIS takes .listener suffix as a request that is interpreted and executed by analysis and decision systems.

3) Execution system

The execution system mainly defines extensive interface of information systems and analyzes the executed results of MIS, and it uses the way of Java class to be defined and implemented.

4) Data system

This module can use Struts + Spring + Hibernate framework for developing, adopting MVC [10] control mode, in accordance with the typical three-layer structure, similar with existing information systems in development mode. Data systems, analysis and decision system, execution system together form a software platform of MIS. Analysis and decision system and execution systems as a connecting bridge between data systems and sensing networks also are an important guarantee to implement MIS automated and intelligent.

5.2. Application Results

We apply our design scheme to a logistics company for detecting the goods out of storage, shown in Figure 5.

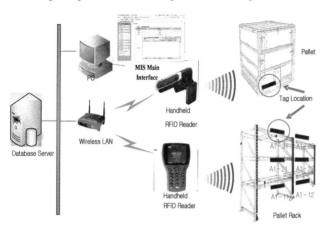

Figure 5. Detection to goods out of storage.

Practical results show that our MIS can display the physical location of goods in real time, all the information on the items can be collected and tracked in real time, and provide a strong support to goods out of storage for its effective management and control.

6. Conclusions

This paper systematically talks about integrating, processing and converting data, fully connects the physical world to the digital world to complete the accurate mapping between the two part, for the manufacturing and service enterprises to provide an enterprise-class product development scheme. The MIS model we present based on Internet of things for manufacturing and service enterprises, can make a complex product-development system more clearly, dynamically and completely controlled in the hands of managers. Thus, quality and reliability of the manufacture products or services has a systemic guarantee, contributing to implement the production and management informatization, and its productivity will have greatly improved, too.

From the application level, on this basis of the conceptual model of management information system based on Internet of things, people can further research to establish general information processing custom rules, and enhance constructing efficiency for MIS. This is certainly conducive to the wide promote of Internet of things technology and its applications.

Acknowledgements

The research was supported by Artificial Intelligence Key Laboratory of Sichuan Province (No. 2013RYY04) and the Sichuan Provincial Education Department's Key Project (No.14ZA0210).

Our work was also supported by university Key Laboratory of Sichuan Province (No. 2013WYY09) and Fund Project of Sichuan Provincial Academician (Experts) Workstation (No.2014YSGZZ02).

References

[1]   Yuan J S, Hu Y. Implementation of RFID Middleware Based on Hash Chain[J]. Applied Mechanics and Materials, 2013:12-15.

[2]   Ghonaim W, Ghenniwa H, Shen W. Towards an agent oriented smart manufacturing system[C]. //Computer Supported Cooperative Work in Design (CSCWD), 2011 15th International Conference on. IEEE, 2011:636 - 642.

[3]   Kopetz H. Real-Time Systems[M]. Springer US, 2011:307-323.

[4]   Li D, Wei Q, Liu C, et al. A novel verification code technology to make web system more secure[C]. //Computer Science & Education (ICCSE), 2011 6th International Conference on. IEEE, 2011:1303 - 1306.

[5]   Kiritsis D. Closed-loop PLM for intelligent products in the era of the Internet of things[J]. Computer-Aided Design, 2011, 43(5): 479-501.

[6]   Ellis G. Control system design guide: using your computer to understand and diagnose feedback controllers[M]. Butterworth-Heinemann, 2012.

[7]   Ostwald D, Porcaro C, Mayhew S D, et al. EEG-fMRI based information theoretic characterization of the human perceptual decision system[J]. PloS one, 2012, 7(4): e33896.

[8]   Foster I, Vockler J, Wilde M, et al. Chimera: A virtual data system for representing, querying, and automating data derivation[C]//Scientific and Statistical Database Management, 2002. Proceedings. 14th International Conference on. IEEE, 2002: 37-46.

[9]   Qu C, Engel T, Meinel C. Implementation of an enterprise-level groupware system based on J2EE platform and WebDAV protocol[C]. //Enterprise Distributed Object Computing Conference, 2000. EDOC 2000. Proceedings. Fourth International. IEEE, 2000:160 - 169.

[10]   Lin Y J, Lin S. Research on E-Commerce Software Framework of MVC Mode Based on .NET[J]. Applied Mechanics and Materials, 2013:2645-2648.

18

Factors associated with low level of health information utilization in resources limited setting, Eastern Ethiopia

Kidist Teklegiorgis, Kidane Tadesse, Gebremeskel Mirutse, Wondwossen Terefe

Department of Public Health, College of Health Sciences, Mekelle University, Mekelle, Ethiopia

Email address:

kidtek6@gmail.com (Teklegiorgis K.), Kiducs98@yahoo.com (K. Tadesse), gebramskelmirutse@yahoo.com (G. Mirutse), kidwonyt4@gmail.com (W. Terefe)

Abstract: Health information system (HIS) is a system that integrates data collection, processing, reporting and use of the information necessary for improving health service effectiveness and efficiency through better management at all levels of health services. Despite the credible use of HIS for evidence based decision making, countries with the highest burden of ill health and the most in-needs for accurate and timely data have the weakest HIS in the vast majority of world's poorest countries. The main of this study was to assess the level of information utilization and identify factors affecting information use in, Ethiopian, health facilities. A cross sectional study was conducted by using structured questioners in Dire Dawa administration health facilities. All unit/department heads from all government health facilities were selected. The data was analyzed using STATA version 11. Frequency and percentages was computed to present the descriptive findings. Association between variables was computed using binary logistic regression. Over all utilization of health information was found to be 53.1%. Friendly format for reporting and managers provide regular feed back to their staff were found to be significantly associated with health information utilization, and their strength were (AOR=2.796,95% CI[1.478,5.288]) and (AOR=2.195,95%CI[1.213,3.974]) respectively. Overall HIS utilization was found to be below the national expectation level. Low utilization of HIS was found in health posts than health centers and hospitals. There was also shortage of assigned HIS personnel, separate HIS office and assigned budget for HIS in majority of units/departments.

Keywords: HMIS, HIS, Ethiopia, Information Utilization

1. Introduction

A health information system (HIS) is a system that integrates data collection, processing, reporting and use of the information necessary for improving health service effectiveness and efficiency through better management at all levels of health services. Maintaining a good HMIS is an essential part in strengthening the health system (1, 2). In 2007, the World Health Assembly (WHA) passed a resolution on strengthening of HIS. The resolution acknowledges that sound information is critical in framing evidence based health policy and making decision and it is fundamental for monitoring program towards internationally agreed health related development goals. Although HMIS forms a backbone for strong health systems, most developing countries still face a challenge in strengthening routine health information systems (3, 4).

In a good HMIS, data collection should be similar with the data requirements of users (only relevant data) and to the available processing capabilities, also the information generated should be simple to obtain and only the minimum required information must be collected, so that analysis can be done quickly. Feedback to the providers of the health data is an essential component of any reporting system (5, 6). The Ethiopian Federal Ministry of Health (FMOH) has emphasized the HMIS as a key component for successful implementation of Health Sector Development Program (HSDP) strategic plan. The core health indicators come from routine health service and administrative records through HMIS and M&E and are complementary processes standardizing of indicator definitions and data recording and reporting forms; integration of data from different programs into a shared channels improves health system efficiency and effectiveness (7-9).

The value of health information is determined by its utilization in decision-making. Public health decision-making is critically dependent on the timely availability of sound data. Developing countries are reported to have a large amount of unreliable health data, poor human resources and poor information technology infrastructure, hence effective HIS are needed to improve these problems. In Ethiopia data quality and utilization of health information remains weak, particularly at primary health care facilities and district levels and the major associated factors includes (10-15).

2. Methods and Materials

2.1. Study Setting

This study was conducted in Dire Dawa administration, Ethiopia, health facilities from March 01-31/2013. Dire Dawa is one of the two chartered cities in Ethiopia (the other being the capital, Addis Ababa). Dire Dawa lies in the eastern part of Ethiopia which is 501 km away from Addis Ababa. The administration has one governmental hospital, 16 health centers and 34 health posts. Except the regional health bureau, it has no zonal or district health bureau.

Based on the 2007 Census conducted by the Central Statistical Agency of Ethiopia (CSA), Dire Dawa has a total population of 342,827, of whom 171,930 were men and 170,897 women; 232,854 or 69.92% of the population are considered urban inhabitants, with an estimated area of 1,231.20 square kilometers [32].

2.2. Study Design

We used a facility based cross sectional study design; all department heads of health facilities have been interviewed at point in time, to assess the level of information utilization and associated factors.

2.3. Study Participants and Sampling

The source population was all governmental health facilities found in Dire Dawa administration. The study population was all unit/department head of hospital, health centers and health posts. Since all health facilities in the administration currently implement HMIS, all unit/department heads from all health facilities were included in the study. In Dire Dawa Administration, there are a total of 267 unit/department heads from all health facilities including health posts. We conduct a census of unit/department heads i.e. all department heads have been included in this study.

2.4. Data Collection Procedures, Instrument, and Quality Management

A face to face interview using structured questionnaires was employed to collect primary data among all unit/department heads of the health facilities. The questionnaire was adopted from the performance of routine information system management framework assessment tool version 3.1. This PRISM tool is useful to get detailed information on the strengths and weaknesses of HIS in its input, process and output and identifies factors affecting its performance. It was prepared in English, translated to Amharic and then back to English by another person to ensure consistency. Two health professionals who are members of HIS monitoring team were assigned as supervisors. Six health professionals who had basic HMIS training and had prior experience on data collection were assigned as data collectors. To maintain data quality, during data collection period, the two supervisors and the principal investigators performed the supervision of data collection procedures on daily bases. Checked every completed questionnaire and gave onsite technical assistance to the data collectors. The data was checked for any missing values and completeness.

2.5. Data Analysis

The Collected data was checked for completeness, coded, entered and cleaned using STATA version 11. Analysis of data was done using the same package. Since all the variables were categorical frequency and percentages was computed to present the descriptive analysis. Associations between the dependent and independent variables were computed using binary logistic regression. A p-value <0.05 was considered as cut-off point for statistical significance.

To check whether the fitted model predicted well or not, the ROC Curve was analyzed and also Hosmer-Lemeshow test used to test overall goodness of fit. Multicollinearity in the variables was checked using Variance Inflation Factor (VIF).Interaction was also checked during the analysis.

2.6. Ethical Issues

Institutional ethical clearance was first sought from Mekelle University, college of health science. Data was collected after written consent from Dire Dawa regional health bureau. During the interview each participant were informed about the aim of the study. The interviewer discussed the issue of confidentiality and. Participants were informed that they have full right to refuse or discontinue participating in the research.

3. Results

3.1. Descriptive Analysis

Out of the total 239 respondents 188(78.7%) were from 16 health centers, 28(11.7%) were from health posts and the remaining 23(9.6%) were from one referral hospital. Of the total departments included on this study 25(10.4%) were from adult OPD, 12(5%) were each from Emergency, Delivery and ART departments, 15(6.3%) were from TB and Leprosy departments, 10(4.2%) were from VCT departments and 15(6.3%) were from under 5 OPD (Table-1).

Table 1. *Distribution of units/departments heads of hospital, health centers and health posts in Dire Dawa Administration health facility, April 2013.*

Unit/departments	Frequency	Percent
VCT	10	4.2
Adult OPD	25	10.4
Under 5 OPD	16	6.7
Laboratory	16	6.7
Pharmacy	16	6.7
Family planning	15	6.3
ANC/PMCT	15	6.3
Emergency	12	5.0
Delivery	12	5.0
Environmental	15	6.3
EPI	15	6.3
TBL	15	6.3
ART	12	5.0
Ward/IPD	9	3.8
Statistics Unit	8	3.3
Health Facility		
Unit/departments of health centers	188	78.7
Unit/departments of hospital	23	9.6
Units of health post	28	11.7

3.2. HIS Input

Majority 150(62.7%) and 154(64.4%) of the respondents reported that there was no assigned HIS personnel and separate HIS office in their department respectively. Majority, 195(81.6%) department heads reported there was no specific budget assigned for HIS. Around 125(52.3%) of the respondents also revealed there was no legislative, regulatory and planning framework in their facility (Table-2).

Table 2. *Health facility department's HIS inputs in Dire Dawa administration, April 2013.*

HIS input	Yes Frequency (%)	No Frequency (%)
Personnel assigned to HIS	89(37.2)	150(62.7)
Separate unit assigned to HIS	85(35.5)	154 (64.5)
Availability of equipment for HIS	149(62.3)	90(37.7)
Adequacy of equipments	68(45.6)	81(54.4)
Specific budget assigned for HIS	44(18.4)	195(81.6)
Mechanism to facilitate HIS resource	117(49.0)	122(51.0)
HIS training for staffs	126(52.7)	113(47.3)
Planning framework to use HIS	114(48.0)	125(52.0)
Duration of training		
Less than 6 months	28(22.2)	
6 months - 1 year	30(23.8)	
More than 1 year	68(54.0)	

3.3. HIS Process

One hundred ninety one (79.9%) unit/department heads reported they collect health data on daily basis. Majority 196(82.0%) of departments also keep patient registration and HIS monthly reports. Among them 137(57.3%) revealed the records were easily accessible to their staffs. Majority 164(68.6%) of heads also reported that they received directives in the last 3 months to check data accuracy, to fill format completely and submit the monthly report timely. In this study 185(77.4%) department heads claimed they submitted HIS report timely (Table 3).

Table 3. *Health facility department's HIS process in Dire Dawa Administration, Apr. 2013.*

HIS process	Yes Frequency (%)	No Frequency(%)
Collecting data on daily activities	191(79.9%)	48(20.1%)
Keep registration and copies of HIS monthly report	196(82.0%)	43(18%)
Accessibility of records for staffs	148(62.0%)	91(38.0%)
Procedures for distributing and reporting data	178(74.5%)	61(25.5%)
Data put at administrative level	205(85.7%)	34(14.3%)
Criteria for verification of completeness and consistency	181(75.7%)	58(24.3%)
Receive directives in the last 3 month	164(68.6%)	75(31.4%)
Timeliness of reported data	185(77.4%)	54(32.6%)
Completeness of reported data	196(82.0%)	43(18.0%)
Consistency of reported data	188(78.7%)	51(21.3%)
Representativeness of data.	195(81.9%)	44(18.1%)

3.4. HIS Output

Compiling of HIS data and reports containing HIS information was reported in 170(71.1%) and 162(67.8%) department heads respectively. Display of key indicators was reported in 145(60.7%) and quarterly and any other feedback reports were also available in 138(57.7%) of departments. Regarding the use of health information for decision making, 156(65.3%) reported they use information to make decision. Among them 72(46.2%) use the information for future reference, 66(42.3%) use to observe trends of service delivery and 18(11.5%) to pass reports for other subsidy health offices respectively (Table -4).

Table 4. *Health facility department's HIS output in Dire Dawa Administration, Apr. 2013.*

HIS Output	Yes Frequency (%)	No Frequency (%)
Department compile HIS data	170(71.1%)	69(28.9%)
Compile any report containing HIS information	162(67.8%)	77(32.2%)
Display key indicators with tables	145(60.7%)	94(39.3%)
Presence of catchment area map	163(68.2%)	76(31.8%)
Display summery of demographic information	177(74.0%)	62(26.0%)
Availability of feedback or other report on HIS data	138(57.7%)	101(42.3%)
Use HIS data for decision making	156(65.3%)	83(34.7%)
Use HIS data for future reference	72(46.2%)	
Use HIS data to observe trends	66(42.3%)	
Use HIS data to pass for subsidy health office	18(11.5%)	
Present target & performance	147(61.5%)	92(38.5%)
Calculation of area coverage	92 (38.5%)	147(61.5%)
Presence of routine review meeting	146(61.1%)	93(38.9%)
Incentive for information use	67(28.1%)	172(71.9%)
Policy for information use	87(36.4%)	152(63.6%)
Dissemination mechanism of health information	154(64.4%)	85(35.6%)

Based on the set criteria for HIS utilization, overall utilization rate was found to be 53.1%. Utilization of HIS was also compared based on health facility type and from the analysis the highest utilization rate was 55.3% by the health centers and 52.2% in hospitals followed by 39.3% in health posts (Figure-1).

Technical determinant characteristics for HIS utilization.

Table 11 revealed that health departments which had standard set of indicators were 2.39 times (COR=2.390, 95% CI [1.294, 4.415]) more likely utilized HIS than those departments which did not have standard indicators. Departments which had well designed format were 2.85 times more likely utilized HIS than those departments which did not have well designed format (COR=2.857, 95%CI [1.448, 5.637]). Similarly departments with friendly format for reporting were 3.12 times more likely utilize HIS than departments without friendly format (COR=3.122, 95%CI [1.671,5.831]). Health departments which had trained staffs to fill format were 3.98 times more likely utilize HIS than

departments without trained staffs (COR=3.986,95%CI [1.981,8.020]). Similarly health departments which had skilled human resource were 2.61 times more likely utilize HIS than departments without skilled human resource (COR=2.611, 95%CI [1.442, 4.725]). Departments which use appropriate technology for data analysis were 92% more likely utilize HIS than those departments which did not use technology for data analysis (COR=1.928,95%CI [1.131,3.286]). However when they are adjusted with other predictor variables, only friendly format for reporting showed statistically significant association (AOR=2.796, 95%CI [1.478, 5.288]). Hence, departments with friendly format for reporting

Was 2.796 times more likely utilizing HIS than departments without friendly format.

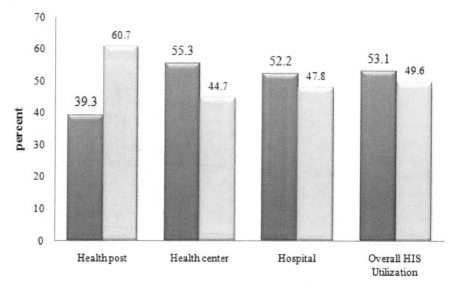

Figure 1. Utilization of HIS by health facility type in Dire Dawa Administration, Apr 2013.

Table 5. Associated Technical determinant characteristics for HIS utilization in all governmental health facilities at Dire Dawa Administration, Apr.2013.

Technical characteristics	HIS utilization	COR	95%CI	AOR	95%CI
Standard set of indicator.	Agree Disagree	2.390 1R	(1.294,4.415)	1.101 1R	(0.514,2.391)
Well designed format.	Agree Disagree	2.857 1R	(1.448,5.637)	1.388 1R	(0.616,3.153)
Trained staff to fill format.	Agree Disagree	3.986 1R	(1.981,8.020)	2.061 1R	(0.911,4.661)
Skilled human resource.	Agree Disagree	2.611 1R	(1.442,4.725)	1.404 1R	(0.672,2.905)
Friendly format for reporting.	Agree Disagree	3.122 1R	(1.671,5.831)	2.796 1R	(1.478,5.288)*
Technology for data analysis.	Agree Disagree	1.928 1R	(1.131,3.286)	1.293 1R	(0.721,2.317)

CI= confidence interval *= p< 0.05, COR= Crude Odds Ratio, AOR= Adjusted Odds Ratio

3.5. Associated Organizational and Behavioral Characteristics for HIS Utilization

Health departments in which their decision was based on supervisor directives were 82% more likely utilize HIS than

departments in which their decision was not based on supervisor directives (COR=1.827, 95%CI [1.023, 3.261]). Managers who provide regular feedback to their staff were 2.42 times more likely utilize HIS than managers who did not provide feedback, (COR=2.420, 95%CI[1.362,4.302]).

Similarly managers who report on data accuracy regularly were 94% more likely utilize HIS than those managers who did not report data accuracy, (COR=1.940, 95%CI [1.107,3.397]), however when they are adjusted with other variables only managers who provide regular feedback to

their staffs was significantly associated with HIS utilization and these managers were 2.195 times more likely utilize HIS than managers who did not provide feedback(AOR=2.195, 95%CI[(1.213,3.974]).

Table 6. Associated organizational and behavioral characteristics for HIS Utilization in all governmental health facilities at Dire Dawa Administration, Apr.2013.

Possible Determinants	HIS Utilization	C OR	95% CI	A OR	95% CI
Decision based on supervisor directive.	Agree	1.827	(1.023,3.261)	1.256	(0.664,2.362)
	Disagree	1ᴿ		1ᴿ	
Managers provide regular feedback.	Agree	2.420	(1.362,4.302)	2.195	(1.213,3.974)*
	Disagree	1ᴿ		1ᴿ	
Manager report on data accuracy.	Agree	1.940	(1.107,3.397)	0.886	(0.773,2.312)
	Disagree	1ᴿ		1ᴿ	

CI= confidence interval *= p< 0.05, COR= Crude Odds Ratio, AOR= Adjusted Odds Ratio

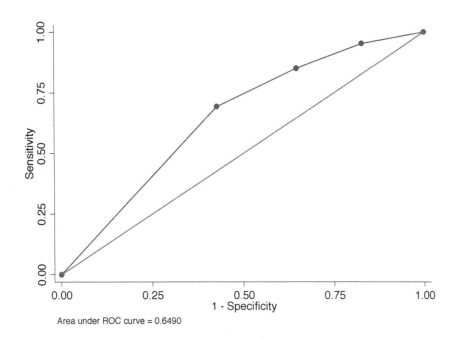

Area under ROC curve = 0.6490

***Figure 2.** Model Adequacy goodness of fit*

The area under the ROC curve (Figure-2) was 0.649 which suggests that the logistic regression model fairly predict (cut-off point=0.50). The significance value of Hosmer-Lemeshow (Goodness-of-Fit) statistic was statistically insignificant (p=0.992) which indicated that the model adequately fit the data. multicolinearity in the variables was checked using Variance Inflation Factor (VIF) and the calculated VIF was 1.03 which is less than 10 and this indicates there was no a problem of multicolinearity.

4. Discussion

Based on PRISM framework using HIS performance diagnostic tools, this study tried to assess the current status of HIS performance at health facility's HIS input, process and output and also tried to identify possible determinant of technical, organizational and behavioral factors for HIS

utilization and data quality.

From the findings of this study 75% of units/departments reported that they had trained staffs and skilled human resources who were capable of performing HIS tasks. Though only 37% of departments reported there were specifically assigned personnel for HIS activity. Similarly 35% and 19% of the facilities have separated HIS office and assigned budget for HIS. These finding was somewhat comparable with other similar study in Bahr-Dar where 45%, 43% and 21% was reported for availability of HIS personnel, HIS office and budget respectively in 2011[27], while only 23.8% was reported for trained staff in North Gonder in 2006 [29] .Regarding availability of HIS equipment, 63% had the necessary equipment. Whereas availability of coordination mechanism to facilitate the use of HIS resources and presence of regulatory and planning framework to use HIS were found to be below 50%. This may be due to less concern given to these issues by majority of the facilities. Considering training on HIS activity, 53% responded for availability of training. It is known that continuous training on HIS activity is important to create awareness, to have trained staff and skilled human resource that are confident and motivated to perform HIS task. When compared to a similar study conducted in Jimma, HIS training was below 50% in 2009 [26].

In order to check the accuracy of the data collected and report at the origin of data source, patient registration and copy of HIS monthly reports should be kept well. According to this study 90% of departments collect health data on daily activity and 82% keep patient registration and HIS monthly reports. These records were also easily accessible to staffs and easily retrieved in 67% of the departments. A similar study done in Jimma reported that all health departments collect data on daily activity and 73% keep their registration and monthly reports. Whereas the study conducted in Bahr Dar revealed that only 77% collect data on daily activity. In this study more than 74% of departments had clear procedure for distributing and reporting the collected data, 85% put the data at administrative level and 75% used a set of criteria to verify completeness and consistency of data before reporting. Regarding availability of supervision 69% of units/ departments had received supervisor directives to check data accuracy, to fill format completely and submit monthly report timely. This was higher when compared with similar studies where availability of supervision was reported below 50% in Bahr-Dar and North Gonder respectively. This may be due to the fact that majority of the health facilities were easily reachable for supervision.

Accurate, consistent, complete and timely information is essential for public health decision-making and action-taking such as policy making, planning, programming and monitoring [13]. In this study 77.4% department heads agreed reports were submitted according to the schedule, which is within 20th to 22nd days of the month for health post and 20th to 24th for health centers and hospital. There was 82.0% department heads also claimed reports were completely filled before reporting while 78.7% of these reports was agreed to be consistent. A similar study in North Gonder showed only 50% HMIS reports were submitted timely while 96% of these reports were completely filled in 2006. Consistency of reports in this study area was slightly high compared to the study in Jimma where 62% of respondents claimed consistency of reports in 2009. This increment may be due to the fact that majority of units/departments had basic HIS training, which in turn had skilled human resource to perform HIS tasks in improving data quality and information use. Another reason could be due to availability of good supervision and feedback given by senior supervisors in this study area.

As originally proposed, HIS performance is defined as improved data quality and continuous use of information. In addition Use of information depends upon the decision power of the people and the importance given to other considerations despite the availability of information [15].

From the finding of this study 71.1% and 67.8% of units/departments compile HIS data and report containing HIS information respectively. It is known that health departments are the primary producers of data and are expected to change this data in to information at the site of data generation. This information is used for evidence based decision making for planning, budget allocation, monitoring and evaluation of program to take immediate action. So based on the set criteria for HIS utilization the overall utilization was found to be 53.1%. This finding was higher when compared with other similar studies in which only 22.5% HIS utilization was reported in North Gonder, 32.9% in Jimma, 45.6% in Bahr Dar, and 44.6% reported in Malawi. On the other hand this finding could be strengthened by the report of progress and lessons on HMIS/M&E implementation from pioneer regions (including Dire Dawa) in 2008 showed that health facilities implementing the new HMIS and M&E achieved considerably high improvements in data quality, information management, and reporting and information use [33].

About 61% units reported there was routine meeting for reviewing managerial and administrative matters. This was higher compared to the assessment report on data quality and information use in selected health facilities in 2011 where only 23.5% facilities had routine review meeting [30]. In this study availability of incentives and policy for information use were found to be below 40%. A similar finding was reported on the study conducted in Bahr Dar where only 18.3% and 42.9% reported for availability of incentives and policy respectively.

Although the PRISM framework allows identifying determinant factors for HIS utilization and data quality, due to lack of similar studies conducted using this framework, it did not allow comparison of the identified determinant factors between different studies.

Among the technical variables friendly format for reporting was found to be significant predictor for HIS utilization. This might be explained by friendly format increase the motivation and confidence of health professionals in performing HIS tasks and saves their time during reporting. Whereas among behavioral and organizational factors managers provide regular feedback to their staffs was also found to be determinant factors for HIS utilization. This might be due to the fact that if there is feedback mechanism, departments will identify their strength and weakness.

Acknowledgements

We are grateful to all research team who dedicated their full time and effort during data collection. We would like to thank Dire Dawa Administrative Health Bureau for their cooperation in undertaking this research and also all department heads of hospital, health centers and health posts for their participation and support in providing the required information for this research.

References

[1] World Health Organization Regional Office for the Western Pacific. Workshops on the assessment and development of national Health Information Systems (HIS) and epidemiological surveillance, WHO 1986.

[2] Chawla R, Bansal AK, Indrayan A. Informatics Technology in Health Care, Nati Med 1997, vol.10 (1): pp31-5.

[3] http//www.who.int/entity/healthmetrics/hmn. Accessed at12:39 12/08/2012

[4] Rwanda Health Information System Assessment Report, RTI international 2006, USAID/Ministry of Health, Rwanda.

[5] Developing Health Management Information System. A practical guide for developing countries, WHO 2004.

[6] WHO, A Framework and Standards for Country Health Information System Development. Geneva; WHO, 2008.

[7] HMIS Reform Team. Health Management Information System / M&E: Information Use Guidelines and Display Tools, Federal Ministry of Health 2007.

[8] GAVI/core: Monitoring national immunization system using core indicators

[9] Tullen University. Tullen University supported HMIS Implementation program Training Manual 2009; Addis Ababa.

[10] Sahay Sundeep. Special Issues on IT and Health Care in Developing Countries, Department of Informatics, University of Oslo 2001, Norway.

[11] Health Metrics Network. Assessing the National Health Information System: An Assessment Tool version 4.

[12] World Health Organization. Assessment of Ethiopian National Health Information System; Final report, 2007.

[13] Lippeveld T, Sauerborn R, Bodart C. Design and implementation of health information systems: World Health Organization 2000, Geneva.

[14] Health Facility's Revised Health Management Information System (HMIS) procedural manual volume-one, Uganda 2010.

[15] Aqil A, Lippeveled T, Dairiku H. PRISM framework: a paradigm shift for designing, strengthening and evaluating routine health information systems; Health Policy and Planning 2009.

[16] MEASURE Evaluation-PRISM: Performance of Routine Information System Management Framework

[17] World Health Organization. Monitoring the building blocks of health systems: a handbook of indicators and their measurement strategies, WHO 2010, Geneva, Switzerland.

[18] Ajzen I. Laws of human behavior: symmetry, compatibility, and attitude-behavior correspondence, 2005..

[19] Odhiambo-Otieno GW. Evaluation criteria for district health management information systems: lessons from the Ministry of Health, Kenya. International Journal of Medical Informatics 2005b. vol.74: pp31-8.

[20] Hackman JR, Oldham GR. Work redesign. Reading, MA: Addison-Wesley, 1980.

[21] Mavimbe JC, Braa J, Bjune G. Assessing immunization data quality from routine reports in Mozambique. BMC Public Health2005. Vol. 11: pp108.

[22] Da Silva AS, Laprega MR. Critical evaluation of the primary care information system (SIAB) and its implementation in Ribeiero Preto, Sau Paulo, Brazil. Cadernos de Saude Publica 2005. Vol.21: pp1821–8.

[23] Mapatano MA, Piripiri L. Some common errors in health information system report (DR Congo). Sante´ Publique 2005. Vol.17: pp551–8.

[24] Odhiambo-Otieno GW. Evaluation of existing district health management information systems: a case study of the district health systems in Kenya. International Journal of Medical Informatics 2005. vol.74: pp733–44.

[25] Nsubuga P, Eseko N, Tadesse W et al. Structure and performance of infectious disease surveillance and response, United Republic of Tanzania, 1998. Bulletin of the World Health Organization2002. Vol. 80: pp196–203

[26] Aqil A, Hotchkiss D, Lippeveld T, Mukooyo E, Asiimwe S. Do the PRISM framework tools produce consistent and valid results? A Uganda study. Working Paper. National Information Resource Center, Ministry of Health, Uganda; MEASURE Evaluation, 2008.

[27] Peter K, Miriam N, Amos N. Development of HMIS in poor countries: Uganda as case study; UMU press 2005, vol.3 (1).pp48-50.

[28] Sultan A, Challi J, Waju B. Utilization of Health information System at district level in Jimma zone, Ethiopian Journal of health science 2011, vol.21: PP.75-79.

[29] Helen T. assessment of the Health Management information System implementation Status in public health facilities in Bahir-Dar city. Master's thesis, school of information science, Addis Ababa University, 2011.

[30] Gebrekidan M, Negus W, Hajira M. Data Quality and Information use: a systematic review to improve evidence in Ethiopia, African health Monitor 2011, Issue No.14 (http/www.aho.afro.who.int/en/ahm/issue14)

[31] Gashaw A. Assessment of utilization of Health Information System at district level with particular emphasis to HIV/AIDS program in North Gonder, Master's thesis, department of community health medical faculty, Addis Ababa University 2006.

[32] HMIS task force. SNNP Regional Government, 2011. http//www.snnprhb.gov.et

[33] Woldemariam H, Habtamu T, Fekadu N, Habtamu A. Implementation of an integrated Health Management Information System and Monitoring and Evaluation (HMIS/M&E) system in Ethiopia: progress and lessons from pioneering regions; Quarterly health Bulletin 2010, vol.3(1): pp48-52.

[34] Central Statistics Agency of Ethiopia, 2007.

19

Lane Detection Method of Statistical Hough Transform Based on Gradient Constraint

Peng Yan-zhou, Gao Hong-feng[*]

College of Information Engineering, Henan University of Science and Technology, Luoyang, China

Email address:

pengyanzhou@sina.com (Peng Yan-zhou), gaohongfenghappy@126.com (Gao Hong-feng)

Abstract: A lane detection method of statistical Hough transform based on gradient constraint is proposed to solve the problem of computational cost and grid quantization precision of classical Hough transform. Statistical Hough transform uses the Gaussian kernel function to model each pixel in the image .The size of initial data set is limited by using the method of gradient constraint. Eventually lane parameters' continuous probability density function is given. The results of the experimentation show that under highway circumstance the provided method can rapidly and robustly detect the lane.

Keywords: Statistical Hough Transform, Gaussian Kernel Function, Gradient Constraint

1. Introduction

With the increase in the number of vehicles, the number of car accident on highway has increased annually. Many accidents are caused by a lack of awareness about driving conditions due to driver carelessness or visual interference. Lane detection and tracking technology based on visual are the key technology on the applications of driver assistance systems for automobiles [1]. Many researchers have done a lot of work on that [2-8]. Road standard in our country formulates that the highway minimum plane curve radius is 650m.Taking the lane line curvature radius of 650m, 40m bending lane line in front of the vehicle can be approximate to straight lines. The approximation in most cases can be established from the experiment image, and near-field vision can ensure the vehicle's safety driving. So the linear model is suitable for the standardization highway road detection and near-field vision in the lane line can be obtained by straight lines model fitting.

Lane detection is still a fertile area of machine vision research[9-11]; variations of the Hough transform are still among the most popular and commonly used methods [8]. It transforms the straight line in the image space to corresponding position of a point in the parameter space, and then the position of the point in the parameter space is formed in the peak after cumulative voting. Through the extraction of the peak, the parameters of the line are obtained. In these approaches, the input images are first preprocessed to find edges using a Canny edge detector or steer able filters, followed by a threshold. The classical Hough transform is then used to find straight lines in the binary image.

Classical Hough transformation works well for line finding when the roads are mostly straight; however, it also has shortcomings as the probability density function of the parameters in classical Hough transform is estimated using a discrete two-dimensional histogram [2], Here are two of them: First, in the classical Hough transform, every pixel in the original image space participate in the transformation from image space to parameter space. At the same time, the voting of the parameter point do not always come from the same line in the image space, also may be caused by the chance to arrange of lane marking points which are not in the same straight line. This not only makes the algorithm increased in computational complexity and time-consuming, also lead to the subsequent lower accuracy. Second, for the grid quantization precision in parameter space, classical Hough transform is very difficult to achieve the optimal. If the grid is quantitative too much, that would be result in double counting in a same straight line, thus increasing the computational complexity. If the grid is not quantitative too much, that would be result in a bad space gathering and not getting the right line parameters.

Base on this, the paper models the classical Hough transform parameters by statistical kernel function, and put each pixel's position and gradient orientation in the image as the observation data. The probability density function of the parameters is continuous and contains more useful information. This also solves the problem of the grid quantitative accuracy effectively. For processing and modeling on every pixel in the image, computational cost is larger. Using the method of gradient threshold limits the size of initial data set. Only keep large gradient pixels modeling by Gaussian kernel function.

This paper is organized as follows. Section 2 introduces the principle of statistical Hough transform. In section 3, the lane detection method of statistical Hough transforms based on gradient constraint is presented. Results and analyses are given in section 4, which introduce experimental results on different road situations. Finally, this paper is concluded in section 5.

2. The principle of Statistical Hough Transform

First rewriting the classical Hough transform equation:

$$\rho = x\cos\theta + y\sin\theta \qquad (1)$$

The variables x、y、θ、ρ are continuous random variables .Some of them may be available in different observation space. In particular, we define the following observation space:

1, $S_{xy} = \{(x_i, y_i)\}_{i=1\cdots N}$ .This is the observation space of variables (x, y) which used in the classical Hough Transform.

2, $S_{\theta xy} = \{(\theta_i, x_i, y_i)\}_{i=1\cdots N}$ .This is the observation space of θ . Indeed, when considering images, the gradient orientation can locally be computed and used as an observation θ .

3, $S_{\theta \rho} = \{(\theta_i, \rho_i)\}_{i=1\cdots N}$ .when knowing θ_i, x_i, y_i , the measure ρ_i can be computed using (1) and also used as an observation.

In addition to the observations, we attached a prior p_i ($\sum_{i=1}^{N} p_i = 1$, $0 \le p_i \le 1$)to each observation i 。 The statistical framework completely generalizes the classical Hough Transform and also takes advantage of the relation (1) between the random variables. This allows us to propose three different estimates of $p_{\theta\rho}(\theta, \rho)$ for each observation space (S_{xy} , $S_{\theta xy}$ and $S_{\theta\rho}$).

Let $G(x, y)$ be the gray image of $f(x, y)$, its first order derivatives are $G_x(x, y)$, $G_y(x, y)$ .The gradient magnitude $\|\nabla G_i\|$ and gradient orientation θ_i for each pixel

i at location (x_i, y_i) are getting from the following formula:

$$\|\nabla G_i\| = \sqrt{G_x^2(x_i, y_i) + G_y^2(x_i, y_i)} \qquad (2)$$

$$\theta_i = \arctan(\frac{G_y(x_i, y_i)}{G_x(x_i, y_i)}) \qquad (3)$$

Variance of θ_i is defined as:

$$\sigma_{\theta_i}^2 = \frac{\sigma^2}{\|\nabla I_i\|^2} \qquad (4)$$

Where σ^2 is the noise variance, generally defined as 1.

2.1. The Probability Density Function Under Different Observation Space

We propose three estimates of the probability density function $p_{\theta\rho}(\theta, \rho)$ for observation space $S_{\theta\rho}$, $S_{\theta xy}$, S_{xy} using kernel modeling.

First, kernel function model is used to give the probability density function $p_{\theta\rho}(\theta, \rho)$ in the observation space $S_{\theta\rho}$.

$$\hat{p}_{\theta\rho}(\theta, \rho | S_{\theta\rho}) = \sum_{i=1}^{N} \frac{1}{h_{\theta_i}} k_\theta(\frac{\theta - \theta_i}{h_{\theta_i}}) \bullet \frac{1}{h_{\rho_i}} k_\rho(\frac{\rho - \rho_i}{h_{\rho_i}}) p_i \qquad (5)$$

Where h_{θ_i} and h_{ρ_i} are the variable bandwidths. Their estimations are explained in next section. The kernels $k_\theta(\bullet)$ and $k_\rho(\bullet)$ have been chosen Gaussians so that (5) gives a continuous and smooth estimate of the density $p_{\theta\rho}(\theta, \rho)$.

For the observation space $S_{\theta xy}$, using the Bayes formula, we can write:

$$p_{\theta\rho xy}(\theta, \rho, x, y) = p_{\rho|\theta xy}(\rho|\theta, x, y)p_{\theta xy}(\theta, x, y) \qquad (6)$$

Under the observation space $S_{\theta xy}$,the variable x, y, θ are known, the variable ρ is deterministic by formula (1). Therefore, we propose to model the conditional probability as follows:

$$p_{\rho|\theta xy}(\rho|\theta, x, y) = \delta(\rho - x\cos\theta - y\sin\theta) \qquad (7)$$

Where $\delta(\bullet)$ is the Dirac distribution. As a consequence, only $p_{\theta xy}(\theta, x, y)$ is to estimate using kernels with the observation space $S_{\theta xy}$:

$$\hat{p}_{\theta xy}(\theta, x, y | S_{\theta xy}) = \sum_{i=1}^{N} \hat{p}_{\theta xy}(\theta, x, y | \theta_i, x_i, y_i)p_i = \sum_{i=1}^{N} \frac{1}{h_{x_i}} k_x(\frac{x - x_i}{h_{x_i}}) \frac{1}{h_{y_i}} k_y(\frac{y - y_i}{h_{y_i}}) \frac{1}{h_{\theta_i}} k_\theta(\frac{\theta - \theta_i}{h_{\theta_i}})p_i \qquad (8)$$

Note that we have assumed the variables x , y , θ independent given their observation space (θ_i, x_i, y_i) .The estimate can be computed:

$$\hat{p}(\theta, \rho | S_{\theta xy}) = \sum_{i=1}^{N} \frac{1}{h_{\theta_i}} k_\theta(\frac{\theta - \theta_i}{h_{\theta_i}}) R_i(\theta, \rho)p_i \qquad (9)$$

with:

$$R_i(\theta,\rho) = \iint \delta(\rho - x\cos\theta - y\sin\theta)\frac{1}{h_{x_i}}k_x(\frac{x-x_i}{h_{x_i}}) \times \frac{1}{h_{y_i}}k_y(\frac{y-y_i}{h_{y_i}})dxdy$$

In the observation space S_{xy} which is the classical Hough transform observation space, the only available thing is the position (x, y). No prior information is available on the variable θ, therefore, its kernel can be replaced in (9) by the uniform distribution as:

$$\frac{k_\theta(\theta - \theta_i)}{h_{\theta_i}} = \frac{1}{\pi}$$

Then, expression (9) becomes:

$$\hat{p}_{\theta\rho}(\theta,\rho|S_{xy}) = \frac{1}{\pi}\sum_i R_i(\theta,\rho)p_i = \frac{1}{\pi}R(\theta,\rho) \quad (10)$$

with,

$$R(\theta,\rho) = \iint \delta(\rho - x\cos\theta - y\sin\theta)\hat{p}_{xy}(x,y|S_{xy})dxdy \quad (11)$$

And,

$$\hat{p}_{xy}(x,y|S_{xy}) = \sum_{i=1}^{N}\frac{1}{h_{x_i}}k_x(\frac{x-x_i}{h_{x_i}})\frac{1}{h_{y_i}}k_y(\frac{y-y_i}{h_{y_i}})p_i \quad (12)$$

Equation (10) gives a kernel estimate for the classical Hough transform.

2.2. Kernels and Bandwidths

It is usually acknowledged that the choice of the kernel $k(\bullet)$ is very important, we have chosen the kernels k_θ and k_ρ as Gaussian and now we discuss the choice of kernels k_x and k_y. Various kernels k_x and k_y can be used such as:

1. The Dirac kernels are defined as:

$$\begin{cases} \dfrac{k_x(x-x_i)}{h_{x_i}} = \delta(x-x_i) \\ \dfrac{k_y(y-y_i)}{h_{y_i}} = \delta(y-y_i) \end{cases} \quad (13)$$

In this case, no bandwidths are needed. The corresponding kernel $R(\theta,\rho)$ in the Hough space is then also a Dirac:

$$R_i(\theta,\rho) = \delta(\rho - x_i\cos\theta - y_i\sin\theta) \quad (14)$$

2. The Gaussian kernels are defined as:

$$\begin{cases} \dfrac{k_x(x-x_i)}{h_{x_i}} = N(x_i, h_{x_i}^2) \\ \dfrac{k_y(y-y_i)}{h_{y_i}} = N(y_i, h_{y_i}^2) \end{cases} \quad (15)$$

The corresponding kernel $R(\theta,\rho)$ in the Hough space is:

$$G_i(\rho,\theta) = \frac{1}{\sqrt{2\pi(\sigma_{x_i}^2\cos^2\theta + \sigma_{y_i}^2\sin\theta)}}\exp(\frac{-(\rho - x_i\cos\theta - y_i\sin\theta)^2}{2(\sigma_{x_i}^2\cos^2\theta + \sigma_{y_i}^2\sin^2\theta)}) \quad (16)$$

In this paper, we have chosen the kernels as Gaussian. The Dirac kernel is then just a special case of the Gaussian kernel when the bandwidth goes toward 0.

For the variables θ and ρ, we naturally set the bandwidths $h_{q_i} = s_{q_i}$, $h_{r_i} = s_{r_i}$. The bandwidths (h_{x_i}, h_{y_i}) are estimated in a similar fashion as the variable bandwidth for θ. (h_{x_i}, h_{y_i}) reflect the uncertainty attached to the observation space (x_i, y_i) of the variables (x, y). Because of the digitalization process, the observation spaces of the variables (x, y) have a precision ± 1. Then, we set

$$h_{x_i} = h_{y_i} = 1 \quad (17)$$

3. Lane Detection Method of Statistical Hough Transform Based on Gradient Constraint

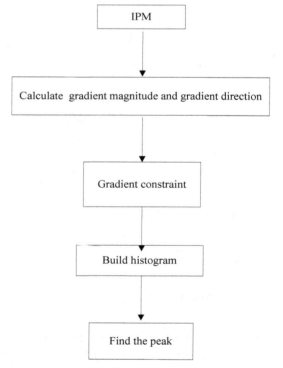

Figure 1. The flow chart of lane detection algorithm.

Based on the statistical Hough transform method described in the previous section, we implement a robust lane detection method based on gradient constraint. The proposed method starts from an inverse perspective mapping algorithm, then each pixel gradient magnitude and gradient orientation are calculated. The gradient constraint method is performed as a selection step, when the pixel gradient magnitude is greater than the threshold; this pixel is selected to model by Gaussian kernel function .Then build a 3D histogram based on the probability density function. The peaks in the histogram are the desired lane parameters. The flow chart of lane detection algorithm is shown in Fig.1.

3.1. IPM

Based on the flat ground hypothesis with known extrinsic and intrinsic parameters of the camera, IPM can remove the perspective effect. It remaps pixels from the original image to the other image that has a different coordinate system. This remapping procedure can be done by a fast lookup table with distortion compensation. As the resolution for near and further object is different in the original image, an interpolation process is needed in the IPM algorithm [3][4]. The resulting image is shown in Fig. 2.We can see from Fig 2 that IPM creates a somewhat cleaned up and less complex image where distracters (sky, objects, etc.,) are downplayed.

(a)   (b)   (c)

Figure 2. (a) Original image. (b) Gray image. (c)IPM image.

3.2. Gradient Constraint

The probability density function of lane parameters is estimated by multiple kernel density, and the uncertain variables are modeled by Gaussian kernels. Statistical Hough transform can directly work on the gray image and it is more robust than the classical Hough transform against noise. But computing the Statistical Hough Transform on an image is more computationally expensive than the classical Hough transform because all pixels of the image are used. The gradient constraint method used to decrease the number of the pixel, in addition, would not cause histogram sparse.

the distribution figure of it, as shown in fig.3.We can get the minimum and maximum gradient magnitude is 0 and 126,respectively. Most of the pixels' gradient magnitudes in the image are relatively small. The number of pixel with gradient magnitude varies from 0 to 20 is the most. These pixels not only increase the complexity of modeling, but also have little chance on the lane line. So, we take those pixels as the basis pixels and get rid of the pixel whose gradient magnitude is zero to calculate the gradient magnitude threshold T . Pixels whose gradient magnitude is greater than the threshold is to participate in statistics Hough transform. The threshold is obtained as:

$$T = G_{\min} + \frac{\left| G_{\max} - G_{\min} \right|}{10} \qquad (18)$$

Where $G_{\min}$ is the minimum gradient magnitude, $G_{\max}$ is the maximum gradient magnitude. Here, we define $G_{\min} = 20$, $G_{\min}$ value can decide by the actual gradient magnitude range.

Introducing the gradient constraint method to statistical Hough transform on the one hand keeps the on lane line pixels modeled by Gaussian as far as possible, on the other hand reduces the amount of calculation of building histogram.

3.3. Build Histogram

This section we applied the kernels function to lane detection. Distribution of lane parameters is determined by

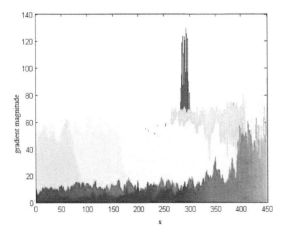

Figure 3. Gradient distribution of Figure 2-c.

Here, we analysis gradient magnitude of the image and get

the position of each pixel in the image given by (x_i,y_i) and the orientation of the pixel θ_i , giving the observation space $Q_{xy\theta}$, the lane parameters probability density function can be represented as $p(\rho,\theta\,|\,Q_{xy\theta})$ .It can be written according to Bayes rule [3]:

$$p(\rho,\theta,x,y\,|\,S_{xy\theta}) = p(\rho\,|\,x,y,\theta,S_{xy\theta})p(x,y,\theta\,|\,S_{xy\theta}) \quad (19)$$

In (19), the first probability $p(r\,|\,x,y,q,S_{xyq})$ is determined by (1), and the second probability $p(x,y,q\,|\,S_{xyq})$ can be modeled by a Gaussian kernel function, thus (19) becomes:

$$p(\rho,\theta,x,y\,|\,S_{xy\theta}) = \delta(\rho-x\cos\theta-y\sin\theta)\frac{1}{N}\sum_i K_x K_y K_\theta \quad (20)$$

Where $\delta(\bullet)$ is the Dirac function, $K_x \sim \mu(x_i,\sigma_{x_i}^2)$, $K_y \sim \mu(y_i,\sigma_{y_i}^2)$, $K_\theta \sim \mu(\theta_i,\sigma_{\theta_i}^2)$ are Gaussian kernels. The distribution $p(r,q\,|\,S_{xyq})$ can be obtained by integrating (20) over (x, y):

$$p(\rho,\theta\,|\,S_{xy\theta}) = \frac{1}{N}\sum_i G_i(\rho,\theta) \quad (21)$$

Where

$$G_i(\rho,\theta) = \frac{1}{\sqrt{2\pi(\sigma_{x_i}^2\cos^2\theta+\sigma_{y_i}^2\sin^2\theta)}}\exp(\frac{-(\rho-x_i\cos\theta-y_i\sin\theta)^2}{2(\sigma_{x_i}^2\cos^2\theta+\sigma_{y_i}^2\sin^2\theta)})$$

Let $\theta\in[-\frac{\pi}{2},\frac{\pi}{2}]$, $\rho\in[-\rho_j,\rho_j]$, where $\rho_j=\frac{w}{2}\cos(a\tan(\frac{h}{w}))+\frac{h}{2}\sin(a\tan(\frac{h}{w}))$,And w and h are the width and height of the IPM image. Then compute the probability for selected pixels according to (21). The variance of x , y , θ are defined as $\sigma_{x_i}^2=1,\sigma_{y_i}^2=1$, $\sigma_{\theta_i}^2=\frac{1}{\|\nabla G_i\|^2}$ 。 Fig.4 shows the histogram of fig.2-c.

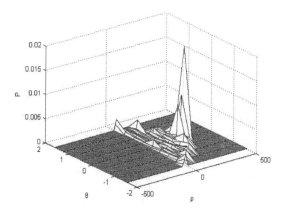

Figure 4. Histogram of statistics Hough transforms.

4. Results and Analyses

Test images on our experiments are captured using on-board system. To demonstrate the performance of the algorithm, we apply it on various situations on the highway under the environment of laboratory. This paper selected 3000 frames of images under various scenarios for testing, a total of 2780 frames correctly detect the lane line, and the correct detection probability is up to 92.7%.

Figure 5 contains two groups' lane detection results, each group consists two parts, the upper part is the original image, and the lower part is the test results. Group (a) is the detection result of no obstacle in the vision field; Group (b) is the detection result of cars or other obstacles occlude in the lane. As can be seen from the test results, under different highway situations, the proposed method detects the lane location in the real range, in case of a small amount of vehicles or obstacle; the robust algorithm can still detect the lane line correctly.

Figure 5. Lane detection results.

Using the gradient constraint method limits the size of

initial data set. Only keep large gradient magnitude pixels modeling by Gaussian kernel function to reducing the amount of calculation. Tab.1 shows the processing speed and the total number of pixels participates in the histogram before and after gradient constraint for Fig.2-c. Before gradient constraint, the processing speed is 1.1s per frame, after gradient constraint, the processing speed is 0.64s per frame. The detection results in Fig 5 reveal the gradient constraint method does not affect the validity of the results.

Table 1. Total number of pixels and processing time contrast before and after gradient constraint.

	total number	processing speed
Before gradient constraint	127600	1.10second/per frame
After gradient constraint	53208	0.64 second/per frame

5. Conclude

A lane detection method of Statistical Hough transform based on gradient constraint is proposed on analyzes the advantages and disadvantages of classical Hough transform. Statistical Hough transform uses the Gaussian kernel function to model each pixel in the image solving the problem of the classical Hough transform grid quantization accuracy. Using the method of gradient constraint limits the size of initial data set for reducing the amount of calculation and improving the follow-up detecting accuracy. Eventually lane parameters of continuous probability density function are given. The results of the experimentation show that under highway circumstance the provided method can rapidly and robustly detect the lane.

References

[1]   Aharon Bar Hillel, Ronen Lerner, Danlevi, Guy Raz. "Recent progress in road and lane detection: a survey", Machine Vision and Application, vol. 10, no. 4, pp.727-745, 2014.

[2]   Rozenn Dahyot, "Statistical Hough transform", IEEE Transactions on pattern analysis and machine intelligence, vol. 31, no.8, pp.1502-1509, 2009.

[3]   G.Liu, F.Wörgötter, I.Markelic´, "combining statistical Hough transform and particle filter for robust lane detection and tracking", In Proceeding(s) of IEEE Intelligent Vehicles Symposinm University of California,pp.993-997,2010

[4]   G.Liu, F.Wörgötter, I.arkeli, "Stochastic lane shape estimation using local image descriptors", IEEE Transactions on intelligent transportation systems, IEEE, vol. 14, no. 1, pp.13-21, 2013.

[5]   H.Yoo, U.Yang, K.Sohn, "Gradient-enhancing conversion for illumination-robust lane detection", IEEE Transactions on intelligent transportation systems, IEEE, vol. 14, no.3, pp.1083-1094, 2013.

[6]   R.Gopalan,T.Hong,M.Shneier. "A learning approach towards detection and tracking of lane markings", IEEE Transactions on intelligent transportation systems, IEEE, vol. 13, no.3, pp.1088-1098, 2012.

[7]   Z.Kim. "Robust lane detection and tracking in challenging scenarios", IEEE Transactions on intelligent transportation systems, IEEE, vol. 9, no.1, pp.16-26, 2008.

[8]   Amol Borkar, Monson Hayes,Mark T.Smith. "A novel lane detection system with efficient ground truth generation", IEEE Transactions on intelligent transportation systems, IEEE, vol.13, no.1, pp.365-374, 2012.

[9]   J.C.McCall, M.M.Triedi, "Video based lane estimation and tracking for driver assistance:Survey,system and evaluation". IEEE Transactions on intelligent transportation systems, IEEE, vol.7, no.1, pp.20-37, 2006.

[10]   Guangtao Cui, Junzheng Wang, Jing Li, "Robust multilane detection and tracking in urban scenarios based on LIDAR and mono-vision ", IET Image Processing, vol.8, no.5, pp.269-279, 2014.

[11]   Y Wang, N.Dahnoun, A.Achim. "A novel system for robust lane detection and tracking".Signal Processing, vol.92, no.2, pp.319-334, 2012.

20

Influence of task characteristics on adoption of project management information system in non-governmental organizations' projects in Nakuru Town (Kenya)

Tobias Oyugi[1, *], Harriet Kidombo[2], Ouinter Omware[1]

[1]Department of Education and External Studies, University of Nairobi, Nairobi, Kenya
[2]School of Continuing and Distance Education, University of Nairobi, Nairobi, Kenya

Email address:
koyugibft@gmail.com (T. Oyugi), harrietkidombo@yahoo.com (H. Kidombo), qokeyo@gmail.com (Q. Omware)

Abstract: In the world today, Management Information System (MIS) is a buzz in all aspects of our economy in managing people and organizational processes; this is aimed at enhancing economic competitiveness and guaranteeing customer satisfaction. Whereas there is consensus that MIS has huge effect on a firm's productivity, the effects are only realized if and when, MIS is accepted and used. It is essential therefore to understand the determinants of MIS adoption so as to appreciate the enormous benefits attached to it. An understanding of how MIS adoption theories can be beneficial to the attainment of the said benefits is important and especially in the non-governmental organizations (NGO's) sector where the focus of this study was. This study sought to determine the influence of Task Technology Fit Framework on the adoption of Project Management Information System (PMIS) in NGO projects in Nakuru town. The study objectives were to establish the influence of task characteristics on adoption of PMIS by NGO's, to examine the influence of technology characteristics in ascertaining adoption by NGO's, to assess the influence of the individual characteristics in adoption of PMIS by NGO's and to establish organizational management expectations that influence adoption of PMIS by NGO's. The study was carried out in Nakuru town with focus on 40 NGO's that were purposively selected. A study sample of 40 project managers and 80 project coordinators were used. The study adopted descriptive case study research design. The study samples were selected using systematic sampling approach for the identification of NGO's (project managers) and simple random sampling in selection of project coordinators. Data was collected using two sets of questionnaires and interviews. Data collected was then analyzed using SPSS and Microsoft Excel software's. The results were then presented in a tabular summaries form. The study revealed that there was a positive relationship between the nature of task characteristics. The study further implores researchers to keenly investigate all PMIS systems that are in use by NGO's and to standardize their design and usage as seen in the construction industry. The study findings could be used by software developers in designing systems that work best and as well guide management of NGO's in implementing successfully the integration of PMIS.

Keywords: Task Characteristics, Project Management Information System, Non-Governmental Organizations' Projects

1. Introduction

Information systems (IS) cannot be defined exclusively without highlighting its key enabler which in the modern world is referred to as Information Technology (IT). The word technology in the 21st century has a connotation to computing and a myriad of electronic devices that are a hallmark of our living rooms, streets and the environment in its entirety. By definition "Technology" refers to the theoretical and practical knowledge, skills, and artifacts that can be used to develop products and services as well as their production and delivery systems (Burgelman et al.,1996). Information technology thus can be said to be the practical knowledge, artifacts and skills that is required in information management. A system by its nature constitutes several components that work together not in isolation but in an integrated manner with a purpose to achieving a common goal. An IS as used in this study refers to all components and resources necessary to deliver information and information processing functions to the organization; these includes hardware, software, people and a network interface (Gabber, 2004).

According to the RAND organization (Hundley, 2004, p 2), "Advances in information technology are affecting most segments of business, society, and governments today in many if not most regions of the world. The changes that IT is bringing about in various aspects of life are often collectively called the "information revolution." Drawing from history, revolutions have been experienced in many shades and colors; in 2011, the Arab world had an upsurge of protests as modern technology provided an opportunity in the social media to force leadership change in their countries and in particular Egypt and Tunisia. Were it not for IT probably the story would be different. Over the last few decades we have moved from invention of the written book in Greece around 1000 BC to Gutenberg's printing press and engraving, around AD 1450 (Brandon, D 2006). The latest of revolutions that have changed the way we live was the emergence of the internet and convergence of systems across the world. In his essay on this modern information revolution, business guru Peter Drucker (2004) noted, "This revolution will surely engulf all major institutions of modern society," and "this revolution will force us to redefine what the business enterprise actually is the creation of value and wealth." Modern project management in not a new thing and by the turn of the 20th century (Brandon, D, 2004) use of engineering and management principles pervaded its design and implementation.

"Around that time, managers of such projects faced pressure from proponents of scientific management to organize in a centralized way and control not just what was done but the details of how and when it was done" (Yates, 2000).

PMIS as a part of IS refers to the tools and techniques used to gather, integrate, and disseminate the outputs of project management processes. It is used to support all aspects of the project from initiation through closing, and can include both manual and automated systems (PMI, 2008). This study focuses on automated systems in management of poverty alleviation projects in Nakuru Town. In its design PMIS adoption is tied to the ICT literacy of the users, nature of organizational task and thus a critical evaluation of the workforce competency in usage of related ICT systems is valuable. Nakuru is the one most populated town in Kenya, having a density of 181 persons per km². Nakuru Town is the most densely populated division, where most of the people live in divisions like Kaptembwo, Langalanga, Ponda Mali and Mwariki. The town has been growing at a very high rate while provision of basic facilities has not expanded at the same rate to serve the population (Nakuru district strategic plan 2008).

1.1. Statement of the Problem

In a study to augment TTF, a social Technical gap was established among those using social networking information systems. The Social Technical Gap is "the divide between what we know we must support socially and what we can support technically (Ackerman, 2000)." The Social Technical Gap as captured in the Social network study can be conceived of as a specific instance of task technology fit. Social requirements are a sub-set of requirements that make up social tasks, such as communication, coordination, and cooperation that are elements of PMIS. Thus the Social Technical Gap explains the lack of fit between social requirements and technical solutions. By its design, task technology fit as a theory in the IS lifecycle portends that at the integration phase of PMIS focus is on the role of PMIS in mainstreaming IS solutions into functional departments (Nolan 1979). The three elements of Task Technology Fit underscore this argument by highlighting task, technology and individual characteristics as an appropriate mix to achieving sound adoption of PMIS in realizing performance. NGO's have people who have unique characteristics and personal attributes but whose influence are essential in adoption of PMIS use. The nature of social tasks that is characteristic of a PMIS like communication, scheduling, budgeting, planning and control must be integrated in system design for it to be adopted as fit for use. The technology that drives PMIS completes the triangulation of TTF.

1.2. Purpose of the Study

The purpose of this study was to assess the adoption of PMIS using the Task Technology Fit (TTF) framework in NGO projects. This evaluation was hinged on the perceived strengths and weaknesses of the TTF theoretical framework in establishing adoption of PMIS use among NGO's in Nakuru Town. With studies gearing to bridging the gaps in TTF theory, the study delved into improving the TTF theory to meeting its goodness in adoption of PMIS by Non-governmental organizations in Nakuru Town.

1.3. Objectives of the Study

This study was guided by four objectives that were drawn from the independent variables forming the TTF theory. These were:

1. To establish the influence of task planning on adoption of PMIS by NGO's
2. To examine the influence of task communication on adoption by NGO's
3. Assess the influence of task scheduling on adoption of PMIS by NGO's
4. To establish how task controlling influence adoption of PMIS by NGO's
5. To determine how task reporting influence adoption of PMIS by NGO's

1.4. Hypotheses of the Study

The study was guided by the following hypotheses;

Ho_1: There is no significant relationship between task planning and PMIS adoption.

Ho_2: There is no significant relationship between task communication and PMIS adoption.

Ho_3: There is no significant relationship between task scheduling and PMIS adoption.

Ho_4: There is no significant relationship between task controlling and PMIS adoption.

Ho$_5$: There is no significant relationship between task reporting and PMIS adoption.

1.5. Significance of the Study

This research was meant to be of immense significance to the NGO sector in Kenya. It did assess whether TTF theory of adoption as integrated in PMIS implementation by most NGO's yields the desired maximum PMIS adoption status in the local context. This was expected to inform donors and NGO management in policy formulation as regards performance improvement and planning their activities in the developing world. The research gives recommendations on the appropriate mix of variables that guarantee adoption of any new technology based on TTF and further advice integration with other MIS adoption theories.

This research further informs best adoption practices among emerging local and international NGO's and other organizations who are intending to adopt some sort of MIS or those that are already implementing MIS. In the interest of living with technology; and the need to meeting our developmental objectives at its best, the study sought to establish if PMIS adoption and usage mitigate pilferage, increase customer satisfaction, motivate project teams and keep the donor community committed to continuous funding in their areas of interest. The successes aforementioned were seen to be the driving factors behind the choice of an adoption strategy in PMIS implementation.

2. Literature Review

2.1. Task Characteristics

This section describes the characteristic requirements of task that are part of PMIS. These include scheduling, planning, reporting, progress review and resource management.

2.1.1. Project Planning

Enterprise guidance and project background information form the basis for planning the project. This information should be a part of the PMIS. The PMIS supports the full range of the project life cycle to include pre-project analysis and post project reviews (Turner 1999).

The PMIS should interface with larger organizational information systems to permit smooth, efficient interchange of information in support of organizational and project objectives and goals (Thomsen 2011). Planning for a PMIS requires that information be selectively included and irrelevant information omitted to preclude an overabundance of data and little relevant information.

2.1.2. Resource Management

Information is needed to manage the project, which is to plan, organize, evaluate, and control the use of resources on the project. The PMIS should be able to apply algorithms such as resources leveling and smoothing to manage the project. The PMIS should be able to check for and help resolve over allocation of resources (Clements, Gido 2006).

2.1.3. Tracking and/or Monitoring

An important purpose served by a PMIS is that it can track at the work package level for early identification of schedule slippage or significant cost overruns on detailed work areas. Early identification of small problems permits the attention to detail before there are major impacts on higher-order work. This is especially important on large projects or projects that have a very rigorous schedule to meet the enterprise's or customer's goals. The PMIS should be prospective and capable of providing intelligence on both the current and probable future progress and status of the project (Thomsen 2011).

2.1.4. Report Generation

Information to manage a project comes from a wide variety of sources, including formal reports, informal sources, observation, project review meetings, and questioning which is aided by formal evaluation and analysis as to what the information says about the status of the project (Thomsen 2011). Reporting capabilities are given a high priority, because the ability to produce extensive and power reports is a feature that most users and stakeholders rate very highly (Clements, Gido 2006). The PMIS should be able to provide reports on the project's status and progress, planning, scheduling, individual tasks and resources.

2.1.5. Integration with other Systems

The PMIS should provide integration with distributed databases, spread sheets, and even object-orientated databases. Furthermore, the system should be able to import and export information to and from word processing and graphics packages (Gido 2006). The system should also do this through e-mail and other communication avenues provided for in the system. Information provides the basis for continuation of the project in the absence of the project manager. The project team can monitor the progress of the project and compare it to the project plan to assure that work is progressing satisfactorily. An effective PMIS provides the information that demonstrates when the project is on track or when it has exceeded the allowable limits of performance. A PMIS should be able to track the progress of tasks, durations, costs, committed or spent, and resources.

2.2. Project Management Information System

Project management information system is an open collaborative system that is used to manage projects. It provides business processes and procedures which are either virtual in integration and access or are standalone systems which operate within an organization. It houses data and provides routes along which appropriate workflow demands, information log trail and record generation are managed. Constant communication between stakeholders that are geographically a part allows for timely feedback eliminating misinformation. In the past companies used unrelated tools to manage projects; tools like email communication, paper processes and document storage were dispersed in location making it quite difficult to track and report on project status.

Today PMIS manages several projects with an escalation of its adoption across the globe.

The true innovation in PMIS is the way it facilitates communication between the management, site workers, middle management, affiliate organizations and other stakeholders. PMIS combines project management and technology to produce a global collaborative network. All stakeholders, owners, vendors all work in single system with a single set of data. As the system records, routes, tracks and notifies, it creates a documented trail of decision making that follows established processes across the entire organization that ultimately reduces failures. PMIS creates an environment that enables full compliance and consistency across the projects in key areas that include communication, administration of employees, document storage, sharing lessons learnt, manage gained knowledge, track, analyze, report projects and manage working relationships among the work force.

2.3. Successes of Project Management Information Systems

Project success consists of two separate components, namely project management success and project product success (Baccarini 1999). Project management success focuses on the project management process and in particular on the successful accomplishment of the project with regards to cost, time and quality. These three dimensions indicate the degree of the 'efficiency of project execution'. Project product success on the other hand focuses on the effects of the project's end-product. Even though project product success is distinguishable from project management success, the successful outcomes both of them are inseparably linked. 'If the venture is not a success, neither is the project' (Pinkerton 2003). McLean (2003) illustrates the components and requirements within the project management success as; within time, specification and budget and product success as; system quality, information quality, service quality, information usage, user satisfaction, individual impact, and organizational impact.

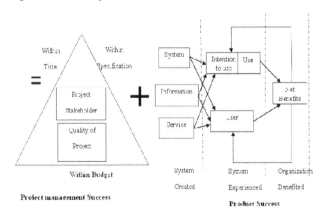

Source: Delone and Mclean (2003).

Figure 1. Adding project management success to the Delone and Mclean Success Model.

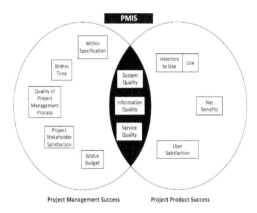

Source: Fitzgerald (2004)

Figure 1. Adapted from common dimensions in project management success with PMIS overlap.

Consequently, it is clear that a Project Management Information System is the golden midway for project management towards project success. This is illustrated below in Figure 2-3: Adapted Common dimensions in project management success and project product success with PMIS overlap (Fitzgerald 2004).

Essentially, the task of PMIS has been described as subservient to the attainment of project goals and the implementation of project strategies; it provides project managers with essential information on the cost-time performance parameters of a project and on the interrelationship of these parameters (Raymond et al., 1987). In the IT industry today, Gartner research estimates that 75% of projects managed with PMIS support will succeed while 75% of projects without such support will fail (Light M., et.al., 2005). In light of this, research also cautions that only a small number of projects utilize all PMIS tools during the project management life cycle such as planning, scheduling, risk management, cost estimates, document management, communicating, and reporting (Herroelen,2005; Love & Irani 2003).

2.4. Information Systems Task Technology Fit Theory

The core of a task technology fit theory is a formal construct known as task-Technology Fit (TFT), which is the matching of the capabilities of the technology to the demands of the task, that is, the ability of IT to support a task (Goodhue and Thompson 1995). TTF model have three key constructs, Task characteristics, Technology characteristics, which inadvertently affect the third construct Task Technology Fit, which in turn affects the outcome variable, either performance of utilization of technology. This model propose that technology that does not offer the perceived usefulness will not easily be adopted for use; technology will only be used if and only if the said functionality element in its design support the activities and processes that the user expects it to accomplish. A common addition to TTF theory is the individual's abilities that enable them to use the technology (Goodhue 1988, Goodhue and Thompson 1995). The inclusion of Individual abilities is supported by both Work Adjustment Theory from which TTF was originally derived and recent MIS studies in which Experience with a particular IT is generally associated with higher utilization of that IT (Guinan et al.1997, Thompson et al.1994)

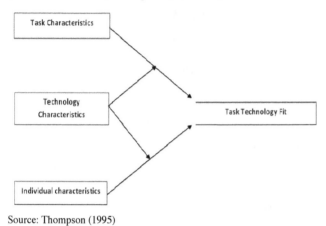

Source: Thompson (1995)

Figure 3. *A model of the task technology Fit framework.*

2.5. PMIS Adoption Challenges and its Requirements

Organizations are constantly shrouded with many ongoing internal and external pressures that influence the way they operate; this portend a potential for changes either within their operations or in their management approach. Such pressures usually dictate the necessity for potential shift in infrastructural arrangements of the IS's that are in use; organizations are therefore forced to take on challenges of implementing new IS's or accept whatever consequences that might follow due to failure to switch gear in this endeavor. Whereas businesses must continuously grow organically to survive, NGO's must constantly adapt to the changes in the market place and diversify to meet the changing global demands. This means that the requirements of the PMISs will also change and utilize the power of technology to meet the ongoing needs of the organization (Senn, 1990).

With the development of PMIS's there is always the hope for seamless PMIS implementation and the projects for which the services are intended expects that there will be no interruptions in delivery of outlined outputs and impacts. However, there are many opportunities for things to go wrong during PMIS implementation and NGO's take the number of risks when embarking on this course of action (Moguire, 2002). The challenges identified by studies done over the years are split into three categories which mirror the variables in this study. These include; operational issues, task characteristics, individual human characteristics and technological issues.

2.6. Conceptual Framework

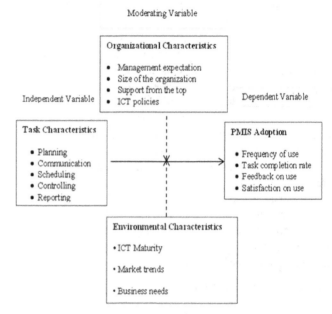

Figure 4. *Conceptual Framework*

3. Methodology

3.1. Research Design

A research design is the scheme, outline, plan, structure or a strategy of investigation conceived so as to obtain answers to research questions and control variables; it constitutes a blueprint for the collection, measurement, and analysis of data (Kothari, 2003). This study adopted descriptive and correlational survey research design employing a triangulation approach where both quantitative and qualitative approaches are integrated.

3.2. Target Population

The target population for this study was the 90 non-governmental organizations within Nakuru town which could be local to Nakuru or are international in their service delivery which already employing PMIS in their financial systems. In stratifying the selected geographical area, the study categorizes the NGO's as international and local. The study then further sought to only involve NGO's that have operations outside the town that requires remote linkage with the main office assumed to be in Nakuru for local NGO's and international headquarters for those that are international. Within these NGO's, the study focused on Project managers and the functional project coordinators in each of their project areas.

3.3. Sampling Procedure and Sample Size

Purposive sampling approach was applied in this study; this is courtesy of the stated study objectives which ties the study to elements of TTF as applied in PMIS adoption. Because not all NGO's have PMIS within their operations the target is the 90 out of the 145 with operations in Nakuru town. A sample of 53 NGO's was picked from the 90 that have operations remote to Nakuru Town and which forms the research population. This is 62 % of the total number of NGO's that are in Nakuru town. From each NGO selected samples of 2 project coordinators were chosen randomly using simple random sampling. The project managers being averagely 1 per project were clustered into NGO's that have more than 1 project manager and those that have only one and from which 1 was chosen from each cluster.

The determination of the sample size was done using Cochran's (1977) formulas. Cochran's sample size for categorical data is:

$$n = t^2pq/d^2 = (1.96)^2 (.50)(.50)/(.50)^2$$

$$n \text{ thus } = 384$$

Where: n = desired sample size

t = value of selected alpha level of 0.25 in each tail = 1.96 (the alpha level of 0.5 indicates the level of risk the researcher is willing to take; the true margin of error may exceed the margin of acceptable margin of error.

pq = estimate of variance =0.25 (maximum possible proportion (.50) producing maximum possible sample size)

d = acceptable margin of error

Therefore for a population of 90 NGO's (270) with PMIS the required sample size is calculated as follows:

$n_f = N/(1+n/population)$

$n_f = 384/(1+(384/270))$

$n_f = 160$

The study will use a sample size of 159 respondents comprising project managers and coordinators distributed across all selected 53 NGO's which mathematically fit within the 1:2 ratio though not 160 as above.

3.4. Data Collection

Questionnaire and an in depth interview were used to collect primary data. The project managers and project coordinators were the major targets. Focus group discussion was also be used to help clarify issues pertaining to interview questions in the in depth interview schedule. Different questionnaires were used for both the project managers and project coordinators. While the majority of questions were different, a number were similar for validity and reliability reasons. Both open ended and closed ended questions were used. The questionnaires were emailed to the respondents and also hard copies provided at their offices in an effort to try and increase the return rate. In depth interviews were mainly conducted with the project manager's in every organization. In cases where project managers were not available program coordinators in charge were considered.

3.5. Data Analysis

Filled up questionnaires were checked for completeness, consistency and clarity. The responses were coded by assigning a numerical value to each; this was to make them quantitative for ease of possible capture by the computer in SPSS for Windows Version 19 analysis. In order to clean up the data averages like mean and median as well as distributions like standard deviations were performed on the data sets in order to discover any anomalies and appropriate corrections done. Descriptive statistics such as frequencies, percentages, median and mode were used for quantitative analysis of the data. To establish the extent to which several NGO have adopted use of PMIS, a Pearson product correlation moment coefficient of selected variables were generated to obtain a general view of the respondents' opinions on the influence on PMIS adoption. To establish the magnitude of relationships as captured by the hypotheses, a cross tab chi-square coefficient guided the acceptance on non –acceptance of p -values based on a statistical standard of measure at (0.05) 95% confidence level.

4. Research Findings

4.1. Response Rate

Table 1. Response rate.

Category of respondents	Feedback (Number of questionnaires returned)	Target No. of questionnaires (Sample size)	Response rate
Project mangers	40	53	76.9 %
Project Coordinators'	80	106	74.1%

4.2. Type of NGO by Affiliation

Table 2. Type of NGO by Affiliation.

NGO type	Frequency	Percent
Local	23	57.5
International	17	42.5
Total	40	100.0

The study show that majority at 57.5 % of the respondents were drawn from the local NGO affiliation. 42.5 % of the NGO's are international which gives a fair share of all interest in development. The implication of this distribution on its own does not have any statistical significance and neither would it point conclusions in any direction.

Comparing the affiliation of the NGO's and the years PMIS have existed reflects however a very weak negative correlation (r (40) = -0.001) as shown in Table 7 below. It is thus confirmatory that with maturity of an organization it is not likely it will embrace PMIS. The international NGO's are expected to have an edge over their local counterparts when it comes to existence of PMIS in their functional units since they connect quite often in reporting to their headquarters abroad. This again disputes the notion of PMIS use and adoption among NGO's based on affiliation.

4.3. Year's Organization has Used PMIS

The findings to how long the organization has used PMIS for both project manager and project coordinators are shown in a Table 8 below. It should be noted that only 40 organizations were considered in the study thus the findings from the project managers reflects exactly what the project coordinators did fill in. Each project manager had 2 project coordinators considered in the study from the same organization.

Table 3. Years Organization has used PMIS.

Years of PMIS use	Frequency	Percent
Between 1 and 5	11	27.5
Between 6 and 10	11	27.5
Between 11 and 15	6	15
Between 16 and 20	10	25
>20	2	5
Total	40	100

Most of the organization appeared to have used PMIS for more than 20 years with a cumulative frequency of 95 % use over the last 20 years. A paltry 5 % of the organizations involved had used PMIS for the last 30 years. These findings are a pointer to the fact that PMIS is not a new thing among NGO's in Nakuru and based on these figures adoption and full use of PMIS begged answers owing to such a huge percentage of PMIS use over the years.

4.4. The Influence of Task Characteristics in Ascertaining Adoption by NGO's

This section presents the findings related to the influence of task characteristic indicators of a PMIS that define key operations by a given NGO in its adoption and usage.

4.4.1. Task Characteristics Indicators

Table 4. Task characteristics indicators.

Task characteristic indicators	Category	Frequency	Percent
Planning within a PMIS	Y	66	82.5
	N	14	17.5
Task scheduling within a PMIS	Y	42	52.5
	N	38	47.5
Progress review within a PMIS	Pert chart	63	78.8
	Gantt Chart	8	10
	Other	9	11.3
Mode of communication	E-mail	40	100
Format of reporting	Brief	35	43.8
	Comprehensive	43	53.8
	Other	2	2.5

4.4.2. Task Scheduling within a PMIS

Task scheduling is a key component of any standard PMIS; it does allow users to schedule activities that they wish to accomplish over a given period of time. 52.5% of the respondents are in agreement that their system allows scheduling of activities with 47.5% not being able. This therefore implies that as a task characteristic in a PMIS the influence might be negative in enhancing adoption levels as the sole purpose of scheduling is to bring order especially where a project involves a large group who are geographically displaced. The figures provide an insight as to the need to have the necessary standard task characteristic in any given PMIS for the lack of any influences to a larger extent adoption levels.

4.4.3. Progress Review within a PMIS

The results above shows that most organizations have within their PMIS task characteristics which is a project review tool that helps in monitoring the progress of a project. 78.8% have a project evaluation and review technique tool integrated within their systems, 10% have a Gantt chart while 11.3% uses a spreadsheet, mobile phones and project forums under other techniques. The implication here is that most organizations have a review tool of some sort meaning as a task characteristic within a PMIS, the use of a review tool is crucial in influencing adoption and usage of a PMIS.

4.4.4. Planning within a PMIS

The results above shows 82.5% of the respondents plan their work using the PMIS system. 17.5% do not plan their work within the system but use other software techniques in doing so. Planning being a key task characteristic component of a PMIS it is implied therefore that its inclusion is very essential in influencing adoption and usage of PMIS. Though a smaller percentage does not plan within the PMIS it was clear from the interviews that other mechanisms are used while planning and in some cases attributed to lack of integration in certain systems.

4.4.5. Mode of Communication Preferred within PMIS

It is clear from the results obtained that all the reporting and communication within any PMIS used by NGO's in Nakuru is 100% email. The implication of these results is that despite the availability of other modes of communication email still ranks top meaning that these other communication modes need not be included in the PMIS so as to only have what is fit for use thereby making the PMIS interface less confusing.

4.4.6. Format of Reporting to Upper Management

The Table shows comprehensive (53.8%) reporting as the preferred mode compared to brief (43.8%) and others (2.5%). The implication here is that whatever the nature of the report as a task characteristic there must be an element of reporting in PMIS if it is to be effectively of use and relevance to the users. From a management information systems view point the top management requires very brief but synthesized reports that can then assist in decision making. The fact that 53.8% of the project coordinators do provide comprehensive reports it was clear from the interview that the project managers usually require both the brief and the comprehensive report in aiding full comprehension of the facts as presented.

4.4.7. Promptness' on Feedback and Frequency of Reporting

The table below presents findings on promptness' on feedback and frequency of reporting as other indicators of task characteristic in PMIS.

Table 5. Task Characteristics Indicators (2).

Task indicators	Hourly	Daily	Weekly	Fortnightly
Promptness of feedback	5	60	14	1
Percent	6.3	75	17.5	1.3
Frequency of reporting	4	47	24	5
Percent	5	58.8	30	6.3

4.4.8. Frequency of Reporting to Upper Management

The results shows that majority (58.8%) report on a daily basis compared to 30.0% weekly reporting, 6.3% monthly reporting and hourly reporting at 5.0%. These figures imply that there is less pressure on the system at any given time during the day as the project coordinators report mainly at close of business. Drawing a comparison with the nature of reports which shows 53.8% giving descriptive reports a conclusion is thus derived at that it is the project managers that will condense the obtained information into a succinct form for onward transmission to other stakeholders'. This in effect guarantees that the usage of the PMIS in quite mandatory at the project managers level.

4.4.9. Promptness of Feedback from Project Manager

The findings as shown in the Table above is that 75% get feedback daily from the project managers compared to 17.5% who get weekly feedback, 6.3% who get hourly feedback and a paltry 1.3% who get fortnightly feedback. The findings imply that reports given to project managers are quickly acted upon and any clarifications are obtained within a day. These findings point to a very efficient communication within the PMIS which is task component met within its usage.

5. Conclusions and Recommendations

Tasks that are integrated within a PMIS have a very significant influence on the level of adoption and usage within a PMIS. The inherent task characteristics that were identified by the study to be significant included the planning tool, task scheduling tool, project review tool (Pert chart), communication, different report export/import tools to other auxiliary software's. Task integration of all these components appeared to influence much the appreciation of the systems capability and to larger extent the conviction by user that PMIS is a good thing.

Based on the findings, the researcher recommended that besides the choice of PMIS it is cognizant that policies be put in place that guides its full implementation. The entire process of systems analysis and design must be fully embraced and both feasibility study on the user expectations and their feedback at each stage of implementation be adhered to fully.

During this study the researcher identified some areas that require further research. Having analyzed the task, technology fit framework and recognizing the characteristic nature of this theory the study thus confirms that technology adoption is not only a Fit element from the design angle but the characteristic nature of individual as well as the control on the users. This study recommends that further research be done in establishing why there is unanimity that PMIS is a good thing yet with training and support still the benefits that are expected to accrue from its usage does not translate to increased level of performance especially among those working in NGO's. This analogy is captured on the different PMIS systems that are in use by most NGO's. Unlike PMIS used in other organizations where standards are set and only

few systems are in use with maximum outputs very little interest is coming from the developers to entrenching certain standards in NGO PMIS's that can translate to maximum benefits for the these organizations.

References

[1] Ackerman, M. S. (2000). The intellectual Challenge of CSCW: The Gap between Social Requirements and Technical Feasibility. Human-Computer Interaction, 15 (2), 179-203.

[2] Adams, D. A., Nelson, R. R. & Todd, P. A. (1992). Perceived usefulness, ease of use, and usage of information technology: A replication. *MIS Quarterly*. 16(2), 227-248.

[3] Ahlemann F. (2008), Project Management Software Systems Requirements, Selection Processes and Products, 5th Edition. Wurzburg: BARC.

[4] Ajzen, I.; and Fishbein, M. *Understanding Attitudes and Predicting Social Behavior*. Englewood Cliffs, NJ: Prentice-Hall, 1980.

[5] Ajzen, I. (1985). From intentions to Actions: A Theory of Planned bBehavior. In J. Kuhl & J. Beckman (Eds.), *Action-control: From cognition to Behavior* (pp. 11-39). Heidelberg: Springer Press.

[6] Anderson, Eugene W. and Mary W. Sullivan (1993), "The Antecedents and Consequences of Customer Satisfaction for Firms," *Marketing Science*, 16 (2), 129-45.

[7] Baccarini, D 1999, 'The Logical Framework Method for Defining Project Success', *Project*

[8] *Management Journal*, vol. 30, no. 4, pp. 25-32.

[9] Bergeron, F., Raymond, L., Rivard, S. & Gara, M. F. (1995). Determinants of EIS Use: Testing a Behavioral Model. *Decision Support System*, 14 (1), 131-146.

[10] Brandon, D. (2002). Issues in the Globalization of Electronic Commerce. In V. K. Murthy

[11] & N. Shi (Eds.), *Architectural Issues of Web-enabled electronic business*. Hershey,

[12] PA: Idea Group Publishing.

[13] Brandon, D. (2004). Project Performance Measurement. In P. Morris & J. Pinto (Eds.), *The*

[14] *Wiley Guide to Managing Projects*. New York: Wiley.

[15] Burgelman R.A., Maidique M.A. and Wheelwright S.C. 1996. 'Strategic Management of Technology and Innovation'. Irwin. Chicago. USA. Second Edition.

[16] Burke, R. J. 2001a, 'Spence and Robbins' Measures of Workaholism Components: Test-Retest

[17] Stability', *Psychological Reports*, Vol. 88, no. pp. 882-888.

[18] Caldwell, R. (2004). *Project Management Information System: Guidlines for Planning, Implementing, and Managing a DME Project Information System*. New York: CARE Press.

[19] Cleland, D. I. (2004b). *Project Management Information System in Project Management: Strategic Design and Implementation* (5th ed.). New York: McGraw-Hill Press.

[20] Clements, J. P. & Gido, J. (2006). *Effective Project Management*. Canada: Thomson South-Western.

[21] Cochran, W. G. (1977) Sampling Techniques. John Wiley & Sons:New York, 1977. pp.74-76.

[22] Cragg, P. B. and King, M. (1993). Small-Firm Computing: Motivators and Inhibitors. *MIS Quarterly,* 17 (1): 47-60.

[23] Dabholkar, P. A. and Bagozzi, R. (2002) *An Attitudinal Model of Technology-Based Self-Service: Moderating Effects of Consumer Traits and Situational Factors,* Journal of the Academy of Marketing Science, 30 (3), pp. 184-201.

[24] Davis, F.D., Bagozzi, R.P. & Warshaw, P.R. 1989, " User Acceptance of Computer Technology: A Comparison of two Theoretical models.", *Management Science,* vol. 35, no. 8, pp. 982–1003.

[25] Davis, F. D. (1989). Perceived Usefulness, Perceived Ease of Use, and User Acceptance of Information Technology. *MIS Quarterly.* 13(3), 319-339.

[26] DeLone, W.H., and Mclean, E.R. (1992), Information Systems Success: The Quest for the Dependent Variable, Information Systems Research, 3(1), 6095.

[27] De Lone, W.H., and Mclean, E.R. (2003), The DeLone and McLean Model of Information Systems Success: A TenYear Update, Journal of Management Information Systems, 19(4), 930.

[28] Dishaw, M. T. & Strong, D. M. (1998a). Experience as a Moderating Variable in a Task-Technology Fit Model Presented at the Fourth Americas Conference on Information Systems. Baltimore.

[29] Dishaw, M.T. & Strong, D. M. (1998b). Supporting Software Maintenance with Software Engineering Tools: A Computed Task-Technology Fit Analysis. *Journal of Systems and Software,* 44, 107-120.

[30] Fenech, T. (1998).Using Perceived Ease of Use and Perceived Usefulness to Predict Acceptance of the World Wide Web. *Computer Networks and ISDN Systems,* 30 (7), 629-630.

[31] Gabber, E., The Case Against User-level NetworkingProceedings of the Third Annual Workshop on System-Area Networks (SAN-3), February 2004, Madrid Spain.

[32] Garson, G. D. (2008). Multiple regression. Retrieved January 28, 2008, from

[33] http://www2.chass.ncsu.edu/garson/pa765/regress.htm

[34] Goodhue, D. L. (1995). Understanding User Evaluations of Information Systems. *Management Science*, 41(12), 1827-1844.

[35] Goodhue, D. L. & Thompson, R. L. (1995). Task-Technology Fit and Individual Performance. *MIS Quarterly*, 19 (2), 213-236.

[36] Gupta, A. (2000) Enterprise resource planning: the emerging organizational value systems, Industrial Management & Data Systems, April, 2000, Volume 100, Issue 3, p114-118.

[37] Havelka, D., & Rajkumar, T.M. (2006), Using the troubled project recovery framework: Problem recognition and decision to recover. E-Service.Journal, 5(1), 4373.

[38] Herroelen W. (2005), Project scheduling theory and practice. Prod Oper Manage, 14(4):41332.

[39] Huber, G. P. (1990) „A Theory of the Effects of Advanced Information Technologies on Organizational Design, Intelligence, and Decision Making", The Academy of Management Review 15 (1), pp. 47-71.

[40] Hundley, R., et al. (2004). The global course of the information revolution: recurring themes and regional variations. Retrieved from www.rand.org/publications/MR/MR1680/

[41] Kothari, C.R.,1985, Research Methodology- Methods and Techniques, New Delhi, Wiley Eastern Limited.

[42] Kwon, T. H.; and Zmud, R. W. "Unifying the Fragmented Models of Information Systems Implementation." In J. R. Boland, and R. Hirshheim (eds.), *Critical Issues in Information Systems Research*, New York: John Wiley, 1987, pp. 227-251.

[43] Laudon, K., & Laudon, J. P. (2009). *Management Information Systems* (11th ed.). New York: Pearson press.

[44] Light M, Rosser B, Hayward S. (2005), Realizing the benefits of projects and portfolio management. Gartner, Research ID G00125673, 131.

[45] Maciaszek, L. A. (2001). *Requirements Analysis and System Design: Developing Information Systems with UML*. Harlow: Addison-Wesley Press.

[46] Maguire, S. (2000) Towards a "Business-led" Approach to Information Systems Development, Information Management & Computer Security, December, 2000, retrieved May 10th 2006, from: http://www.emeraldinsight.com.

21

Parallel image processing using algorithmic skeletons

Sare Eslami Khorami

Islamic Azad University South Tehran Branch, Tehran, Iran

Email address:

sare.eslami@gmail.com

Abstract: In the last few decades, image processing has achieved significant theoretical and practical progress. It has been so fast that image processing can be easily traced in several disciplines and industries. At present, various methods have been proposed to implement image processing. The present paper aims to present a technique for image processing which utilizes design and analysis of parallel algorithms. It employs a new approach called "algorithmic skeletons" which is composed of a set of programming templates; hence facilitating the programmers' work.

Keywords: Image Processing, Algorithmic Skeletons, Face Detection and Recognition

1. Introduction

Image processing has two major sections: image enhancement and machine vision. Image enhancement includes methods such as using fading filters and increasing contrast to enhance image visibility, picture thickness, and to make sure they are correctly displayed in the target environment (such as a printer or a monitor)[15]. Machine vision involves methods to understand the content of images to be used in area such as robotics and axis images [17]. Parallel processing has accelerated processing such as computing speed of computer systems [1]. As image processing is capable of parallelism, this paper addresses image processing by using parallelism.

2. Algorithmic Skeletons

Algorithmic skeletons are general models for parallel programming [1]. It provides a programming language which is not only simple and independent of machine architecture but also highly efficient. Skeletons are algorithmic patterns used in parallel programming. They are usually integrated with a host language and they are considered the only source of parallelism in that language. For example, mapping skeletons run a function on all items in a list in parallel. FARM skeletons implements master-slave in parallel or D&C represents divide and conquer parallelism [16]. A task is recursively sub-divided until a condition is met, then the sub-task is executed and results are merged while the

recursion is unwound. The most important feature of a skeleton is its generality that is the ability to be used in different applications [1]. In most algorithmic skeletons, there are a set of functions that has to be defined by the user. Once defined by the user, these functions are compiled into a specific location in the skeleton and then they are executed after a pre-processing. Usually every skeleton has a performance model which is presented as a mathematical formula and the user is able to predict the performance time by compiling the related parameters in this model.

3. Classification and Skeletonization of Image Operations

Image processing operations can be classified as low-level, intermediate-level and high-level (Table 1); Based on this classification, it is possible to define a skeleton library for image operations.

Table 1. Image operations.

Image operations	Source	Output
Low-level	Image	Image
Intermediate-level	Image	Object/vector-data
High-level	Object/vector-data	Object/vector-data

3.1. Low-Level Image Operations

Low-level image processing operations use the values of image pixels to modify individual pixels in an image. They can be divided into point-to point, neighborhood-to-point and global-to-point operations [5]. Point-to-point operations depend only on the values of the corresponding pixels from the input image and the parallelization is simple. Neighborhood operations produce an image in which the output pixels depend on a group of neighboring pixels around the corresponding pixel from the input image. Operations like smoothing, sharpening, filtering, noise reduction and edge detection are highly parallelizable. Global operations depend on all the pixels of the input image, like Discrete Fourier Transform (DFT) and they are also parallelizable.

3.2. Intermediate-Level Image Operations

Intermediate-level image processing operations work on images and output other data structures, such as detected objects (e.g., faces) or statistics, thereby reducing the amount of information. Operations such as Hough transform [10] (to find a line in an image), center-of-gravity calculation[11], labeling an object[12], are examples of intermediate-level image operations. They are more limited from the aspect of data parallelism when compared to low level operations. They can be defined as image to-object operations.

3.3. High-Level Image Operations

High-level image processing operations work on vector data or objects in the image and return other vector data or objects. They usually have irregular access patterns and thus are difficult to run data parallel. They can be divided into object-to-object or object-to-point operations. Position estimation [13] and object recognition theory [14] are examples of this category.

3.4. Skeletons for Image Operations

It is possible to use the data-parallelism paradigm with the master-slave approach for low level, intermediate-level and high-level image processing operations. A master processor is selected for splitting and distributing the data to the slaves. The master can also process a part of the image (data). Each slave processes its received part of the image (data) then, the master gathers and assembles the image (data) back. Based on the above observation, we identify a number of skeletons for parallel processing of low-level, intermediate-level and high-level image processing operations. They are named according Eto the type of the operator. Headers of some skeletons are shown in code 1.

```
//skeleton for point to point operations
void PixelToPixelOp(E_IMG *in, E_IMG
*out,void(*op)());
//skeleton for neighborhood to point operations
void NeighborToPixelOp(E_IMG *in, E_IMG *out,
E_WIN *win,void(*op)());
//skeleton for global to point operations
void GlobalToPixelOp(E_IMG *in, E_IMG *out,
void(*op)());
//skeleton for image to object operations
void ImageToObject(E_IMG *in, E_OBJ *out,
void(*op)());
//skeleton for object to object operations
void ObjectToObject(E_OBJ *in, E_OBJ *out,
void(*op)());
//skeleton for object to point/value operations
void ObjectToPoint(E_OBJ *in, E_Point *out,
void(*op)());
```
Code 1. Skeleton library

Each skeleton can be executed on a set of processors. From this set of processors, a host processor is selected to split and distribute the image to the other processors. The other processors from the set receive a part of the image and the image operation which should be applied to it. Then the computation takes place and the result is sent back to the host processor. The programmer of the image processing application should only select the skeleton from the library and returns the appropriate operation as a parameter.

4. Face Detection and Recognition

For recognizing a face from an image, first, it is necessary to separate it from the image, and then, it should be recognized from a data base of known faces. So, the face recognition process can be divided in two parts:

4.1. Face Detection

For detecting faces, we have proposed an algorithm [3] by searching for the presence of skin tone colored pixels or groups of pixels. We have used the YUV color domain, because it separates the luminance (Y) from the true color (UV). In the RGB color space, the components represent not only color but also luminance, which varies from one situation to another (due to the fact that changing light causes the reliability to be decreased). By using the YUV color domain, not only the detection has become more reliable but also the skin-tone identification has become easier, because the skin tone can now be indicated in a 2−dimensional space. By measuring the UV values of human skin-tone, the skin-tone region has been identified as a rectangle in the UV spectrum (Figure 1) and every non-skin color out of the "skin box" is seen as non face (Figure 2).

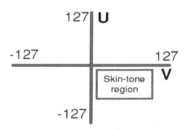

Figure 1. *Skin region in UV spectrum.*

Figure 2. Skin-tone result.

The face (skin) detection part separates the skin-tone from the image and sends only the luminance and the coordinate of the skin to the recognition part. It should be mentioned that the recognition part distinguishes faces from other parts of the body such as hands and feet that have the same skin color. Furthermore, if an image is coded in the RGB color space, it is first converted to YUV.

4.2. Face Recognition

The next step of the process is the recognition part. Through this process, an area of skin, detected in the previous step, is identified with respect to a face database. For this purpose, a Radial Basis Function (RBF) neural network is used [6]. The reason for using an RBF neural network is its ability to cluster similar images before classifying them [4]. An RBF neural network structure is demonstrated in Figure 3.

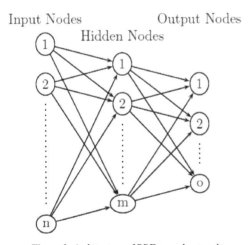

Figure 3. Architecture of RBF neural network

Its architecture is similar to that of a traditional three layer feed forward neural network. The input layer of this network is a set of n units, which accepts the elements of an n-dimensional input feature vector. (Here, the RBF neural network input is the face which is gained from the face detection part. Since it is normalized to a 64 * 72 pixel face, it follows that n = 4608.) The input units are completely connected to the hidden layer with m hidden nodes. Connections between the input and the hidden layers have

fixed unit weights and, consequently, it is not necessary to train them. The purpose of the hidden layer is to cluster the data and decrease its dimensionality. The RBF hidden nodes are also completely connected to the output layer. The number of the outputs depends on the number of people to be recognized (o equals the number of persons plus one according to Figure).

The output layer provides the response to the activation pattern applied to the input layer. The change from the input space to the RBF hidden unit space is nonlinear, whereas the change from the RBF hidden unit space to the output space is linear.

For the recognition part, a skin area should be fed to the neural network input. Subsequently, the output should be calculated for each person from the database. The network node has one output node for each person from the database and the maximum value between the output nodes is considered to be the recognized person. For distinguishing a face from other parts of the body and from noise, we have preserved one of the outputs of the neural network.

5. Skeletonizing

This section shows how it is possible to skeletonize image processing applications via a skeletons library. According to Section 4, face recognition can be divided into two main tasks:

Detecting skin in the image, which can be further dived into two parts:

Finding the skin-tone in the image; we can map this part of the program as low-level image processing operations, because the input of this part is an image and the output is also an image.

Separating the skin-tones from the image as objects, and determining the coordinates of each of these skin-tones. So we map this part as intermediate level image processing operations, because the input is an image and the output is a set of objects (faces).

Sending each of the skin-tones (faces) to the neural network for identification, according to the faces which are in the data base. We map this part as high-level image processing operations, because the input is an object and the output is the number of the recognized person.

Code 2 shows the C-code of face recognition.

```
/*find skin tone*/
for (y=1; y < HEIGHT-1; y++){
for (x=1; x < WIDTH-1; x++){
/* convert color */
Convertcolor(R[x][y],G[x][y],B[x][y],
U[x][y],V[x][y]);
/* find skin-tone */
if( MIN_U<U[x][y]&&U[x][y]< MAX_U &&
MIN_V<V[x][y]&&V[x][y]< MAX_V)
out[x][y] = 1;
else out[x][y] = 0;        }
}
/*label the image*/
for (y=1; y < HEIGHT-1; y++)
```

```
for (x=1; x < WIDTH-1; x++)
if(out[x][y])
label(label[x][y]);
/*Neural network*/
for (h=0;h< HIDDEN_NODE; h++){
out_hidden[h]=0;
for (i=0;i< INPUTE_NODE; i++){
out_hidden[h] += input[i]*i2h_weight[h][i];
}
out_hidden[h] = ActiveFunc(out_hidden[h]);
}
for (o=0;o< OUTPUT_NODE; o++){
out_rbf[o]= 0;
for (h=0;h< HIDDEN_NODE; h++){
out_rbf[o] += out_hidden[h]*h2o_weight[o][h];
}
}
person = 0;
max = 0;
for (o=0;o< OUTPUT_NODE; o++){
if( out_rbf[o] > max){
max= out_rbf[o];
person = o;
}
}
```

Code 2: Face recognition

The main parts of the program are the parts which are inside the loops and they have the same operations for each pixel in an image or for each object (face). For being able to bring data parallelism into the program, we use skeletons as mentioned in Code 1. The code can be divided into the following tasks:

- Convert color: Since in our setup input is in RGB, for detecting the skin tone in the UV domain, the values of U and V should be calculated for each pixel.
- Binarization: For each pixel, it should be checked whether it is within the skin-tone box or not (see Figure 3).
- Labeling: For separating the faces from the image, the same label should be assigned to pixels which are nearby in the skin-tone.
- Neural network: The neural network for recognizing the objects which are detected in the previous part.

The main function of the skeletonized code is shown in Code 3 where (the first three tasks are mapped onto the first three skeletons; and the neural network is mapped onto the second three skeletons).

```
PixelToPixelOp(RGB, UV, &yc2ycbcr);
PixelToPixelOp(UV, skin, &Binarization);
ImageToObject(skin, obj, &labeling);
for( i= 0; i < num_object; i++){
ObjectToObject(obj,hidden, &NeuralNet_hiddennode);
ObjectToObject(hidden,out, &NeuralNet_outputnode);
ObjectToValue(out, person, &Find_max);
}
```

Code 3: Main function of skeleton code for face recognition

6. Evaluation and Discussion

We have implemented the skeletons library for the IMAP-board. Each implemented skeleton follows a standard template: first, the control processor reads the image or data from the external memory; Then, it distributes the data between the PEs; After that, it sends the determined operations (instructions) from the skeletons to the PEs; Finally, it gathers the result from the PEs and writes it in the external memory.

Table 2 shows the execution time for each skeleton in the program. The image size that we have used is 256 * 240 pixels and the neural network that we have used has 4608 input nodes, 15 hidden nodes and 6 (5 persons + 1 noise) output nodes.

Table 2. *execution time.*

Skeleton	Time(ms)
PixelToPixelOp(RGB, UV, &yc2ycbcr)	1.9
PixelToPixelOp(UV, skin, &Binarization)	1.75
ImageToObject(skin, obj, &labeling)	1.58
ObjectToObject(obj, hidden, &NeuralNet_hiddennode)	2.1
ObjectToObject (hidden, out, &NeuralNet_outputnode)	0.567

We have also implemented a manually optimized version of face recognition (without using the skeletons) on the IMAP-board. The difference is that each skeleton reads the image (object) from the external memory, distributes it between the PEs, and again stores the results in this external memory, whereas in the optimal solution it is not always necessary to read and write data from/to the external memory. We have measured the execution time for reading, distributing and gathering an image (256 * 240 pixels) for each skeleton and it is 0.16ms. The average time for running each skeleton is 1.58ms (Table 2).

Consequently, the execution time for sending and gathering an image, takes 11% of skeleton execution time $(0.16/(1.58-0.16) = .11)$. Note that in general, it is not necessary to send/collect the entire image to/from a skeleton (For instance, for the neural network, it's only necessary to send the skin-tone region). From these measurements, we may deduce that in general the execution time for skeletonized code is in the order of 10% worse than the execution time of an optimized program (on the IMAP-board and assuming that similar types of skeletons are used in the application).

For the face recognition case study, the skeletonized code takes 8.21ms and the optimized code takes 7.8ms, which is an overhead of approximately 5%. Based on this initial experience, we expect that skeletonization can be used as a very convenient programming and implementation method which does not result in an excessive execution time overhead. It relieves the programmer from many tedious low level implementation and parallelization details.

References

[1] H. Gonz´alez-V´elez, M. Leyton, "A Survey of Algorithmic Skeleton Frameworks: High-Level Structured Parallel Programming Enablers," in Research Monographs in Parallel and Distributed Computing. MIT Press, 2008.

[2]   Aldinucci, M.; Danelutto, M.; Antoniu, G.; Jan, M. "Fault-Tolerant Data Sharing for High-level Grid: A Hierarchical Storage Architecture". Achievements in European Research on Grid Systems, 2008.

[3]   Wang, Q., Wu, J. Long, C. Li, B, "P-FAD: Real-time face detection scheme on embedded smart cameras ," in Distributed Smart Cameras (ICDSC), 2012 Sixth International Conference,2012.

[4]   Y. Hu and J. Hwang, Handbook of neural network signal processing. CRC Press, 2002.

[5]   C. H. Chu, E. J.Delp, L.H. Jamieson,H. J. Siegel, F. J.Weil, and A. B. Whinston, "A model for an intelligent operating system for executing image understanding tasks on a reconfigurable parallel architecture," Journal of Parallel and Distributed Computing, vol. 6, pp. 598–662, June 1998.

[6]   J. Haddadnia, K. Faez, and P. Moallem,"Human face recognition with moment invariants based on shape information," in Proceedings of the International Conference on Information Systems, Analysis and Syn-thesis, vol. 20, (Orlando, Florida USA), International Institute of Informatics and Systemics(ISAS), 2001.

[7]   Mario Leyton, Jose M. Piquer. "Skandium: Multi-core Programming with algorithmic skeletons", IEEE Euro-micro PDP 2010.

[8]   G. Yaikhom, M. Cole, S. Gilmore, and J. Hillston. "A structural approach for modelling performance of systems using skeletons." Electronic Notes in Theoretical Computer Science, 190(3):167–183,2007.

[9]   N. Zhang, Y. Chen, W. Jian-Li," Image parallel processing based on GPU ," Advanced Computer Control (ICACC), 2010 2nd International Conference, March 2010.

[10] S. Eghtesadi, M. Sandler, "Implementation of the Hough transform for intermediate-level vision on a transputer network", Journal of Parallel and Distributed Computing, Volume 13, Issue 3, Pages 212–218, April 1989.

[11] R. Boynton, "Measuring weight and all three axes of the center of gravity of a rocket motor without having to re-position the motor", presentation at the 61st Annual Conference of the Society of Allied Weight Engineers Virginia Beach, Virginia May 20-22, 2002.

[12] Z. Fang , X. Li , "A parallel processing approach to image object labeling problems", CSC '87 Proceedings of the 15th annual conference on Computer Science, Page 423, New York, 1987.

[13] C.Papamanthou, F. Preparata, R.Tamassia, "Algorithms for Location Estimation Based on RSSI Sampling", Springer-Verlag Berlin Heidelberg, 2008.

[14] S. Bohlhalter, C.Fretz, B. Weder, "Hierarchical versus parallel processing in tactile object recognition: a behavioural-neuroanatomical study of aperceptive tactile agnosia", Brain ,2002.

[15] P. Jonker and W. Caarls, "Application driven design of embedded real-time image processing," in Proceedings of ACIVS 2003 (Advanced Concepts for Intelligent Vision Systems), (Gent, Belgium), 2003.

[16] J. darlingtons, Y. Guo, H.W. To, J. Yang, "Functional Skeletons for Parallel coordination", proceeding of 1st EuroPar Conference, Stokholm, Sweden, pp. 55-66, Agust 1995.

[17] R. Jones, "Machine vision applications", science direct, Volume 1, Issue 4, 1991, Pages 439–446.

22

Bread Shrimp Microbe Growth Simulation and Prediction System Based on Neural Network

Xiao Laisheng[1], Zheng Yuandan[2]

[1]Educational Information Center, Guangdong Ocean University, Zhanjiang, China
[2]Information College, Guangdong Ocean University, Zhanjiang, China

Email address:
xiaolaisheng@163.com (Xiao Laisheng)

Abstract: According to the requirements of a scientific research project, a set of bread shrimp microbial growth simulation and prediction system is designed and implemented in detail. The system is established by taking vibrio parahemolyticus in bread shrimp as research objects, according to effects of temperature, salt and time on their growth, and employing neural network technology. In order to improve its compatibility, the system is developed by using C# on Visual Studio 2008 platform, and its design and implementation are based on AForge.NET framework and sliding-window modeling method. The system consists of three parts: data management, data simulation and data prediction, which would provide an effective analytical tool for bread shrimp safe production. After tested carefully, the system can meet the requirements of the project design.

Keywords: Neural Network, AForge.NET, Simulation and Prediction System, Microbial Growth, Bread Shrimp

1. Introduction

Intelligent simulation and prediction for microbial growth refers to that under the premise of without microbial detection and analysis and according to the characteristic data of the food microbe in different processing, storage and circulation, the dynamic changes of the growth and survival of main pathogenic bacteria and spoilage bacteria in food is going to be determined by processing with computers, thus the quality and safety of food can be evaluated and predicted quickly. According to the existing limited experimental data, using neural network prediction algorithm, and through intelligent simulation and prediction neural network-based microbial growth simulation and prediction system can provide more data than one that come from real experiments, which could provide reference data for safe food production.

According to the requirements of a research project, sub project of National Science and Technology Support Program of China: Key Integrated and Demonstrated Technologies for Quality and Safety Control in Aquatic Product Processing Process (No. 2012BAD29B06), the authors of this paper have developed a set of bread shrimp microbial growth simulation and prediction system. The system is established by taking

vibrio parahemolyticus in bread shrimp as research objects, according to effects of temperature, salt and time on their growth, and employing neural network technology. The system consists of three parts: data management, data simulation and data prediction, which would provide an effective analytical tool for bread shrimp safe production.

In order to improve its compatibility, the system is developed by using C# on Visual Studio 2008 platform, and its design and implementation are based on AForge.NET framework and sliding-window modeling method. Through intelligent simulation and prediction in the system, users can predict vibrio parahemolyticus growth and survival data in various conditions only providing a limited number of experimental vibrio parahemolyticus growth and survival data in the conditions. By this way, users do not need to perform experiments in each condition, greatly reducing the number of experiments and saving experimental time and costs.

2. Related Work

Food simulation and prediction microbiology is a new science based on the subjects such as microbiology, mathematics, statistics and computer applications, which needs the research foundation that a series of models that can be able to describe and predict microbial growth and survival in specific conditions should be designed. The core of food microbe simulation technology is to form mathematical models, through which the rules of growth, live and death of microbe can be described [1-2].

Up to now, domestic scholars have done a lot of research for microbial growth simulation modeling [3-7]. In their work, all of the models including level-one, level-two and level-three models described microbial growth with mathematical equations, such as level-one model with linear model, Logistic model, Gompertz model, Baranyi & Roberts model etc, level model with square root model, Al Leave equation etc. In recent years overseas scholars have also done a lot of research for microbial growth simulation modeling [8-15], but they only put emphasis on mathematical modeling too. As imagined, microbial growth is a dynamic and continuous process, it is difficult to use single mathematical equation to simulate. Artificial neural network is a network constructed manually to simulate human brain function, absorbing some advantages of biological nerve, such as high parallelism, non-linear global role, good fault-tolerance and associative memory function, and very strong self adaptive and self learning ability. Therefore, neural network has very outstanding qualities of adaptive learning, parallel computing, distributing storage, associative memory. Theory has proved that neural network can approach any continuous real function with arbitrary precision. Hence, it is feasible to take neural network to simulate microbial growth process.

Just for that reason, scholars over the world have carried out a great deal of research on the aspect of applying neural network to microbial growth simulation [16-23]. From these related research literatures, we can know that the application of neural network applied to microbial growth was also carried out a more extensive research, and a good simulation effect was achieved too. But so far, applying neural network to simulate and predict growth for vibrio parahemolyticus in bread shrimp is still not reported. Moreover, in [24] one author of the paper tried to develop a universal platform for microbial growth simulation modeling with VC++ and MATLAB, but

its compatibility is not good. In the light of such reasons, in order to meet the requirement of the research project (No. 2012BAD29B06) and to improve the compatibility of system, in this paper we have developed an intelligent simulation and prediction system for bread shrimp microbial growth by using C# on Visual Studio 2008 platform, and its design and implementation are based on AForge.NET framework and sliding-window modeling method.

3. AForge.NET

AForge.NET is an open source C# framework designed for developers and researchers in the fields of computer vision and artificial intelligence - image processing, neural networks, genetic algorithms, fuzzy logic, machine learning, robotics, etc.

The framework is comprised by the set of libraries and sample applications, which demonstrate their features. Typically, AForge.NET is comprised of a series of components, such as AForge.Imaging, AForge.Vision, AForge.Video, AForge.Neuro, AForge. Genetic, AForge.Fuzzy, AForge.Robotics, AForge.MachineLearning, etc. AForge.Imaging is a library with image processing routines and filters; AForge.Vision is a computer vision library; AForge.Video is a set of libraries for video processing; AForge.Neuro is a neural networks computation library; AForge.Genetic is an evolution programming library; AForge.Fuzzy is a fuzzy computations library; AForge.Robotics is a library providing support of some robotics kits; AForge.MachineLearning is a machine learning library. The framework is provided not only with different libraries and their sources, but with many sample applications, which demonstrate the use of this framework, and with documentation help files, which are provided in HTML Help format. The documentation is also available on-line. [25]

When a neural network-based system is developed, a neural networks computation library, AForge.Neuro, should be used. The C# library on AForge.Neuro contains six main entities shown in Figure 1.

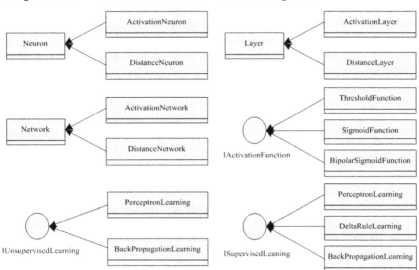

Figure 1. Six main entities in C# library on AForge.Neuro.

From Figure 1, we can see that there are six main entities in C# library on AForge.Neuro, namely, Neuron, Layer, Network, IActivationFunction, ISupervisedLearning, IUnsupervisedLearning. Neural network is made of a collection of neurons, in which each neuron is described by Neuron. Neuron is a base abstract class for all neurons, which encapsulates such common entities like a neuron's weight, output value, and input value. Other neuron classes inherit from the base class to extend it with additional properties and specialize it. Neural network is also made of some layers, in which each layer is described by Layer. Layer represents a collection of neurons. This is a base abstract class, which encapsulates common functionality for all neuron's layers. A network consists of a collection of neuron's layers, which is described be Network, what is a base abstract class, which provides common functionality of a generic neural network. To implement a specific neural network, it is required to inherit the class, extending it with specific functionalities of any neural network architecture. IActivationFunction is an activation function's interface. Activation functions are used in activation neurons - the type of neuron, where the weighted sum of its inputs is calculated and then the value is passed as input to the activation function, and the output value becomes the output value of the neuron. ISupervisedLearning is an interface for supervised learning algorithms - the type of learning algorithms where a system is provided with sample inputs, with desired output values during the learning phase. The aim of the system is to generalize learning data, and learn to provide the correct output value when it is presented with the input value only. IUnsupervisedLearning is an interface for unsupervised learning algorithms - the type of learning algorithms where a system is provided with sample inputs only during the learning phase, but not with the desired outputs. The aim of the system is to organize itself in such a way to find correlation and similarities between data samples.

The C# library on AForge.Neuro provides the following two types of neural network architectures: Activation Network and Distance Network. In engineering practice, we can select one of the two types of neural network architectures, but how to make a choice depends on concrete problems. Activation Network is commonly used neural network where each neuron computes its output as the activation function's output, and the argument is a weighted sum of its inputs combined with the threshold value. The network may consist of a single layer, or of multiple layers. Trained with supervised learning algorithms, the network allows to solve such tasks as approximation, prediction, classification, and recognition. Another neural network is Distance Network where each neuron computes its output as a distance between its weight values and input values. The network consists of a single layer, and may be used as a base for such networks like Kohonen Self Organizing Map, Elastic Network, and Hamming Network.

The C# library on AForge.Neuro also provides abundant learning algorithms, which could be used to train different neural networks and to solve different problems. Primary learning algorithms include Back Propagation Learning, Perceptron Learning, SOM Learning, Delta Rule Learning, Elastic Network Learning. Back Propagation Learning is one of the most popular, known and commonly used algorithms for multi-layer neural network learning. Because the algorithm is able to train multi-layer neural networks, the range of its applications is very great, and includes such tasks as approximation, prediction, object recognition, etc. Perceptron Learning could be used with a one-layer activation network, where each neuron has a threshold activation function. SOM Learning treats neural network as a 2D map of nodes, where each node may represent a separate class. The algorithm organizes a network in such a way, that it becomes possible to find the correlation and similarities between data samples. Delta Rule Learning utilizes the activation function's derivative, and may be applicable to single-layer activation networks only, where each neuron has a continuous activation function instead of a threshold activation function. The most popular continuous activation function is the unipolar and bipolar sigmoid function. Elastic Network Learning is similar to the idea of the SOM learning algorithm, but it treats network neurons not as a 2D map of nodes, but as a ring. During the learning procedure, the ring gets some shape, which represents a solution. [26]

Software design process based on AForge.NET could be described as follows:

Firstly in order to use the classes and interfaces of AForge. Neuro to construct and train the neural network model, it is needed to open VisualStudio2008 software and add the three dynamic link libraries AForge. Controls. dll, AForge. dll and AForge. Neuro. dll in its solution manager.

Secondly the activation network or distance network class should be introduced to instantiate the neural network model in accordance with the actual requirements. Subsequently, it is needed to choose a suitable learning algorithm for each model from the classes of BP Learning, Delta rule Learning, Perceptron Learning, SOM Learning or Elastic Network Learning, and set the parameters such as relevant learning rate and impulse value.

Finally the neural network model can be trained by using the training data sets generated by sliding-window method. At the same time, the error curves in the training process can be drawn onto the Chart control provided by AForge.NET framework so as to view the data conveniently. When the error of neural network is less than the preset error or the number of training is reached, the training process will be stopped [27].

Nowadays, C#-based AForge.NET is widely used in scientific and engineering research, industry applications, such as motion video detection, eye-tracking control system, diagnostics of products, etc. [28-31].

4. Neural Network Sliding-Window Modeling Method

In general, neural network modeling uses sliding-window

method. In order to facilitate computer programming, a neural network sliding-window modeling method is theoretically derived in detail by one of the authors of the paper Xiao Laisheng [32]. Specific method is described as follows.

4.1. Neural Network Architecture for Sliding-Window Modeling

Figure 2 Shows neural network architecture for sliding-window modeling.

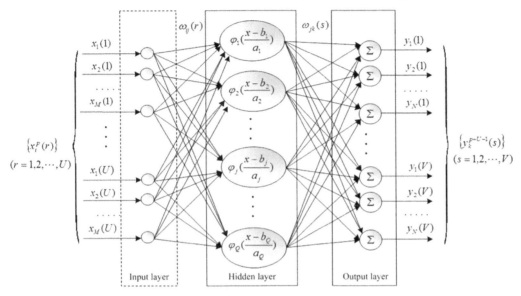

Figure 2. Neural network architecture for sliding-window modeling.

In Figure 2, assume that M is total number of nodes in input layer, $i = 1, 2, \cdots, M$; Q is total number of nodes in hidden layer, $j = 1, 2, \cdots, Q$; N is total number of nodes in output layer, $k = 1, 2, \cdots, N$; P is total number of input samples, $p = 1, 2, \cdots, P$; $\{x_i^p\}$ are inputs of network, $\{y_k^p\}$ are outputs of network, $\{d_k^p\}$ are their corresponding target outputs; ω_{ij} are connection weights between neurons in input layer and neurons in hidden layers, ω_{jk} are connection weights between neurons in hidden layer and neurons in output layers; a_j is scale parameter and b_j is translation parameter of wavelet. When Sliding-Windows is adopted, U is sliding-window input parameter, V is sliding-window output parameter. In this case, input weights of network ω_{ij} are extended equally to the number of $\omega_{ij} \times U$, which are marked as $\omega_{ij}(r), r = 1, 2, \cdots, U$, and output weights of network ω_{jk} are extended equally to the number of $\omega_{jk} \times V$, which are marked as $\omega_{jk}(s), s = 1, 2, \cdots V$.

Then input of *jth* neuron of wavelet basis can be expressed as $s_j^p = \sum_{i=1}^{M} \omega_{ij} x_i^p$, its output is $t_j^p = \phi(\frac{s_j^p - b_j}{a_j})$, output of *kth* level component in output layer is $y_k^p = \sum_{j=1}^{Q} \omega_{jk} t_j^p$, total error function is defined as $E = \frac{1}{P} \sum_{p=1}^{P} E^p = \frac{1}{2P} \sum_{p=1}^{P} \sum_{k=1}^{N} (d_k^p - y_k^p)^2$.

4.2. Learning Algorithm

When sliding-window is used, the learning algorithm of wavelet neural network is described as follows.

Step one, Initialize network weights, thresholds, scale and translation parameters of wavelet function.

Give corresponding initial values for each of the following parameters: scale parameter a_j and translation parameter b_j of the wavelet, weights of the network $\omega_{ij}(r), r = 1, 2, \cdots, U$ and $\omega_{jk}(s), s = 1, 2, \cdots V$, learning rate η and momentum factor λ.

Set sample counter $p = 1$ and number of iterations $n = 1$, and provided maximum number of iterations is N.

Step two, Input learning sample s$\{x_i^p(r)\}, r = 1, 2, \cdots, U$ and corresponding sliding-window desired outputs $\{d_k^{p+U-1}(s)\}, s = 1, 2, \cdots, V$, and calculate outputs of hidden layer $\{t_j^p\}$ and sliding-window outputs of output layer $\{y_k^{p+U-1}(s)\}, s = 1, 2, \cdots, V$.

Inputs of hidden layer are

$$s_j^p = \sum_{i=1}^{M} (\sum_{r=1}^{U} \omega_{ij}(r) x_i^p(r)), \ j = 1, 2, \cdots, Q \quad (1)$$

Outputs of hidden layer are

$$t_j^p = \phi(\frac{s_j^p - b_j}{a_j}) = \phi(\frac{\sum_{i=1}^{M}(\sum_{r=1}^{U} \omega_{ij}(r) x_i^p(r)) - b_j}{a_j}), \ j = 1, 2, \cdots, Q \quad (2)$$

Sliding-window outputs of output layer are

$$y_k^{p+U-1}(s) = \sum_{j=1}^{Q} \omega_{jk}(s)t_j^p, \quad k=1,2,\cdots,N. \quad s=1,2,\cdots V \quad (3)$$

In equations (1), (2), and (3), $x_i^p(r)$ is input of input layer, s_j^p is input of hidden layer, t_j^p is output of hidden layer, $y_k^{p+U-1}(s)$ is sliding-window output of output layer, $\phi(\cdot)$ is wavelet basis function.

Step three, Calculate target error and gradient vectors.

Define target error function E^p as

$$E^p = \frac{1}{2}\sum_{k=1}^{N}\sum_{s=1}^{V}(d_k^{p+U-1}(s) - y_k^{p+U-1}(s))^2 \quad (4)$$

Where, $\{d_k^{p+U-1}(s)\}$ is sliding-window desired outputs of output layer, $y_k^{p+U-1}(s)$ is sliding-window calculated outputs of output layer.

Energy function gradient respectively are

$$\delta_{ij}^p(r) = \frac{\partial E^p}{\partial \omega_{ij}(r)} = \frac{\partial E^p}{\partial y_k^{p+U-1}(s)}\frac{\partial y_k^{p+U-1}(s)}{\partial t_j^p}\frac{\partial t_j^p}{\partial \omega_{ij}(r)}$$

$$= -\sum_{k=1}^{N}\sum_{s=1}^{V}(d_k^{p+U-1}(s) - y_k^{p+U-1}(s))\omega_{jk}(s)\phi'(\frac{s_j^p - b_j}{a_j})\frac{x_i^p(r)}{a_j} \quad (5)$$

Where, $\omega_{ij}(r)$ can affect all level component of output layer, so

$$\frac{\partial E^p}{\partial y_k^{p+U-1}} = -\sum_{k=1}^{N}\sum_{s=1}^{V}(d_k^{p+U-1}(s) - y_k^{p+U-1}(s))$$

$$\delta_{jk}^p(s) = \frac{\partial E^p}{\partial \omega_{jk}(s)} = \frac{\partial E^p}{\partial y_k^{p+U-1}(s)}\frac{\partial y_k^{p+U-1}(s)}{\partial \omega_{jk}(s)}$$

$$= -(d_k^{p+U-1}(s) - y_k^{p+U-1}(s))t_j^p$$

$$= -(d_k^{p+U-1}(s) - y_k^{p+U-1}(s))\phi(\frac{s_j^p - b_j}{a_j}) \quad (6)$$

But, $\omega_{ij}(s)$ can only affect *kth* level component of output layer, so

$$\frac{\partial E^p}{\partial y_k^{p+U-1}} = -(d_k^{p+U-1}(s) - y_k^{p+U-1}(s))$$

$$\delta_{aj}^p = \frac{\partial E^p}{\partial a_j} = \frac{\partial E^p}{\partial y_k^{p+U-1}(s)}\frac{\partial y_k^{p+U-1}(s)}{\partial t_j^p}\frac{\partial t_j^p}{\partial a_j}$$

$$= -\sum_{k=1}^{N}\sum_{s=1}^{V}(d_k^{p+U-1}(s) - y_k^{p+U-1}(s))\omega_{jk}\phi'(\frac{s_j^p - b_j}{a_j})(\frac{s_j^p - b_j}{a_j^2}) \quad (7)$$

$$\delta_{bj}^p = \frac{\partial E^p}{\partial b_j} = \frac{\partial E^p}{\partial y_k^{p+U-1}(s)}\frac{\partial y_k^{p+U-1}(s)}{\partial t_j^p}\frac{\partial t_j^p}{\partial b_j}$$

$$= -\sum_{k=1}^{N}\sum_{s=1}^{V}(d_k^{p+U-1}(s) - y_k^{p+U-1}(s))\omega_{jk}\phi'(\frac{s_j^p - b_j}{a_j})(-\frac{1}{a_j}) \quad (8)$$

Step four, Error back propagation and modify network parameters.

Computational formulas are

$$\omega_{ij}(r)(t+1) = \omega_{ij}(r)(t) - \eta\delta_{ij}^p(r) + \lambda[\omega_{ij}(r)(t) - \omega_{ij}(r)(t-1)] \quad (9)$$

$$\omega_{jk}(s)(t+1) = \omega_{jk}(s)(t) - \eta\delta_{jk}^p(s) + \lambda[\omega_{jk}(s)(t) - \omega_{jk}(s)(t-1)] \quad (10)$$

$$a_j(t+1) = a_j(t) - \eta\delta_{aj}^p + \lambda[a_j(t) - a_j(t-1)] \quad (11)$$

$$b_j(t+1) = b_j(t) - \eta\delta_{bj}^p + \lambda[b_j(t) - b_j(t-1)] \quad (12)$$

Step five, Input next sample, namely set $p = p+1$. If $p \le P$, then go to *Step two*.

Step six, Calculate total error of the network

$$E = \frac{1}{P}\sum_{p=1}^{P}E^p = \frac{1}{2P}\sum_{p=1}^{P}\sum_{k=1}^{N}\sum_{s=1}^{V}(d_k^{p+U-1}(s) - y_k^{p+U-1}(s))^2 \quad (13)$$

And judge if E is smaller than preset progress value $\varepsilon(\varepsilon > 0)$. If $E < \varepsilon$ or $n > N$, stop the learning of network, otherwise, set $n = n+1$ and $p = 1$, go to Step two.

It is needed to explain that, in the process of derivation as an example the wavelet function is taken as activation function of the neural network. In fact, other functions can be used as activation functions too, such as Sigmoid Function: S shape function. But in engineering practice how the final effects to use these functions are depends on a series of simulation experiments, in which a lot of tests and comparisons should be done.

5. System Design and Implementation

5.1. Overa Design

5.1.1. Requirement Regulation

Firstly, users acquire the number of bacterial colonies on temperature, salinity, PH, low temperature, temperature +PH and temperature + salinity at several time points by experiments. Secondly the system storages related experimental data, and begins neural network simulation according to the experimental data and finally predicts the number of bacterial colonies of vibrio parahaemolyticus on each time point.

This system consists of the following three parts.

Data management

Data management includes data addition, data deletion, data loading, data query. Users add the experimental data into the database for management through data addition and can delete the added data if needed.

According to the experimental conditions, the number of bacterial colonies of vibrio parahaemolyticus could be inquired through data query. Data loading can load experimental data into the system under certain conditions. It is needed to load the relevant data before simulation.

Data simulation

According to the experimental data of a certain state, the

number of bacterial colonies at all time points in the state could be simulated through the BP neural network algorithm.

Data prediction

According to the experimental data of a certain state, the number of bacterial colonies at a certain time point in the state could be predicted through the BP neural network algorithm. This time point can be the one that the user has not acquired by experiments. In this way, users can predict the number of bacterial colonies at each time point through a limited number of experiments.

5.1.2. Overall Function Structure

According to the demand, the system is divided into three parts: data management module, data simulation module, data prediction module. Data management module includes functions of data addition, data deletion, data query and data loading. Overall function structure diagram is as shown in Figure 3.

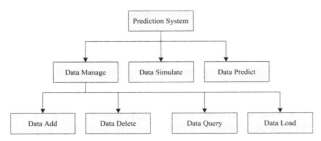

Figure 3. Overall function structure.

5.1.3. Basic Process Flow

The process of data simulation and prediction is shown in Figure 4. The growth experiment data of vibrio parahaemolyticus in bread shrimp in the six states of temperature, salinity, pH, temperature, temperature + PH, temperature + salinity at some time points are acquired through experiments in the laboratory. Then, these data are made as initial input data to a neural network and processed as input normalization, and finally the algorithm of Back Propagation Learning is taken for training the neural network. The trained neural network can be used for predicting the number of bacterial colonies of vibrio parahaemolyticus for each time point.

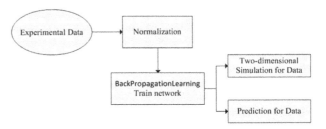

Figure 4. Process of data simulation and prediction.

5.1.4. Overall Scheme

The system is developed as an easy-to-use microbial growth simulation and prediction system, in which the growth experimental data of vibrio parahaemolyticus in bread shrimp in the six states of temperature, salinity, pH, low temperature, temperature + PH, temperature + salinity at some time points are taken as input data for neural network. Neural network algorithm, Back Propagation Learning, is used for neural network simulation. The program structure of the system is to take Visual Studio 2008 as its front, SQL Server2008 as its database, and use open source AForge.NET for its framework. The front desk interface displays two-dimensional data graphics, while in the background the system loads experimental data stored in the database, applies open source framework AForge.NET for neural network simulation, and outputs the prediction results to the front desk interface.

5.2. Detailed Design

5.2.1. Database Design

The background database of the system uses SQL Server database, which is used to store the experimental growth data of vibrio parahaemolyticus. Interface connects to the database through the System. Data. SqlClient provided by the C# namespace method. Experimental data of vibrio parahaemolyticus in bread shrimp in six states of temperature, salinity, pH, low temperature; temperature + PH, temperature + salinity are provided by experiments in laboratory, which can be changed with a certain period of time. Six pieces of corresponding data tables in the database are established to store data.

i. Temperature table: Temperature table is designed for storing the experimental growth data of vibrio parahaemolyticus in bread shrimp in different temperature and time. The temperature table is shown in Table 1.

Table 1. Temperature table.

Field name	Field description	Data type	Can be empty	Constraint	Remarks
temperature	temperature	float		Combined primary key	
hour	time	float		Combined primary key	
amount	number of bacterial colonies	float	no		

ii. Salt table: Salt table is designed for storing the experimental growth data of vibrio parahaemolyticus in bread shrimp in different salt and time. The salt table is shown in Table 2.

Table 2. *Salt table.*

Field name	Field description	Data type	Can be empty	Constraint	Remarks
salt	salt	float		Combined primary key	
hour	time	float		Combined primary key	
amount	number of bacterial colonies	float	no		

iii.   PH table: PH table is designed for storing the experimental growth data of vibrio parahaemolyticus in bread shrimp in different PH and time. The PH table is shown in Table 3.

Table 3. *PH table.*

Field name	Field description	Data type	Can be empty	Constraint	Remarks
PH	PH	float		Combined primary key	
hour	time	float		Combined primary key	
amount	number of bacterial colonies	float	no		

iv.   LowSurvival table: LowSurvival table is designed for storing the experimental growth data of vibrio parahaemolyticus in bread shrimp in different low temperature and time. The LowSurvival table is shown in Table 4.

Table 4. *LowSurvival table.*

Field name	Field description	Data type	Can be empty	Constraint	Remarks
Low Temperature	low temperature	float		Combined primary key	
hour	time	float		Combined primary key	
amount	number of bacterial colonies	float	no		

v.   TempreturePh table: TemperaturePh table is designed for storing the experimental growth data of vibrio parahaemolyticus in bread shrimp in different temperature, PH and time. The temperature+PH table is shown in Table 5.

Table 5. *TemperaturePh table.*

Field name	Field description	Data type	Can be empty	Constraint	Remarks
temperature	temperature	float		Combined primary key	
ph	ph	float		Combined primary key	
hour	time	float		Combined primary key	
amount	number of bacterial colonies	float	no		

vi.   TemperatureSalt table: TemperatureSalt table is designed for storing the experimental growth data of vibrio parahaemolyticus in bread shrimp in different temperature, salt and time. The temperature+salt table is shown in Table 6.

Table 6. *TemperatureSalt table.*

Field name	Field description	Data type	Can be empty	Constraint	Remarks
temperature	temperature	float		Combined primary key	
salt	salt	float		Combined primary key	
hour	time	float		Combined primary key	
amount	number of bacterial colonies	float	no		

5.2.2. System Function Module Detailed Design

i.   *Neural network training module:* The basic principle of neural network training is that experimental data are used as its inputs and needed to be normalized, and the network is trained through an activation function. In the system we use Sigmoid Function as its activation function. After training, the network can be used to perform data prediction. The key codes are as follows.

privateconstint trempreture = 0;// trempreture -0，salty -1，ph-2，lowSurvival -3，tremprePh ph-4，tempreSalty -5
    privateconstint salty = 1;
    privateconstint ph = 2;
    privateconstint lowSurvival = 3;

privateconstint tremprePh = 4;
privateconstint tempreSalty = 5;

//Two-dimensional
constint inputNum = 1;
constint outputNum = 1;
//Training data
int trainNum;
double[][] trainInput;
double[][] trainOutput;
//The maximum and minimum data are used for normalization
    double[] maxInput = newdouble[inputNum];
    double[] minInput = newdouble[inputNum];

```
double[] maxOutput = newdouble[outputNum];
double[] minOutput = newdouble[outputNum];
//Construct chart data
double[,] data;

privateActivationNetwork network; //neural network

public BPNeural()
        {
                init();
        }

privatevoid init()
        {

        }

publicvoid setChart(Chart chart)
        {
this.chart = chart;
        }

//Input normalization
    privatedouble premnmxInput(double num, double min,
double max)
        {
    double xFactor = 2.0 / (max - min);
    return (num - min) * xFactor - 1.0;
        }

//Output normalization
    privatedouble premnmxOutput(double num, double min,
double max)
        {
    double yFactor = 1.7 / (max - min);
    return (num - min) * yFactor - 0.85;
        }

//Output counter normalization
    privatedouble getOriginalOutput(double num, double min,
double max)
        {
    double yFactor = 1.7 / (max - min);
    return (num + 0.85) / yFactor + min;
        }

//Training sample data
    privatevoid getTrainData()
        {
    string queryString = null;
    if (category == tempreture)
            queryString = "SELECT hour,amount
FROM tempreture WHERE tempreture = " + condition1;
    if (category == salty)
            queryString = "SELECT hour,amount
FROM salt WHERE salt = " + condition1;
    if (category == ph)
```

```
            queryString = "SELECT hour,amount
FROM ph WHERE ph = " + condition1;
    if (category == lowSurvival)
            queryString = "SELECT hour,amount
FROM lowSurvival WHERE tempreture = " + condition1;
    if (category == temprePh)
            queryString = "SELECT hour,amount
FROM tempreturePh WHERE tempreture = " + condition1
+" AND ph = "+condition2;
    if (category == tempreSalty)
            queryString = "SELECT hour,amount
FROM tempretureSalt WHERE tempreture = " + condition1
+ " AND salt = " + condition2;

    //Initial max min data
    for (int i = 0; i < inputNum; ++i)
            {
                maxInput[i] = double.MinValue;
                minInput[i] = double.MaxValue;
            }
    for (int i = 0; i < outputNum; ++i)
            {
                maxOutput[i] = double.MinValue;
                minOutput[i] = double.MaxValue;
            }

    // read maximum 50 points
    int maxTempNum = 50;
    double[][] tempInputData = newdouble[maxTempNum][];
    double[][]          tempOutputData          =
newdouble[maxTempNum][];
    int num = 0;

    using        (SqlConnection        connection        =
newSqlConnection(connectionString))
            {
    SqlCommand command = newSqlCommand(queryString,
connection);
                connection.Open();
    SqlDataReader reader = command.ExecuteReader();
    try
            {
    while ((num < maxTempNum) && reader.Read())
            {
    //handle data
    //train input
                        tempInputData[num]        =
newdouble[inputNum];
    for (int j = 0; j < inputNum; j++)
            {
                        tempInputData[num][j]
= double.Parse(reader[0].ToString());
    // search for min value
    if (tempInputData[num][j] < minInput[j])
                        minInput[j]        =
tempInputData[num][j];
    // search for max value
```

```
if (tempInputData[num][j] > maxInput[j])
                                    maxInput[j]          =
tempInputData[num][j];
                            }
    // trainOutput
                            tempOutputData[num]          =
newdouble[outputNum];
    for (int j = 0; j < outputNum; j++)
                            {
                                    tempOutputData[num][j]
= double.Parse(reader[1].ToString());
    // search for min value
    if (tempOutputData[num][j] < minOutput[j])
                                    minOutput[j]         =
tempOutputData[num][j];
    // search for max value
    if (tempOutputData[num][j] > maxOutput[j])
                                    maxOutput[j]         =
tempOutputData[num][j];
                            }
                            num++;

    // allocate and set trainInput trainOutput
                            trainNum = num;
                            trainInput           =
newdouble[trainNum][];
                            trainOutput          =
newdouble[trainNum][];
    for (int j = 0; j < trainNum; j++)
                            {
                                    trainInput[j]        =
newdouble[inputNum];
                                    trainOutput[j]       =
newdouble[outputNum];
                            }
    Array.Copy(tempInputData, 0, trainInput, 0, num);
    Array.Copy(tempOutputData, 0, trainOutput, 0, num);
                            }
                    }
finally
                    {
// Always call Close when done reading.
                            reader.Close();
                            connection.Close();
                    }

//Construct data displayed in chart
                    data = newdouble[trainNum, 2];
    for (int i = 0; i < trainNum; i++)
                    {
                            data[i, 0] = trainInput[i][0];
                            data[i, 1] = trainOutput[i][0];
                    }

// Display chart boundary label
                    labelMinHour.Text            =
minInput[0].ToString();
```

```
                    labelMaxHour.Text            =
maxInput[0].ToString();
                    labelMinAmount.Text          =
minOutput[0].ToString();
                    labelMaxAmount.Text          =
maxOutput[0].ToString();

    // normalization
    for (int i = 0; i < trainNum; ++i)
                    {
    for (int j = 0; j < inputNum; ++j)
                            {
                                    trainInput[i][j]     =
premnmxInput(trainInput[i][j], minInput[j], maxInput[j]);
                            }
    for (int j = 0; j < outputNum; j++)
                            {
                                    trainOutput[i][j]    =
premnmxOutput(trainOutput[i][j],            minOutput[j],
maxOutput[j]);
                            }
                    }
            }
    }

    privatevoid trainNetwork(int inputNum, int hideNode, int
    outputNum, double learningRate, double Momentum, int
    iterate)
            {
//Training network

//create multi-layer neural network
                    network                      =
newActivationNetwork(newBipolarSigmoidFunction(2),
inputNum, hideNode, outputNum);
    //create teacher
    BackPropagationLearning         teacher      =
newBackPropagationLearning(network);
    //set learning rate and momentum
                    teacher.LearningRate = learningRate;
                    teacher.Momentum = Momentum;

    int iteration = 0;
    double error = 0;

    while (iteration < iterate)
                    {
                            error = teacher.RunEpoch(trainInput,
trainOutput) / trainNum;
                            ++iteration;
                    }
            }
```

ii. *Two-dimensional simulation of data:* The trained
     neural network can predict the growth of vibrio
     parahaemolyticus at any time, and the predicted value
     can be simulated by a two-dimensional image. The

key codes are as follows.
```
//Two-dimensional simulation
privatevoid simulateTwoDimension()
        {
                chart.RangeX                            =
newRange((float)minInput[0], (float)maxInput[0]);
                chart.UpdateDataSeries("data", data);
                chart.UpdateDataSeries("solution", null);

        double[,] solution = newdouble[50, 2];
        double[] networkInput = newdouble[1];

        // calculate X values to be used with solution function
        for (int j = 0; j < 50; j++)
                {
                        solution[j,  0]  =  chart.RangeX.Min  +
(double)j * chart.RangeX.Length / 49;
                }

        // calculate solution
        for (int j = 0; j < 50; j++)
                {
                        networkInput[0]                         =
premnmxInput(solution[j,        0],        minInput[0],
maxInput[0]);//normalization
                        solution[j,        1]        =
getOriginalOutput(network.Compute(networkInput)[0],
minOutput[0], maxOutput[0]);
                }
                chart.UpdateDataSeries("solution",
solution);


        }
```
iii. *Data prediction:* The trained neural network can
    predict the growth of vibrio parahaemolyticus for a
    single time entered by user. The key codes are as
    follows.
```
publicdouble predict(double input)
        {
        double[] networkInput = newdouble[1];
                networkInput[0]  =  premnmxInput(input,
minInput[0], maxInput[0]);//normalization
        return
getOriginalOutput(network.Compute(networkInput)[0],
minOutput[0], maxOutput[0]);
        }
```

5.3. System Implementation

5.3.1. Implementation of Data Management Module

In the data management module, the experimental data can
be added, deleted, queried, and data can be also loaded from
the database.

Data addition is as shown in Figure 5. Enter data that is
needed to add in the input box, and then click the Add button
to add.

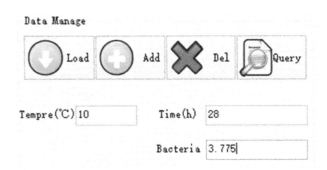

Figure 5. Data Add.

Data query interface is similar to data addition, enter the
data into the corresponding input boxes to temperature and
time, and then click on the Query button to search. If the
queried data does not exist in the database, it will give tips.

Data loading is as shown in Figure 6, after clicking on the
Load button, the experimental data of the corresponding state
in the database will be loaded into the table.

Tempre(°C)	Time(h)	lgNt(cfu/mL)
10	0	2.977
10	20	3.35
10	28	3.775
10	44	4.172
10	52	4.365
10	68	5.129
10	74	5.85
10	94	6.418
10	100.5	7.066
10	120	8.07
10	138	9.395
10	145	9.926
14	0	3.082
14	14.5	3.361
14	24	4.175
14	38.5	4.875
14	47.5	5.671
14	62.5	6.146
14	70.5	6.939
14	88	7.593
14	94.5	7.998
14	110.5	8.455
14	120	8.612

Figure 6. Data loading.

Data deletion interface is similar to data loading interface,
select a record in the table, and then click the Del button, you
can delete the data from the database.

5.3.2. Implementation of Data Simulation Module

Data simulation is as shown in Figure 7. Select the
condition that is needed to be simulated at the top of the list
box, and then click on the Simul button, you can perform
neural network training and two-dimensional data simulation.

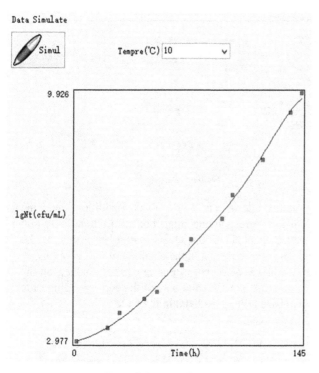

Figure 7. Data simulation.

5.3.3. Implementation of Data Prediction Module

Data prediction is as shown in Figure 8. Enter the prediction condition in the corresponding condition box, and then click the Pred button, and the results of the prediction will be displayed on the bacterial value box.

Figure 8. Data prediction.

6. Conclusions

According to the requirements of a research project, sub project of National Science and Technology Support Program of China: Key Integrated and Demonstrated Technologies for Quality and Safety Control in Aquatic Product Processing Process (No. 2012BAD29B06), the authors of this paper have developed a set of bread shrimp microbial growth simulation and prediction system. The system is established by taking vibrio parahemolyticus in bread shrimp as research objects, according to effects of temperature, salt and time on their growth, and employing neural network technology. The system consists of three parts: data management, data simulation and data prediction, which would provide an effective analytical tool for bread shrimp safe production. In order to improve its compatibility, the system is developed by using C# on Visual Studio 2008 platform, and its design and implementation are based on Aforge.NET framework and sliding-window modeling method.

The system is developed as an easy-to-use microbial growth simulation and prediction system, in which experimental growth data of vibrio parahaemolyticus in bread shrimp in the six states of temperature, salinity, pH, low temperature, temperature + PH, temperature + salinity at some time points are taken as input data for neural network. Neural network algorithm, Back Propagation Learning, is used for neural network simulation. The program structure of the system is to take Visual Studio 2008 as its front, SQL Server2008 as its database, and use open source AForge.NET for its framework. The front desk interface displays two-dimensional data graphics, while in the background the system loads experimental data stored in the database, applies open source framework AForge.NET for neural network simulation, and outputs the prediction results to the front desk interface. After tested carefully, the system can meet the requirements of the project design.

Through intelligent simulation and prediction in the system, users can predict vibrio parahemolyticus growth and survival data in various conditions only providing a limited number of vibrio parahemolyticus growth and survival data in the conditions. By this way, users do not need to perform experiments in each condition, greatly reducing the number of experiments and saving experimental time and costs.

Acknowledgment

This research work was funded by the sub project of National Science and Technology Support Programof China under Grant No. 2012BAD29B06 and the Science and Technology Project of Guangdong Province under Grant No. 2014B040401014.

References

[1]   Xiao Laisheng, A Neural Network-Based Multi-Dimensional Simulation Modeling Approach for Food Microbial Growth, Advanced Science Letters, ISSN: 1936-6612, Volume 6, Pages 400-405(15 March 2012).

[2]   Wang Zhengxia, Xiao Laisheng, "Prediction Model of Ocean Food Microbe Growth Based on Neural Network and Its Simulation", CCCA2011, Volume II, p160-165, ISBN: 978-1-61284-102-1, 2011.

[3]   Zhou Kang, Liu Shouchun, Li Pinglan, Ma Changwei, Peng Zhaohui, New Advances in Predictive Food Microbial Growth Model, Microbiology, APR 20, 2008, 35(4): 589-594.

[4]   Zhang Yuting, Meng Yaquan, Yan Guoting, Application of Matlab in microbial growth forecast model, Hebei Chemical Industry, Vol. 31, No.1, Jan. 2008, pp.20-22.

[5]   Zhang Yuting, Wu Kun, Zhang Chunhui, Wang Yufeng, Selection and application of microorganism growth model in cold fresh pork, Meat Industry, 2005, No.11, Totally 295, pp.23-25.

[6]   Yang Hongju, Nan Qingxian, Establishment of main corruption microbial growth model in cold pork, Storage and Process, 2004, No.3, pp.7-10.

[7] Liu Xinyou, Nan Haijun, Hao Yaqing, Gao Yuanjun, Tang Xueyan, Zhang Fang, Research on microbial growth model for fresh cut apples in storage period, Journal of Henan Agricultural Sciences, 2007, No.3, pp.88-91.

[8] I. Stamati, F. Logist, E. Van Derlinden, J.-P. Gauchi, J. Van Impe, Optimal experimental design for discriminating between microbial growth models as function of suboptimal temperature, Mathematical Biosciences 250 (2014) 69–80.

[9] I. Stamati, F. Logist, S. Akkermans, E. Noriega Fernández, J. Van Impe, On the effect of sampling rate and experimental noise in the discrimination between microbial growth models in the suboptimal temperature range, Computers and Chemical Engineering 85 (2016) 84–93.

[10] Si Zhu, Guibing Chen, Numerical solution of a microbial growth model applied to dynamic environments, Journal of Microbiological Methods 112 (2015) 76–82.

[11] Anastasia Lytou, Efstathios Z. Panagou, George-John E. Nychas, Development of a predictive model for the growth kinetics of aerobic microbial population on pomegranate marinated chicken breast fillets under isothermal and dynamic temperature conditions, Food Microbiology 55 (2016) 25e31.

[12] Albert Ibarz • Pedro E. D. Augusto, An autocatalytic kinetic model for describing microbial growth during fermentation, Bioprocess Biosyst Eng (2015) 38:199–205.

[13] Long Liu • Zhiguo Guo • Jianjiang Lu •Xiaolin Xu, Kinetic model for microbial growth and desulphurisation with Enterobacter sp., Biotechnol Lett (2015) 37:375–381.

[14] María Jesús Munoz-Lopez, Maureen P. Edwards, Ulrike Schumann and Rober s. Anderssen, Multiplicative modelling of four-phase microbial growth, Pacific Journal ofMathematics for Industry (2015) 7: 7.

[15] Yury V. Bukhman • NathanW. DiPiazza • Jeff Piotrowski • Jason Shao• Adam G. W. Halstead • Minh Duc Bui • Enhai Xie • Trey K. Sato, Modeling Microbial Growth Curves with GCAT, Bioenerg. Res. (2015) 8: 1022–1030.

[16] Yong-guang Yin, Yun Ding, A close to real-time prediction method of total coliform bacteria in foods based on image identification technology and artificial neural network, Food Research International 42 (2009) 191–199.

[17] M. Hajmeer, I. Basheer, A probabilistic neural network approach for modeling and classification of bacterial growth/no-growth data, Journal of Microbiological Methods 51 (2002) 217–226.

[18] M. Cheroutre-Vialette, A. Lebert, Application of recurrent neural network to predict bacterial growth in dynamic conditions, International Journal of Food Microbiology 73 (2002) 107–118.

[19] A. H. Geeraerd, C. H. Herremans, C. Cenens, J. F. Van Impe, Application of artificial neural networks as a non-linear modular modeling technique to describe bacterial growth in chilled food products, International Journal of Food Microbiology 44 (1998) 49–68.

[20] Adolf Willem Schepers, Jules Thibault, Christophe Lacroix, Comparison of simple neural networks and nonlinear regression models for descriptive modeling of Lactobacillus helveticus growth in pH-controlled batch cultures, Enzyme and Microbial Technology 26 (2000) 431–445.

[21] Francisco Fernández-Navarroa, Antonio Valero, César Hervás-Martínez, Pedro A. Gutiérrez, Rosa M. García-Gimeno, Gonzalo Zurera-Cosano, Development of a multi-classification neural network model to determine the microbial growth/no growth interface, International Journal of Food Microbiology 141 (2010) 203–212.

[22] Francisco Fernández-Navarroa, César Hervás-Martíneza, M. Cruz-Ramírez, Pedro Antonio Gutiérrez, Antonio Valero, Evolutionary q-Gaussian Radial Basis Function Neural Network to determine the microbial growth/no growth interface of Staphylococcus aureus, Applied Soft Computing 11 (2011) 3012–3020.

[23] Daniel S. Esser • Johan H. J. Leveau • Katrin M. Meyer, Modeling microbial growth and dynamics, Appl Microbiol Biotechnol (2015) 99:8831–8846.

[24] Wang Zhengxia, Xiao Laisheng, Lin Honghong, Qiu Shuzhong, Huang Chiyun, Lei Xiaoling, Intelligent General Predictive Platform for Sea Food Microorganism Growth, Computer Knowledge and Technology, Vol 7, No. 19, July 2011.

[25] http://www.aforgenet.com/aforge/framework/.

[26] http://www.codeproject.com/Articles/16447/Neural-Networks-on-C.

[27] Xiao-sheng LIU, Xiao HU, Ting-li WANG, Rapid assessment of flood loss based on neural network ensemble, Trans. Nonferrous Met. Soc. China 24(2014) 2636−2641.

[28] Chengying Gong, Hui He, Research of AForge.NET in Motion Video Detection, Applied Mechanics and Materials Vols. 496-500 (2014), pp 2150-2153.

[29] Suraj Verma*, Prashant Pillai and Yim-Fun Hu, Development of an eye-tracking control system using AForge.NET framework, Int. J. Intelligent Systems Technologies and Applications, Vol. 11, Nos. 3/4, 2012.

[30] ŽIDEK Kamil, RIGASOVá Eva, Diagnostics of Products by Vision System, Applied Mechanics and Materials Vol. 308 (2013) pp 33-38.

[31] Ondrej Krejcar, Utilization of C# Neural Networks Library in Industry Applications, ICeND 2011, CCIS 171, pp. 61-72, 2011.

[32] Laisheng Xiao, "A sliding-window modeling approach for neural network", International Journal of Control and Automation, ISSN 2005-4297, Vol.7, No.8, Aug. 2014.

23

Vehicle Fault Diagnostics Using Text Mining, Vehicle Engineering Structure and Machine Learning

Yi Lu Murphey, Liping Huang, Hao Xing Wang, Yinghao Huang

Department of Electrical and Computer Engineering, University of Michigan-Dearborn, Dearborn, USA

Email address:

yilu@umich.edu (Y. L. Murphey)

Abstract: This paper presents an intelligent vehicle fault diagnostics system, SeaProSel(Search-Prompt-Select). SeaProSel takes a casual description of vehicle problems as input and searches for a diagnostic code that accurately matches the problem description. SeaProSel was developed using automatic text classification and machine learning techniques combined with a prompt-and-select technique based on the vehicle diagnostic engineering structure to provide robust classification of the diagnostic code that accurately matches the problem description. Machine learning algorithms are developed to automatically learn words and terms, and their variations commonly used in verbal descriptions of vehicle problems, and to build a TCW(Term-Code-Weight) matrix that is used for measuring similarity between a document vector and a diagnostic code class vector. When no exactly matched diagnostic code is found based on the direct search using the TCW matrix, the SeaProSel system will search the vehicle fault diagnostic structure for the proper questions to pose to the user in order to obtain more details about the problem. A LSI (Latent Semantic Indexing) model is also presented and analyzed in the paper. The performances of the LSI model and TCW models are presented and discussed. An in-depth study of different term weight functions and their performances are presented. All experiments are conducted on real-world vehicle diagnostic data, and the results show that the proposed SeaProSel system generates accurate results efficiently for vehicle fault diagnostics.

Keywords: Vehicle Fault Diagnostics, Text Data Mining, Machine Learning, Vehicle Diagnostic Engineering Structure, TCW, LSI

1. Introduction

As computers and networks grow more powerful and data storage devices become more plentiful and less costly, the amount of information in digital form is exploded. The majority of such digital data are in text form. Text data mining has many applications including text document search and categorization, website search, customer services, and automatic diagnostic systems [1~4].

In this research we focus on text documents that are casually typed or recorded. Many text mining applications require processing casual text data, which often are in semi-structured or unstructured text, such as clinical document analysis [3, 5], emails, instant messages, free-text of medical records, operational notes, emails, instant messages, etc., and the application of this research is in automotive diagnostic text mining.

In automotive industry there are abundant information

available in casual natural language description form that contain valuable vehicle fault diagnostic knowledge, marketing information, consumer evaluation or satisfaction of certain vehicle models, styles, accessories, etc [6]. For example, several thousands of vehicle problems are reported daily to various auto service shops. It is important to find root-cause of a vehicle problem quickly and accurately. In a typical vehicle fault diagnostic process, vehicle problems are first described by customers in casual words and terms. A service advisor records the customer's complaints or description of symptoms verbatim on the repair order, and then searches for a diagnostic code that matches the description. The diagnostic code is used to guide the diagnosis and repairing processes. Due to the complexity of modern vehicles, the number of diagnostic codes can be in hundreds, which makes manual searching of correct diagnostic code difficult and may lead to a lengthy and less accurate diagnosis and repair process, and, possibly, unnecessary part replacements. In order to improve the accuracy and efficiency of vehicle fault diagnostics, it is important to develop an automated system that can help customers to report problems described in casual words and terms, and technicians to quickly find the correct diagnostic code, i.e., the root cause of the problems. There are several challenges involved in this problem.

The descriptions of vehicle problems provided by customers are often ill-structured. Most of such descriptions do not follow the English grammar, and contain many misspelled words, self-invented acronyms and shorthand descriptions.

The descriptions of a problem by different people vary based on the education and/or cultural background of the customers, and their familiarity of vehicle terminologies and knowledge of automotive engineering. For example, the term "trunk" used United States means the same thing as the term "boot" used in UK. One faulty symptom, for example, "a noise is heard from the engine and the engine runs rough" can be described by customers in various ways, such as engine knocks, hood squeak, engine misses idle, engine lopes, etc. The following are examples of customer descriptions of the same vehicle problem:

Customer 1: "WENT ON A SALES ROAD TEST WITH CUST, VEHICLE WOULDNOT START,"

Customer 2: "CHECK CAR WONT START,"

Customer 3: "CK BATTERY HARD TO START."

High dimensions of terms and document classes. Since there are typos and self-invented acronyms and abbreviations frequently occurring in customer descriptions, the number of distinct terms used in these documents is several times more than formally printed documents. For example, the word "engine" has more than 20 different spellings in customers' descriptions in our data collections. Since the output vector represents all the diagnostic codes used by a car manufacturing company, there can easily be several hundreds of different document classes. These two high dimension issues pose challenges for generating efficient and effective response for a given problem description.

In this paper we present an intelligent vehicle fault diagnostics system, Search-Prompt-Select(SeaProSel), which is developed by combining automatic text categorization techniques with vehicle engineering structure and machine learning to provide effective search functions for the diagnostic code that accurately matches a given problem description. The SeaProSel system uses machine learning techniques to automatically learn words, terms and their variations commonly used in verbal description of vehicle problems from training data, and incorporate a vehicle fault diagnostic engineering structure into the search process to provide accurate diagnostic code that matches the problem description. This paper is organized as follows. Section 2 presents a brief overview of the state-of-art technologies for text mining and document categorization, Section 3 presents the proposed system, SeaProSel, Section 4 presents the experiment results generated from real-world vehicle diagnostic data, and Section 5 concludes the paper.

2. Research in Text Mining and Document Classification

Until the late '80s, the most popular approach to text categorization are based on knowledge engineering [7~9]. These approaches usually consist of a set of predefined rules that are encoded with expert knowledge. Each rule is represented as a disjunctive normal form (DNF formula) followed by a category name. A document is classified under a specific category if it satisfies the DNF formula of the category. This DNF expression is mostly defined by domain experts. If categories are updated or ported to a different domain, domain experts need to intervene to redefine DNF expressions for new categories from scratch. In recent years most techniques used in text document classification and categorization are developed based on machine learning technologies, which automatically build document classifiers by learning the characteristic of document categories from a set of training documents. The advantage of machine learning is that it does not heavily rely on manual labors during the model construction stage. Its effectiveness level, in many cases, is superior to that of professional human work. Consequently, automatic text categorization has become a major research area of machine learning. Many text categorization systems have been developed using different machine learning algorithms, including k-nearest neighbor (K-NN), neural networks, latent semantic indexing, probabilistic models, support vector machine, and etc.

The initial application of k-Nearest Neighbor (K-NN) to text document categorization and classification was introduced by Masand and his colleagues [7, 10], and later it became a widely used method in text classification [11~13]. In text document classification and categorization, a document is often represented as a vector composed of a series of selected words called as feature vector. A K-NN based text categorization system is to find the K documents in the training data that are most similar to an input unknown document. The category contains the majority among the K best matched documents is considered as the category to which the unknown document belongs. The similarity between the unknown document and each training document is measured by a similarity function, which is critical in generating accurate results [11~13].

Neural networks (NNs) have been popular in text categorization and document retrieval [14~16]. The most popular neural network architecture for text classification is a multilayer neural network trained with the well-known backpropagation algorithm using supervised learning [17~22].

Self-Organized Map(SOM), also known as the Kohonen network [23], is a popular unsupervised neural network used in text classification. A SOM network attempts to cluster the training data while preserving the topological properties of the input space. During the training process, it builds the network, i.e. the map, by applying a competitive process to input examples. A fully trained SOM network can be used as a pattern classifier [3]. SOM has also been used in feature selection for text categorization [24] and text clustering [25, 26].

Probabilistic Modeling has been used in text document classification. A widely used framework of probabilistic model for text document classification is derived from the Bayesian theorem of conditional probability [8, 27]:

$$P(c_i \mid \vec{d_j}) = \frac{P(c_i)P(\vec{d_j} \mid c_i)}{P(\vec{d_j})},$$

where dj is the input document, $\vec{d_j}$ is the feature vector that represents dj, ci is the ith document class, $P(\vec{d_j})$ is the probability that a document dj represented by vector $\vec{d_j}$ occurs randomly, $P(c_i)$ the probability of a randomly picked document belongs to category ci, $P(\vec{d_j} \mid c_i)$ is the probability of document $\vec{d_j}$ occurring given that document dj is in document class ci, and $P(c_i \mid \vec{d_j})$ is the probability of dj , represented by vector $\vec{d_j}$ belonging to document class ci. To simplify the calculation of the conditional probability, Naïve Bayes (NB) classifier has been applied to document classification [9]. A Naïve Bayes classifier assumes that the conditional probability of each term in the feature vector for a given class is independent of the conditional probability of other terms in the feature vector for a given class. This assumption is called class conditional independence. It makes the computation of the NB classifier far more efficient than the exponential complexity of a non-naïve Bayes approach since it does not require the term combination as predictors. Studies comparing different classification models have shown the performance of Naïve Bayes classifier is comparable with neural network classifiers and batch linear classifier [28, 29].

Support vector machine (SVM) approach was developed based on the structural risk minimization theories in statistical learning [30]. A SVM maps the input feature space to a high dimensional space through a kernel function. It then chooses the hyperplane with the maximum margin that can separate the positive from negative examples in the feature space. According to the structural risk minimization, the generalization error is bounded by the sum of the training set error and a term derived from the Vapnik-Chervonenkis (VC) dimension of the learning machine. Unlike traditional artificial neural networks (ANNs), which minimize the empirical training error, SVM aims at minimizing the upper bound of the generalization error, which represents the error on unseen data for a classifier. Thus high generalization performance can be achieved. SVM can potentially learn a larger set of patterns and be able to scale better than artificial neural networks [31]. Many published literatures show that SVM learning can lead to high performance in a broad range of pattern classification applications [31~34].

SVMs have been popular in text classification and categorization [35, 36]. SVM is designed for two-class pattern classification. However in text document classification, most applications involve more than two categories of documents. Therefore a text categorization system developed using SVMs usually use one of the following two approaches to build a multiclass SVM system. Let $N > 2$ be the number of text categories. The first approach would design N SVM classifiers, each of which discriminates the kth class against the remaining N-1 classes, $k = 1$ to N. The SVM associated with the class k seeks a decision surface in the feature space that separates class k from all other classes. Collectively the N SVM models result in N decision boundaries [37]. When a new document x is submitted to the system, all N SVMs are applied to x, and the class represented by the SVM that generates the largest output value is assigned to the input document x. The second approach is to train $N(N-1)/2$ SVMs, each of which is trained to pair-wisely separate two different classes in the training data set. Different voting strategies, such as Max-Wins [37] or directed acyclic graph (DAG) can be used to make the final classification decision based on the results from the $N(N-1)/2$ pair-wise SVMs [38].

Even with the advanced technologies discussed above text mining continuous to be a challenging research area. In this paper we present an innovative technique that combines automated text document classification with domain knowledge to derive a search result that precisely matches the input query.

3. SeaProSel: an Intelligent Vehicle Fault Diagnostic System

All automotive companies develop its own diagnostic codes that are used in their vehicle fault diagnostic processes. Some companies may have several sets of diagnostic codes with names such as CSC (Customer Symptom Codes), CCC (Customer Concern Codes), and etc. Without losing generality, we refer to such a code system as a vehicle diagnostic code (VDC). The SeaProSel system is designed to map a query description to a specific VDC that accurately matches the problem description. This query-to-VDC mapping is a M-to-M mapping. Multiple descriptions can be mapped to the same VDC, and one query can be mapped to multiple VDCs due to ambiguity in language. For example, the three customer descriptions given in Section 1 have the same diagnostic code that represent the problem of "ENGINE WOULD NOT START."

In addition to the synonymy and polysemy problems existing in general text documents, the documents occurring in vehicle fault diagnostics pose particular challenges: typos, grammar errors, self-invented terms and acronyms, inappropriate usages of punctuations, and etc. The proposed SeaProSel is designed to deal with these challenging issues in order to generate a unique VDC that accurately matches the input query. SeaProSel has a hierarchical matching and searching system that uses text data mining technology to quickly retrieve diagnostic code that accurately matches the query, i.e. the problem description provided by a user. In the cases that no unique diagnostic code is found, the system will follow the given automotive diagnostic system to prompt questions to user in an attempt to obtain more information from the user about the vehicle problem. It then uses the answer provided by the user to search for the correct diagnostic code. This prompt and search process can be repeated until a unique diagnostic code is found.

Figure 1 illustrates the system architecture of the SeaProSel. At the first stage the SeaProSel directly searches for a VDC that matches the input query by using a Vector Space Model. We present two approaches, first is a Term-Code-Weight (TCW) model and the second a latent semantic indexing (LSI) model. The TCW model is a weighted matrix that is obtained through a machine learning algorithm. The LSI model uses the reduced-rank matrices to approximate the original TCW matrix. Each category and query is converted into a low-dimensional vector in a LSI space. Both models along with the critical research issues related to the two models, such as term selection and weight functions, are discussion in depth in section 3.A. If no exactly matched VDC is found, and the system outputs a list of best matched VDCs and then enters the second stage, *Prompt & Select*, which follows the vehicle diagnostic engineering hierarchy to prompt questions for user to select the more detailed and better described vehicle problem. Based on the user's answers, the system generates a new list, VDC_list2, which is a sublist of VDC_list1 and contains the VDCs that satisfy the user selected descriptions. The *Prompt & Select* process is repeated until a satisfactory VDC is found. This process is described in Section 3.B.

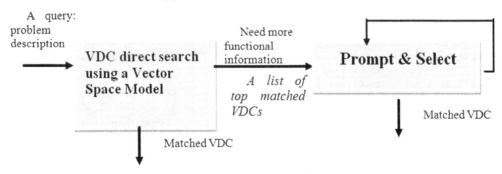

Figure 1. Overview of SeaProSel System.

A. Building a diagnostic document classification model using machine learning

In text data mining, a Vector Space Model (VSM) is an algebraic representation of text documents that contains vectors of identifiers or index terms such as words or phrases [39, 40]. In a VSM, all documents are represented in term weighted vectors. In this research we investigate two VSM models, TCW(Term-Code-Weight) matrix and LSI matrix. Both models are built using machine learning algorithms to represent vehicle fault diagnostic knowledge.

The two-dimensional TCW matrix, denoted as A_{MxN}, is generated from a training data set Tr, where M is the number of effective terms in Tr, and N is the number of diagnostic categories in Tr.

The training data set contains samples of customer descriptions of vehicle problems, and each description is associated with a correct diagnostic code assigned by automotive diagnostic experts. The machine learning algorithm consists of two major computational components: Term Extraction, and TCW Matrix Construction. The Term Extraction process involves the detection of a list of distinctive and effective terms, removal of punctuations and stopping words, word stemming and word variation detection. The TCW matrix contains M terms generated by the Term Extraction process, and N vehicle diagnostic codes, which represent document classes. An entry in a TCW, $A_{MxN}(i,j)$, represents the weight of the ith term associated with the jth diagnostic code, which is generated based on the statistical analysis of the ith term occurring in the training documents labeled with j^{th} diagnostic code. The TCW matrix is used to map directly from a problem description to the best matched diagnostic codes. The TCW matrix is built using a machine learning algorithm that contains the following major processes,

Document preprocessing

Document indexing

Term weight generation

Once we obtain the TCW matrix, the VDC that matches an input document can be generated by the process, *Vehicle Fault Diagnostics* using a similarity function.

1) *Document Preprocessing:* Two data noise problems associate with casual text documents, one is improper use of punctuations and special symbols, and another mislabeling document categories in training data. The misuse of punctuations in the text documents makes the text categorization less accurate. For example, the punctuations in 'ACCEL.', 'Dead.NEEDS' make the two terms different from their correct forms, 'ACCEL' and 'Dead' and 'NEEDS'. The existence of such inappropriate use of punctuation results in a lot of additional entries in the term list that actually should not exist, and cause misleading statistics. Three different types of processes are implemented. First type of processes involves the search for special symbols or punctuations appearing at one end or both ends of a word, for example, 'ACCEL.', '*DIESEL*', '****

TOW', and 'IN ****'. These symbols can be removed directly without any possibility of alternating the meaning of the word. The second type of processes is to search for special symbols or punctuations such as ".",'(', ')', '&', '*', ' / ', '+', etc, These symbols are either removed or replaced by a space. The third type of processes is more sophisticated. It mainly concerns the punctuations such as ',', ':', '.', etc. When they occur as a part of initials, numerical or time/date formats, such as 'A.C.', 'P.I.D.', '2,000', '16.00', '4:00', '4×4', they are kept as part of the original string. If they occur between two words for example, 'engine,check', the punctuations are replaced with a space.

In supervised machine learning, each training data sample is assigned a target class code, i.e. diagnostic code in our application. The class code assignment is still been done largely by diagnostic experts. Some documents may have the class code missing, others may be assigned of multiple codes because the person who assign the class codes is not sure which one is correct. We developed the following procedure to deal with this problem.

For all the documents with missing labels, we build a standard diagnostic code matrix, DC, based on standard descriptions of diagnostic code, which are available in mechanics' handbook. We extract the training documents with specific diagnostic codes to form a subset of training data, denoted as TrC, which is then used to generate the TCW matrix $C \in R^{p \times q}$ and term list T_Lc, where p is the number of index terms, and q is the number of codes. For a document q with n labels, X1, X2, ..., Xn, the relevance between q and Xi is calculated using the cosine similarity function shown below:

$$s_i = sim(\vec{q}, \overrightarrow{C_{X_i}}) = \frac{\sum_{j=1}^{p} q_j (C_{X_i})_j}{\left(\sum_{j=1}^{p} (q_j)^2 \sum_{j=1}^{p} ((C_{X_i})_j)^2 \right)^{\frac{1}{2}}}.$$

Let the similarity scores between q and the n diagnostic code vectors be $s_1, s_2, ..., s_n$, and $S_{max} = Max\{s_i \mid i = 1, ..., n \}$. The diagnostic code corresponding to S_{max} is assigned to document q. In the cases that multiple diagnostic codes are useful, we set a threshold th, and if the difference between S_{max} and s_i is smaller than th, diagnostic code X_i is also assigned to the document q.

2) *Document Indexing:* The terms used in the TCW matrix need to be derived automatically from training documents, and carefully selected so they effectively represent document contents. We developed the following document indexing algorithm to extract effective indexing terms automatically from training data. Let us assume a collection of documents are to be classified into N diagnostic codes or categories, (C1, C2, ... CN), and we have training documents Tr1, Tr2, ..., TrN, where Tri contains the training documents belonging to category i, i = 1, ..., N. The objective of the following algorithm is to generate a list of indexing

terms, T_L, where each term $t_i \in T\_L$ that effectively represents the contents in the documents contained in Tr, where Tr = $Tr_1 \cup ... \cup Tr_N$. The document indexing algorithm contains the following major computational components.

Step 1: Extract all distinct terms from Tr to form an initial term list T_L.

Step 2: Generate a stop word list, stop_word list, which is used to make sure those words do not occur in the term list T_L. T_L contains the words, such as "the", "about", "an", "and", etc. that provide little information for document class discrimination. It also contains words have no specific meaning in a given application domain. For example, in vehicle fault diagnostic documents, terms such as 'customer', 'states', 'said', 'ck', 'cust', 'driving', etc. occur in documents of all classes.

Step 3: We implemented the well-known Porter Stemming algorithm (or 'Porter stemmer') [41] and applied it to the training data to generate groups of words that have the same stem, and the variant word forms is represented by one root word.

The Porter Stemming algorithm is based on the idea that the suffixes in the English language mostly consist of a combination of smaller and simpler suffixes. It has five computational processes. In each step, if a suffix rule matches with a word, then the conditions attached to that rule are tested on the resulting stem. A condition, for example, may be the number of stem length after suffix removal must be greater than the threshold. For example, the suffix of 'ing' can be safely removed from the word "singing", and the remaining part, i.e. the stem "sing" replaces the original word. Stemming word processing reduces the dimensionality to the word list significantly.

Step 4: Eliminating low-frequency words. Two frequency thresholds d_th, w_th, are defined to remove words occurring infrequently. A term is removed from T_L if its occurring frequency in the number of different vehicle diagnostic code categories is less than d_th or its occurring frequency in all training documents is less than w_th times. The optimal values for d_th and w_th can be obtained through experiments.

Step 5: Eliminating words evenly distributed across all categories. Words that have even distributions among all document categories are also removed from T_L, since they appear in the same frequency over all document categories.

Step 6. Output T_L, which is used for building the TCW matrix described below.

3) *Modeling diagnostic documents using a TCW Matrix:* An entry in a TCW matrix A_{MxN}, denoted as $a_{i,j}$, is the weight of the ith term in T_L belonging to the jth VDC, for $i = 1, ..., M$ and $j = 1, ..., N$. The weight in each entry in A_{MxN} is a function of the occurrence frequency of a term with respect to a category. The function is referred to a weight function. Term weighting is an important component for improving performance in the VSM based text mining [42]. Terms need to be weighted according to their importance for a particular

document category and for the whole document collection. A useful index term must fulfill a dual function: it occurs in the documents of the same category with high frequency so as to render the document retrievable, and it is useful to distinguish the documents of one category from the others. A term weight function is usually a combination of a local weight and a global weight function. The following describes three popular local weight functions.

Term Frequency: $l_{ij} = \text{tf}_{ij}$, which is the occurrence frequency of term i within document category j,

$$\text{Binary: } B_{ij} = \begin{cases} 0 & \text{if } tf_{ij} = 0 \\ 1 & f_{ij} > 0 \end{cases},$$

and

$$\text{Log function: } l_{ij} = \text{Log}_2(\text{tf}_{ij} + 1).$$

A local weight function provides a measure of how well that a term describes the document contents in a particular category. However, using only local weight is not enough to evaluate the importance of a term in the document classification. Some terms, due to their rarity use in a particular category of documents, are more important in identifying these documents than others do. Some terms, however, because they appear in many documents, are not useful to discriminate documents in one category from the others. A global weight measure is used to reflect the overall importance of the index term in the entire document collection. Four well-known global weights introduced by

Dumais [43] are:

$$\text{Normal: } \sqrt{\frac{1}{\sum_j tf_{ij}^2}},$$

$$\text{Gfldf: } \frac{gf_i}{df_i},$$

$$\text{Idf: } \log_2\left[\frac{ndocs}{df_i}\right] + 1,$$

$$\text{Entropy: } 1 - \sum_j \frac{p_{ij}\log(p_{ij})}{\log(ndocs)} \text{ where } p_{ij} = \frac{tf_{ij}}{gf_i},$$

where df_i, the document frequency, is the total number of documents in the document collection, i.e. training data, that contain term i, gf_i, the global frequency, is the frequency of term i occurring in the entire document collection, and $ndocs$ is the total number of documents in the document collection.

Different weight functions transform the raw occurrence frequency of a term in a document to different weights. In general, the entry $a_{i,j}$ of a TCW matrix A is a function of a local and a global weight components. The most commonly used term weight functions are listed in Table 1. These weight functions have been evaluated through extensive experiments and the results are discussed in Section 4. Based on these experiments, the proposed SeaProSel system uses the tf-idf weight function in its VCD direct search component.

Table 1. Popular weight functions.

Entropy	Gfidf	Normal	tf-idf	B-idf
$tf_{ij} * (1 - \sum_j \frac{p_{ij}\log(p_{ij})}{\log(ndocs)})$	$tf_{ij} * \frac{gf_i}{df_i}$	$tf_{ij} * \sqrt{\frac{1}{\sum_j tf_{ij}^2}}$	$tf_{ij} * \log\left[\frac{ndocs}{df_i}\right] + 1$	$B_{ij} * \log\left[\frac{ndocs}{df_i}\right] + 1$
B-normal $B_{ij} * \sqrt{\frac{1}{\sum_j tf_{ij}^2}}$	Log-idf $\log(tf_{ij}+1) * (\log\left[\frac{ndocs}{df_i}\right]+1)$	Log-entropy $\log(tf_{ij}+1) * (1 - \sum_j \frac{p_{ij}\log(p_{ij})}{\log(ndocs)})$	log-Gfidf $\log(tf_{ij}+1) * \frac{gf_i}{df_i}$	log-norm $\log(tf_{ij}+1) * \sqrt{\frac{1}{\sum_j tf_{ij}^2}}$

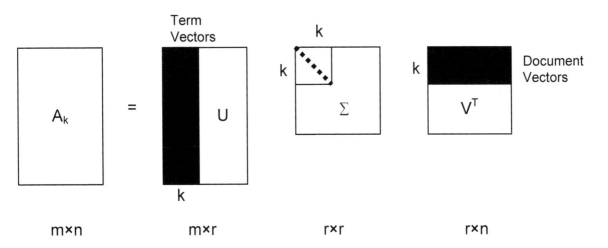

Figure 2. A rank-k approximation matrix.

4) *Modeling diagnostic documents using a LSI Matrix:* A popular variant of TCW matrix is constructed using latent semantic indexing (LSI) method [44~46]. It uses the reduced-rank matrices to approximate the original TCW matrix. Each category and query is converted into a low-dimension vector and mapped into the LSI space. Relevance measures for the user query are also performed in this space.

A LSI matrix is built from the TCW matrix. A is decomposed into the product of three matrices $A = U \Sigma V^T$, where $U^T U = V^T V = I_n$, and $\Sigma = diag(\sigma_1,...,\sigma_n)$, $\sigma_i > 0$ for $1 \leq i \leq r, \sigma_j = 0$ for $j \geq r+1$. Matrices U and V contain left and right singular vectors of A, respectively, and diagonal matrix Σ contains singular values. A rank-k approximation to A is represented $A_k = U_k \Sigma_k V_k^T$, where Uk and Vk are constructed by taking only the k largest singular values of Σ along with their corresponding columns in the matrices U and V respectively. Ak is the unique matrix of rank k that is closest in the least squares sense to A. Fig. 2 illustrates the relationship between A and Ak.

The SVD method attempts to capture most important underlying structure in the association of terms and documents. Since k is usually much smaller than the number of terms m, some "noise" are eliminated by deleting low ranking columns. Because SVD is a strictly mathematical method, the contents of the matrices are not interpretable with respect to the documents or terms it analyzes. The best rank k in the SVD model depends on the training data, which will be further discussed in the experiment section. However, it is a powerful technique to reduce the dimension of any term-by-document matrix.

5) *Vehicle Fault Diagnostics using TCW and LSI matrices:* The objective of vehicle fault diagnostics is to classify the user query to a diagnostic code that accurately matches the input query. Vehicle Fault Diagnostics using TCW algorithm consists of two processes, formulating query vector, and measuring similarity between the term vector and a column vector in the TCW. An input problem description d is firstly preprocessed using the same procedures as described earlier, including removing unnecessary punctuations, stop words and word stemming, etc. It is then transformed into a term vector $\bar{q}$ with the same length M of T_L. Let $\bar{q} = (q_1,...,q_M)^T$, where q_i is the frequency of the ith term on T_L occurred in the query document d, i = 1, ..., M. The classification decision on which VDC category that best matches with $\bar{q}$ is made based on the similarity measure between $\bar{q}$ and each column vector of A. Let the column vectors of A be $\bar{a}_j = (a_{1j},...,a_{Mj})^T$, j=1, ..., N. We use the following cosine based similarity measure to generate a similarity score between the vector $\bar{q}$ and the column vector $\bar{a}_j$,

$$r_j^c(\bar{q}, \bar{a}_j) = \frac{\bar{q} \bullet \bar{a}_j}{\|\bar{q}\| \bullet \|\bar{a}_j\|} = \frac{\sum_{i=1}^{M} q_i a_{ij}}{\sqrt{\sum_{i=1}^{M} q_i^2 \sum_{i=1}^{M} a_{ij}^2}}$$

After similarity score is obtained for every VDC category and the input query, there are two approaches by which our system can use to determine if the diagnostic codes with the best similarity score should be returned as matched code class. One method is to use a threshold: all diagnostic categories with similarity scores larger than the threshold are regarded as relevant and assigned to the query. The second method is to output the VDC category represented by the column vector in the TCW matrix that has the highest similarity score with the input query vector.

In the LSI model, a user's query is represented by a vector in the reduced-rank space. From a user query, we first construct the same term vector $\bar{q}$ as in the TCW model. Then $\bar{q}$ is converted into the vector in the reduced-rank space by the following formula: $\bar{q}_k = \bar{q}^T U_k \Sigma_k^{-1}$. The classification decision on which VDC category that best matches with $\bar{q}_k$ is made based on the similarity measure between $\bar{q}_k$ and each column vector of Ak, the same process as in the TCW classification process described above.

Both TCW based and LSI based VDC direct search system will be evaluated in Section 4.

B. Integrating automatic search with vehicle engineering structure

The proposed vehicle fault diagnostic system, SeaProSel, is an integration of direct search using the TCW matrix and the progressive prompt and select process based on a hierarchical vehicle fault diagnostic engineering structure. A diagnostic code system is usually organized in a hierarchical structure that contains multiple levels of functional descriptions, and each level provides descriptions about a class of symptoms, specific function or component faults, conditions, and etc. In this representation, the vehicle fault diagnostic codes are represented in the leaf nodes, the root of the tree is the entire vehicle system, and the subsequent levels represent the hierarchies of subsystems, components or devices. Figure 3 shows an example. The highest layer has three function groups. Under each function group, there are sub-function groups. For each function group at level 2, there are component groups. Under each component group, there are different categories of deviations, under each of which, there is a layer of conditions. Each node in the tree is accompanied with a brief description. For example, a description for a function group could be "Engine with mountings and equipment," a description for a component category under the function group could be "starting," the descriptions for conditions under such function group could be "engine turns", "cold start" or "unsure when", and a description for a VDC could be, "ENGINE WOULD NOT START."

The SeaProSel system uses the TCW matrix to directly obtain highly matched diagnostic codes, interacts with user by prompting diagnostic questions based on the vehicle engineering structure, takes user's selection/answer to either generate a diagnostic code that accurately match the user's answers or lead to the next level of functional prompts. Figure 4 shows the architecture of the SeaProSel system developed based on the vehicle fault diagnostic system illustrated in Figure 3. In Figure 4, SQ_1 represents the input problem description, SQ_2 represents the selected level 2 function group, and SQ_3 represents the selected component/functionality. The SeaProSel algorithm has the following major computational steps.

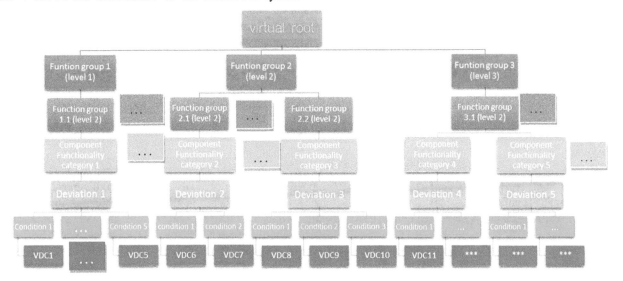

Figutre 3. *A hierarchical vehicle fault diagnostic system architecture.*

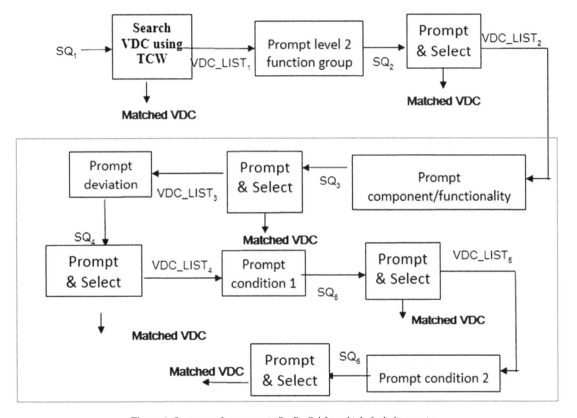

Figure 4. *Overview of processes in SeaProSel for vehicle fault diagnostics.*

Step 1: process the input query document SQ1 using the procedure, *VDC Direct Search using TCW*. Let the output of the procedure be F1 (SQ1) = {VDC_1, $conf_1$, ..., VDC_k, $conf_k$} , where $conf_1 \leq conf_2 \leq ..., \leq conf_k$

Step 2: If $\Delta 1 = conf_1 - conf_2$ is high, then output VDC_1 and exit

Step 3: Find $c \leq k$ such that $\Delta c = conf_c - conf_{c+1}$ is high

Step 4: Find the node H in the tree structure such that

Found_Codes = {VDC$_1$, ..., VDC$_c$} are all H's descendants, and no other nodes in the tree has this property except H's parent nodes.

Example 1: If Found_Codes = {VDC$_8$, VDC$_9$, VDC$_{10}$ } , the H code is "Deviation 3".

Example 2: If Found_Codes = {VDC$_6$, VDC$_9$, VDC$_{10}$ } , the H code is "Function Group 1".

Step 5: Call the following *Prompt & Select* procedure.

Step 5.1 Following the H node's direct descendants, and present the descriptions associated with the descendants to the user.

For example 1, the descriptions of "Condition 1," "Condition 2" and "Condition 3" under "Deviation 3" are presented to the user

Step 5.2 Based on the user selection, if the unique VCD is found, output the VCD and exit the program.

Step 5.3 Follow the descendant node selected by the user and find the VCDs that match the user's selections, and denote them F2 (SQ2) = {VDC'$_1$, conf'$_1$, ..., VDC'$_{k1}$, conf'$_{k1}$} , where conf'$_1$ ≤ conf'$_2$ ≤ ..., ≤ conf'$_{k1}$

Step 5.4 If Δ2 = conf'$_1$ – conf'$_2$, is high, then output VDC'$_1$ and exit

Step 5.5: goto Step 3.

4. Experiments

We were provided by an automotive company with the hierarchical vehicle fault diagnostic system illustrated in Figure 3. The hierarchical vehicle fault diagnostic system has 540 vehicle diagnostic codes, and each node is accompanied with a general description of the vehicle problems the node covers.

We conducted three different sets of experiments to evaluate, respectively, different weight functions, TCW matrix verse the LSI matrix, and the entire SeaProSel system.

The TCW and LSI matrices were all trained on a data set of 200,000 real-world customer descriptions of vehicle problems. After removing extraneous documents and eliminating documents with wrong labels, we had 199,552 valid documents as training data. After data preprocessing such as punctuation preprocessing, Portel stemming and typo removal, the number of index terms generated from the training data were reduced from 7033 to 3883. The TCW and LSI components as well as the weight functions were evaluated on TEST6K, a testing set of 6000 vehicle diagnostic documents collected from different retailer service shops in USA during one week time period. All test documents were labeled with true diagnostic codes by auto technicians.

The following evaluation criteria are used to analyze system performances. For each input query, two levels of matching accuracy are measured: the low level of matching (LLM) and high level matching (HLM). If the *VDC Direct Search* system using either TCW or LSI matrix returns the correct VDC code, i.e. it exactly matches one of the leaf nodes in the hierarchical vehicle fault diagnostic system shown Figure 3, then it is a low level matching. In this case, the ProSeaSel system will output the VDC code and terminate the search. If the VDC Direct Search system returns the code that does not match any of the leaf nodes but matches the correct higher level categories in the hierarchical system shown in Figure 3, then it is a high level matching. For example, if an input query's true VDC is "vdc1", but the output of the VDC Direct Search system is "vdc5". Since "vdc1" and "vdc5" have the same deviation category, the system has a wrong LLM, but a correct HLM. Based on these two types of matching criteria, we define two accuracy measures of system performances when a batch of test queries is used as test data, Exact Match Rate (EMR) and Category Match Rate (CMR). EMR is defined as the number of correct matched outputs in LLM over the size of the training data, and CMR the number of correct outputs in HLM over the size of the training data.

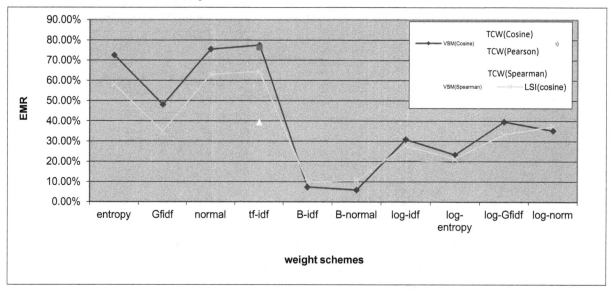

Figure 5. Effects of Weight Schemes and Similarity Functions.

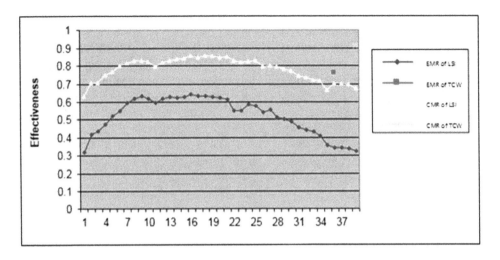

Figure 6. *Performances of the LSI systems of various K-values.*

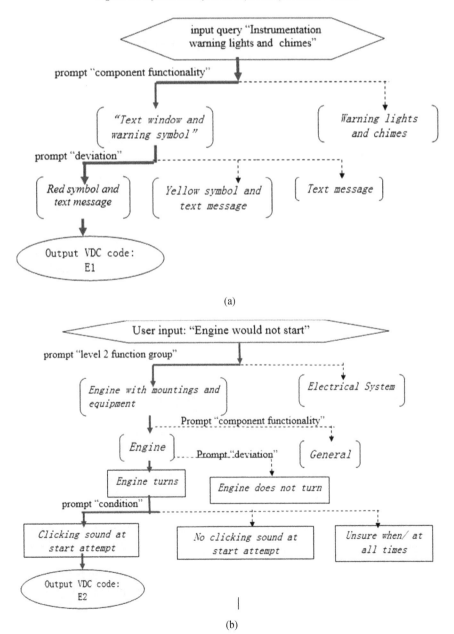

(a)

(b)

Figure 7. *Two examples of query processes by SeaProSel system*

A. Evaluation of weight functions

As described before, several weight schemes can be used in both TCW and LSI models. All weight functions shown in Table 1 were implemented in both the VSM and the LSI models. We used three different similarity functions: Cosine, Pearson, and Spearman in the query classification processes. The results are shown in Figure 5. It shows that the best result is generated by the TCW model that uses the tf-idf weight function combined with cosine similarity function. Pearson similarity measure used in the TCW model combined with the tf-idf weight function achieved the similar performance to that of cosine measure. Both of them are better than the Spearman similarity function.

B. Evaluation of TCW and LSI models

The accuracy of the LSI model is heavily affected by value of rank, K. Since the results above indicates that the weight scheme tf-idf combined with cosine measure produced the highest EMR, they are used in both TCW and LSI systems. In order to explore the effects of parameter K, we applied various K values to construct the singular value decomposition matrices, $A_k = U_k \Sigma_k V_k^T$, and compared the performances of these SVD matrices with the TCW matrix. Theoretically, the range of K-value is between 1 to the number of columns of TCW matrix. However, our experiments shows that EMR degrades rapidly when K-value is larger than 40 in this application. Figure 6 showed that the CMR and EMR of LSI models with K values between 1 and 40, as well as the performances of the TCW classification system. It appears that the best performance has been achieved with K equal to 17. But the TCW outperformed the best LSI system by more than 11%.

C. Evaluation of SeaProSel

We tested the entire SeaProSel system on a set of 3273 query examples, none of which were included in the training data. The performances are analyzed as follows. 97% of the test queries were answered with unique and correct VDCs by the *VDC direct search using TCW Model* without going to the *Prompt & Select* process. The other 3% of the test queries were processed through subsequent Prompt & Select processes. At the end of the processes, correct VDCs were found for all test queries. Overall the prompt and select process was used at the rate of 0.065/query.

Figure 7 shows the processes of two test queries by the SeaProSel system. In Figure 7 (a), the test query was "Instrumentation warning lights and chimes". The *VDC direct search* component returned multiple mached VDCs. By finding the H node of these VDCs, the *Prompt & Select* component present to the user the descriptions of different problems at the component functionality level (see Figure 3) related to the input query. After the user selected "Text window and warming symbol", the SeaProSel went on to the questions at the "deviation" level. When the user selected "Red symbol and text message", a unique VDC code is found that matches the input query as well as the answers selected by the user during the *Prompt & Select* processes.

In the second example (see Figure 7 (b)), the test query is "Engine would not start". The *VDC direct search* component returned multiple VDCs, which is represented as VDC_List1. By finding the H node of these VDCs on the VDC_list1, the *Prompt & Select* component gave descriptions of different problems at level 2 function groups related to the VDC_List1. After the user selected "Engine with mountings and equipment", the SeaProSel went on to display the questions under the selected node at the "Component Functionality" level. When the user selected "Engine", the SeaProSel went on to display the questions under the selected node at the "Deviation" level. When the user selected "Engine turns", the SeaProSel went on to display the questions under the selected node at the "Condition" level. When the user selected "clicking sound at start attempt", a unique VDC, E2, is found that matches the input query as well as the answers selected by the user during the *Prompt & Select* processes.

5. Conclusion

We have presented an intelligent vehicle fault diagnostic system, SeaProSel. SeaProSel consists of two major components, *VDC Direct Search* using a VSM, and *Prompt & Select*. Two VSM technologies were developed, implemented and evaluated, a TCW model and a LSI model. Both models were developed based on machine learning and text mining techniques. The *Prompt & Select* component is a system that is built upon a vehicle fault diagnostic engineering structure with a progressive process of query, select, and search to achieve efficient and accurate classification of vehicle problem descriptions. We also presented algorithms for preprocessing text documents that contains spelling errors, typos and self-invented terms, choosing effective weight functions, and building an effective TCW matrix and LSI matrices from a given training data set. We have conducted extensive experiments to evaluate the algorithms and the entire SeaProSel system.

Based on our experimental results we conclude that, in the application domain of vehicle fault diagnostic text documents, the tf-idf weight function gives the best performance when it is used in either TCW or LSI models with the similarity function being either Cosine or Pearson. In terms of the optimal ranks in the LSI systems, our experiments show that the optimal K values are in the range of K=13 through K=19, with K=17 giving the best performance. When we compare the performances of the TCW model with the best LSI model, i.e. the LSI system used K=17, we notice that the TCW model outperforms the best LSI system by more than 11%.

The SeaProSel system is implemented based on a real-world vehicle diagnostic code system with 540 different code classes, and is evaluated on 3273 query documents, which are verbatim vehicle problem descriptions by customers. The SeaProSel system achieved 97% accuracy in finding the diagnostic codes directly based on the *VDC Direct Search using TCW*. Through the innovative processes of *Prompt and Select* procedure, the SeaProSel was able to find the correct diagnostic code 100% for all test queries.

Our major contributions are summarized as follows.

(1) Presented an innovative computational framework, SeaProSel, that combines automatic search with engineering structural search through a Prompt & Select strategy. Experimental results show that SeaProSel is effective in searching for diagnostic code accurately matching a given problem description.

(2) Presented new algorithms for learning automotive diagnostic code using TCW matrix and LSI model. Based on our experimental results, TCW is more effective in the application of casual text document categorization

(3) Presented new algorithms for preprocessing engineering diagnostic documents.

Although the application domain we presented is in the area of vehicle fault diagnostic documents, some techniques we presented are applicable to other applications that involve processing casual text documents such as automated question answering services, and classification of Tweets, instant messages, and e-mail messages.

References

[1] Fang, J., Guo, L., Wang, X. D., & Yang, N. 2007. Ontology-Based Automatic Classification and Ranking for Web Documents. *Fourth International Conference on Fuzzy Systems and Knowledge Discovery -FSKD* , 2007.

[2] Zhuang, F. Z.; Luo, P.; Shen, Z. Y.; He, Q.; Xiong, Y. H.; Shi, Z. Z. & Xiong, H. 2012. Mining Distinction and Commonality across Multiple Domains Using Generative Model for Text Classification. *IEEE Transactions on Knowledge and Data Engineering,* Volume: 24 , Issue: 11, Page(s): 2025 – 2039, 2012.

[3] Huang, Y.H., Seliya, N., Murphey, Y. L., & Friedenthal, R. B. 2010. Classifying Independent Medical Examination Reports using SOM networks. *Proceeding of the 6th International conference on Data Mining*, Las Vegas, Nevada, USA, 2010, p58-64.

[4] Mencıa, E. L., Park, S. H., & Fürnkranz, J. 2010. Efficient voting prediction for pairwise multilabel classification. *Neuro computing* 73 pp.1164–1176, 2010.

[5] Zeng, Q.; Zhang, X.; Zhang, W.; Li, Z. & Liu, L. 2010. Extracting Clinical Information from Free-text of Pathology and Operation Notes via Chinese Natural Language Processing. *2010 IEEE International Conference on Bioinformatics and Biomedicine Workshops*, pp 593-597, Hong Kong, 2010.

[6] Huang, Y. H., Murphey, Y. L., & Ge, Y. 2013. Automotive diagnosis typo correction using domain knowledge and machine learning. *IEEE Symposium Series on Computational Intelligence*, 2013.

[7] Creecy, R.M., Masand, B. M., Smith, S. J., and Waltz, D. L. 1992. Trading MIPS and memory for knowledge engineering: classifying census returns on the Connection Machine, *Communications of the ACM*, 35(8): p. 48—63, 1992.

[8] Sebastiani, F. 2002. Machine learning in automated text categorization. *ACM Computing Surveys*, 2002. 34(1): p. 1-47.

[9] Yang, Y. & Liu, X. 1999. A re-examination of text categorization methods. *Proc. 22th ACM Int. Conf. on Research and Development in Information Retrieval (SIGIR'99)*. 1999. Berkeley, CA.

[10] Masand, B., Linoff, G., & Waltz, D. 1992. Classifying news stories using memory based reasoning. *Development in Information Retrieval*, 1992: ACM Press, New York, US.

[11] Radovanović, M. & Ivanović, M. 2008. Text mining: approaches and applications, *Novi Sad J. Math.* Vol. 38, No. 3, 2008, 227-234

[12] Lu, F. & Bai, Q. Y. 2010. Refined weighted K-Nearest Neighbors algorithm for text categorization. *International Conference on Intelligent Systems and Knowledge Engineering (ISKE)*, 2010.

[13] Bijalwan. V., Kumar, V., Kumari, P., & Pascual, J. 2014. KNN based Machine Learning Approach for Text and Document Mining. *International Journal of Database Theory and Application*, Vol. 7, No. 1, 2014, pp. 61 – 70.

[14] Baeza-Yates, R., Ribeiro-Neto, B., *Modern Information Retrieval*, 1999: Addison Wesley.

[15] Syu, I., Lang, S.D. & Deo, N.; 1996. Incorporating latent semantic indexing into a neural network model for information retrieval. *Proceedings of the fifth international conference on Information and knowledge management*, 1996.

[16] Chen. Z.H., Ni, C. W. and Murphey, Y. L., 2006. Neural Network Approaches for Text Document Categorization. *IEEE International Joint Conference on Neural Networks,* July, 2006.

[17] Zhang, M.L. and Zhou, Z. H. 2006. Multilabel Neural Networks with Applications to Functional Genomics and Text Categorization. *IEEE Transaction in Knowledge and Data Engineering*, Vol. 18, Issue 10, Oct. 2006.

[18] Cho, S.B. and Lee, J. H., 2003. Learning Neural Network Ensemble for Practical Text Classification. *Lecture Notes in Computer Science*, Volume 2690, Pages 1032– 1036, 2003.

[19] Yu, B.; Xu, Z. B. & Li, C. H. 2008. Latent semantic analysis for text categorization using neural network. *Knowledge-Based Systems*, 21- pp. 900–904, 2008

[20] Thi, H. N. T.; Huu, O. N. & Ngoc, T. N. T.;2013. A supervised learning method combine with dimensionality reduction in Vietnamese text summarization. *IEEE Computing, Communications and IT Applications Conference (ComComAp)*, 2013.

[21] Vinodhini, G. & Chandrasekaran, R.M.; 2014. Sentiment classification using principal component analysis based neural network model. *2014 International Conference on Information Communication and Embedded Systems (ICICES)*, 2014

[22] Li, C. H. and Park, S. C., 2009. An efficient document classification model using an improved back propagation neural network and singular value decomposition. *Expert Systems with Applications,* 36, pp- 3208–3215, 2009.

[23] Kohonen, T. 1990. The self-organizing map. *Proc. of the IEEE*, 9, 1464-1479, 1990.

[24] Manomaisupat, P., and Abmad k. Feature Selection for text Categorization Using Self Orgnizing Map. *2nd International Conference on Neural Network and Brain, 2005*, IEEE press Vol 3, pp.1875-1880, 2005.

[25] Liu, Y.C.; Wang, X.L.; & Wu, C.; 2008. ConSOM: A conceptional self-organizing map model for text clustering. *Neurocomputing*, 71(4-6), 857-862, 2008.

[26] Liu, Y.C., Wu, C., & Liu, M. 2011. Research of fast SOM clustering for text information. *Expert Systems with Applications*, 38(8), 9325-9333, 2011.

[27] Lewis, D.D. 1998. Naive (Bayes) at forty:The independence assumption in information retrieval. *Proceedings of ECML-98.* Springer Verlag, Heidelberg, 1998.

[28] Friedman, N.; Geiger, D.; Goldszmidt. M.; 1997. Bayesian Network Classifiers. *Machine Learning*, November 1997, Volume 29, Issue 2-3, pp 131-163.

[29] Theodoridis, S.; 2015. Machine Learning: A Bayesian and Optimization Perspective. *Academic Press*, 2015.

[30] Vapnik, V.; 1995. The Nature of Statistical Learning Theory. *Springer Verlag, New York*, 1995.

[31] Mukkamala, S., Janoski, G., Sung, A H.. 2002. Intrusion Detection Using Neural Networks and Support Vector Machines. *Proceedings of IEEE International Joint Conference on Neural Networks*, IEEE Computer Society Press, pp.1702-1707.

[32] Murphey, Y.L.; Chen, Z.H.; Putrus, M. & Feldkamp, L.A. 2003. SVM learning from large training data set. *IEEE International Joint Conference on Neural Networks*, July, 2003.

[33] Hong, H.B.; Murphey, Y.L.; Gutchess, D. & Chang, T.S. 2005. Identifying knowledge domain and incremental new class learning in SVM. *IEEE International Joint Conference on Neural Networks*, July, 2005.

[34] Chapelle, O. & Vapnik, V. 2000. Model selection for support vector machines. In S.A. Solla, T.K. Leen, and K.R. Muller, editors, *Advances in Neural Information Processing Systems*, volume 12. MIT Press, Cambridge, MA, 2000.

[35] Zhang, W.; Yoshida, T.; & Tang, X. 2008. Text Classification based on Multi-word with Support Vector Machine. *Knowledge-Based Systems*, vol. 12, 2008.

[36] Feinerer, I. & Karatzoglou, A., 2010. Support Vector Machines for Large Scale Text Mining in R. *19th International Conference on Computational Statistics*, 2010.

[37] Hsu, Chih-Wei and Lin, Chih-Jen, 2002. A Comparison of Methods for Multiclass Support Vector Machines. *IEEE Transactions On Neural Networks*, VOL. 13, NO. 2, MARCH 2002.

[38] Platt, J. C., Cristianini, N., and Shawe-Taylor, J., 2000. Large margin DAG's for multiclass classification. *Advances in Neural Information Processing Systems*. Cambridge, MA: MIT Press, vol. 12, pp. 547–553, 2000.

[39] Huang, L.P. 2006. Intelligent Systems for text categorization and retrieval. *M.S. Thesis, Department of Electrical and Computer Engineering*, University of Michigan-Dearborn, 2006.

[40] Raghavan, V.V., & Wong, S.K.M. 1986. A Critical Analysis of Vector Space Model for Information Retrieval. *Journal of the America Society for Information Science*, 1986. 37(5): 279-287.

[41] Porter, M.F. 1997. An algorithm for suffix stripping. *Readings in Information Retrieval*, 1997. Morgan Kaufmann Publishers Inc. San Francisco, CA, USA.

[42] Dumais, S.T., 1991. Improving the retrieval of information from external sources. *Behavior Research Methods, Instruments and Computers*, 1991. 23(2): p. 229-236.

[43] Dumais, S.T., 1990. *Enhancing performance in latent semantic indexing (LSI) retrieval. Technical Report Technical Memorandum*, Bellcore, 1990.

[44] Dumais, S.T., Furnas, G. W., Landauer, T. K. and Deerwester, S. 1988. Using latent semantic analysis to improve information retrieval,. *In Proceedings of CHI'88: Conference on Human Factors in Computing*. 1988. New York: ACM.

[45] Jessup, E. R., & Martin, J.H., 2001. Taking a new look at the latent semantic analysis approach to information retrieval. *Computational information retrieval*, 2001: p. 121-144.

[46] Sebastiani, F. & Ricerche, C. N., 2002. Machine learning in automated text categorization. Journal of ACM Computing Surveys, Volume 34, Issue 1, March 2002.

24

Organization of Multi-Agent Systems

Hosny Ahmed Abbas[1, *], Samir Ibrahim Shaheen[2], Mohammed Hussein Amin[1]

[1]Department of Electrical Engineering, Assiut University, Assiut, Egypt
[2]Department of Computer Engineering, Cairo University, Giza, Egypt

Email Address:
hosnyabbas@aun.edu.eg (H. A. Abbas), sshaheen@eng.cu.edu.eg (S. I. Shaheen), mhamin@aun.edu.eg (M. H. Amin)

Abstract: In complex, open, and heterogeneous environments, agents must be able to reorganize towards the most appropriate organizations to adapt unpredictable environment changes within Multi-Agent Systems (MAS). Types of reorganization can be seen from two different levels. The individual agents level (micro-level) in which an agent changes its behaviors and interactions with other agents to adapt its local environment. And the organizational level (macro-level) in which the whole system changes it structure by adding or removing agents. This chapter is dedicated to overview different aspects of what is called MAS Organization including its motivations, paradigms, models, and techniques adopted for statically or dynamically organizing agents in MAS.

Keywords: Multi-Agent Systems, Organization, Organizational Models, Dynamic Reorganization, Self-Organization

1. Introduction

Complexity and highly distribution are the key characteristics of modern real world systems. The complexity of the near future and even present applications can be characterized as a combination of aspects such as great number of components taking part in the applications, knowledge and control have to be distributed, the presence of non-linear processes in the system, the fact that the system is more and more often open, its environment dynamic and the interactions unpredictable [3]. Further, the increasing complexity, heterogeneity, and openness of modern software systems have reached a point that imposes new demands on their engineering technologies. It is expected that conventional engineering approaches will stand powerless in front of future systems increase in scale and complexity either vertically (control and information layers) or horizontally (physical distribution). It doesn't mean that conventional engineering techniques will become obsolete and have to be thrown away. Absolutely, they only need to be integrated with new engineering styles where concepts such as, decomposition, autonomy, modularity, and adaptivity can be collectively combined in one system. MAS are considered as a promising engineering (i.e., architectural) style for developing adaptive software systems able to handle the continuous increase in their complexity as a result of their open, heterogeneous, and continuous evolution nature. They model the system as distributed autonomous agents cooperate together to achieve system goals. The ability of agents to dynamically reorganize to adapt working environment dynamic changes is a key feature provided by MAS. It is obvious that the natural way to model a complex system is in terms of multiple autonomous components that can act and interact in flexible ways in order to achieve their objectives, and also that agents provide a suitable abstraction for modeling systems consisting of many subsystems, components and their relationships [22]. Ferber [23] described how agents, as a form of distributed artificial intelligence, are suitable for use in application domains which are widely distributed. MAS are currently considered as the most representatives among artificial systems dealing with complexity and highly distribution [24]. MAS allow the design and implementation of software systems using the same ideas and concepts that are the very founding of human societies and habits. These systems often rely on the delegation of goals and tasks among autonomous software agents, which can interact and collaborate with others to achieve common goals [34]. In other words, an agent falls somewhere between a simple event-triggered program and one with human collaborative abilities [36].

In contrast to initial MAS research, which concerned individual agents' aspects such as agents' architectures, agents' mental capabilities, behaviors, etc, the current research trend of MAS is actively interested in the adaptivity, environment, openness and the dynamics of these systems. Also, there is a great attention towards the MAS technique as a way to design self-organized systems. In open environments, agents must be able to adapt towards the most appropriate organizations according to the environment conditions and their unpredictable changes. Agent organizations are considered as an emergent area of MAS research that relies on the notion of openness and heterogeneity of MAS and imposes new demands on traditional MAS models [44]. MAS that have the ability to dynamically reorganize (regardless of the type of reorganization, self or enforced) will be adaptive enough to survive against their dynamic and continuously changing working environments. Dynamic reorganization can take many forms, for instance, agents can dynamically change their roles, behaviors, locations, acquaintances, or the whole system organization structure can be dynamically changed.

An agent organization can also be defined as a social entity composed of a specific number of members (agents) that accomplish several distinct tasks or functions and that are structured following some specific topology and communication interrelationships in order to achieve the main aim of the organization. Thus, agent organizations assume the existence of global common goals, outside the objectives of any individual agent, and they exist independently of agents [64][65].

This chapter is dedicated to provide a comprehensive overview of MAS organization including its motivations, paradigms, and familiar organizational models. The remaining of this chapter is organized as follows: Section 2 explores MAS literature to identify the motivations towards agent organizations. Section 3 presents different approaches and paradigms used to organize agents within multi-agent systems. Section 4 introduces what is called organizational models, which concern the abstractions, languages, approaches and techniques for modeling dynamically reorganized MAS. And Section 5 concludes the article and highlights future work.

2. Motivations to MAS Organization

This section is dedicated to identify from MAS literature the suggested motivations to give increasing attention to MAS organization. Basically, a MAS is formed by the collection of autonomous agents situated in a certain environment, respond to their environment dynamic changes, interact with other agents, and persist to achieve their own goals or the global system goals. There are two viewpoints of MAS engineering, the first one is the agent-centered MAS (ACMAS) in which the focus is given to individual agents. With this viewpoint, the designer concerns the local behaviors of agents and also their interactions without concerning the global structure of the system. The global required function of the system is supposed to emerge as a result of the lower level individual agents interactions in a bottom-up way.

Picard et al. [13] stated that the agent-centered approach takes the agents as the "engine" for the system organization, and agent organizations implicitly exist as observable emergent phenomena, which states a unified bottom-up and objective global view of the pattern of cooperation between agents. Further, Picard gives the ant colony [15] as an example, where there is no organizational behavior and constraints are explicitly and directly defined inside the ants. The main idea is that the organization is the result of the collective emergent behavior due to how agents act their individual behaviors and interact in a common shared and dynamic environment.

The key problems of the ACMAS viewpoint are unpredictability and uncertainty. Because the whole is more than the sum of its parts [14], this approach can lead to undesirable emergent behaviors that may impact system performance, as a result, this approach might be not suitable to design and engineer complex multi-agent systems. The MAS applications engineered by the ACMAS approach are closed for agents that are not able to use the same type of coordination and behavior, and that all global characteristics and requirements are implemented in the individual agents and not outside them [10].

Weyns [11] stated that giving the responsibility of system organization implicitly to individual agents, as in the ACMAS approach, in addition to their functional responsibilities is not adequate because it is a type of dual responsibility, which is very complex to engineer and not suitable for handling real world complexity and other emerged characteristics such as highly distribution, unpredictability, uncertainty, and continuous evolution.

The second viewpoint of MAS engineering is what is called organization-centered MAS (OCMAS) in which the structure of the system is given a bigger attention through the explicit abstraction of agent organization. With that approach, the designer designs the entire organization and coordination patterns on the one hand, and the agents' local behaviors on the other hand. It is considered as a top-down approach because the organization abstraction imposes some rules or norms used by agents to coordinate their local behaviors and interactions with other agents.

The OCMAS viewpoint has been promoted by many pioneers in MAS research. For instance, Jennings and Wooldridge [2] stated that MAS contribute to the software engineering (SE) discipline as a way to simplify the design of complex software systems but considering MAS with no real structure isn't suitable for handling current software systems complexity, and higher order abstractions should be used and some way of structuring the society is typically needed to reduce system complexity, to increase system efficiency, and to more accurately model the problem being tackled. Odell et al. [4] stated that the current practice of MAS design tends to be limited to individual agents and small face-to-face groups of agents that operate as closed systems which is not adequate to model and design of complex adaptive systems. Also Gutknecht and Ferber [66] argued that taking organizational concepts, such as groups, roles, structures, dependencies, etc, as first class citizens, and relating them to the behavior of agents is a key issue for building large scale and complex systems. In another article, Ferber [6] also stated that representing a MAS as an organization consists of roles enacted by agents arranged (statically or dynamically) to form groups of agents, can handle many drawbacks such as system complexity, uncertainty, and system dynamism.

Gasser [3] stated that we simply have hardly any real experience building truly heterogeneous realistically coordinated multi-agent systems that work together and almost no basis for systematic reflection and analysis of that experience. Further, Horling et al. [5] stated that our real world getting more complex and highly distributed and that should be reflected in new software engineering paradigms such as MAS. Therefore, the adoption of higher order abstract concepts like organizations, societies, communities, and groups of agents can reduce systems complexity, increase its efficiency, and improve system scalability.

Establishing an organizational structure that specifies how agents in a system should work together helps the achievement of effective coordination in MAS [39]. Broek [7] stated that complexity of real world applications needs to be tackled from higher abstraction order such as organizations which can be used to limit the scope of interactions, provide strength in numbers, reduce or manage uncertainty, and formalize high-level goals which no single agent may be aware of. Further, Hübner [8] confirmed that organizations provide a framework for structuring and managing agents' interactions and serve as a kind of tuning of the agents autonomy level. Furthermore, Burns et al. [12] stated that in organization theory [25][26], it is commonly accepted that different types of organizational structure are suitable for particular environmental conditions and one of the main reasons for creating organizations is to provide stable means for coordination that enable the achievement of global goals.

Moreover, Corkill et al. [36] stated that as agent-based systems become more widespread and complex, designed organization will become an important aspect of effective system performance, and they suggested the possible situations where organization design will be very important such as, large number of agents, long duration of agent activities, more repetitive activities, more activities require shared resources, more collaborative the activities, more specialized agents, less capable agents, and less slack resources are available. Also, they emphasized that no one organization is right for every situation.

In nutshell, proposing a way for statically or dynamically organizing MAS, has been given great attention by MAS researchers, as a promising approach for handling the challenging issue of engineering complex and large-scale software systems. The adoption of the ACMAS or OCMAS viewpoints mainly depends on the nature of application domain and the degree of system complexity. The developers interested in bottom-up self-organized systems will prefer the ACMAS approach and the developers interested in top-down system reconfiguration will prefer the OCMAS approach. In the MAS literature there are two communities each adopts and concerns one of the two engineering approaches. The first one is SASO (Self-Adaptive and Self-Organizing systems) which concerns the ACMAS viewpoint. And the second one is COIN (Coordination, Organization, Institutions and Norms in agent systems) which concerns the OCMAS viewpoint.

The OCMAS viewpoint is more adequate for engineering complex adaptive multi-agent systems, which are expected to be, in the near future, the mainstream approach for engineering large-scale and even ultra-large scale application domains especially with the evolving topic of the Internet of Things (IoT) [17], which concerns devices capable to communicate via the Internet and manipulate an enormous amount of data. Examples of such application domains are CPS (Cyber-Physical Systems) [16], Smart Grids [18], global SCADA (Supervisor Control and Data Acquisition) [19], Pervasive Computing [20], Ubiquitous Computing [21], etc. The next section explores the familiar paradigms of MAS organization.

3. Paradigms of MAS Organization

Originally, the organization abstract is inspired from business human organizations, which are constituted of a number of roles, so a key concept in the design of OCMAS is that of roles, which define normative behavioral repertoires for agents [4]. A role is defined as an abstract description of some activity or functionality, for instance in a business human organization we may see a role like Manager who is responsible of the organization management and the coordination between other organization members (roles). In MAS, agents are supposed to enact roles according to the capabilities of each agent. It is also possible that one agent can enact many roles in the same time. The role enacted by an agent has a direct effect on the agent behavior and interaction with other roles (agents). Odell et al. [27] described two familiar ways for assigning roles to agents, endogenously by emergent self-organization as the system runs, or exogenously by the system designer when the system is constructed or modified. The adoption of human organization theory was the focus of distributed systems in general before multi-agent systems, which are themselves distributed systems [30][31][32][33].

Modern organizations (real or virtual) are characterized by their complex structure, dense information flows, and incorporation of information technology, they also characterized by highly dynamic, constantly changing, organic structure and show hardly identified, not formalized, non-linear behavior [28][29]. These challenges enforce the urgent need to a new way of engineering multi-agent systems.

Inspired from human organizations, Galbraith [37] described an agent organization as an entity that is composed of a set of agents, working together to achieve a shared purpose through a division of labor, integrated by decision processes continuously through time. Further, Galbraith pointed out that an organization consists of patterns of behavior and interaction that are relatively stable and change slowly over time.

Shehory [1] defined MAS organization as the way in which multiple agents are organized to form a multi-agent system. The relationships and interactions among the agents and specific roles of agents within the organization are the focus of multi-agent organization. The use of organizations provides a new way for describing the structures and the interactions that take place in MAS. Dignum [10] stated that agent organization can be understood from two perspectives: organization as a process and organization as an entity. In other words, organizations can be considered as the process of organizing a set of individual agents, thus in this sense it is used to refer to constraints (structures, norms and patterns) found in a social context that shape the actions and interactions of agents [53]. In other situations, it can be considered as an entity in itself, with its own requirements and objectives and is represented by (but not identical to) a group of agents. In fact, agent organizations demand the integration of both perspectives and rely for a great extent on the notion of openness and heterogeneity of MAS.

Figure 1 illustrates how a MAS can be seen from two levels, the individual agents' level and the organizational level. The organizational level presents a higher order abstraction of the lower agents' level.

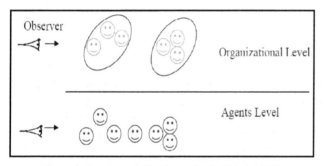

Figure 1. Organizational level vs. individual level in MAS.

Ferber et al. [6] proposed a set of general principles that should be taken into account when designing MAS with organizational dimension:

1. The organizational level describes the "what" and not the "how". In other words, the organizational level imposes a structure into the pattern of agents' activities, but does not describe how agents behave.
2. No agent description and therefore no mental issues at the organizational level. The organizational level should not say anything about the way agents would interpret this level.
3. An organization provides a way for partitioning a system, each partition (or agent group) constitutes a context of interaction for agents. Thus, a group is an organizational unit in which all members are able to interact freely.

Ferber principles provide important general guidelines for OCMAS research. They identify precisely the logical relation between agents and their organization regardless of the nature of organization (i.e. a process or an entity). The first principle concerns the autonomy of agents. Agents should be autonomous but they may be guided by some general organizational norms or constraints. Full autonomy is not a preferred agent characteristic in MAS research, we can only find a type of full autonomy with humans because they have perfect rational minds, but agents (software or hardware)

designed for specific missions in certain application domains and the concept of safety imposes some constraints on agents' autonomy, in these situations, a designed organization, where agents give up some degree of self-motivation and autonomy can be an appropriate choice [36].

The second principle concerns the unawareness of agents about the existence of the organizational level, which according to Ferber should be transparent from agents. In other words, agents should be affected indirectly by the change of system organization (i.e., through environment). The third principle concerns system modularity. Organizations provide a way for, statically or dynamically, decomposing the system. Modularity and flexibility of system decomposition enhance system maintainability.

Horling and Lesser [5] also stated that organizational design employed by an agent system can have a significant, quantitative effect on its performance characteristics, and they surveyed the major organizational paradigms used in multi-agent systems. These include hierarchies, holarchies, coalitions, teams, congregations, societies, federations, markets, and matrix organizations. Also, they provided a description of each paradigm, and discuss its advantages and disadvantages, further, they provided examples of how each organization paradigm may be instantiated and maintained. Table 1 provides a summary of Horling and Lesser [5] work. The Table contains a number of methods by which MAS could be organized and highlights the key characteristics, benefits, and drawbacks of each organization paradigm. Similar work was provided by Carley and Gasser [35]. The main conclusion of these surveys is that no single organization paradigm is necessarily better than all others in all situations. The selection made by a designer should be dictated by the needs imposed by the system's goals, the resources at hand, and the environment in which the participants will exist. In other words, an organization paradigm that can be described as a fit-to-all paradigm does not exist (at least till now!). A MAS can be statically (in design time) organized using any of the organization paradigms presented in Table 1, not only this but also hybrids of these and others in addition to dynamic changes from one organization style to another are also possible [1] with the price of implementation complexity. The later case is called dynamic reorganization which is currently a very active research area within MAS discipline. The next subsections present in more details the concept of dynamic reorganization and its captivating relevant concepts, self-organization and emergence.

3.1. Dynamic Reorganization

Earlier proposed MAS organization mechanisms tackled with organizational aspects at design time, that approach requires some important initial knowledge about the exact purposes and objectives of the system-to-be and every interaction to which it may be confronted in the future have to be known in design time [41]. However, the openness, complexity, and heterogeneity of modern software systems impose new demands and requirements on agent-oriented software engineering (AOSE) [71], which is concerned with the development of feasible, effective, and adaptive MAS. Building adaptive MAS (AMAS) able to handle openness, complexity, and highly distribution of modern real world applications has recently attracted great attention.

Table 1. Analysis of Some of Possible MAS Organization Paradigms (adopted from [5]).

Paradigm	Key Characteristic	Benefits	Drawbacks
	Decomposition	Maps to many common domains; handles scale well	Potentially brittle, can lead to bottlenecks or delays
Holarchy	Decomposition with autonomy	Exploit autonomy of functional units	Must organize holons, lake of predicable performance
Coalition	Dynamic, goal-directed	Exploit strength in number	Short-term benefits may not outweigh organization construction costs
Team	Group level cohesion	Address larger grained problems; task-centric	Increased communication
Congregation	Long-lived, utility-directed	Facilitates agent discovery	Sets may be overly restrictive
Society	Open system	Public services; well defined conventions	Potentially complex, agents may require additional society-related capabilities
Federation	Middle-agents	Matchmaking, brokering, translation services, facilitates dynamic agent pool	Intermediaries become bottlenecks
Market	Competition through pricing	Good at allocation, increased utility through centralization, increased fairness through bidding	Potential for collusion, malicious behaviour, allocation decision complexity can be high
Matrix	Multiple managers	Resource sharing, multiple influenced agents	Potential of conflicts, need for increased agent sophistication
Compound	Concurrent organizations	Exploit benefits of several organizational styles	Increased sophistication, drawbacks of several organizational styles

AMAS designed to be capable to adapt themselves to unforeseen situations in an autonomous manner. They can be realized by enabling the system to dynamically reorganize to adapt its environment changes [42]. Dynamic reorganization is a way to design and develop AMAS. It can be described as the change of MAS structure and behavior as a result of internal (local) or external (supervisory) demand. The external demand can be for example human intervention. The internal demand emerges from the system itself as an autonomous system to adapt environments changes. Generally, dynamic reorganization in MAS takes place as a result of individual agents' interactions. However, in many application domains the environment can stimulate MAS reorganization (e.g., when removing or adding environment resources), the system may reorganize to adapt the change of environment. In other words, reorganization is the answer to change in the environment.

Dignum et al. [40] identified two types of MAS dynamic reorganization, emergent Organization in which global behavior cannot be specified in advance, but emerges from the interaction of local behaviors. In other words, agents' interactions may eventually create dynamic organizations [44]. Thus, emergent organizational behavior is primarily a bottom-up process in which agents look for interaction and local control decisions that have been effective in the past and give similar decisions preference in the future. The ACMAS viewpoint concerns this type of reorganization. The other type of reorganization is called designed organization, which has an explicit interaction structure that determines the coordination of the agents participating. Designed systems are created using organization design knowledge and task-environment information to develop an explicit organizational structure, that is then elaborated by the individual agents into appropriate behaviors. Designed organization exhibits predicable and controllable behavior, dynamic change implies the need for highly intelligent and communicative agents (at least some of them) that can reason about and negotiate change. Designed organization is the main concern of the OCMAS approach. In human organizations, it has been proven that designed organizations perform better than those that emerge naturally. This viewpoint holds for agent organizations as well, that is because the global behavior of emergent organizations cannot be predicted and changes cannot be guided, which makes this type less suitable for situations where coordinated and goal-directed global action is required.

Picard et al. [13] added the agents' awareness /unawareness of the existence of the organization structure as a dimension of the organization modification process and he identified four cases:

1. The agents don't represent the organization, although the observer can see an emergent organization. In some sense, they are unaware that they are part of an organization.

2. Each agent has an internal and local representation of cooperation patterns which it follows when deciding what to do. This local representation is obtained either by perception, communication or explicit reasoning.

3. The organization exists as a specified and formalized schema, made by a designer but agents don't know anything about it and even do not reason about it. They simply comply with it as if the organizational constraints were hard-coded inside them.

4. Agents have an explicit representation of the organization which has been defined. The agents are able to reason about it and to use it in order to initiate cooperation with other agents in the system. The agents are able to reason about it and to use it in order to initiate cooperation with other agents in the system.

Case 1 and 2 considered as ACMAS and case 3 and 4 considered as OCMAS. The importance of Picard classification of MAS dynamic reorganization is that nearly most of known reorganization methods fit to a specific case or multiple cases. Similar classification proposed by Sichman et al. [44], but he used the concept of observer in the same position as the agent awareness of the organization. Table 2 provides the global picture of possible types of MAS

organization with examples. As shown in the table MAS organization is classified according to the awareness/unawareness of individual agents about the presence of the organizational level.

Table 2. *The global picture of MAS organization.*

	Agents unaware	Agents aware
ACMAS=Emergent organization	Organization is observed. It is implicitly programmed in agents, interactions, and environment.	Organization is observed. Coalition mechanisms programmed in the agents.
Concerned Community	SASO	COIN
Examples	Swarm-based systems [72]	Contract-Net Interaction Protocol [73]
OCMAS = Designed organization	Organization is a design model. It may be hard coded in the agents.	Organization is programmed in the agents and/or in specialized middleware services.
Concerned Community	COIN	COIN
Examples	AOSE methodologies such as: MASE [74], INGENIAS [75].	Organizational models such as: AGR [58] MOISE+ [67]

Picard also, after finishing his valuable study proposed a comprehensive definition of dynamic reorganization as follows:

"Reorganization is a process, endogenous or exogenous, concerning systems in which organization is explicitly manipulated through specifications, constraints or other means, in order to ensure an adequate global behavior, when the organization is not adapted. Agents being aware of the organization state and structure, they are capable of manipulating primitives to modify their social environment. This process can be both initiated by an external entity or by agents themselves, by reasoning directly on the organization (roles, organizational specification) and the cooperation patterns (dependencies, commitments, powers)."

This definition assumes that the agents are aware of the existence of the organizational level, thus it concerns the OCMAS viewpoint. But, what if agents are unaware of the organization level? According to Picard, in this case the dynamic reorganization process is called self-organization which defined by Picard as follows:

"Self-organization is an endogenous and bottom-up process concerning systems in which only local information and representations are manipulated by agents unaware of the organization as a whole, in order to adapt the system to the environmental pressure by modifying indirectly the organization, therefore by changing directly the system configuration (topology, neighborhoods, influences, differentiation), or the environment of the system, by local interactions and propagation, by avoiding predefined model biases."

This definition states that self-organization represents the ACMAS viewpoint. In a self-organized system, agents are unaware of the organization level, the reorganization process is decentralized, implicit, endogenous, and agents are responsible of the system dynamic reorganization, which is often initiated by an environmental change. In a dynamically reorganizing system where agents are aware of the organization level, this process can be decentralized or not, but always explicit and directly performed by entities (designer or

agents) manipulating organizational primitives. Therefore, the awareness is a key dimension added by Picard to identify self-organized MAS. The next section provides detailed review of the self-organization concept in MAS.

3.2. Self-Organization

Self-* properties [43] (i.e., self-organization, self-healing, self-adaptation, self-configuration, etc) are the most captivating concepts recently appeared in software engineering. They remind us of Einstein ideas about Time Machine, which was and still a far dream of human to travel through time. Human also dreams to design a system, regardless of its nature (software or hardware), able to do all things by itself. A system has all known self-* properties will be amazing. Actually, this type of systems is imaginary (at least till now!); we can only see this system in science fiction movies. However, it is possible to design systems with one or more of self-* properties for predefined purposes and under certain circumstances.

The first use of the term self-organization returns to Ashby [56], in 1947, he stated that a system is said to be self-organized if it changed its own organization rather than being changed by an external entity. Self-organization in software systems received great attention since the last few years. It is an attractive way to handle the dynamic requirements in software in general and MAS in specific. It refers to a process where a system changes its internal organization to adapt to changes in its goals and its working environment without explicit external control. Understanding the mechanisms that can be used to model, assess and engineer self-organizing behavior in MAS is currently an issue of major interest [38].

Picard's definition of self-organization (see previous section) can be rephrased as follows: Self-organization is a process where some form of overall order or coordination arises out of the local interactions between the components of an initially disordered system. This process is spontaneous: it is not necessarily directed or controlled by any agent or subsystem inside or outside of the system. It is often triggered by random fluctuations, which are triggered and amplified by positive feedback. The resulting organization is wholly decentralized or distributed over all the components of the system, it is typically very robust and able to survive and self-repair substantial damage or perturbations.

The roots of the term self-organization return to the work of Glansdorff and Prigogine [46] through thermodynamics studies. They discovered that open systems decrease their entropy (order comes out of disorder) when an external energy is applied on the system. Matter organizes itself under this external pressure to reach a new state where entropy has decreased.

Nature is full of self-organization forms and patterns, for instance social behavior of insects like ants or termites, which formed as a result of indirect communication through environment without the need for any type of direct interaction, this type of interaction is called Stigmergy. Social behavior of humans is also self-organized and gives rise to emergent complex global behaviors. Human beings typically work with local information and through local direct or indirect interactions producing complex societies [45].

Researchers from variety of disciplines who were interested in self-organization in nature found MAS as the adequate engineering style for modeling and simulation of the self-organization phenomena and after a period of time the situation reversed as the MAS researchers, who are concerned with AOSE gave a greet attention to bio-inspired models for developing complex, open, and heterogeneous MAS-based applications. Self-organization and emergence are currently the main focus of AOSE researchers. The adoption of naturally inspired methods and approaches for engineering self-organized MAS is currently a very active research area [47][48]. Mechanisms such as direct interactions [49], Stigmergy [50], reinforcement [51], and agents' cooperation [52] are widely used to design MAS with self-organization behavior.

Another relevant and interesting concept is that of emergence, which can be considered as a process takes place in complex systems (which may or may not be self-organized). Self-organization results from emergence, but there is no guarantee that a self-organized system will always generate emergent phenomena. Understanding how to engineer systems that are capable of presenting self-organized behavior and desirable emergence is currently a very active research area too. The next section introduces briefly the concept of emergence.

3.3. Emergence

A lot of confusion exists about the meaning of the two relevant terms emergence and self-organization. One of the sources of the confusion comes from the fact that a combination of both phenomena often occurs in dynamical systems [53]. In MAS domain, self-organization and emergence concepts are recently getting great focus as a way to engineer open, heterogeneous, and complex MAS-based applications such as complex adaptive systems (CAS) [54], which are fluidly changing collections of distributed interacting components that react to both their environments and to one another. The familiar definition of emergence is as a phenomenon where global behavior arises from the interactions between the local parts of the system. This general and vague definition indicates that still there is no consensus of a clear definition for emergence. Also, it indicates the absence of clear understating of its nature. In contrast to the reductionism theory [55], which allows a system to be reduced to the sum of its parts, the emergent global behavior cannot be predicted by observing its parts local behaviors. An accepted operational definition of emergence was proposed by De Wolf and Holvoet [53] as follows:

"A system exhibits emergence when there are coherent emergents at the macro-level that dynamically arise from the interactions between the parts at the micro-level. Such emergents are novel with respect to the individual parts of the system."

This definition uses the concept of an 'emergent' as a general term to denote the result of the process of emergence, i.e., properties, behavior, structure, patterns, etc. The 'level' mentioned refers to certain points of view. The macro-level considers the system as a whole and the micro-level considers the system from the viewpoint of the individual entities that make up the system. The concept of emergence is very complex and it is not fall in the scope of this article, interested readers are invited to explore the emergence relevant references.

3.4. Discussion

Static design of MAS is not adequate for modern real world applications, which characterized by their increasing complexity heterogeneity, and openness. Even closed systems in which the number of agents is constant with time should have a type of adaptive dynamic behaviors. All possible behaviors of modern systems cannot be captured at design time and that requires these systems to be adaptive able to adapt changes in their working environments. Dynamic reorganization is currently a familiar way for developing adaptive MAS. As shown in Section 2, the adoption of organizational aspects within MAS is promoted and recommended by pioneers of MAS research. Dynamic reorganization can be described as the change of MAS structure and behavior as a result of internal or external demand. The external demand can be for example human intervention. The internal demand emerges from the system itself as an autonomous system to adapt environments changes. Self-organization is a dynamical and adaptive process where systems acquire and maintain structure themselves, without external control. In self-organizing systems, robustness is used in terms of adaptivity in the presence of perturbations and change. A self-organizing system is expected to cope with that change and to maintain its organization autonomously.

Emergence emphasizes the presence of a novel coherent macro-level emergent (property, behavior, structure, etc) as a result of the interactions between micro-level parts. A combination of emergence and self-organization is a promising approach to engineer large-scale multi-agent systems. In most systems that are considered in MAS literature, emergence and self-organization occur together. Research in MAS and CPS communities focuses on such systems. In very complex (multi-agent) systems, i.e. distributed, open, large, situated in a dynamic context, etc., the combination of emergence and self-organization is recommended.

When a researcher proposes an approach to dynamically reorganize a multi-agent system to adapt environments' changes, he actually proposes what the MAS domain consensus agreed to call as an Organizational (or organization) Model. MAS organizational models will play a critical role in the development of future larger and more complex MAS. The main concern of organizational models is to describe the structural and dynamical aspects of organizations [9]. They have proven to be a useful tool for the analysis and design of multi-agent systems. Furthermore, they provide a framework to manage and engineer agent organizations, dynamic reorganization, self-organization, emergence, and autonomy within multi-agent systems. The next section introduces organizational models in some details.

4. Organizational Models

Organizational models have been recently used in agent theory for modeling coordination in open systems and to ensure social order in MAS applications [64]. The adoption of organizational models is currently given great importance within most agent-oriented software engineering methodologies. The motivation to this direction is that in open environments, agents must be able to adapt towards the most appropriate organizations according to the environment conditions and their unpredictable changes. As a result, organizational models should guarantee the ability of organizations to dynamically reorganize as a response to dynamic environment changes. Organizational models are responsible of how efficiently and effectively organizations carry out their tasks, they have been recently used in agent theory for modeling coordination in open systems and to ensure social order in multi-agent system applications [7].

From the business management discipline an organizational model, also called as organizational structure, defines an organization through its framework, including lines of authority, communications, duties and resource allocations. A model is driven by the organization's goals and serves as the context in which processes operate and business is done. The ideal model depends on the nature of the business and the challenges it faces. In turn, the model determines the number of roles needed and their required skill sets. In MAS, the purpose of an organizational model is to enhance the analysis and design of OCMAS, so it's usually integrated with a particular agent-based software engineering methodology.

Before exploring some of the familiar organizational models proposed for modeling complex MAS, it is a suitable time to show the difference between them and MAS development methodologies. In general, a methodology is a body of methods employed by a discipline. A method is a procedure for attaining something. A methodology aims to prescribe all the elements necessary for the development of a software system [57]. AOSE community concerns creating development methodologies suitable for the development of agent-oriented or agent-based software. Typically, a development methodology (agent-oriented or not) comprises an ordered set of phases such planning, analysis, design, implementation, validation, and deployment. An organizational model is a tool adopted within a development methodology for modeling the system-to-be. Typically, it starts in the analysis phase but can expand through design and implementation phases, or in other cases it can expanded through the whole development life cycle.

The next section explores some of familiar proposed MAS organizational models focusing in their tackled organizational aspects, their advantages, and their disadvantages.

4.1. Familiar Organizational Models

There is a lot of MAS organizational models proposed in the literature; each of them tackles MAS organization from a different viewpoint. Some of them adopt the ACMAS viewpoint, others adopt the OCMAS viewpoint, and some adopt a hybrid approach concerns both ACMAS and OCMAS viewpoints. In what follows, three of familiar organizational models are introduced.

4.1.1. AGR and AGRE

Ferber et al. [6] proposed a very concise and minimal OCMAS model called AGR, for Agent/Group/Role, also known as the AALAADIN model [58]. The authors of AGR model proposed a set of notations and a methodological framework to help the designer to build MAS using AGR. Further, they presented a set of diagrams (organizational structure, cheeseboard diagram, and organizational sequence diagrams), which may represent the different aspects (static and dynamic) of OCMAS. Their model is based on the dynamic creation of agents groups (agents partitioning) and dynamic forming of hierarchies of groups (Holarchies). They pointed out that their AGR-based model can be integrated with Gaia [59] MAS development methodology to complete the analysis and design phases of MAS development. Figure 2 presents the AGR meta-model.

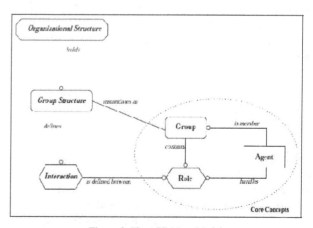

Figure 2. The AGR Meta-Model.

The core concepts on which the AGR model is based are agent, group and role. The agent in AGR is assumed to be an active, communicating entity which plays roles within groups, with no restrictions on its internal architecture. The group is defined as the basic unit of agent aggregation. Each agent is part of one or more of these groups. The role is an abstract representation of an agent function, service or identification within a group. Each agent can handle several roles, and each role handled by an agent remains local to a group. Other important abstract concepts are also shown the AGR meta-model shown in Figure 9.1, they are Group Structure and Organizational Structure. The group structure is an abstract representation of the roles required in this group and their interaction relationships and protocols. The organization structure is the set of group structures expressing the design of a multi-agent organizational scheme.

In other paper, Ferber et al. [60] presented an extension of the AGR organizational model, called AGRE (AGR + Environment), which includes physical (or simply geometrical) environments. This extension is based on the concept of a space which can be seen either as a physical area or as a social group.

The main advantages of the AGR/AGRE models are: supporting of heterogeneous agents architectures, heterogeneous communication languages, and dynamic role-group relationships. On the other hand, the disadvantages are multi-role agents which make agents internally complex; roles sharing between Groups can cause overloaded agents, agents ask to join groups which require highly knowledgeable agents, use of mediator agents (brokers) which can be a source of bottlenecks, and very few known real applications.

4.1.2. MOISE

Hannoun et al. [67] proposed MOISE (Model of Organisation for multI-agent SystEms); for modeling organizational aspects of MAS. Similar to the AGR model, their model is based on three major concepts: roles, organizational links (roles relations), and groups. What distinguishes the MOISE model is that it tries to integrate both viewpoints, ACMAS and OCMAS. By this way MOISE gives the chance to the designer to model totally or partially the social behavior of system agents by specify the possible organizational structures and that will be useful for system verification and validation. On the other hand, for the sake of flexibility, agents should be able to reason about their social behaviors and have a direct influence on system dynamic reorganization.

The MOISE model is structured along with three levels: (i) for each agent, definition of the tasks that it is responsible of (individual level), (ii) aggregation of agents in large structures (aggregate level), (iii) global structuring and interconnection of the agents and structures with each other (society level). The organization in MOISE is viewed as a normative set of rules that constrains the agents' behaviors [67].

The MOISE organizational model was extended by Hübner et al. to MOISE$^+$ [68] to create an organization-centered

model for independently specify the structural and functional aspects then link them by a deontic aspect. Another extension to MOISE$^+$ [69] was done to add dynamic reorganization process to adapt environment changes.

4.1.3. MACODO

Weyns et al. [61] presented an organizational model for context-driven dynamic agent organizations. The model defines abstractions that support application developers to describe dynamic reorganization. The organizational model is part of an integrated approach, called MACODO (Middleware Architecture for COntext-driven Dynamic agent Organizations); in this model, the life-cycle management of dynamic organizations is separated from the agents, organizations are first-class citizens, and their dynamics are governed by laws. Moreover, the authors provided a formal specification to describe and specify the semantics of their organizational model abstractions using Z specification language [62], which is based on set theory and first order predicate calculus. The main concern of MACODO is to directly relate organization dynamics to context changes in the environment.

We argue that the main drawback of the MACODO organizational model is the pure dynamically created organization; we argue that an organization should be tackled from the two perspectives, static and dynamic for the sake of long-term system stability. Dynamically creating and vanishing of organizations without keeping an amount of static behavior can impact system stability and prevents it from reaching an equilibrium state. In other words, there should be an amount of balance between static and dynamic organizational behaviors. The authors applied their model to traffic monitoring application. To our best knowledge, there is no any other real world application designed with MACODO.

4.2. Discussion

In MAS literature, there is large number of organizational models proposed by MAS researchers from all over the world to support the organizational aspects within MAS. Some of these models adopt the ACMAS viewpoint, others are concerned with the OCMAS viewpoint, and others adopt a hybrid approach combines both viewpoints. For the sake of this article size, it is not possible to explore all proposed organizational models in details, but interested readers can see [70], which is a handbook of research on MAS organizational models contains many of recent organizational model. Bellow, we provide our remarks about these models:

- This large number of organizational models indicates that concerning organizational aspects within MAS is currently a very interesting research area.
- It also emphasize that till now there is no a fit-to-all organizational models that can be used to design MAS-based systems in all application domains.
- Nearly, each of these models was dedicated to specific real world application domain and it is not applied to other applications.

- Some of these organizational models tackle with organization structure issues at design time (pure static), and others tackle them at will (pure dynamic).
- In some of them the organization abstraction is not explicit and the responsibility of dynamic reorganization is given to individual agents in addition to their functional responsibilities.
- Most of them considered the intra-organization and did not tackle with inter-organization reorganization. How to model the interaction among organizations?
- Few organizational models tackled both static and dynamic aspects of organizations and environments.
- In most of them the individual agent initiates to join a certain organization and this require that the agent has a reasonable knowledge about the services of each organization to select the appropriate one to join. We argue that letting the organization itself to select suitable agents to award it a role is the better approach because organization knowledge is more global than that of an individual agent.

Based on these remarks and limitations of most previously proposed MAS organizational models, we proposed a novel organizational model for engineering complex large-scale MAS-based applications. The new MAS organizational model was called NOSHAPE and conceptually presented in [76]. NOSHAPE is supposed to handle all the limitations of other related models. It exploits the overlapping relationships among higher order abstraction entities such as organizations of agents, worlds of organizations, and even universes of worlds within MAS to realize and utilize their captivating characteristics.

5. Conclusion and Future Work

MAS organization can be considered as a process to dynamically reorganize the system-to-be to adapt environment dynamic changes. Or, it can be considered as an entity facilitates the partitioning of the system-to-be. Organizations are a typical way to structure and manage interactions among agents. Establishing an organizational structure that specifies how agents in a system should work together helps the achievement of effective coordination in MAS. This chapter provided a comprehensive overview about MAS organization including its motivations, paradigms, models, and other related concepts such as self-organization and emergence. In MAS literature, we found very large number of organizational models proposed to support dynamic reorganization of the MAS, this large number of organizational models indicates that concerning organizational aspects within MAS is currently a very active and interesting research area and that till now there is no a fit-to-all MAS organizational model that can be used for engineering all possible application domains. This conclusion motivates us to propose a novel organizational model for engineering complex and highly distributed large-scale MAS such as modern industrial networks (i.e., SCADA [19]).

References

[1] Shehory, O. Architectural properties of multi-agent systems. Technical Report CMU-RI-TR-98-28, The Robotics Institute, Carnegie Mellon University, Pittsburgh, Pennsylvania 15213, 1998.

[2] Jennings, N. R., & Wooldridge, M. Agent-Oriented Software Engineering. in Bradshaw, J. ed. Handbook of Agent Technology, AAAI/MIT Press, 2000.

[3] Gasser, L. (2001). Perspectives on Organizations in Multi-Agent Systems. In Multi-Agent Systems and Applications, Michael Luck et al (pp. 1–16). Berlin: Springer-Verlag. doi:10.1007/3-540-47745-4_1.

[4] Odell, J. J., Parunak, H. V. D., & Fleischer, M. (2003). The role of roles in designing effective agent organizations. In Software Engineering for Large-Scale Multi-Agent Systems (pp. 27–38). Springer Berlin Heidelberg. doi:10.1007/3-540-35828-5_2.

[5] Horling, B., & Lesser, V. (2004). A survey of multi-agent organizational paradigms. The Knowledge Engineering Review, 19(4), 281–316.doi:10.1017/ S0269888905000317.

[6] Ferber, J., Gutknecht, O., & Michel, F. (2004). From agents to organizations: an organizational view of multi-agent systems. In Agent-Oriented Software Engineering IV (pp. 214–230). Springer Berlin Heidelberg. doi:10.1007/978-3-540-24620-6_15.

[7] Van Den Broek, E. L., Jonker, C. M., Sharpanskykh, A., & Treur, J. (2006). Formal modeling and analysis of organizations. In Coordination, Organizations, Institutions, and Norms in Multi-Agent Systems (pp. 18-34). Springer Berlin Heidelberg.

[8] Hübner, J. F., Vercouter, L., & Boissier, O. (2009). Instrumenting multi-agent organisations with artifacts to support reputation processes. In Coordination, Organizations, Institutions and Norms in Agent Systems IV (pp. 96–110). Springer Berlin Heidelberg. doi:10.1007/978-3-642-00443-8_7.

[9] Ferber, J., Michel, F., & Báez, J. (2005). AGRE: Integrating environments with organizations. In Environments for multi-agent systems (pp. 48-56). Springer Berlin Heidelberg.

[10] Dignum, V. (2009). The role of organization in agent systems. Handbook of Research on Multi-Agent Systems: Semantics and Dynamics of Organizational Models, 1-16.

[11] Weyns, D., Haesevoets, R., & Helleboogh, A. (2010). The MACODO organization model for context-driven dynamic agent organizations. ACM Transactions on Autonomous and Adaptive Systems (TAAS), 5(4), 16.

[12] Burns, T., & Stalker, G. (1961). *The Management of Innovation*, Tavistock, London.

[13] Picard, G., Hübner, J. F., Boissier, O., & Gleizes, M. P. (2009, June). Reorganisation and self-organisation in multi-agent systems. In 1st International Workshop on Organizational Modeling, ORGMOD (pp. 66-80).

[14] Upton, J., Janeka, I., & Ferraro, N. (2014). The whole is more than the sum of its parts: aristotle, metaphysical. Journal of Craniofacial Surgery, 25(1), 59-63.

[15] A. Drogoul, B. Corbara, and S. Lalande. MANTA: New experimental results on the emergence of (artificial) ant societies. In Nigel Gilbert and Rosaria Conte, editors, Artificial Societies: the Computer Simulation of Social Life, pages 119–221. UCL Press, London, 1995.

[16] Rajkumar, R. R., Lee, I., Sha, L., & Stankovic, J. (2010, June). Cyber-physical systems: the next computing revolution. In Proceedings of the 47th Design Automation Conference (pp. 731-736). ACM.

[17] Mattern, F., & Floerkemeier, C. (2010). From the Internet of Computers to the Internet of Things. In From active data management to event-based systems and more (pp. 242-259). Springer Berlin Heidelberg.

[18] James Momoh (2012), Smart Grid: Fundamentals of Design and Analysis, Wiley-IEEE Press; 1 edition (March 20, 2012).

[19] Abbas, H. A. (2014). Future SCADA challenges and the promising solution: the agent–based SCADA. International Journal of Critical Infrastructures, 10(3), 307-333.

[20] Saha, D., & Mukherjee, A. (2003). Pervasive computing: a paradigm for the 21st century. Computer, 36(3), 25-31.

[21] Friedewald, M., & Raabe, O. (2011). Ubiquitous computing: An overview of technology impacts. Telematics and Informatics, 28(2), 55-65.

[22] Jennings NR (2001) An agent-based approach for building complex software systems. Communications of the ACM 44 (4):35–41

[23] Ferber J (1999) Multi-Agent Systems: An Introduction to Distributed Artificial Intelligence. Addison-Wesley, Harlow, England.

[24] Wooldridge, M.: An Introduction to Multi-Agent Systems. Wiley, New York (2002).

[25] Posey, Rollin B. (March 1961). "Modern Organization Theory edited by Mason Haire". Administrative Science Quarterly 5 (4): 609–611.

[26] Hertz, D. and R. Livingston. (1950). Contemporary Organizational theory: A review of current concepts and methods. Human Relations, 3 (4), 373-394.

[27] Odell, J. J., Parunak, H. V. D., & Fleischer, M. (2003). The role of roles in designing effective agent organizations. In Software Engineering for Large-Scale Multi-Agent Systems (pp. 27-38). Springer Berlin Heidelberg.

[28] Van Den Broek, E. L., Jonker, C. M., Sharpanskykh, A., & Treur, J. (2006). Formal modeling and analysis of organizations. In Coordination, Organizations, Institutions, and Norms in Multi-Agent Systems (pp. 18-34). Springer Berlin Heidelberg.

[29] Miles, R. E., Snow, C. S., Mathews, J. A., Miles, G., & Coleman, H. J. (1997). Organizing in the knowledge age: Anticipating the cellular form. The Academy of Management Executive, 11(4), 7-20.

[30] Lesser, V. R., & Corkill, D. D. (1981). Functionally accurate, cooperative distributed systems. Systems, Man and Cybernetics, IEEE Transactions on,11(1), 81-96.

[31] Corkill, D. D. (1980). An organizational approach to planning in distributed problem-solving systems. Technical Report 80-13, Department of Computer and Information Science, University of Massachusetts, Amherst, Massachusetts 01003.

[32] Jay Galbraith. Designing Complex Organizations. Addison-Wesley, 1973.

[33] Fox, M. S. (1981). An organizational view of distributed systems. Systems, Man and Cybernetics, IEEE Transactions on, 11(1), 70-80.

[34] Giovanna Di Marzo Serugendo et al (2011), "Self-organizing Software, From Natural to Artificial Adaptation", Springer.

[35] M. Carley and L. Gasser. Computational organization theory. In G. Weiss, editor, Multiagent Systems: A Modern Approach to Distributed Arti_cial Intelligence, pages 299.330. MIT Press, 1999.

[36] Corkill, D. D., & Lander, S. E. (1998). Diversity in agent organizations. Object Magazine, 8(4), 41-47.

[37] Jay R. Galbraith. Organization Design. Addison-Wesley, 1977.

[38] Giovanna di Marzoserugendo et al, "Self-organization in multi-agent systems", The Knowledge Engineering Review, Vol. 20:2, 165–189., 2005, Cambridge University Press.

[39] K. S. Barber and C. E. Martin, 'Dynamic reorganization of decisionmaking groups', in Proceedings of the 5th Autonomous Agents, (2001).

[40] Dignum, V., Dignum, F., & Sonenberg, L. (2004, September). Towards dynamic reorganization of agent societies. In Proceedings of Workshop on Coordination in Emergent Agent Societies at ECAI (pp. 22-27).

[41] Bernon, C., Camps, V., Gleizes, M. P., & Picard, G. (2005). Engineering adaptive multi-agent systems: The adelfe methodology. Agent-oriented methodologies, 172-202.

[42] Guessoum, Z., Briot, J. P., Marin, O., Hamel, A., & Sens, P. (2003). Dynamic and adaptive replication for large-scale reliable multi-agent systems. InSoftware engineering for large-scale multi-agent systems (pp. 182-198). Springer Berlin Heidelberg.

[43] Berns, A., & Ghosh, S. (2009, September). Dissecting self-* properties. In Self-Adaptive and Self-Organizing Systems, 2009. SASO'09. Third IEEE International Conference on (pp. 10-19). IEEE.

[44] Sichman, J. S., Dignum, V., & Castelfranchi, C. (2005). Agents' organizations: a concise overview. Journal of the Brazilian Computer Society, 11(1), 3-8.

[45] Serugendo, G. D. M., Gleizes, M. P., & Karageorgos, A. (2006). Self-Organisation and Emergence in MAS: An Overview. Informatica (Slovenia),30(1), 45-54.

[46] P. Glansdorff and I. Prigogine. Thermodynamic study of Structure, Stability and Fluctuations. Wiley, 1971.

[47] Mano, J. P., Bourjot, C., Lopardo, G., & Glize, P. (2006). Bio-inspired mechanisms for artificial self-organised systems. Informatica, 30(1), 55-62.

[48] Giovanna (2011) Di Marzo Serugendo et al, "Self-organizing Software, From Natural to Artificial Adaptation", Springer, 2011.

[49] Zambonelli, F., Gleizes, M. P., Mamei, M., & Tolksdorf, R. (2004, May). Spray computers: frontiers of self-organization. In Autonomic Computing, 2004. Proceedings. International Conference on (pp. 268-269). IEEE.

[50] Karuna, H., Valckenaers, P., Saint-Germain, B., Verstraete, P., Zamfirescu, C. B., & Van Brussel, H. (2005). Emergent forecasting using a stigmergy approach in manufacturing coordination and control. In Engineering Self-Organising Systems (pp. 210-226). Springer Berlin Heidelberg.

[51] Weyns, D., Schelfthout, K., Holvoet, T., & Glorieux, O. (2004). Role based model for adaptive Agents. In *Fourth Symposium on Adaptive Agents and Multiagent Systems at the AISB'04 Convention.*

[52] M.P. Gleizes, V. Camps, and P. Glize. A theory of emergent computation based on cooperative self-organisation for adaptive artificial systems. Fourth European Congress of Systems Science. Valencia, 1999.

[53] De Wolf, T., & Holvoet, T. (2004). Emergence and self-organisation: a statement of similarities and differences. *Engineering Self-Organising Systems, 3464,* 1-15.

[54] Akgün, A. E., Keskin, H., & Byrne, J. C. (2014). Complex adaptive systems theory and firm product innovativeness. Journal of Engineering and Technology Management, 31, 21-42.

[55] Streng, W. (2005). Reductionism versus Holism–Contrasting Approaches.Consilience. Interdisciplinary Communications, 2006, 11-14.

[56] Ashby, W.R.: Principles of self-organizing dynamic systems. Journal of General Psychology 37 (1947) 125–128.

[57] Giorgini, P., & Henderson-Sellers, B. (2005). Agent-oriented methodologies: an introduction. *Agent-oriented Methodologies,* 1-19.

[58] Ferber, J. and Gutknecht, O., Aalaadin: a meta-model for the analysis and design of organizations in multi-agent systems. in Third International Conference on Multi-Agent Systems, (Paris, 1998), IEEE, 128-135.

[59] Wooldridge, M., Jennings, N. R., & Kinny, D. (2000). The Gaia methodology for agent-oriented analysis and design. Autonomous Agents and Multi-Agent Systems, 3(3), 285-312.

[60] Ferber, J., Michel, F., & Báez, J. (2005). AGRE: Integrating environments with organizations. In Environments for multi-agent systems (pp. 48-56). Springer Berlin Heidelberg.

[61] Weyns, D., Haesevoets, R., & Helleboogh, A. (2010). The MACODO organization model for context-driven dynamic agent organizations. ACM Transactions on Autonomous and Adaptive Systems (TAAS), 5(4), 16.

[62] Spivey, J. M. (1989). The Z notation (Vol. 1992). New York: Prentice Hall.

[63] Coutinho, L. R., Sichman, J. S., & Boissier, O. (2005, October). Modeling organization in mas: A comparison of models. In First Workshop on Software Engineering for Agent-oriented Systems (pp. 1-10).

[64] Argente, E., Palanca, J., Aranda, G., Julian, V., Botti, V., Garcia-Fornes, A., & Espinosa, A. (2007). Supporting agent organizations. In Multi-Agent Systems and Applications V (pp. 236-245). Springer Berlin Heidelberg.

[65] Dignum, V., Dignum, F.: A Landscape of Agent Systems for the Real World. Tech. Report Utrecht University (2007)

[66] Gutknecht, O., & Ferber, J. (1998). A model for social structures in multi-agent systems (Vol. 98040). Technical Report RR LIRMM.

[67] Hannoun, M., Boissier, O., Sichman, J. S., & Sayettat, C. (2000). MOISE: An organizational model for multi-agent systems. In Advances in Artificial Intelligence (pp. 156-165). Springer Berlin Heidelberg.

[68] Hübner, J. F., Sichman, J. S., & Boissier, O. (2002, July). Moise+: towards a structural, functional, and deontic model for mas organization. In Proceedings of the first international joint conference on Autonomous agents and multiagent systems: part 1 (pp. 501-502). ACM.

[69] Hübner, J. F., Sichman, J. S., & Boissier, O. (2004). Using the MOISE$^+$ for a Cooperative Framework of MAS Reorganisation. In Advances in artificial intelligence–SBIA 2004 (pp. 506-515). Springer Berlin Heidelberg.

[70] Dignum, V. (Ed.). (2009). Handbook of Research on Multi-Agent Systems: Semantics and Dynamics of Organizational Models: Semantics and Dynamics of Organizational Models. IGI Global.

[71] Jennings, N. R. (1999). Agent-oriented software engineering. In Multiple Approaches to Intelligent Systems (pp. 4-10). Springer Berlin Heidelberg.

[72] Duan, Junhua, Yi-an Zhu, and Shujuan Huang. "Stigmergy agent and swarm-intelligence-based multi-agent system." Intelligent Control and Automation (WCICA), 2012 10th World Congress on. IEEE, 2012.

[73] Smith, R. G. (1980). The contract net protocol: High-level communication and control in a distributed problem solver. IEEE Transactions on computers, (12), 1104-1113.

[74] S.A. DeLoach. Methodologies and Software Engineering for Agent Systems. The Agent-Oriented Software Engineering Handbook Series : Multiagent Systems, Artificial Societies,and Simulated Organizations, volume 11, chapter The MaSE Methodology. Kluwer Academic Publishing (available via Springer), 2004.

[75] Juan Pav'on and Jorge J. G'omez-Sanz. Agent oriented software engineering with ingenias. In Vladim'ır Mar'ık, J"org P. M"uller, and Michal Pechoucek, editors, CEEMAS, volume 2691 of Lecture Notes in Computer Science, pages 394–403. Springer, 2003.

[76] Abbas, H. A. (2014). Exploiting the Overlapping of Higher Order Entities within Multi-Agent Systems. International Journal of Agent Technologies and Systems (IJATS), 6(3), 32-57. doi:10.4018/ijats.2014070102.

25

Improving honeyd for automatic generation of attack signatures

Motahareh Dehghan, Babak Sadeghiyan

Department of Computer Engineering and Information Technology, Amirkabir University of Technology (AUT), Tehran, Iran

Email address:

Motahareh479@aut.ac.ir (M. Dehghan), basadegh@aut.ac.ir (B. Sadeghiyan)

Abstract: In this paper, we design and implement a new Plugin to Honeyd which generates attack signature, automatically. Current network intrusion detection systems work on misuse detectors, where the packets in the monitored network are compared against a repository of signatures. But, we focus on automatic signature generation from malicious network traffic. Our proposed system inspects honeypot traffic and generates intrusion signatures for unknown traffic. The signature is based on traffic patterns, using Longest Common Substring (LCS) algorithm. It is noteworthy that our system is a plugin to honeyd - a low interaction honeypot. The system's output is a file containing honeypot intrusion signatures in pseudo-snort format. Signature generation system has been implemented for Linux Operating System (OS) but due to the common use of Windows OS, we implement for Windows OS, using C programming language.

Keywords: Honeypot, Honeyd, Signature, Intrusion Detection System (IDS), Longest Common Substring (LCS) Algorithm

1. Introduction

Nowadays, in order to reduce the effects of network attacks and prevent network intrusion, several security equipments are designed and implemented. One of them is honeypot.

Honeypot offers a variety of services and attracts attackers.

In this paper, we acquire patterns from honeypot's traffic on basis of packets sent to multiple hosts from attackers, which have approximately similar content. Then, from these patterns we generate signatures. The system's output is a file containing intrusion signatures in pseudo- snort format. As illustrated in Figure 1, our proposed system is a plugin to honeyd-low interaction honeypot that designs appropriate responses based on these signatures [1]. Also, these signatures can be used to filter the traffic directed towards the honeypot, in order to reduce the amount of traffic needed to be processed by the honeypot sensors.

2. Data and Materials

2.1. Honeypot

As mentioned by Grønland [2], honeypot is a system which

is built and set up in order to be hacked. Besides this, honeypot is also a trap system for the attackers which is deployed to counteract the resources of the attacker and slow him down, thus he wastes his time on the honeypot instead of attacking the production systems.

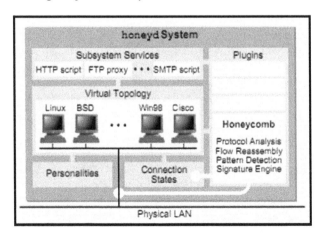

Figure 1. Honeyd and Proposed System.

- Types of honeypots include [3,4] Honeypots in terms of reality Physical honeypots
- A physical honeypot is a real machine in network which

has a particular IP address.
- Virtual honeypots A virtual honeypot is simulated by another machine.
- Honeypots in terms of interaction by attacker Low interaction honeypots A low-interaction honeypot will

typically run or emulate a small number of services on a real or emulated operating system.
- High interaction honeypots A high-interaction honeypot is often a real computer running a real operating system (Figure 2).

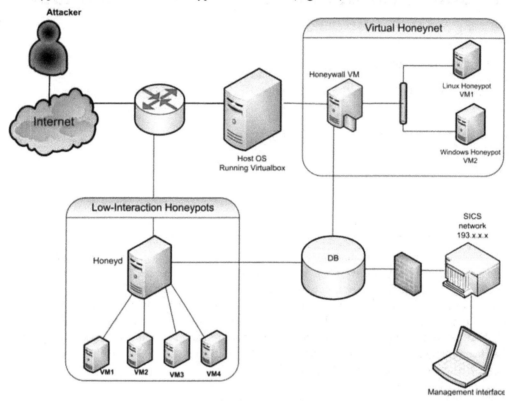

Figure 2. Types of Honeypots.

2.2. Honeyd

Honeyd is an Open Source low-interaction honeypot implemented for UNIX and Windows Operating Systems (OS) [5]. Every attacker which intends to communicate network with useless Internet Protocol (IP) Address, is disconnected and interacted by honeyd disconnects this connection and interacts with him. Honeyd is a framework for virtual honeypots which allows thousands of IP addresses to communicate with virtual machines. Thus, it should be able to simulate network topology. Honeyd is a central machine which captures the traffic directed towards the virtual honeypots and simulates appropriate responses [6].

2.3. Longest Common Substring of Two Strings

The longest common substrings of a set of strings can be found by building a generalised suffix tree for the strings, and then finding the deepest internal nodes which have leaf nodes from all the strings in the subtree below it [7]. The figure on the right is the suffix tree for the strings "ABAB", "BABA" and "ABBA", padded with unique string terminators, to become "ABAB$0", "BABA$1" and "ABBA$2". The nodes representing "A", "B", "AB" and "BA" all have descendant leaves from all of the strings, numbered 0, 1 and 2.

2.4. Cygwin

Cygwin is a UNIX-compatible environment that runs on Windows systems. It consists of cygwin1.dll, a library that takes POSIX calls and translates them into Win32 calls; a shell (GNU BASH, the shell used on most Linux systems, is the default); an implementation of the X Window System as well as GCC [8].

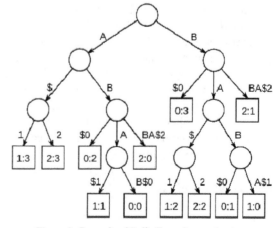

Figure 3. Generalized Suffix Tree of a set of strings.

3. Research Methodology

3.1. System Architecture

The proposed system architecture consists of following parts:
- Local Control Unit
  - Analysis Unit
- Communication Unit
- Database
- Known-Attack Filter
- Network Intrusion Prevention System
- Global Control Unit

Each unit is described as follow:

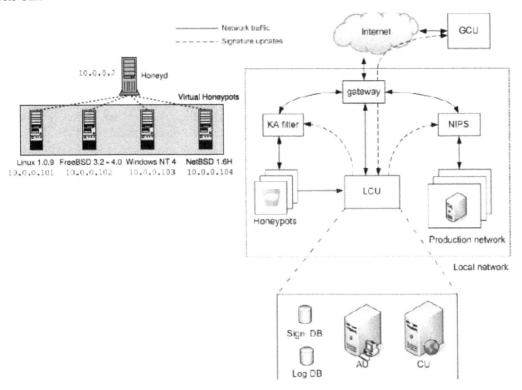

Figure 4. Proposed System Architecture

- *Local Control Unit*

This unit has a simplified version that is only able to receive signature updates from the Global Control Unit (GCU) and use these in NIPS to protect the production network. But in a complicated version, LCU consists of behind units:

  - *Analysis Unit – (AU)*

The AU's main task is to correlate the incoming honeypot events and create signatures for possible worms. When receiving new events from a honeypot, the following procedure is executed:

- Step 1: The incoming events are stored in the log database and correlated with older events. If a similar chain of events has been received a certain number of times before, it is assumed that the events are caused by a worm and step 2 is carried out. If not, the events are simply stored and the AU returns to idle state.
- Step 2: The network packets causing the same chain of events are compared. If a common substring (larger than a given threshold) is found between these traffic traces, a signature is created.
- Step 3: Before storing the newly generated signature in the database, it is compared with the already existing ones. It can then either be stored directly in the database as a new entry or help to improve one of the older ones.

  - *Communication Unit – (CU)*

The CU's main purpose is to exchange signatures with the Global Control Unit (GCU) as well as issuing signature updates to the Known-Attack (KA) filter and Network Intrusion Prevention System (NIPS).

  - *Databases*

The signature database is used to store locally generated as well as received signatures. The log database is used to store the logged events along with relevant data.

- *Known-Attack Filter – (KA Filter)*

The main purpose of the KA filter is to look for known attacks (based on the signatures received from the LCU) in the traffic directed towards the honeypots.

- *Network Intrusion Prevention System – (NIPS)*

The NIPS is placed in the system to protect the production network. It can filter traffic that is unwanted based on certain ports as specified by the network administrator, as well as traffic that have been declared malicious as a result of signature updates from the LCU. Similar to the KA filter, it is also possible for the NIPS to report back to the LCU on the activity level of the received signatures.

- *Global Control Unit – (GCU)*

The GCU serves as a central signature storage and distribution unit. It receives signature updates from the distributed LCUs and is able to correlate received data from different locations to compose improved signatures. Based on the received data, it issues periodic updates to the LCUs. As the GCU is a potential single point-of-failure and the effects can be catastrophic if it is compromised, the requirements regarding security are strict. All communication between the GCU and LCUs should be authenticated and encrypted in order to avoid forged signature updates.

3.2. Implementation

The implementation is based on traffic patterns, using Longest Common Substring (LCS) algorithm. Our system output is a file containing honeyd intrusion signatures in pseudo-snort format to filter unwanted production network traffic. Also the proposed architecture introduces the use of a Known-Attack (KA) filter. The main purpose of this filter is to remove known attacks from the traffic directed towards the honeypots. This filter reduces the amount of traffic needed to be processed by the honeypot sensors.

Signature generation system is implemented in Linux OS, but due to the common use of Windows OS, our implementation is also in Windows OS, using C programming language.

According to [5, 9, 10], for implementing the system we use below items:

1 Winpcap to capture packets
2 Cygwin compiler
3 Libevent library: The libevent API provides a mechanism to execute a callback function when a specific event occurs on a file descriptor or after a timeout has been reached [11].
4 Libdnet library: libdnet provides a simplified, portable interface to several low-level networking routines [12].
5 Libstree library: libstree is a generic suffix tree implementation, written in C [13].
6 Python

4. Results and Analysis

Signatures are periodically reported to an output module which implements the actual logging of the signature records. At the moment, there are modules that convert the signature records into pseudo-Snort format and a module that dumps the signature strings to a file. Our proposed system generated 53 signatures during a roughly 18-hour period and we captured 224 KB of traffic, comprising 560 TCP connections, 120 UDP connections and 24 ICMP pings. 25 signatures were created containing flow content strings. These are relatively long; on average they contain 136 bytes. The signatures format is as follow:

alert tcp 61.0.0.0/8 any → 129.241.196.0/24 80 (msg: "Hello!!! "; flags: PA+; flow: established; content: "GET http://lookfreebies.com/prx1.php HTTP/1.0|0D

0A|Accept: */*|0D 0A|Accept-Language: en-us|0D 0A|User-Agent: Mozilla/4.0 (compatible; MSIE 6.0; Windows NT 5.0)|0D 0A|Host: lookfreebies.com|0D 0A|Connection: Keep-Alive|0D 0A 0D|";) As mentioned in

[14], rule options are:
- The direction operator → indicates the orientation, or direction of the traffic that the rule applies to. The IP address and port numbers on the left side of the direction operator is considered to be the traffic coming from the source.
- The generated signature has TCP protocol that the source IP address is 61.0.0.0/8 and the destination IP address is 129.241.196.0/24 and its port is 80.
- The msg rule option tells the logging and alerting engine the message to print along with a packet dump or to an alert.
- The content keyword is one of the more important features of Snort. It allows the user to set rules that search for specific content in the packet payload and trigger response based on that data.
- The flags keyword is used to check if specific TCP flag bits are present.

5. Conclusion

In Summary, an automated signature generation system for Windows OS designed and implemented. This system considered as honeyd plugin. Our tests show the proposed system is particularly good at generating attack signatures.

Acknowledgements

I would like to thank Mr. Erfan Khosravian for valuable feedbacks and Comments.

References

[1] Vusal Aliyev, "Using honeypots to study skill level of attackers based on the exploited vulnerabilities in the network". Master of Science Thesis in the Master Degree Programme, Secure and Dependable Computer Systems, Department of Computer Science and Engineering Division of Computer Security. Goteborg, Sweden, 2010.

[2] Grønland, Vidar Ajaxon. "Building IDS rules by means of a honeypot". Master's Thesis, Master of Science in Information Security, Department of Computer Science and Media Technology Gjøvik University College, 2006.

[3] Noordin, Yusuff, Mohamed. "HONEYPOTS REVEALED". IT Security Officer. Specialist Dip. Info Security, MA. Internet Security Mgmt.

[4] Mark Mcijerink, Jonel Spellen. "Intrusion Detection System honeypots". Master Program System and Network Administration, University of Amsterdam, 2006.

[5] Baumann, Reto. "Honeyd – A low involvement Honeypot in Action". Originally published as part of the GCIA (GIAC Certified Intrusion Analyst) practical, 2003.

[6] Provos, Niels. "Honeyd- A Virtual Honeypot Daemon". Center for Information Technology Integration, University of Michigan. 2003.

[7]   Sung, Wing-Kin; Melvin, Zhang Zhiyong. "Suffix Tree and Suffix Array". Knowledge Discovery and Data Mining Conference,2005.

[8]   Moody, George. "An Introduction To Cygwin". Harvard-MIT Division of Health Sciences and Technology.

[9]   Provos, Niels; Mathewson, Nick. "Libevent – an event notification library", 2011. URL: http://libevent.org/

[10] Van Rossum, Guido; "Introduction to Python". LinuxWorld, New York City, Documented in https://www.python.org/doc. 2002.

[11] Libevent – an event notification library: http://libevent.org.

[12] Libdnet: http://libdnet.sourceforge.net.

[13] Christian Kreibich;   libstree: http://www.icir.org/christian/ libstree .

[14] Roesch,Martin; Green, Chris. "SNORT Users Manual 2.8.5", The Snort Project (https://manual.snort.org), 2009.

26

Effective load balancing in cloud computing

Zeinab Goudarzi[*], **Ahmad Faraahi**

Department of Computer Engineering and Information Technology, Payame Noor University, PO BOX 19395-3697 Tehran, Iran

Email address:

z1990_good@yahoo.com (Z. Goudarzi), afaraahi@pnu.ac.ir (A. Faraahi)

Abstract: Internet, from its beginning so far, has undergone a lot of changes which some of them has changed human's lifestyle in recent decades. One of the latest changes in the functionality of the Internet has been the introduction of Cloud Computing. Cloud Computing is a new internet service, which involves virtualization, distributed computing, networking, software etc. This technology is becoming popular to provide various services to users. Naturally, any changes and new concepts in the world of technology have its own problems and complexities. Using Cloud Computing is no exception and has many challenges facing the authorities in this area such as load balancing, security, reliability, ownership, data backup and data portability. Load balancing is one of the essential factors to enhance the working performance of the Cloud service provider by shifting of workload among the processors. Proper load balancing aids in minimizing resource consumption, implementing fail-over, enabling scalability, avoiding bottlenecks and over- provisioning etc. Given the importance of the process of load balancing in Cloud Computing, the aim of this paper is to review the process and to compare techniques in this field.

Keywords: Cloud Computing, Load Balancing, Metrics

1. Introduction

Cloud Computing is a new technology, which provides on-demand network access to a shared pool of computing resources. Cloud is a pay-go model where the consumers pay for the resources utilized instantly, which necessitates having highly available resources to service the requests on demand [1]. It was intended to enable computing across widespread and diverse resources, rather than on local machines or at remote server farms [2].

Services in a Cloud are of 3 types as given in [3]: (1) Software as a Service (SaaS): with SaaS, the users don't need to install the software on their machines. SaaS provider maintains and manages software, supplies the hardware facilities and the users can use software directly from the cloud. For small business, SaaS is the best way to use advanced technology. (2) Platform as a Service (PaaS): PaaS provides a platform on which users can directly develop and deploy their own applications and transfer to other customers through their server and internet. Microsoft Azure is one example of PaaS. (3) Infrastructure as a Service (IaaS): IaaS offers the hardware as a service to the customers and provides an environment for deploying, running and managing virtual machines and storage.

Cloud Computing by using the resources, information, software and shared equipment provides a client's service within a specific time. Of course, regarding the time which is spent on the Internet, the whole Internet can be considered as a Cloud. Operating and capital costs can be reduced by using Cloud Computing [4]. Due to the spread of Cloud Computing in recent years, from the perspective of market presence, understanding the effect of load balancing in the Cloud is important. Cloud Computing Platform, is a fully automated service platform that allows users to buy, create distance, dynamic scalability, and management of the system [5].

The load measuring is mechanized so as to avoid disruption in delivery of a service when one or more components of the system are in trouble. In this case, the system components are constantly monitored, and when a component fails to respond, load balancing comes up and do not sent traffic on it. Often, problems can be minimized with proper load balancing that not only reduce costs and create green computing, but keeps the pressure minimum on the unique circuits that makes them potentially longer life [6].

Load balancing in Cloud Computing systems is really a challenge now. It is a mechanism that distributes the dynamic local workload evenly across all the nodes in the whole Cloud to avoid a condition in which some of the nodes are over loaded while some others are idle or under loaded. It helps to achieve a high user satisfaction and resource utility of the system. It also ensures that every computing resource is distributed efficiently and fairly [7].

The load considered here can be in terms of CPU load, amount of memory used, delay or network load [8]. Load balancing ensures that all the processor in the system or every node in the network does approximately the equal amount of work at any instant of time [9]. Load balancing algorithms are placed in three categories on the basis of who starts the process of load balancing: sender initiated, receiver initiated, symmetric (combination of sender initiated, receiver initiated types) and are placed in two categories based on the current state of the system: static and dynamic [6].

With load balancing, the load can be balanced by active transferring of local workload from a machine to the machine in the remote node or machine that is used less [10]. Load balancing is also required in the Clouds to meet the Green Computing. In this way, it can reduce the amount of energy by avoiding excessive interaction or virtual machines considering the workload, and by reducing the energy consumption, carbon emissions are reduced and, we thus achieve the Green Computing. As given in [7], [11] and [12] the goals of load balancing are:

i Have a backup plan to build a fault tolerant system
ii Substantial improvement in performance
iii Stability maintain the system
iv Accommodate future modification in the system

When a given workload is applied on any cluster's node, this given load can be efficiently executed if the available resources are efficiently used. So that, there must be a mechanism for choosing the nodes that have these resources. Scheduling is a component or a mechanism, which is responsible for the selection of a cluster node, to which a particular process will be placed. This mechanism will investigate the load balancing state. Hence, scheduling needs algorithms to solve such problems [9].

2. Important Resources and Metrics of Load Balancing

Important resources in load balancing as discussed by Hamo and Saeed [13] include:

i Computer processor time: it is the most important resource in operating system. When distributed system is used this resource need to be balanced.

ii Computer memory: another important resource in the computer is memory. When these computers are connected across the grid, memory resources, need to be balanced.

iii Computer I/O: I/O resources, which is depends on the effective usage of storage, in addition to that of CPU and memory, need to be balanced.

In Cloud Computing, load balancing is a necessary mechanism to increase the service level agreement (SLA) and better uses of the resources [8].

Various metrics in load balancing Techniques in Cloud Computing are discussed in Table 1.

Table 1. Metrics of Load Balancing [6], [9], [10]

Metric	Illustration
Throughput	It is used to calculate the no. of tasks whose execution has been completed. This metric should be high to achieve good load balancing and improve the performance of the system.
Overhead	It determines the amount of overhead involved while implementing a load balancing algorithm. It is composed of overhead due to movement of tasks, inter-processor and inter-process communication. This metric should be minimized so that a load balancing technique can work efficiently.
Fault Tolerance	Is the ability of an algorithm to perform uniform load balancing in case of link failure. The load balancing should be a good fault-tolerant technique, in order to achieve a high user satisfaction and improve the performance of the system.
Response Time	It is the amount of time taken to respond by a particular load balancing algorithm in a distributed system. It should be minimized.
Resource Utilization	It is used to check the utilization of resources. It should be optimized for an efficient load balancing.
Scalability	It is the ability of an algorithm to perform load balancing for a system with any finite number of nodes. This metric should be improved for load balancing.
Performance	It is used to check the efficiency of the system. This has to be improved at a reasonable cost, e.g., reduce task response time while keeping acceptable delays.
Migration Time	Is the time to migrate the jobs or resources from one node to other. It should be minimized in order to enhance the performance of the system.
Energy Consumption	Determines the energy consumption of all the resources in the system. Load balancing helps in avoiding overheating by balancing the workload across all the nodes of a Cloud, hence reducing energy consumption.

3. Load Balancing Algorithms

3.1. Static Load Balancing

Static load balancing algorithms allocate the tasks to a node only based on the node's ability for processing the new request. This process is based solely on prior knowledge of the properties of nodes, which can include the node processing power, memory, and storage capacity and so on. Static load balancing algorithms usually do not consider the changes that occur at run time for these attributes and cannot adapt to changes in runtime. Their goal is to minimize execution time and limit the communication overhead and delay [10].

In fact, static load balancing allocates a work that enters the system to a processor or a fixed node, and each time the system is restarted, the same processor will be responsible for executing the work. It is possible that the allocated task to the same processor does not work, but allocating the new coming tasks is in a fixed order or model. The static load balancing is either Deterministic or Probabilistic. In the Deterministic load balancing, tasks are connected to the smallest queue of work stations since routing decisions are based on the state of the system. In Probabilistic load balancing, tasks are randomly sent to the stations with equal probability [13].

3.2. Dynamic Load Balancing

Dynamic load balancing algorithms take into account the various features of nodes, capabilities and network bandwidth. Most of these algorithms rely on a combination of information about the nodes in the cloud which have already been collected and properties of collection time. The algorithm may actively re-allocate the tasks to the nodes based on the information gathered just after allocating the tasks to the nodes. So they need constant monitoring over the nodes and tasks stream, and are usually more difficult to implement. But on the other hand, they enjoy a higher accuracy and can produce a more efficient load balancing results [15].

An important advantage to dynamic load balancing is that load balancing decisions are based on the current state of the system which contribute to better overall performance of system with dynamic migration of loads [10]. A dynamic strategy is usually performed several times and may re-allocate a scheduled task to a new node based on the dynamic state of the system environment [13].

Dynamic load balancing algorithms fall into two categories: distributed and Non-distributed. In distributed type, the task of balancing the load is for all the nodes in the system. Interaction between nodes to achieve load balancing can be in two forms: cooperation and non-cooperative. In the first form, the nodes cooperate with each other to reach a common goal such as improving the time of the total response. And in the second form, each node works independently toward a local target like improving the response time of a local work [9].

However, in Non-distributed form, one node or a group of nodes are doing load balancing task. The Non-distributed dynamic load balancing algorithms can be classified into two types of Centralized and Semi-Distributed. In Centralized type, the load balancing algorithm is performed only over one node of system, so called central node. This node solely has the duty of load balancing of the entire system. The other nodes only have interactions with the central node. In the type of Semi-Distributed, the nodes of system have been divided into clusters in which load balancing of each cluster is centralized. By using appropriate techniques for each cluster, a node can be selected to look after the load balancing in cluster. Hence, the total load balancing of system is done by the central nodes of each cluster [4].

The distributed dynamic load balancing algorithms produce more messages than their Non-Distributed counterparts since each node within the system needs to communicate with any other node. The advantage of this method is lack of bottleneck in the system, which in turn affect the system performance partly. The distributed dynamic load balancing can put an enormous pressure on a system in which each node needs to exchange situational information with any other node. This method is more effective when most of the nodes work independently with little interaction with other nodes. Since the centralized dynamic load balancing receive fewer messages, the total number of interactions within the system is diminished as compared to the semi distributed type. However, the centralized algorithms can create bottleneck on the central node, and also the load balancing pattern become useless when the central node crashes. So this algorithm is more suitable for small-sized networks [10].

4. Load Balancing Techniques

4.1. Honeybee Foraging Algorithm

The main idea behind the algorithm is derived from the behavior of honey bees for finding and reaping food. There is a class of bees called the forager bees which forage for food sources, upon finding one, they come back to the beehive to advertise this using a dance called waggle dance. The display of this dance, gives the idea of the quality or quantity of food and also its distance from the beehive. Scout bees then follow the foragers to the location of food and then began to reap it. They then return to the beehive and do a waggle dance, which gives an idea of how much food is left and hence results in more exploitation or abandonment of the food source.

In case of load balancing, as the webservers demand increases or decreases, the services are assigned dynamically to regulate the changing demands of the user. The servers are grouped under virtual servers (VS), each VS having its own virtual service queues. Each server processing a request from its queue calculates a profit or reward, which is analogous to the quality that the bees show in their waggle dance. One measure of this reward can be the amount of time that the CPU spends on the processing of a request. The dance floor in case of honey bees is analogous to an advert board here. This board is also used to advertise the profit of the entire colony. Each of the servers takes the role of either a forager or a scout. The server after processing a request can post their profit on the advert boards with a probability of pr. A server can choose a queue of a VS by a probability of px showing forage/explore behavior, or it can check for advertisements (see dance) and serve it, thus showing scout behavior. A server serving a request, calculates its profit and compare it with the colony profit and then sets its px. If this profit was high, then the server stays at the current virtual server; posting an advertisement for it by probability pr. If it was low, then the server returns to the forage or scout behavior [4].

4.2. Based Random Sampling

Biased Random Sampling is a distributed and scalable load balancing approach that uses random sampling of the system domain to achieve self-organization thus balancing the load across all nodes of the system. Here a virtual graph is constructed, with the connectivity of each node (a server is treated as a node) representing the load on the server. Each server is symbolized as a node in the graph, with each in degree directed to the free resources of the server each server is symbolized as a node in the graph, with each in degree directed to the free resources of the server. Regarding job execution and completion,

i Whenever a node does or executes a job, it deletes an incoming edge, which indicates reduction in the availability of free resource.

ii After completion of a job, the node creates an incoming edge, which indicates an increase in the availability of free resource.

The addition and deletion of processes is done by the process of random sampling. The walk starts at any one node and at every step a neighbor is chosen randomly. The last node is selected for allocation for load. Alternatively, another method can be used for selection of a node for load allocation, that being selecting a node based on certain criteria like computing efficiency, etc. Yet another method can be selecting that node for load allocation which is under loaded i.e. having highest in degree. If b is the walk length, then, as b increases, the efficiency of load allocation increases. We define a threshold value of b, which is generally equal to log n experimentally. A node upon receiving a job, will execute it only if its current walk length is equal to or greater than the threshold value. Else, the walk length of the job under consideration is incremented and another neighbor node is selected randomly. When, a job is executed by a node then in the graph, an incoming edge of that node is deleted. After completion of the job, an edge is created from the node initiating the load allocation process to the node which was executing the job. Finally what we get is a directed graph. The load balancing scheme used here is fully decentralized, thus making it apt for large network systems like that in a Cloud [4].

4.3. Active Clustering

Active Clustering works on the principle of grouping similar nodes together and working on these groups. The process involved is:

i A node initiates the process and selects another node called the matchmaker node from its neighbors satisfying the criteria that it should be of a different type than the former one.

ii The so called matchmaker node then forms a connection between neighbors of it which is of the same type as the initial node.

iii The matchmaker node then detaches the connection between itself and the initial node.

The above set of processes is followed iteratively [4].

The performance of the system is enhanced with high resources thereby in-creasing the throughput by using these resources effectively. It is degraded with an increase in system diversity. This algorithm optimizes job assignment by connecting similar services by local re-wiring and performs better with high resources.

4.4. Carton

This technique is used to equally distribute the load balancing tasks among different servers. Therefore, the corresponding costs can be reduced and limited distribution rates are used to ensure a fair allocation of resources [15].

4.5. Event-Driven

A load balancing algorithm has suggested an event-driven method for the real time Massively Multiple Player Online Games. This algorithm after receiving the incoming capacity as input analyzes its own components in the context of resources and the overall state of play settlement. As a result, the activities of load balancing produce the game session [16].

4.6. Server-Based Load Balancing for Distributed Internet Services

A new service-based load balancing policy for Web servers that are distributed throughout the world has been suggested. This policy helps to reduce the time of service through limiting the number of deviances of a request to the closest server of remote path without making them the overhead. A middleware has been described for the implementation of this protocol which uses a discovery method for helping the Web servers to bear the load [17].

4.7. Black-Box and Gray-Box Strategies

Wood et. al, [18] adopt Black-Box and Gray-Box strategies for Virtual Machine (VM) migration in large data centers. Black-Box technique has been designed to monitor the system resource usage, detect hotspots and initiate the necessary migrations, that can make these decisions by simply observing each Virtual Machine from the outside and without any knowledge of the application resident within each Virtual Machine, and Gray-Box technique has been designed to access a small amount of OS level statistics to better inform the migration algorithm. The authors have designed the Sandpiper system to support techniques. Sandpiper imposes negligible overheads and that Gray-Box statistics enable Sandpiper to make better migration decisions when alleviating memory hotspots.

4.8. Min-Min

This algorithm work by considering the execution and completion time of each task and begins with a set of all unassigned tasks. First, minimum execution time for all tasks is found. Then, the task with the least execution time among all the tasks on any resources is selected. The algorithm assigned the task to the resource that produces the minimum completion time. Until all tasks are scheduled the same procedure is repeated [19].

4.9. Max-Min

This algorithm is almost same as the Min-Min algorithm but, it schedules larger tasks first of all i.e. After finding out minimum execution times, the maximum value is selected which is the maximum time among all the tasks on any resources. Until all tasks are scheduled the same procedure is repeated [19].

4.10. The Message Oriented Model

Clusters offer the opportunity of using the distributed applied programs by different computers on the networks. This is associated with the introduced clusters in the network performance. If the total load in distribution network is loaded by a computer, it makes the network slower. To prevent this situation, the resource management can be used as software metrics for traffic distribution between stations to keep the network performance in a high level. The Web services are mainly used in the "quick online message programs". This technology is for the real time communication between different sides; however, the availability of functional program is important. One model has been presented that uses XMPP for load balancing. The clients of XMPP send the prepared information to the prepared server of XMPP and XML flows contain the details of the prepared information of the customers generated by these servers. Using a load balancing on top of a XMPP server allows incoming requests from public services to be prioritized and applied [20].

4.11. OLB + LBMM

This method uses a combination of two algorithms for a better implementation and maintaining the load balancing of system. The OLB scheduling algorithm, keeps each node in the mode of work to reach the goal of load balancing, and LBMM scheduling algorithm is used to reduce the time each task is run on a node which leads to reduction in total run time. The usage environment of this algorithm is three dimensional cloud computing networks [21]. This combination algorithm makes better use of the resources, increases productivity and provides better results compared to honeybees exploration, random sampling and active clustering.

4.12. Fuzzy Logic

The paper in [22] proposes the novel load equalization technique using Fuzzy Logic in Cloud Computing, within which load equalization could be a core and difficult issue in

Cloud Computing. In this work, the authors have designed a new load balancing algorithm based on Round Robin in Virtual Machine environment of Cloud Computing in order to achieve better response time and processing time. The load balancing algorithm is done before it reaches the processing servers the job is scheduled based on various parameters like processor speed and assigned load of Virtual Machine and etc. It maintains the information in each VM and numbers of request currently allocated to VM of the system. It identify the least loaded machine, when a request come to allocate and it identified the first one if there are more than one least loaded machine. In this architecture, the fuzzifier performs the fuzzification process that converts two types of input data like processor speed and assigned load of Virtual Machine and one output like balanced load which are needed in the inference system. The design also considers the processor speed and load in Virtual Machine as two input parameters to make the better value to balance the load in Cloud using Fuzzy Logic. These parameters are taking as inputs to the fuzzifier, which are used to measure the balanced load as the output. Two parameters named as the processor speed and assigned load of virtual Machine of the system are jointly used to evaluate the balanced load on data centers of Cloud Computing environment through Fuzzy Logic.

4.13. Join-Idle-Queue Algorithm

This algorithm suggests a load balancing algorithm for active scalability of Web services. This algorithm provides load balancing in large-scale with distributors of the dispatchers. First, the load balancing of idle processors is done across the dispatchers for access of any idle processor to each dispatcher and then allocation of tasks to processors is performed to reduce the average queue length of each processor [23]. By removing the load balancing work of the vital routes of processing requests, this algorithm effectively reduces the system load in which no communicative overhead is occurred while entering tasks, and real response time is not raised as well.

4.14. The Central Load Balancing Policy for Virtual Machines

This policy balances the load evenly in a computing cloud or distributed virtual machine and increases the overall performance of the system by about 20%, but does not take into account those systems that have a fault tolerance. This method uses information of general mode for load balancing decisions [24].

4.15. Power Aware Load Balancing Strategy

The strategy proposed in [25] is an energy conscious, power aware load balancing strategy based on adaptive migration of Virtual Machines. This strategy will be applied to Virtual Machines on Cloud, considering higher and lower thresholds for migration of Virtual Machines on the servers. If the load is greater or lower then defined upper & lower thresholds, VMs will be migrated respectively, boosting resource utilization of the Cloud data center and reducing their energy consumption.

The system models that used in this paper consist of global and local manager. The local managers, which are part of VM monitor, resides on each node and are responsible for keeping continuous observation on when to migrate a VM and utilization of the node. The end-user refers its service request along with some CPU performance parameters to a global manager which in turns intimates the VM monitor for VM Allocation. The local manager reports the global manager about the utilization check of its node. And thus, global manager keeps the check of overall utilization of the resource. To reduce number of migration they integrate minimum migration time policy.

4.16. Dynamic Load Balancing Approach

The paper in [26] proposes the load balancing method based on the remaining storage capacity. The method considers the load and the node's remaining storage capacity of the node. The method uses a hybrid structure model using two layers of load balancing strategies. The lower layer manages the local load information. The upper layer manages the compressed load information. Each level uses the different balance strategy. This will not only be able to timely balance local load, the scheduler can balance the global load in the upper. This model is not a bottleneck. It spends small resources to improve overall system performance. According to the different hotspots of the data, it uses two strategies that include migrating and replicating data to reduce the load.

4.17. Efficient Load Balancing Approach

Zuhori [27] presented Round Robin Algorithm for efficient load balancing in Cloud Environment. This algorithm is Round Robin to reschedule the CPUs. Here at first consumer's request submitted into the Service Accepter and Service Accepter search for free VMs. When it finds one it starts to serve the services to those VMs using Round Robin Algorithm .In Round Robin algorithm the time is divided into multiple slices and each node is given a particular time slice or time interval. The decision of a service acceptation or rejection is taken by the service accepter. The total work of this thesis work is done for ten servers. Here, the real Cloud environment has not used and the procedure of the process scheduled is not dynamic.

4.18. Cost and Energy Optimization

The paper in [28] proposes an Optimized Load Balancing algorithm (OLB) which not only balances the load among the servers but also reduces energy consumption and SLA violation. This paper uses Local regression (LR) for deciding whether host is overloaded or not and uses Minimum Migration Time policy to select the VMs to be migrated away from that host. In this paper under loaded Host Detection has been used to move VMs to other hosts so that this under loaded host can be put to sleep thus saving energy.

4.19. GFTLBS

Yao [29] presented a novel guaranteeing fault-tolerant

requirement load balancing scheme (GFTLBS) to guarantee the fault-tolerant level of all services provided by the data center while balancing the load based on VM migration among the hosts. With GFTLBS, by moving CPU state, memory content, storage content and network connections of VM, VMs can be migrated from the host with the heaviest load to the lightest one while not violating the fault-tolerant requirements of all the services. Based on VM migration, the hardware utilization, power savings, availability, security and scalability can be increased without disrupting the customer applications running in the VMs. In this article all the VMs of different services are assumed to have the same capacity and the same load level. GFTLBS can balance the load among all the hosts in the data center and also guarantee the fault-tolerant level of all services provided in the data center and works well with various groups of the number of VMs and hosts.

4.20. Avoid Deadlocks

Rashmi [1] presented a load balancing algorithm to avoid deadlocks among the Virtual Machines while processing the requests received from the users by VM migration. The proposed algorithm avoids the deadlock by providing the resources on demand resulting in increased number of job executions. In this paper, hop time and wait time may be considered. Hop time is the duration involved in migration of the job from the overloaded VM to the underutilized VM for providing the service. Wait time is the time after which the VMs become available to service the request. Various users submit their diverse applications to the Cloud service provider through a communication channel. The Cloud Manager in the Cloud service provider's datacenter is the prime entity to distribute the execution load among all the VMs by keeping track of the status of the VM. The Cloud Manager maintains a data structure containing the VM ID, Job ID and VM Status to keep track of the load distribution. The VM Status represents the percentage of utilization. The Cloud Manager allocates the resources and distributes the load as per the data structure and analyzes the VM status routinely to distribute the execution load evenly. In processing, if any VM is overloaded then the jobs are migrated to the VM which is underutilized by tracking the data structure. If there are more than one available VM then the assignment is based on the least hop time. The Cloud Manager automatically updates the data structure on completion of the execution.

5. Discussion and Conclusion

In this section we discuss the different techniques that were discussed in Section 4. We also compare these techniques based on the Metrics discussed in Section 2.

Table 2 shows a comparison among the reviewed techniques. The comparison shows the positives and negative points of each technique. For example, The Honeybee Foraging Algorithm achieves global load balancing through local serve actions and does not increase the throughput as the system size increases. However Performs well as system diversity increases. Furthermore, Active Clustering and Based

Random Sampling perform better with high and similar population of resources, but have not good performance when system diversity increases. Based Random Sampling achieves load balancing across all system nodes using random sampling of the system domain. In addition, OLB + LBMM algorithm makes better use of the resources, increases productivity and provides better results compared to Honeybee Foraging Algorithm, Based Random Sampling and Active Clustering. As for the Carton approach, we can see that this approach with very low computation and communication overhead is simple and easy to implement. Event-driven is able to either increase or decrease the scale of the play in several resources based on the variable load of the user, while violation of the quality of service is happened every now and then. Message oriented architecture as a middleware model has been pointed out to improve load balancing in distributed networks. Based on messaging techniques XMPP allowed resources to be monitored and provide availability of cloud resources. This technology is open for real time communication between various parties.

Table 2. Advantages and Disadvantages of Load Balancing Techniques

Techniques	Advantages and Disadvantages
Honeybee Foraging Algorithm	Performs well as system diversity increases. Does not increase the throughput as the system size increases.
Based Random Sampling	Performs better as the number of processing nodes is increased. Performs not well as system diversity increases.
Active Clustering	Performs better as the number of processing nodes is increased. Performs not well as system diversity increases.
Carton	With Very low computation and communication overhead is Simple and easy to implement.
Event-driven	Is able to either increase or decrease the scale of the play in several resources based on the variable load of the user. Quality of services (QOS) breaches.
Server-based load balancing	Reduces service response time.
Black-Box & Gray-Box	Has a drawback in the migration phase.
Min-Min Algorithm	Has a major drawback that it chooses smaller tasks first which makes use of resource with high computational power. Thus, this scheduler when number of smaller tasks exceeds the large ones is not optimal and it can lead to starvation.
Max-Min Algorithm	The waiting time of smaller tasks and the make-span may increase in this scheduler.
Message Oriented Model	As a middleware model has been pointed out to improve load balancing in distributed networks. This technology is open for real time communication between various parties.
OLB + LBMM	Efficient utilization of resources. Enhances system performance.
Fuzzy Logic	Can balance the load with decreases the processing time as well as improvement of overall response time, which are leads to maximum use of resources.
Join-Idle-Queue algorithm	Reduces the system load in which no communicative overhead is occurred while entering tasks, and real response time is not raised as well.
Central Load Balancing	Achieves high performance. Does not consider fault tolerance.
Power Aware LB Strategy	Reduces number of migrations.
Dynamic LB Approach	Is not a bottleneck. Improves overall system performance.
Efficient LB Approach	Tries to reduce response time. Is not dynamic.
Cost and Energy Optimization	Reduces energy consumption. Reduces SLA violation.
GFTLBS	Balance the load and guarantee the fault-tolerant level of all services.
Avoid Deadlocks	Enhances the number of jobs to be serviced Improving working performance.

Based on the Discussed metrics, the reviewed techniques have been compared in Table 3.

Table 3. Comparison of reviewed Load Balancing Techniques Based on Discussed Metrics

Techniques	Considered Metrics in each Technique
Honeybee Foraging Algorithm	Throughput, Performance & Scalability
Based Random Sampling	Throughput, Performance & Scalability
Active Clustering	Throughput, Performance & Scalability
Carton	Performance, Overhead &Resource Utilization
Event-driven	Resource Utilization
Server-based load balancing	Performance & Response Time
Black-Box & Gray-Box	Overhead & Response Time
Min-Min Algorithm	Throughput, Overhead, Response Time, Resource Utilization & Performance
Max-Min Algorithm	Throughput, Overhead, Response Time, Resource Utilization & Performance
Message Oriented Model	Response Time & Performance
OLB + LBMM	Performance & Resource Utilization
Fuzzy Logic	Response Time & Resource Utilization
Join-Idle-Queue algorithm	Response Time, Performance & Overhead
Central Load Balancing	Response Time, Performance, Throughput
Power Aware LB Strategy	Resource Utilization, Performance & Energy Consumption
Dynamic LB Approach	Response Time, Performance
Efficient LB Approach	Response Time, Performance
Cost and Energy Optimization	Performance, Migration Time & Energy Consumption
GFTLBS	Fault Tolerance, Resource Utilization & Scalability
Avoid Deadlocks	Response Time, Performance & Overhead

Load balancing is one of the main challenges in Cloud Computing. It is required to distribute the load evenly at every node to achieve a high user satisfaction and resource utilization ratio by making sure that every computing resource is distributed efficiently and fairly. So in this paper we compared different load balancing algorithms in Cloud Computing and concluded that we can use a special algorithm based on our needs. However Cloud Computing covers wide areas and as already stated, none of the above algorithms do not satisfy all the criteria. Therefore, the need to develop an adaptive method is necessary which is suitable for heterogeneous environments.

References

[1] K. S. Rashmi, V. Suma and M. Vaidehi, "Enhanced Load Balancing Approch to Avoid Deadlocks in Cloud," Special Issue of International Journal of Computer Applications (0975 – 8887) on Advanced Computing and Communication Technologies for HPC Applications (ACCTHPCA), June 2012, pp. 31–35.

[2] M. Randles, D. Lamb and A. Taleb-Bendiab, "A Comparative Study into Distributed Load Balancing Algorithms for Cloud Computing," 24th International Conference on Advanced Information Networking and Applications Workshops, Liverpool, 2010, pp. 1-6.

[3] S. Zhang, H. Yan and X. Chen, "Research on Key Technologies of Cloud Computing, " International Conference on Medical Physics and Biomedical Engineering(2012), Hebei Province, China, pp. 1791–1797.

[4] R. P. Padhy and G. P. Rao, "Load Balancing in cloud computing Systems," Bachelor Thesis, Department of Computer Science and Engineering National Institute of Technology, Rourkela Rourkela-769 008, Orissa, India May 2011, pp. 1-46.

[5] P. Membrey, D. Hows and E. Plugge, "Load Balancing in the Cloud," pp.211 – 224, 2012.

[6] S. Begum and C.S.R. Prashanth, "Review of Load Balancing in Cloud Computing, " IJCSI International Journal of Computer Science Issues , Vol.10, Issue 1,2013.

[7] A. M. Alakeel, "A Guide to dynamic Load balancing in Distributed Computer Systems," International Journal of Computer Science and Network Security (IJCSNS), vol. 10, No. 6, June 2010, pp. 153–160.

[8] T. Sharma, V.K. Banga, "Proposed Efficient and Enhanced Algorithm in Cloud Computing," International Journal of Engineering Research & Technology (IJERT), vol. 2, Issue 2, 2013, pp. 1-6.

[9] Y. Ranjith Kumar, M. Madhu Priya and K. Shahu Chatrapati, "Effective Distributed Dynamic Load Balancing For The Clouds," International Journal of Engineering Research & Technology, vol. 2, 2013, pp. 1-6.

[10] A. Khetan, V. Bhushan and S. Ch. Gupta, "A Novel Survey on Load Balancing in Cloud Computing," International Journal of Engineering Research & Technology (IJERT) , Vol.2, Issue 2 ,2013.

[11] D. Escalnte and A. J. Korty, "Cloud Services: Policy and Assessment", EDUCAUSE Review, vol. 46, July/August 2011.

[12] P. V. Patel, H. D. Patel and P. J. Patel, "A Survey on Load Balancing in Cloud Computing" IJERT, vol. 1, November 2012.

[13] A. Hamo, A. Saeed, "Towards a Reference Model for Surveying a Load Balancing," IJCSNS International Journal of Computer Science and Network Security, vol. 13, No. 2, 2013, pp. 42-47.

[14] K. Nuaimi, N. Mohamed, M. Nuaimi and J. Al-Jaroodi, "A Survey of Load Balancing in Cloud Computing: Challenes and Algorithmsg," 2012 IEEE Second Symposium on Network Cloud Computing and Applications, 2012.

[15] R. Stanojevic and R. Shorten, "Load balancing vs. distributed rate limiting: a unifying framework for cloud control", Proceedings of IEEE ICC, Dresden, Germany, August 2009, pp. 1-6.

[16] V. Nae, R. Prodan, and T. Fahringer, "Cost-Efficient Hosting and Load Balancing of Massively Multiplayer Online Games", Proceedings of the 11th IEEE/ACM International Conference on Grid Computing (Grid), IEEE Computer Society, October 2010, pp. 9-17.

[17] A. M. Nakai, E. Madeira and L. E. Buzato, "Load Balancing for Internet Distributed Services Using Limited Redirection Rates", 5th IEEE Latin-American Symposium on Dependable Computing (LADC), 2011, pp. 156-165.

[18] T. Wood, P. Shenoy, A. Venkataramani and M. Yousif, "Black-Box and Gray-Box Strategies for Virtual Machine Migration," Proc. 4th USENIX Symposium on Networked Systems Design; Implementation, Cambridge, April 11–13, 2007, pp. 229–242.

[19] T. Kokilavani and G. Amalarethinam, "Load Balanced Min-Min Algorithm for Static Meta-Task Scheduling in Grid Computing" International Journal of Computer Applications, vol. 20, No. 2, April 2011, pp. 43-49.

[20] Z. Chaczko, V. Mahadevan, Sh. Aslanzadeh and Ch. Mcdermid, " Availability and Load Balancing in Cloud Computing, " 2011 International Conference on Computer and Software Modeling, IACSIT Press, Singapore, vol.14, pp. 134-140.

[21] S. Wang, K. Yan, W. Liao, and S. Wang, "Towards a Load Balancing in a Three-level Cloud Computing Network", Proceedings of the 3rd IEEE International Conference on Computer Science and Information Technology (ICCSIT), Chengdu, China, September 2010, pp. 108-113.

[22] S. Sethi, A. Sahu and S. K. Jena, "Efficient load Balancing in Cloud Computing using Fuzzy Logic," IOSR Journal of Engineering (IOSRJEN), vol. 2, 2012, pp. 65-71.

[23] Y. Lua, Q. Xiea, G. Kliotb, A. Gellerb, J. R. Larusb and A. Greenber, "Join-Idle-Queue: A novel load balancing algorithm for dynamically scalable web services", An international Journal on Performance evaluation, In Press, Accepted Manuscript, Available online 3 August 2011.

[24] A. Bhadani and S. Chaudhary, "Performance evaluation of web servers using central load balancing policy over virtual machines on cloud", Proceedings of the Third Annual ACM Bangalore Conference (COMPUTE), January 2010.

[25] Kh. Maurya and R. Sinha, "Energy Conscious Dynamic Provisioning of Virtual Machines using Adaptive Migration Thresholds in Cloud Data Center," International Journal of Computer Science and Mobile Computing, IJCSMC, vol. 2, March 2013, pp.74-82.

[26] J. Zhang, S. Zhang, X. Zhang, Y. Lu, S.Wu, "A Dynamic Load Balancing Approach Based on the Remaining Storage Capacity for Mass Storage Systems," Proceedings of the International Conference on Information Engineering and Applications (IEA) 2012, Springer-Verlag London 2013, pp. 1-7.

[27] T. Zuhori, T. Shamrin, R. Tanbin and F. Mahmud, "An Efficient Load Balancing Approach in Cloud Environment by using Round Robin Algorithm," International Journal of Artificial Intelligence and Mechatronics, vol. 1, 2013, pp. 1-4.

[28] J. Bodele and A.Sarje, "Dyanamic Load Balancing With Cost And Energy Optimization In Cloud Computing," International Journal of Engineering Research & Technology (IJERT) , vol. 2, Issue 4, 2013, pp. 1006-1010.

[29] L. Yao, G. Wu, J. Ren, Y. Zhu and V. Li, "Guaranteeing Fault-Tolerant Load Requirement Balancing Scheme," Published by Oxford University Press on behalf of The British Computer Society, 2013, pp. 1-8.

27

Local search heuristic for multiple knapsack problem

Balbal Samir[1], Laalaoui Yacine[2], Benyettou Mohamed[1]

[1]Computer science Department, USTOMB, Oran, Algeria
[2]IT Department, Taif University, Taif, Kingdom of Saudi Arabia

Email address:
belbelsamir@gmail.com (Balbal S.), y.laalaoui@tu.edu.sa (Laalaoui Y.), med_benyettou@yahoo.fr (Benyettou M.)

Abstract: In this paper we will present a heuristic method to solve the Multiple Knapsack Problem. The proposed method is an improvement of the IRT heuristic described in [2].the experimental study shows that our improvement leads some gain in time and solution quality against IRT, MTHM, Mulknap and ILOG CPLEX.

Keywords: Multiple Knapsack Problem, Local Search, Heuristic

1. Introduction

The Multiple Knapsack Problem (MKP) is a variant of the knapsack problem (KP) whose resolution is much more difficult, the fact that we have this problem in areas as different application than the economy, industry, transport, cargo loading and distributed computing, gives it a great practical interest [1].

Viewpoint Artificial Intelligence, the problem of Multiple Knapsack is strongly NP-complete. This means that the resolution of this problem cannot be done in polynomial time. In other words, an exact algorithm is required for optimal resolution.

The objective of this work is to improve the performance of a heuristic proposed by IRT Laalaoui [2], and solve the problem of multiple Knapsack in a way we approached using local search.

2. Presentation of the Multiple Knapsack Problem

The Multiple Knapsack Problem (MKP) is a generalization of the standard 0-1Knapsack Problem where instead of considering only one knapsack, one tries to fill m knapsacks of different capacities [3]. Consider a set $N = \{1... n\}$ of items to be loaded into m knapsacks of capacity c_i with $i \in \{1, ... m\}$. Each item $j \in N$ is characterized by its weight w_j, and its profit p_j and its decision variable x_{ij} which is worth 1 if the item j is loaded into the knapsack i and 0 otherwise. It is then to find m disjoint subsets of N (where each subset corresponds to

filling a knapsack) that maximize the total profit made by the sum of the selected items. The mathematical formulation of the problem MKP is as follows:

$$MKP: \begin{cases} \max \sum_{i=1}^{m} \sum_{j=1}^{n} p_j x_{ij} \\ s.c \ \sum_{j=1}^{n} w_j x_{ij} \le c_i \ , \ i \in \{1, ..., m\} \\ \sum_{i=1}^{m} x_{ij} \le 1 \ , \ j \in \{1, ..., n\} \\ x_{ij} \in \{0,1\}, i \in \{1, ..., m\}, j \in \{1, ..., n\}. \end{cases} \quad (1)$$

Where p_j, c_i and w_j are positive integers.

In order to avoid any trivial case, we make the following assumptions.

All items have a chance to be packed (at least in the largest knapsack):

$$\underset{j \in \{1..n\}}{\text{Max}} w_j \le \underset{i \in \{1,...,m\}}{\text{Max}} c_i \quad (2)$$

The smallest knapsack can be filled at least by the smallest item:

$$\underset{j \in \{1..n\}}{\text{Min}} w_j \le \underset{i \in \{1,...,m\}}{\text{Min}} c_i \quad 3)$$

There is no knapsack which can be filled with all items of N:

$$\sum_{j=1}^{n} w_j > \underset{i \in \{1,...,m\}}{\text{Max}} c_i \quad (4)$$

3. Resolution Method of MKP

The approaches proposed in the literature to solve the problems of the family of the backpack are either exact methods are heuristics. The exact methods are able to solve a problem to optimality but in exponential time [4]. Heuristic methods provide an approximate solution, good quality in reasonable periods of time [4]. Heuristics are either simple heuristic are meta-heuristics.

3.1. The Exact Method

The exact methods proposed in the literature to solve problem MKP are based on the Branch-and-Bound (B &B).

Ingargiola and Korsh [5] proposed a branch-and-bound algorithm which used a reduction procedure based on dominance relationships between pairs of items.

Hung and Fisk [6] proposed a method based Branch and Bound with depth-first strategy as a journey. The upper bounds are obtained using Lagrangian relaxation, with a decreasing scheduling capacity c_i.

The algorithm of Martello and Toth [7] improves proposed by Hung and Fisk with the calculation of upper bounds using surrogate relaxation and taking the minimum of the Lagrangian upper bounds and surrogate relaxation method.

Martello and Toth[8] proposed an algorithm (bound and bound) algorithm improves the Martello and Toth[7]a powerful base of B&B to solve the MKP. This algorithm, called MTM (Method Martello and Toth), applies heuristics Greedy, which involves solving a series of problems with m single Knapsack.

Pisinger[9] improved the algorithm MTM by incorporating an efficient algorithm for calculating higher and better reduction rules for determining the items that can be set to zero terminals and a method that attempts to reduce the ability of backpacks. This new algorithm is called Mulknap. Power Mulknap located in allocating 100000 items in one second. So Pisinger has succeeded with Mulknap resolve cases problems with very large (n = 100 000, m = 10) in a second. But at the same time it fails to resolve cases in smaller problem (n = 45, m = 15), when the ratio n/m is between 2 and 5 ($2 \leq n/m \leq 5$).

Fukunaga and Korf [10] proposed the bin-completion method is a technique based branch- and-bound. It uses the strategy depth first. Each node of the search tree represents a maximum possible allocation for a particular knapsack member.

A. Fukunaga [11] improved bin-completion method in the case of relatively large bodies (n = 100). But the ratio n/m is the major problem in all existing algorithms.

3.2. Existing Solvers

There are many solvers have been developed for solving the problem of the backpack. We distinguish between free software and commercial software. Commercial software often has superior performance to the free solvers. There are two principal existing business software is: The commercial solver IBM ILOG CPLEX and XPRESS-MP solver. There exist also two principal free software are: GLPK and Boob ++.

3.3. Heuristics

Heuristic methods have been proposed for the problem of multiple bag back in order to find good solutions within a reasonable time, heuristic MTHM, CRH and IRT are proposed to solve the problem MKP.

The heuristic (MTHM) of Martello and Toth [12] is a very efficient heuristic to solve the problem MKP It takes place in stages present in the following Figure.

Heuristic: MTHM
Input: n, p_j, w_j, y_j, z, c_i
Output : y_j, z
Begin
　[Initial solution] : Procedure GREEDYS
　[Rearrangement]
　[First improvement]
　[Second improvement]
End

Fig. 1. Heuristic MTHM

The heuristic RCH described by Lalami et al. in [13] is a heuristic with a polynomial time complexity for solving the MKP. Unfortunately, this heuristic resolve any problems that could be solved using optimality Mulknap i.e. instances of problems with a large n/m ratio, which is where the Mulknap gives the best results in less second. The authors fail to describe the interesting case of problems with a small ratio n/m.

In [2], Laalaoui proposed a heuristic to solve the problem completely dependent exchanges found in MTHM and also to increase the efficiency of the latter method (improved profit). This new heuristic integrates three simple heuristics (Replace-One-By-One, Replace-Two-By-One and Replace-One-By-Two) with MTHM by two different techniques: the first technique is simple (SRT) and the second iterative (IRT).

3.4. Metaheuristics Methods

Among the proposed literature to solve the problem MKP methods that uses genetic algorithms metaheuristic methods, methods are located: HGGA (Hybrid Grouping GA) [14], WCGA (Weighted Coding GA) [15], Ugga (Undominated Grouping GA) [16] and Representation-RSGA (Switching GA) [17].

4. Local Search Heuristic for MKP

Local Search is used by many metaheuristic. It is about making incremental improvements to the current solution through a basic transformation until no improvement is possible. The solution is called local optimum found with respect to the transformation used, as shown in Fig.2.

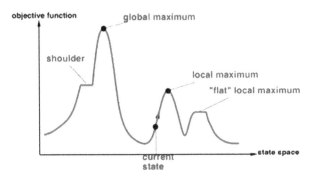

Fig. 2. Local Search

Technically, the local search consists of a series of transformations of the solution to improve it every time. The current solution S is replaced by a better solution S' ∈ N(S) in its vicinity. The process stops when it is no longer possible to find-improving solution in the vicinity of S, such that the algorithm written Fig. 3

```
Algorithm: Local Search
Input: S
Output: N
best ← true
While best = true do
best ← false
for(S' ∈ N(S)) do
if (S' is best of S)
S←S'
best ← true
return
```

Fig. 3. Algorithm for Local Search

Our proposal to solve the problem MKP with local search method is using the following steps:
Step 01: initial solution;
Step 02: Perturbation solution
Step 03: improve the solution;
Step 04: repeating the process a number of times.

4.1. Initial Solution

For the initial solution of this method we will use the IRT technique written by Y. Laaloui in [2].

4.2. Perturbation Solution

We know that one of the disadvantages of IRT and MTHM is the lack of randomness .This drawback severely limits the ability to better search space exploration.

In our new technical we introduce some randomness to the solution of step disturbance. The principle of perturbation solution is to randomly remove one item or several items of the solution as mentioned in the procedure Perturbation.

4.3. Improve the Solution

For the third step the procedures for exchanging items is applied (Replace-One-By-One, Replace-Two-By-One, Replace-One-By-Two) and the steps are repeated for a number of times. The figure (Fig .4) shows the general

algorithm of the method of local search for MKP.

```
Algorithm Local Search Heuristic for MKP ;
Inputs : n , p_j ,w_j , y_j ,z, i ,c̄_i
Outputs : y_j ,z
Begin
01.    MTHM
02.    Replace-Two-By-One
03.    Replace-One-By-Two
04.    Replace-One-By-One
05.    if( prev_z < z )
06.       prev_z = z :
07.       goto step 02.
08.    if(tmpz == z)
09.    tmpz = z :
10.    for (j = 1; j ≤ d; j + +)
11.       tmpx[j] = x[j];
12.    for (j = 1; j ≤ b; j + +)
13.       tmpcr[j] = cr[j] :
14.    else
15.    z = tmpz ;
16.    for (j = 1; j ≤ d; j + +)
17.       x[j] = tmpx[j] ;
18.    for (j = 1; j ≤ b; j + +)
19.       cr[j] = tmpcr[j] ;
20.    if(testmore <= nbretest)
21.       Perturbation()
22.       testmore = testmore + 1
23.       goto step 02.
End.
```

Fig. 4. Local Search Heuristic for MKP

5. Experimental Results

To measure the effectiveness of our work, we have implemented in C programming language, this choice is justified by the speed of the language. And we used the system Lunix (Ubuntu) as a platform for development, since it is widely used in the academic community, and to use shell scripts. The technical Mulknap work is written in C1 .While the code of the implementation MTHM is written in FORTRAN2 and we converted to C using the f2c converter.

We used the optimization tool IBM ILOG CPLEX commercial solver version 12.2.5. All techniques are established in the same environment using the GCC compiler. All tests were performed on a 2.2 GHz Intel Core Duo 2 processor with 2GB of RAM. We have used A. Fukunaga's data-set which was used in [16][17]. This benchmark is a set of 12 problem instances, four instances in each one of the three types: strongly correlated, weakly correlated and multiple subset-sum. The number of knapsacks is 100; the number of items is 300 in each problem instance.

Results of our experimental study are shown in tables 1, this contains a comparison to IRT, MTHM, Mulknap techniques and IBM ILOG CPLEX solver on a data-set from literature [16,17], It is clear that the method attendant gives a result better than Mulknap and CPLEX solver either as a solution or as a time over the local search method for MKP

1http://www.diku.dk/Pisinger/codes.html
2http://www.or.deis.unibo.it/staff-pages/Martello/cvitae.html

improves the results obtained by the IRT technique with a time greater than the time of the latter method, although it remains our proposal novella usable in real time because time does not exceed one second.

Table 1. Results on Uncorrelated,strongly correlated and multiple subset-sum Instances compared to IRT ,MTHM , Mumknap techniques and ibm ilog cplex solver. Time columns show the time in seconds.

Uncorrelated instances

	MTHM		IRT		Mulknap		Cplex		Local Search	
	Z	Time	Z	Time	Z	Time	Z	Time	Z	Time
S 1	806906	0.004	830575	0.293	843374	180	843509	180	842322	0.571
S 2	778781	0.005	791931	0.372	801497	180	802111	180	793371	0.838
S 3	723833	0.008	730805	0.276	740210	180	746721	180	751760	0.683
S 4	755329	0.001	769366	0.404	780777	180	785264	180	782453	0.67

Strongly correlated instances

	MTHM		IRT		Mulknap		Cplex		Local Search	
	Z	Time	Z	Time	Z	Time	Z	Time	Z	Time
S 1	699757	0.001	752146	0.295	745837	180	751391	180	752423	0.388
S 2	681330	0.001	766349	0.42	767114	180	767667	180	767724	0.55
S 3	629253	0.001	710742	0.28	708087	180	710182	180	711614	0.385
S 4	673521	0.001	726563	0.44	722244	180	725484	180	726493	0.61
S 5	711381	0.001	773263	0.401	765050	180	773154	180	773197	0.532
S 6	661103	0.001	738439	0.28	734766	180	738229	180	738307	0.378
S 7	669063	0.001	742562	0.335	742112	180	743073	180	742773	0.449
S 8	704983	0.005	756424	0.233	749965	180	756468	180	756576	0.332
S 9	688309	0.001	753506	0.346	756370	180	756597	180	754527	0.444
S 10	720932	0.004	785382	0.368	783801	180	785191	180	785644	0.476

Multiple subset-sum instances

	MTHM		IRT		Mulknap		Cplex		Local Search	
	Z	Time	Z	Time	Z	Time	Z	Time	Z	Time
S 1	747026	0.009	750145	0.189	744773	180	749527	180	750145	0.287
S 2	762816	0.008	767355	0.182	764293	180	765203	180	767355	0.27
S 3	707080	0.018	709369	0.18	706549	180	708524	180	709369	0.266
S 4	722512	0.008	725203	0.243	721480	180	724154	180	725203	0.377

6. Conclusion

In this article we described an improvement of IRT technique. The proposed method succeeds to give better results compared to IRT, Mulknap and CPLEX with reasonable.

The future work on this new heuristic approach includes a depth experimental study in large-scale data-sets.

References

[1] M. Lalami,M. Elkihel, D. Baz and V.Boyer, "A procedure-based heuristic for 0-1 Multiple Knapsack Problems", International Journal of Mathematics in Operational Research, vol. 4, No. 3, pp. 214-224, 2012.

[2] Y. Laalaoui, "Improved Swap Heuristic for the Multiple Knapsack Problem" IWANN 2013, Part I, LNCS 7902, pp. 547–555, 2013.

[3] S. Martello, P. Toth. "Knapsack problems: algorithms and computer implementations". J Wiley. 1990.

[4] J. Dréo, A. Petrowski, D. Taillard, P. Siarry"Métaheuristiques pour L'optimisation difficile" ,Eyrolles (Editions), November 2003

[5] G. Ingargiola and J.F. Korsh, "An algorithm for the solution of 0-1 loading problems", Operations Research, 23(6):1110--1119, 1975.

[6] M.S. Hung and J.C. Fisk, "An algorithm for the 0-1 multiple knapsack problem", Naval Research Logistics Quarterly, 571--579, 1978.

[7] S. Martello and P. Toth., "Solution of the zero-one multiple knapsack problem", European Journal of Operational Research, 4, 1980.M. Young, The Technical Writer's Handbook. Mill Valley, CA: University Science, 1989.

[8] S. Martello and P. Toth., "A bound and bound algorithm for the zero-one multiple knapsack problem", Discrete Applied Mathematics, vol. 3, pp. 275--288, 1981.

[9] D. Pisinger,"An exact algorithm for large multiple knapsack problems", European Journal of Operational Research, vol. 114, pp. 528--541, 1999.

[10] A. Fukunaga, R.E Korf, "Bin Completion Algorithms for Multicontainer Packing, Knapsack, and Covering Problems", Journal of Artificial Intelligence Research, vol. 28, pp. 393--429, 2007.

[11] A. Fukunaga, "A branch-and-bound algorithm for hard multiple knapsack problems", Annals of Operations Research, vol. 184, N. 1, pp. 97--119, 2011.

[12] S. Martello and P. Toth., "Heuristic algorithms for the multiple knapsack problem", Computing, vol. 27, pp. 93--112, 1981.

[13] M. Lalami,M. Elkihel, D. Baz and V .Boyer, "A procedure-based heuristic for 0-1 Multiple Knapsack Problems, International Journal of Mathematics in Operational Research, vol. 4, No. 3, pp. 214--224, 2012

[14] E. Falkenauer, "A hybrid grouping genetic algorithm for bin packing", Journal of Heuristics, pages 2:5 - 30, 1996.

[15] R. Raidl, "The multiple container packing problem: A genetic algorithm approach with weighted codings", ACM SIGAPP Applied Computing Review, pages 22 - 31, 1999.

[16] A. Fukunaga., "A new grouping genetic algorithm for the multiple knapsack problem", In Proc. IEEE Congress on Evolutionary Computation, pages 2225--2232, 2008.

[17] A. Fukunaga and Satoshi Tazoe, "Combining Multiple Representations in a Genetic Algorithm for the Multiple Knapsack Problem", In Proc of the 11th IEEE Congress on Evolutionary Computation, pages 2423 - 2430, 2009.

28

A new organization model for self-organizing multi-agent systems based on self-adaptation features

Amin Rahmanzadeh, Ali Farahani, Eslam Nazemi

Self-* Laboratory, Faculty of Electrical and Computer Engineering, Shahid Beheshti University, Tehran, Iran

Email address:

a.rahmanzadeh@mail.sbu.ac.ir (A. Rahmanzadeh), a_farahani@sbu.ac.ir (A. Farahani), nazemi@sbu.ac.ir (E. Nazemi)

Abstract: Complexity of information technology systems is increasing continually. A very good solution would be using agents in implementing and controlling these systems. Multi-Agent Systems are good examples of using agents for system control and implementation. On the other hand, Multi-Agent systems need to be controlled and managed too. Using organizations is one of the best solutions. Many research studies have been done in this field. In this paper we will try to introduce, explain, and compare some related works. We will extract their pros and cons. For the weaknesses of this research studies, we have proposed some solutions. In this paper we propose our model of organization, which implements Self-Adaptation features using Self-Organization and can improve extracted problems of existing models. Altogether, we have tried to analyze and compare some of main proposed models for Multi-Agent systems' organization. Finally we have proposed a model to improve Self-Organized organizations of Multi-Agent systems.

Keywords: Multi-Agent Systems, Organization, Organization Model, Organization in Multi-Agent Systems, Self-Organization, Self-Adaptation

1. Introduction

Agents are software or hardware units and their general task is to receive a task, process, execute and give the result as an output to a system or another agent. In any organizations, agents get assigned to a role and have particular tasks according to their assigned role. Multi-Agent systems are defined as a combination of agents and societies from their birth. But, typically the focus is on agents and their stations. These are Agent-Oriented Multi-Agent systems. Recently, this focus is on Organization-Oriented Multi-Agent systems, in which concepts like organization, group, relations, performance, and role are more debated [4].

Multi-Agent systems provide a good situation for implementing autonomous systems that can manage themselves [5]. In [11], Multi-Agent systems are defined as an organization of autonomous agents which are trying to reach their common goals. Multi-Agent systems can be used in any field in which concurrent and complex computation is needed. According to Dignum et.al, [7], organizations are the solution for controlling Multi-Agent systems and according to [2], using organizations a group of simple agents can do big and complex jobs and complexity of the agents is reduced. Also, [11] indicates that organization is a social entity that is coordinated informed. This entity has a specific border and acts based on some basic disciplines to reach a particular goal or a set of goals. Because of complexity in agents, numerous agents, and complexity in the system itself, organization in Multi-Agent systems, is distributed and it is not possible to make it centralized.

One of the main problems is that Multi-Agent systems are generally used in uncertain environments. According to Weyns et.al, [6], environment of an agent is anything other than the agent itself and has a role in the system. As a result, other agents are counted as environment for a particular agent. Change is unavoidable in an uncertain environment. Sometimes these changes can cause a situation in which the current structure of organization does not have suitable and required performance and usefulness. Consequently, using permanent rules for an organization would not be applicable. In another words, the systems should be able to adapt to the environmental changes. As a solution, Self-Organization is proposed in [4, 5]. However based on Horling and Lesser [2], Self-Organization always comes along with emergence.

Emergence is the whole behavior of a distributed system that is arisen from behavior of local parts. Emergence is used against reductionism, which stated that a system can be reduced to the sum of its parts. Emergence can cause undesired situations like a Chaos. So, a control on emergence is also needed.

In 2003 IBM proposed an architectural model for Self-Adaptive systems [8].There are four main parts in this architecture: Monitor, Analyze, Plan, and Execute. These four parts also use a knowledge core. According to this model, a system on which this loop is implemented (Managed Element) is always monitored. As changes happen, this loop collects information, analyzes those information, based on knowledge, decides what to do, and executes necessary actions. In this paper we propose a model in which we combine Self-Adaptive features with Self-Organizing features to solve before-mentioned problems. Our model is an organization model of Multi-Agent systems that uses benefits of an overall control to prevent undesired emergence and the same problems.

The rest of the paper is organized as the following: Related works about organizations in Multi-Agent Systems will be introduced and analyzed in section 2. In section 3, these models will be compared to each other and their advantages and disadvantages will be analyzed. Section 4 proposes some ideas and proposals to improve these models and a model to improve all of before-mentioned weaknesses based on the proposed ideas. Finally, conclusion and references are placed in section 5 and section 6, respectively.

2. Related Works

2.1. AALAADIN, a Meta-Model

Ferber et.al, [1] propose a general Meta-Model for Multi-Agent Systems based on organizational concepts like groups, roles, and structures. This model allows utilization of agents with heterogeneous languages, applications, and structures. This paper claims that the key to design and implement complex and ultra large scale systems is to use mentioned organizational concepts as basic concepts in organization and relating them to behavior of the agents. In this view, without considering agents behavioral principles, organization is considered a method to arrange groups and roles to shape a whole entity.

Figure 1. shows basic concepts of AALAADIN model. In this study, no proposals have been made regarding the internal structure of agents and an agent is defined based on its role in an organization. Also, groups are a set of agents and distinguished according to roles they assign to their agents. An agent can be member of more than one group and consequently, can get more than one role. Each role assigned to an agent is local for that group. Based on this paper, there are concepts in defining organization oriented Multi-Agent Systems other than basic concepts (Role, Group, Agents). Figure 2. shows these concepts. In this figure, "Group Structure" entity is an abstraction of group and

"Organizational Structure" entity is defined as a set of group structures showing the design of an organization of Multi-Agent Systems.

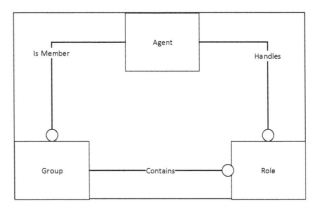

Figure 1. *Conceptual Model of AALAADIN [1]*

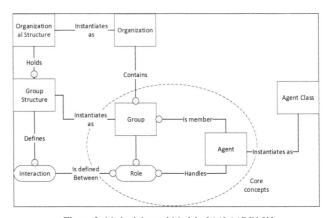

Figure 2. *Methodological Model of AALAADIN [1]*

2.2. Self-Organized Organizations

Kota and et al propose a model for structural adaptation based on Self-Organization in [5]. The method proposed in this paper allows the agents to change their structure of relations to achieve a better distribute of tasks.

The authors believe that decentralized structural adaptation is the best way to obtain Self-Organization. Structural adaptation consists of change in relations of the agents and as a result, redirection in their interactions. The adaptation method is a continuous and centralized process with participation of all agents to decide how and when to update their relations, only based on local accessible information.

The modeling of organization consists of modeling the agents of the organization, organization features, and task environment. In this model, organization of agents consists of a group of collaborating and problem solving agents located in a task environment. Modeling of a task consists of a set of Service Instances (SIs), duals determining a particular service and the amount of process it needs to be executed placed in a tree data structure. The SIs are executed in a prioritized order and a service is executed when all of its nodes are executed too. In other words, the execution of SIs starts from root of the tree and goes towards leaf nodes. Nodes in the same level are executed in a parallel way. Figure 3.a. shows the tree of SIs.

An organization consists of agents that provide these services. Each agent is a dual consisting set of services it can provide and its computational capability. Figure 3.b. shows the organizational structure. The beginning of a task execution starts with assigning the root of a particular SI tree to a randomly chosen agent. So, each agent has two obligations: Task execution and task allocation. There are three kinds of relation among agents in this model: Acquaintance, Peer, and Superior-Subordinate. The agents would often assign SIs to their subordinates rather than its peers. Since an agent has no idea about tasks that will be provided in the future, the structural adaptation method for Self-Organization in this model uses only historical information of agents. Figure 4. shows different types of reorganization. For example, 1(ii)form-sub means that the relation between two agents changes from acquaintance to superior-subordinate.

2.3. MACODO Middleware

Weyns and et al propose architecture of a middleware for Self-Organization in Multi-Agent Systems called MACODO in [6]. In fact, the MACODO middleware is proposed as a middleware to help organization-oriented designation of Multi-Agent Systems in context-based environments. This middleware omits life cycle management from roles of agents and provides reuse capability and easy understanding, design, and management in Multi-Agent Environments. Therefore, whenever there is a change in the system or environment it would be the middleware that adapts the organization. Figure 5. shows organizational model of MACODO.

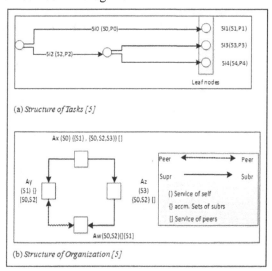

(a) *Structure of Tasks [5]*

(b) *Structure of Organization [5]*

Figure 3. *Examples of Task and Organization [5]*

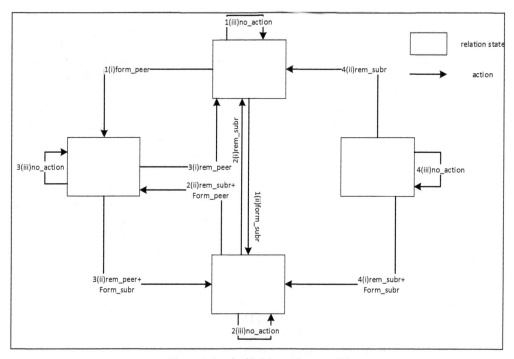

Figure 4. *Graph of Relation Adaptation [5]*

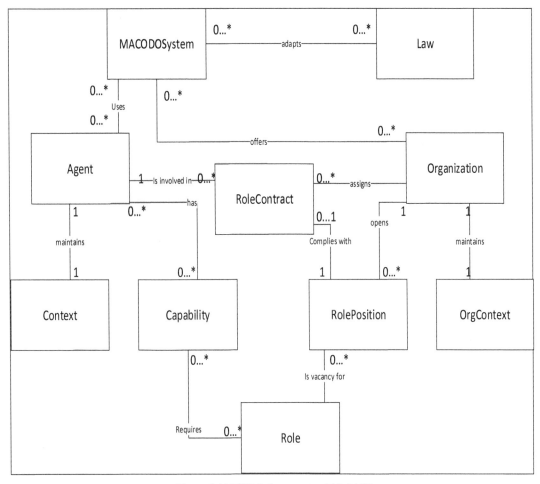

Figure 5. *MACODO Organizational Model [6]*

3. Analysis of models

Among the three, the MACODO middleware is the only model that describes how to implement Self-Organization for Multi-Agent Systems. In this paper, software architecture of agents is proposed and practically tested in a case study about traffic control cameras as agents in roads. Details of advantages and disadvantages of each model are listed in table 1.

Table 1. *Advantages and Disadvantages of Existing Models*

Model name	Advantages	Disadvantages
AALAADIN Model	- Possibility to use heterogeneous agents - Possibility to have more applications for MAS	- No practical proof of efficiency - No internal structure for agents No method to shape groups and organizations and how to adapt
Self-Organizing Organizations	- Agent-oriented and decentralized Self-Organization and - Detailed solution for adaptation - Practical proof of efficiency -Practical and detailed solution for adaptation	- No internal structure for agents - No real implementation in real world
MACODO Middleware	- Internal structure for agents and how they should connect - Real world implementation - Possibility to use heterogeneous agents - Reusability, easy understanding, better design and management	- No more real world implementations

4. Proposed Model for Organization of Self-Organized Multi-Agent Systems

4.1. Overall Proposals

Having no practical implementation in real world mentioned as one of the weaknesses of introduced models in the previous section. To implement a software, the architecture of that software should be available. As a result, a model for Self-Organizing organizations should be architectural. It means, the model should consider system requirements, propose designation, and make implementation and maintenance possible. Therefore, lack of architectural models for Self-Organizing organizations in Multi-Agent Systems can be considered a problem.

Another problem is collaboration of agents that is missing in these models. In Self-Organization for Multi-Agent Systems the direction of orders is bottom-up and agents decide and perform locally. This feature can cause Emergence phenomena in the system. It can be undesired if it is not controlled. An appropriate solution is to reinforce positive emergence or Synergy and decrease and eliminate negative emergence. Therefore, having global coordination and collaboration among the agents whereas they are independent, decide and perform internally, would be a proper solution. This solution can be founded in Self-Adaptation architecture that has a top-down process. In other words, proposing a Self-Adaptive model for Self-Organizing organizations would be the key to control emergence. This model should make Self-Organization process to act in line with main goals of Self-Adaptation process. As a result, it is necessary to propose a view of collaboration among the agents.

4.2. The Necessity of Architecture for Autonomous Systems

According to Garlan and Schmerl [12] and Cheng et.al, [13], while developing Self-Adaptive systems generally, it is necessary to use architecture of system when adding Self-* features. In these research studies, the reasons that we need architecture to develop Self-Adaptive Systems are expressed as below:

- *Isolated concerns:* applying architecture to Self-Adaptive Systems, we can develop Self-Adaptive features in separated and specific areas.
- *System extensibility:* applying architecture to software development, we can easily add more operations to system.
- *Easier maintenance and evaluation:* since using architecture clarifies area of problem and operation, maintenance and evaluation of Self-Adaptive System will be much simpler.
- *Reusability of components, especially Self-Adaptive ones:* if an appropriate level of abstraction is applied on Self-Adaptive components in an architecture based system, they can be easily utilized in other systems with minimum modification.
- *Possibility of using other systems' components in architecture based Self-Adaptive Systems:* if the components are developed based on specific standards, they can be utilized in Self-Adaptive Systems using a simple interpreter.

4.3. The Proposed Model

As mentioned before, one of the problems of existing models for Self-Organization in Multi-Agent systems is that they are not architectural. Then, we discussed the necessity of architecture for autonomous systems. MAPE-K loop on the other hand, is an existing architectural model for autonomous control on an element. In this paper, we say that the MAPE-K loop architecture can be used to control Multi-Agent systems.

Figure 6. shows MAPE-K architecture.

It is true that MAPE-K loop has a centralized control, and Multi-Agent systems are distributed. However, our proposal is not just to use the MAPE-K loop on Multi-Agent systems. In our proposed model, Self-Adaptation, implemented by the MAPE-K loop, determines overall policies, and Self-Organization practically executes the decisions made by the MAPE-K loop. In fact, this is a combination of Self-Adaptation and Self-Organization. In other words, Self-Adaptation monitors the whole system, analyzes the changes, decides what to do, and in execution part, Self-Organization is responsible for execution of decisions made by Self-Adaptation. However, these decisions are about maintenance of the whole system. It means agents are still locally deciding about how to act to emerge to the final goal of the system. Nevertheless, the organization model of Self-Organized Multi-Agent system should support this combination.

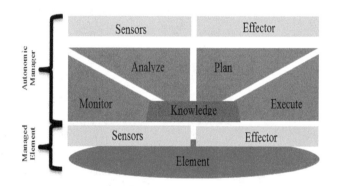

Figure 6. *MAPE-K Control loop [8]*

Horling and Lesser [2] introduce and categorize organizational paradigms for Multi-Agent systems. These paradigms include:

- *Hierarchies:* In Hierarchies, agents are arranged in a structure like trees. It means, the view of agents with a higher level in the tree is more global than that of others in lower levels.
- *Holarchies:* Holons define characteristic of holarchies. Holons can include one or more entities and meanwhile, be a member of one or more superordinate holons.
- *Coalitions:* Consider set A is a population of agents. Each subset of A is a potential coalition. Generally, coalitions are goal directed and have a short life-cycle. It means, coalitions are formed for a specific goal and disappear whenever the goal is reached.
- *Teams:* A common goal is what keeps agents of a team together. In a team, agents work together to reach that common goal. These features make teams and coalitions similar. But, teams try to reach maximum utility of the whole team rather than that of each member. This is what distinguishes teams than coalitions.
- *Congregations:* Like teams and coalitions, agents in congregations work together in a flat organization to reach goals and benefits. The difference is that congregations are not short-lived and formed to reach

multiple goals. They are formed among agents with similar or complementary agents to find more appropriate collaborators.

- *Society:* Societies spontaneously bring a long-lived social collaboration into mind. Societies of agents are fundamentally open systems. It means, agents can join and leave a society if they want. The society acts as an environment in which agents act and interact.
- *Federations:* Federations of agents have many different varieties. Agents of a federation share the common characteristics of a group. They entrust some amount of autonomy to a delegate agent that represents their group. The delegate can have different roles. For example, the delegate can act as an interpreter between agents inside and outside the group, assign tasks to agents inside the group, or, monitor the promotion of other agents.
- *Markets:* In market places, some agents may be buying and some others, seller agents. Buying agents announce their request for some items like resources, tasks, services and goods. On the other hand, selling agents may supply these goods. Sellers or a third party called auctioneer is responsible of processing bids and announcing the winner.
- *Matrix Organizations:* in a strict hierarchical organization, the structure is like a tree in which an agent or a group of agents report to one manager that provides these agents with goals, direction and feedback. This restriction is relaxed in matrix organizational paradigm. In this paradigm, any agent can have multiple managers. Therefore, successful agents can affect multiple entities by their local actions.

From different Organization Paradigms for Multi-Agent systems mentioned above, a combination of federations and hierarchies seems to be the most appropriate paradigm for our model. Figure 7. shows hierarchies and federation paradigm.

Collaboration between agents for coordinating about maintenance and control of the whole system seems to be a good solution for mentioned problems. From paradigms introduced in this part, the most suitable paradigm is the Federation. It means we can choose an agent in each organization to be a representative of the group and transport the information of its own group to other agents. These information can be gathered and transited to an agent in which we have established the so-called MAPE-K loop.

But there is another problem here. What if the agent with MAPE-K roll fails? This architecture makes that specific agent a bottleneck. To solve this problem, we came up with the idea of hierarchical federation. In this model of organization, there is a representative for each organization and these agents can make another organization in a higher level and have another representative.

But, how can this organizational model established in a Multi-Agent system? As you can see in [6], Weyns and et al propose a middleware in which the internal architecture of agents are defined. The agents are responsible for shaping our organizational model, too. Therefore, in agents using our model a component should be defined that is responsible for

roll assignment. There are different reference architectures for Multi-Agents systems:

- OMG's Model: In this model agents are categorized based on their capabilities and organizations.
- FIPA's Model: This model is a foundation for physical intelligent agents and aims pragmatic physical intelligent agents.
- KAoS' Model: This model is for standardization of Multi-Agent systems based on knowledge based and agent oriented view.
- General Magic's Model: This model is a commercial model for Multi-Agent systems in communications area.

We avoid more elaboration of these models. Among these reference models, the FIPA's Model is reference of other models and contains details of inside components of an agent. We choose this model for implementation of agents and the whole Multi-Agent system.

Figure 8. show a hypothetical situation of a Multi-Agent system which is organized using our organizational model. It is interesting to know why same agents are in different levels. For example agent B1 is in level 0 and level 1. Being in a hierarchical federation organization is just a roll and as we know, different rolls can be assigned to one agent. So, agent B1 is in level 0 and level 1 and agent A12 is in level 0, 1, and 2. Also, Figure 8.b. shows the practical situation of a system that is implemented using our model. As you can see, the positions of agents is not changed and the roll of being a representative or being a member of a level is just assigned to agents.

Now, we know that decision about being on which level or organization is made by agents, themselves. This decisions and similar ones can be made based on some specific restrictions like environmental conditions.

5. Discussion and Conclusion

In this paper we analyzed some of the relevant state-of-the-art models for organizations in Multi-Agent Systems. In fact, we studied the ones in which organizations are the control tools of Multi-Agent Systems.

In section 2, the top three research studies in this field were elaborated and analyzed. First of all, AALAADIN model, in which a model for Multi-Agent Systems with heterogeneous agents is proposed, was studied and analyzed. Afterward, Self-Organizing organizations model, in which agents can adapt their structural relations to get a better specification of tasks, is introduced and explained. Finally, the MACODO middleware, in which an architectural model is proposed to design and implement Self-Organization in Multi-Agent Systems, was explained and analyzed. After analyzing and comparing these existing models, we extracted some of their advantages and disadvantages. In the next stage, we stated their problems that the main one was lack of architecture. We showed the necessity of architecture for autonomous systems and finally we propose a model in which architecture is considered and the problems mentioned in section 4.1. are also solved.

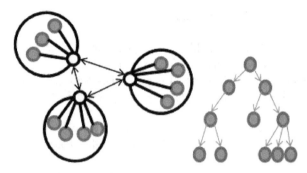

Figure 7. Federation and hierarchical organizational paradigm [2]

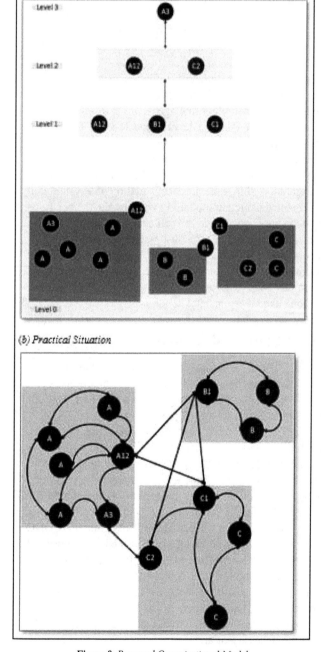

(b) Practical Situation

Figure 8. Proposal Organizational Model

Our new model combines Self-Adaptation features with Self-Organization features. This way, Self-Adaptation control

loop controls the whole system without making it centralized. Self-Organization is the tool of adaptation. Our future work will consist of two main parts: first we should elaborate our model of agents and organization based on FIPA's reference model, and second, we should try to present more details on the restrictions that agents should make decisions based on.

References

[1]   J. Ferber and Gutknecht, "A meta-model for the analysis and design of organizations in multi-agent systems", International Conference on Multi agent systems, pp. 128-135, 1998, France.

[2]   B. Horling and V. Lesser, "A Survey of Multi-Agent Organizational Paradigms", The Knowledge Engineering Review, Vol. 19, Iss. 4, 2004, pp. 281-316.

[3]   K. Y. Rafi, A. Farahani, and E. Nazemi, "An organizational model for autonomic intelligent distributed systems", 2nd World Conference on Information Technology, pp. 624-630, 2012, Turkey.

[4]   J. Ferber, O. Gutknecht, and F. Michel, "From Agents to Organizations: an Organizational View of Multi-Agent Systems", 4th InternationalWorkshop, AOSE, pp. 214-230, 2004, Australia.

[5]   R. Kota, N. Gibbins, and N. R. Jennings, "Self-Organising Agent Organisations", The 8th International Conference on Autonomous Agents and Multiagent Systems, pp. 797-804, 2009, USA.

[6]   D. Weyns, R. Haesevoets, A. Helleboogh, T. Holvoet, and W. Joosen, "The MACODO Middleware for Context-Driven Dynamic Agent Organizations", ACM Transactions on Autonomous and Adaptive Systems (TAAS), Vol. 5, Iss. 1, 2010, pp. 132-160.

[7]   V. Dignum, F. Dignum, L. Sonenberg, "Towards Dynamic Reorganization of Agent Societies", Workshop on Coordination in Emergent Agent Societies, pp. 32-39, 2004, Spain

[8]   An architectural blueprint for autonomic computing, IBM Group, 2003.

[9]   W. Truszkowski, M. Hinchey, J. Rash, and C. Rouff, "NASA's Swarm Missions: The Challenge of Building Autonomous Software", IT Professionals, Vol. 6, Iss. 5, 2004, pp. 47-52.

[10]   P. Mathieu, J. C. Routier, and Y. Secq, "Dynamic Organization of MultiAgent Systems", second international joint conference on Autonomous agents and multiagent systems, pp. 451-452, 2002, USA.

[11]   M. Kolp, P. Giorgini, and J. Mylopoulos, "Multi-Agent Architectures as Organizational Structures", Autonomous Agents and Multi-Agent Systems, Vol. 13, Iss. 1, pp. 3-25, 2006

[12]   D. Garlan and B. Schmerl, "Model-based adaptation for self-healing systems," Proceedings of the first workshop on Self-healing systems - WOSS '02, p. 27, 2002.

[13]   S. Cheng, D. Garlan, and B. Schmerl, "Software Architecture-based Adaptation for Pervasive Systems" International Conference on Architecture of Computing Systems Karlsruhe, pp. 67-82, Germany, April 8–12, 2002

[14] M. Risoldi, J. L. Fernandez-Marquez, G. Di Marzo Serugendo, "Resilience Framework for self-organising systems", Adaptive, Dynamic, and Resilient Systems, G. Cabri and N. Suri (Eds), Taylor and Francis, 2013.

[15] G. Di Marzo Serugendo, J. L. Fernandez-Marquez, "Self-Organising Services", Int. Conf. on Self-Adaptive and Self-Organizing System, Philadelphia, USA, 2013.

[16] G. Stevenson, D. Pianini, S. Montagna, M. Viroli, J.Ye, S. Dobson, "Combining self-organisation, context-awareness and semantic reasoning: the case of resource discovery in opportunistic networks", Proceedings of the 28th Annual ACM Symposium on Applied Computing, Coimbra (POR) March, 2013.

Permissions

All chapters in this book were first published by Science Publishing Group; hereby published with permission under the Creative Commons Attribution License or equivalent. Every chapter published in this book has been scrutinized by our experts. Their significance has been extensively debated. The topics covered herein carry significant findings which will fuel the growth of the discipline. They may even be implemented as practical applications or may be referred to as a beginning point for another development.

The contributors of this book come from diverse backgrounds, making this book a truly international effort. This book will bring forth new frontiers with its revolutionizing research information and detailed analysis of the nascent developments around the world.

We would like to thank all the contributing authors for lending their expertise to make the book truly unique. They have played a crucial role in the development of this book. Without their invaluable contributions this book wouldn't have been possible. They have made vital efforts to compile up to date information on the varied aspects of this subject to make this book a valuable addition to the collection of many professionals and students.

This book was conceptualized with the vision of imparting up-to-date information and advanced data in this field. To ensure the same, a matchless editorial board was set up. Every individual on the board went through rigorous rounds of assessment to prove their worth. After which they invested a large part of their time researching and compiling the most relevant data for our readers.

The editorial board has been involved in producing this book since its inception. They have spent rigorous hours researching and exploring the diverse topics which have resulted in the successful publishing of this book. They have passed on their knowledge of decades through this book. To expedite this challenging task, the publisher supported the team at every step. A small team of assistant editors was also appointed to further simplify the editing procedure and attain best results for the readers.

Apart from the editorial board, the designing team has also invested a significant amount of their time in understanding the subject and creating the most relevant covers. They scrutinized every image to scout for the most suitable representation of the subject and create an appropriate cover for the book.

The publishing team has been an ardent support to the editorial, designing and production team. Their endless efforts to recruit the best for this project, has resulted in the accomplishment of this book. They are a veteran in the field of academics and their pool of knowledge is as vast as their experience in printing. Their expertise and guidance has proved useful at every step. Their uncompromising quality standards have made this book an exceptional effort. Their encouragement from time to time has been an inspiration for everyone.

The publisher and the editorial board hope that this book will prove to be a valuable piece of knowledge for researchers, students, practitioners and scholars across the globe.

List of Contributors

Jia Chunying and Chen Yuchen
College of Electronic and Electric Engineering, Shanghai University of Engineering Science, Shanghai, China

Ding Zhigang
Shanghai Computer Software Technology Development Center, Shanghai, China

Diponkar Paul
Department of EEE, Prime University, Mirput-1, Dhaka, Bangladesh

Md. Rafel Mridha and Md. Rashedul Hasan
World University of Bangladesh, Dhanmondi, Dhaka, Bangladesh

Tingwei Chen and Jing Lei
College of Information, Liaoning University, Shenyang, Liaoning, China

Kidane Tadesse
Biostatistics and Health Informatics, Department of Public Health, College of Health Sciences, Mekelle University, Mekelle, Ethiopia

Ejigu Gebeye
Department of Epidemiology and Biostatistics, Institute of Public Health, College of Medicine and Health Sciences, University of Gondar, Gondar, Ethiopia

Girma Tadesse
Health Informatics, Tulane University Technical Assistant Program to Ethiopia, Addis Ababa, Ethiopia

Ahmed Rashad Khalifa
Systems and Computers Engineering Dept., Faculty of Engineering, Al Azhar University, Cairo, Egypt

Atsuko Nakai
Center for Safe and Disaster-Resistant Society, Okayama University, Okayama, Japan

Shun Motoyoshi and Fuminori Oomori
Graduate School of Natural Science & Technology, Okayama University, Okayama, Japan

Kazuhiko Suzuki1
Center for Safe and Disaster-Resistant Society, Okayama University, Okayama, Japan
Graduate School of Natural Science & Technology, Okayama University, Okayama, Japan

Mohamed Hassine and Hassani Massouad1
LARATSI Lab, ENIM, University of Monastir, Monastir, Tunisia

Lotfi Boussaid
EµE Lab, FSM, University of Monastir, Monastir, Tunisia

Oyugi Tobias and Maina Kairu
Department of Education and External studies, University of Nairobi, Nairobi, Kenya

Familusi E. B. and N. A. Ajayi
University Library, Ekiti-State University, Ado-Ekiti, Ekiti-State, Nigeria

Thomas Kokumo Yesufu
Department of Electronic and Electrical Engineering, Obafemi Awolowo University, Ile-Ife, Nigeria

Abimbola Oyewole Atijosan
Cooperative Information Network, Obafemi Awolowo University, Ile-Ife, Nigeria

Tomas Georgievich Petrov
St. Petersburg State University, Institute of Earth Science, St. Petersburg, Russia

Ali Zeynali Aaq Qaleh
Faculty of Engineering, Islamic Azad University, Qom, Iran

Seyyed Mahdi Haji Mirahmadi
Software Engineer, Young Researchers and Elite Club, Qazvin Branch, Islamic Azad University, Qazvin, Iran

Sara Najari and Iman Lotfi
Computer Department, Payam Noor University, Tehran, Iran

Aalia Hemmati and Sima Emadi
Computer Engineering department, Islamic Azad university of Meybod, Yazd, Iran

Morteza Asghari Reykandeh
Department of Computer Engineering, Islamic Azad University Khoy Branch, Khoy, Iran

Ismaeil Asghari Reykandeh
Department of Computer Engineering, Islamic Azad University Sari Branch, Sari, Iran

Zhengxi Wei
School of Computer Science, Sichuan University of Science & Engineering, Zigong Sichuan 643000, PR China

Kidist Teklegiorgis, Kidane Tadesse, Gebremeskel Mirutse and Wondwossen Terefe
Department of Public Health, College of Health Sciences, Mekelle University, Mekelle, Ethiopia

Peng Yan-zhou and Gao Hong-feng
College of Information Engineering, Henan University of Science and Technology, Luoyang, China

Tobias Oyugi and Ouinter Omware
Department of Education and External Studies, University of Nairobi, Nairobi, Kenya

Harriet Kidombo
School of Continuing and Distance Education, University of Nairobi, Nairobi, Kenya

Sare Eslami Khorami
Islamic Azad University South Tehran Branch, Tehran, Iran

Xiao Laisheng
Educational Information Center, Guangdong Ocean University, Zhanjiang, China

Zheng Yuandan
Information College, Guangdong Ocean University, Zhanjiang, China

Yi Lu Murphey, Liping Huang, Hao Xing Wang and Yinghao Huang
Department of Electrical and Computer Engineering, University of Michigan-Dearborn, Dearborn, USA

Hosny Ahmed Abbas and Mohammed Hussein Amin
Department of Electrical Engineering, Assiut University, Assiut, Egypt

Samir Ibrahim Shaheen
Department of Computer Engineering, Cairo University, Giza, Egypt

Motahareh Dehghan, Babak Sadeghiyan
Department of Computer Engineering and Information Technology, Amirkabir University of Technology (AUT), Tehran, Iran

Zeinab Goudarzi and Ahmad Faraahi
Department of Computer Engineering and Information Technology, Payame Noor University, PO BOX 19395-3697 Tehran, Iran

Balbal Samir and Benyettou Mohamed
Computer science Department, USTOMB, Oran, Algeria

Laalaoui Yacine
IT Department, Taif University, Taif, Kingdom of Saudi Arabia

Amin Rahmanzadeh, Ali Farahani and Eslam Nazemi
Laboratory, Faculty of Electrical and Computer Engineering, Shahid Beheshti University, Tehran, Iran

Index

Printed in the USA
CPSIA information can be obtained
at www.ICGtesting.com
JSHW052021301024
72690JS00004B/132